"Somewhere along the line we have forgotten much of the long and varied tradition of Christian prayer—to our great poverty. Steven Chase's meaty yet readable study helps us to tap this tradition for our own day. Chase uses the metaphor of a tree to describe five models of prayer: conversation (roots), relationship (trunk), journey (branches), transformation (leaves), and presence (fruit). Christian prayer, we discover, has almost infinite variety and interconnection. Chase has done a great service for those who desire to pray more deeply and for those who encourage and accompany them by bringing this treasure back into our contemporary awareness."

—**Elizabeth Liebert,** professor of spiritual life,
San Francisco Theological Seminary

"Without any reservation I recommend this work to persons who are serious about prayer. This is not another fluffy book on how to pray better or how to get what you want from God. Rather, Steven Chase gives us the fruit of his careful research of both the ancient and contemporary literature, drawing from the classical tradition, the Reformers, and contemporary writers to present a rich volume that will be of immense help to a vast array of readers who want a clear, comprehensive, well-documented presentation of the various aspects of prayer. This book will make a valuable contribution to the field of Christian spirituality."

—**Ben Campbell Johnson,** professor emeritus
of Christian spirituality, Columbia Theological Seminary

"A rich and detailed consideration of the length, depth, height, and width of prayer in the Christian tradition, Steven Chase's *Tree of Life* is a lovely and welcome book. Prayer as conversation, relationship, journey, transformation, and presence—these he describes as the roots, trunk, branches, leaves, and fruit of a life-giving approach to the human-divine experience. Focusing more on prayer as a way of life than as a set method, Chase's book allows the deep wisdom of the Christian traditions to enrich us in the contemporary context. The book's poetic imagery invites readers not only to expand their ideas about prayer but also to be drawn into prayer itself."

—**Wendy M. Wright,** professor of theology,
Creighton University

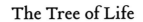
The Tree of Life

The Tree of Life

Models of Christian Prayer

Steven Chase

Baker Academic
Grand Rapids, Michigan

© 2005 by Steven Chase

Published by Baker Academic
a division of Baker Publishing Group
P.O. Box 6287, Grand Rapids, MI 49516-6287
www.bakeracademic.com

Printed in the United States of America

Library of Congress Cataloging-in-Publication Data
Chase, Steven.
    The tree of life : models of Christian prayer / Steven Chase.
       p.   cm.
    Includes bibliographical references and index.
    ISBN 0-8010-2762-4 (pbk.)
    1. Prayer—Christianity. I. Title.
  BV210.3.C45 2005
  248.3′2—dc22
                                                   2005012604

To
the earth's forests
and people in prayer

Lord, teach us to pray.
Luke 11:1

Contents

Acknowledgments

First, I would like to acknowledge my special friends, the general class of birds known as raptors, especially diurnal birds of prey, and especially among these the lovely, hovering kestrels, the deadly sharpies and Cooper's hawks, those wonderful marsh hoverers the northern harriers, desert-fond prairie falcons, peerless peregrines, those comparatively bumbling but nonetheless seldom-starving rough-legged hawks, and the ubiquitous but always delightful and trusty red-tailed hawks. One nocturnal raptor, though it hunts as well during the day, I should also acknowledge is the great snowy owl. I was lucky enough to spot one just outside its normal range one particularly harsh winter in deep snow but only because of the red blood of a recent kill. Many more are rare friends, but these named I see more often and remember most fondly. The fire of God's imagination blazes in them, and more than once these birds have allowed me to see a bit of the flame. When I see no flame, the birds themselves are bold and majestic unto themselves, and I am happy just to catch a moment's glimpse of them alone in the fire of their own majesty.

I would like to acknowledge one red-tailed hawk in particular who taught me about "stilling." There is a small but notable annual southern migration of hawks and falcons on the West Coast that follows the coastline of California and is funneled into a narrow area by the northern peninsula that defines the upper reaches of the San Francisco Bay on the east and the Pacific Ocean on the west. All manner of migrating raptors, preferring land routes as they do, are naturally funneled toward the Golden Gate by this peninsula. Many take an opportunity to rest a while by circling on the updrafts created by the Marin Headlands, which form the southern tip of the peninsula, just before they make

9

their flight across the narrow gate of water as they continue south toward secret nestings.

Some species, however, rest by a flight pattern known as "stilling." To still, a hawk will turn her body into the wind with wings extended and locked in place and with feathers spread. The wind in this area is stiff and shifting, yet through a variety of subtle shifts in wing, feathers, and tail, she is able to remain perfectly still relative to the ground. She sets her wings at a slight tilt or angle to the wind, which thereby secures just the proper pitch crucial for stability and balance. She fans her tail. Her feathers—which seem a vast community in perfect harmony—variously judge and correct for shifts in wind by alternately hugging and thus streamlining her body or flaying out so as to create the slight but needed drag to keep her perfectly still. Her eyes, already seeing eight times the distance ours do, seem to be searching deep into the horizon. Every muscle obeys her purpose of stillness.

One late fall day during the migration, I had climbed to the top of the Headlands. A few people were already there busy systematically counting the birds migrating that year; there were a few others watching with binoculars and birding scopes as well. In a very short time, I noticed that a red-tailed adult female hawk was stilling directly above me. Though familiar among birders who watch raptors with a special enthusiasm, this stilling posture is not all that common, and therefore, I was really quite excited to see it. To top it off, the Headlands at this point rise jagged and abrupt above the bay and the Pacific, and so the red-tailed hawk was not far above me, no more than fifteen or twenty feet at the most. Even without my binoculars, I could make out individual feathers being whipped away by the wind and then brought quickly back into formation with the rest. I could easily make out each feather of the wing and of the tail as it adjusted just slightly from moment to moment to make allowance for the shifting wind. Every nerve and muscle was attentive, ready. Yet in her practiced flight, she was still—still to the wind, still to the earth, an anchor in the sky.

In that moment, I thought that this certainly was prayer. Sharply alert, vigilant, every fiber and feather in play, yet she was perfectly at rest, perfectly still—stillness in motion. The hawk was stilling time. She was in a real sense stopping time, making sabbatical time, stilling time to make a new way of time. She was also telling me that I and the people who shared the moment with me had gathered because we needed time when time was still. We had come because it was time to still time. In stilling time, she showed me constant prayer, an ongoing prayer of connection and relation to the earth, nature, others, myself, and God. Then with one quick dip of a wing, she broke her pattern and ripped across the Golden Gate. Time resumed, but prayer did not stop.

So praise God for sister red-tailed hawk, who is precious and wild and free and whose offspring today are no doubt practicing their stilling to remind us that connections and courage and joy are prayers.

I would also like to acknowledge and thank a few special people who lent me their support, ideas, constructive criticisms, ears, and hearts and without whom this book would not have been completed. Thank you to the Grand Rapids Dominicans and especially the sisters and others on the staff of the Center of Spirituality of the Dominican Center at Marywood, where I was privileged to work in an atmosphere committed to the practice of prayer as an act of mind, body, and spirit.

For insightful comment on an initial proposal or early draft of this work, I thank some of my colleagues in the Society for the Study of Christian Spirituality: Mark Burrows, Joann Wolski Conn, Mary Froehlich, Elizabeth Liebert, Stephanie Paulsell, and Wendy Wright.

Throughout the writing of this book, various other colleagues made comments about the book that got me going again in the right direction or helped me out of a seeming dead end, often without being aware of the help they gave. Especially in this regard I would like to thank Timothy Brown, Curtis Gruenler, Jaco Hamman, and David Stubbs.

During the writing of this book, Rachelle Oppenhuzen, often at just the right moment, would call or write a note just to see how the book was going. I always appreciated her conversation and support. Thank you also to Victor Perry for valuable correspondence on Erasmus's translation of John 1:1, concerning which marginal notes from the 1527 edition read: *sermo rectius quam verbum.* Exactly so.

It is true that one learns best by teaching. The same can be said of the privilege of practicing spiritual direction. And so I would like to thank all the students and directees I have had the pleasure of teaching, guiding, befriending, and learning from. I would especially like to thank two students. Mara Cooper asked a timely question that caught me completely by surprise but went to the heart of a particularly vexing matter. And Randy Smit, during a conversation about the book, said something that has stuck with me: "Just tell the truth." I hope, Randy, with God's help that in some small way I have managed to follow the wisdom of your simple advice.

About my wife, Leanne Van Dyk, I will never be able to say enough in appreciation. Emotionally, psychologically, intellectually, in honesty and in playfulness, she keeps me wanting to be alive. My love and appreciation as always.

Our daughter, Rachel, moving into her teens, is still our angel. May she become a living prayer.

Preface

Seeds of Prayer

> To be a Christian and to pray are one and the same thing.
>
> Karl Barth, *Prayer*

Prayer: The Tree of Life Planted in the Soul

A life of prayer is like a living tree that grows in solitude yet thrives only in an interconnected and mutually supportive ecology.

In the thirteenth century, the Franciscan friar St. Bonaventure wrote *The Tree of Life*, a prayerful meditation on the life of Christ. Bonaventure says that to enkindle our affection, to shape our understanding, and to imprint our memory, he has gathered a "bundle of myrrh" from the forest of the holy gospel. Since imagination aids memory, he asks us to imagine a metaphor of a tree as prayer:

> Picture in your mind a tree whose roots are watered by an ever-flowing fountain that becomes a great and living river with four channels to water the garden of the entire church. From the trunk of this tree, imagine that there are growing twelve branches that are adorned with leaves, flowers, and fruit. Imagine that the leaves are a most effective medicine to prevent and cure every kind of sickness. . . . Let the flowers be beautiful with the radiance of every color and perfumed with the sweetness of every fragrance, awakening and attracting the anxious hearts of men of desire. Imagine that there are twelve fruits, having the sweetness of every taste

(Wisd. 16:20). This fruit is offered to God's servants to be tasted so that when they eat it, they may always be satisfied, yet never grow weary of its taste. This is the fruit that took its origin from the Virgin's womb and reached its savory maturity on the tree of the cross under the midday heat of the Eternal Sun, that is, the love of Christ.[1]

Bonaventure intends that the tree of life be thought of, paradoxically, as an image of the cross of Christ. Christ is the mediator between God and humanity, and the tree of life is a symbol of Christ's mediation between heaven and earth. The cross of Christ is like a seed planted by God, rooted in humanity, with its vertical trunk and horizontal branches stretching to enfold the world in redemptive prayer. Leaves wither and fall on the day of Christ's death but are born anew in Christ's resurrection. We, like Mary and the beloved disciple, are drawn in prayer to the foot of the cross.

For Bonaventure, the tree of life is the cross, but an expansion of his metaphor embraces the life of prayer as well. The tree of life, understood as prayer, planted in the soul bears rich fruit in Christian faith and life as the believer grows and flourishes in God's grace and love.

Bonaventure's *Tree of Life* brings to mind another story of planting and seeds and growth. Jesus tells a parable about a sower who sows seed that falls on a path, among rocks and stones, among thorns, and into good soil. He uses this story to illustrate how people receive, nourish, and harvest the Word of God (Matt. 13:1–23; Mark 4:1–20; Luke 8:4–15). The parable can also be read as an allegory of the life of prayer.

For some, prayer is like seed that is sown randomly with little thought as they walk. They allow a few seeds of prayer to fall on the path. Soon a bird flies down and plucks the exposed seeds from the path. It is as if the seeds were never there at all. For others, initially, prayer is like an unexpected gift; they are walking a new way. They exalt in the gift. They derive joy, harmony, and contentment from prayer. For them, prayer is almost like a drug; euphoria floods their senses. But if sown on rock or stone, this prayer has no root. Having no root, when prayer disappoints, as it goes dark and dry, it simply blows away like sand. For still others, prayer is like seed that falls among thorns. Again, prayer begins to sprout, but it never really gets a chance. Desire exclusively for self and things of the world are like thorns that choke and soon kill prayer. But some sow seed on good soil. The roots of prayer go deep, and the soil nourishes and sustains. Those for whom prayer, like the Word, takes root in good soil, according to Luke, whether in dark or in light, "hold [prayer] fast in an honest and good heart, and bring forth fruit with patience" (Luke 8:15 RSV). They "understand" (Matt. 13:23) and "accept" (Mark 4:20) prayer for what it is and grow in prayer that produces and yields fruit thirty-, sixty-, one hundredfold.

The life of prayer is like a tree sown as seed by God in the human heart. Every such seedling is subject to a life of spiritual conflict and battles for the desires of our heart. Though subject to periods dry with doubt, flooded by illusions, stormed by stress, or weakened by listlessness as though sick through to the heart, the seedling grows slowly into a tree of life. Trees are, more often than not, gnarled and misshapen—but therein lies the unique beauty of each. Their roots of perseverance go deep, and God's soil is good. Prayer in time brings forth fruit. Bonaventure ends his Prologue to *The Tree of Life* with a prayer:

> Feed us with these fruits,
> Shed light upon our thoughts,
> Lead us along straight paths,
> Crush the attacks of the enemy.
> Fill us with your sacred light,
> Breathe holy inspiration,
> Be a peaceful way of life
> For those who love Christ. Amen.[2]

Habitats, Trees, and the Ecology of Prayer

The models of prayer proposed and illustrated in this book are linked metaphorically to the tree of life. The models, or parts of the tree, comprise the central portion of the book. Preceding this core section are the "habitats" of prayer, those aspects of prayer that function as holding environments for the growth and nurture of prayer. Following the models is an "ecology" of prayer suggesting that an interconnected system of practices gives both structure and freedom to those gathered in prayer.

The book proposes and explains five models of prayer. The first model is prayer as conversation, which is represented by the deep roots of the tree of life. Conversational prayer, whether in speech or in silence, in listening or in responding, grounds all prayer in God. Its roots grow deep, anchoring prayer in the rich earth, drawing nutrients from fertile soil, giving support to the entire tree of life.

The second model is prayer as relationship, illustrated in the solid trunk of the tree of life. Relationship in prayer is like the solid wood of the trunk that protects the tree of life from storm and variations in climate and provides constant support, ensuring growth ever upward as if beloved of sky. As essential for the health of prayer as sun, rain, and air for the health of a tree, relationship is the supportive backbone of prayer, providing connection and perseverance in a life often buffeted by sorrow, pain, and grief.

The third model is prayer as journey, illuminated through the many branches of the tree of life. No branch of the tree of life is exactly like another. They sprout at different times, arrange themselves in varied places, and acquire shape and form from exigencies of weather, neighboring branches and trees, sources of light, varieties of species, inborn patterns, qualities of soil, human intervention, and time. Whimsy plays a part as well. As pilgrims in community or in solitude, we travel many different roads by many means and ways. Yet each journey to God grows from the one solid trunk of the tree of life.

The fourth model is prayer as transformation and is reflected in the new leaves of the tree of life. To pray is to change. For new leaves to bud, open, and grow, the old must die. In dying and falling to the ground, the leaves allow the tree, for its survival, to go dormant during harsh cold and long nights. But through the seasons of change and transition, new leaves spring to life, rejuvenating and urging the tree to new growth. Likewise, through the grace of prayer, we are transformed.

The fifth model is prayer as presence, signified by the perfumed fragrance of the flowers and fruits that crown the tree of life. Their sensual aroma is sweet, giving pleasure and evoking gratitude. There is consolation in the fruits of prayer. But more importantly, fruits and flowers from the tree of life represent charity and compassion. These fruits and flowers serve a dual function in prayer: They remind us of the presence of God in all things, and they call us to caring presence before God, ourselves, others, and creation. Within each flower and fruit rests the regenerative potential for new life. Prayer as presence thus adorns the tree of life and contains within it seeds for the continual repopulation of new forest-like communities of faith.

One thing is clear. Prayer in itself does not provide water for the roots, give strength to the trunk, embolden the branches, dazzle the leaves with color, or create the flowers and fruits of the tree of life. God alone loves and commands prayer, tree, and pray-er into being. In prayer, we are privileged to dwell with God and others in such a way that the tree of life takes root in our soul. Some years the rings of this tree of life are wide with exuberant growth. In other years, the rings may be pinched and thin. May God grant you wisdom, protection, and growth during exuberant years and thin. May your prayers be like the giant redwood—always greening, embracing heaven, and grounded in the good soil of earth.

Part 1

Habitats of Prayer

Formation and Tradition

1

Prayer as a Way of Life

Listen! I am standing at the door, knocking; if you hear my voice and open the door, I will come in to you and eat with you, and you with me.

Revelation 3:20

To attend to God in every moment, to love God in the midst of God's creation, raises a question: Does this mean that *everything* is prayer? No. But everything can *become* prayer. Loving intention and attention to God in all ways and in all places create an invitation to prayer. It is the intention of this book to awaken readers to prayer as a way of life.

Prayer, meditation, and contemplation mold us, shape us, guide and form us. They initiate and sustain a habitual way of life. That way of life is prayer. Prayer is indeed a *way*: a path, a pattern, a journey, an adventure, a quest, a gesture, a discipline. And prayer is indeed the stuff of *life*: a way of being, feeling, sensing, understanding, doing, dwelling, caring, seeing, knowing, imagining, reasoning, falling, failing, suffering, relating, and transforming.

To live, one must participate in life; to know prayer, one must pray. Participation and knowledge, in both of these cases, are of the heart as well as of the mind, of the body as well as of the spirit. "Love the Lord your God with all your heart, and with all your soul, and with all your mind" (Matt. 22:37). Prayer, then, is one way of living, just as living is one way of praying.

Reaching the core of the relationship between prayer and life is probably not possible through words alone. Yet part of prayer and part of life is communication, and so we must try. Morton Kelsey confronts this dilemma by framing life and prayer in terms of relationship:

> The practice of prayer and meditation is as complex and varied as human life itself. As we confront the reality of the Other, we bring every part of our being, our ideas and thoughts, our plans for the day, for the week, for our entire life to the Other. . . . What is true of human relationships at their deepest and best is even truer of relationship with God.[1]

Others see prayer in ethical and moral terms. Prayer is life lived in moral conformity to the will of God. In a saying attributed to the hermit monk St. Anthony the Great, "The truly intelligent person [one who avoids that which harms the soul and seeks the good] pursues one sole objective: to obey and to conform to the God of all." There is no profit in prayer unless "one's soul conforms to God's will."[2] Intelligence, in the classic sense of living life well and seeking the good, is a form of action. Prayer likewise is an ongoing act of divinely guided conformity to the will of God. In turn, God's will for us is that we seek and have what is good. Intelligent prayer, therefore, is a way of life.

Fortunately, prayer as a way of life is also for those less intelligent, even stupid, times of our life. Allowing for the broadest parameters of what it means to be human and to live, Simon Tugwell has wisely said:

> Praying frequently, then, really means learning to live our whole lives with God, praying to him out of the very stuff of our lives. Often this will mean that our prayer will seem very trivial, because much that happens to us is trivial. It is in fact a great lesson in humility to have to pray trivial prayers.[3]

In other words, to pray constantly means that sometimes we must pray trivially. Conforming to the will of God in prayer can be as exhausting and trivial as it can be comforting and profound. Prayer is a way of life habituated to the awareness of the presence of God in all things.

Christian prayer is life giving: a stream of living water, a tree of life, intimate connection. But it can also be, over the course of any given life, an agony of darkness, a parched desert, a tear in the fabric of relationship. Prayer as a way of life is wordless and still, conversational and humble, adequate and exalted. It is life changing and life stopping. It blesses us with God's presence and curses us with absence of desire. Prayer can mock, and prayer can console. It is at times a simple yes, and it is at times too deep for words. Prayer is the wisdom of Christ, the advocacy of the Holy Spirit, the gift of a loving God. We are commanded to pray, and we are free to abandon prayer. It is a human response; it is intensely personal and genuinely communal; it reveals what is hidden and often casts a shadow over what is revealed. Prayer is wonder and mystery, and it is as mundane as awakening and "seeing" the breeze that makes new green leaves dance. It engages the body, the mind, and the spirit. It shows us our desires; it is our desire. Prayer shapes and forms us, calls and beckons us, purifies, illuminates, and protects us in our imperfect ways even as it leads us to perfection. Prayer is stillness in constant motion; it is as trivial as it is profound; it is a walk in the forest; it is a pause for tea or espresso in an enlivening but tiring city. It is loneliness. It is communion. Prayer is a way of life.

From the early and formative years of Christian spirituality, contemporary writers are retrieving wisdom that reinforces the claim that prayer is a way of life. Pierre Hadot, in his book *Philosophy as a Way of Life*, traces the roots of this tradition in classical Western philosophy.[4] Hadot describes philosophy as a way of life in the context of a search for wisdom, a wisdom that is as much ethical, practical, and moral as it is a process of knowing. Nuanced by refinements of the relationship between nature and grace, Hadot makes the case that this "quest for wisdom" is also at the very center of Christian contemplative practice lived out in virtue and compassion.

In this sense, Hadot's description of ancient philosophy bears an uncanny resemblance[5] to Christian prayer:

> During this period, philosophy was a *way of life*. This is not only to say that it was a specific type of moral conduct. . . . Rather, it means that philosophy was a mode of existing-in-the-world, which had to be practiced at each instant, and the goal of which was to transform the whole of the individual's life.[6]

Both philosophy and prayer are more than what they might, on the surface, appear to be. Philosophy is not only a way of knowing; prayer is not only a practice. Both make us "be" in the world in a different way.

The idea that prayer is a way of life opens us to contact, conversation, and interaction with creation, others, Scripture, Jesus Christ, the Holy Spirit, and God in new ways. It allows us to enter fully into anxiety, grief, and loss. Prayer as a way of life holds us in a community of care and healing. It fosters self-understanding, relationship, and memory even in the face of pain, suffering, and abandonment. Prayer as a way of life searches without ceasing for the "LORD, who is hiding his face from the house of Jacob" (Isa. 8:17). It is rest as much as it is ceaseless action, charity, and compassion. It is as much listening, stillness, and waiting as it is an arm outstretched to offer bread to the hungry.

But the seemingly endless methods of prayer can confuse or even frighten us. Contemporary author Margaret Guenther has written:

> The resources for prayer are so rich they can threaten to overwhelm us, especially if we are tempted to try everything at once. I have found that certain approaches fit better with some personalities than with others, and there are times in our lives when one method of prayer will be more helpful than another. The way we choose to pray is not as important as where it leads us: the point is to focus on being open to God and not to make an idol of method. Any method can lead us into conversation with God.[7]

If we awaken to the reality that prayer is a way of life, any aspect of our life can lead us into a conversation with God.

Constant Prayer

Q. 116. Why is prayer necessary for Christians?

A. Because it is the chief part of the gratitude which God requires of us, and because God will give his grace and Holy Spirit only to those who sincerely beseech him in prayer without ceasing.

Heidelberg Catechism

The very idea of "constant prayer" can scare one away from prayer altogether. We live in a world of distractions, yet even our distractions can direct us in prayer.

In his letter to the Romans, Paul instructs Christians to "be constant in prayer" (12:12 RSV). In his First Letter to the Thessalonians, he says in simple, quick repetition, "Rejoice always, pray without ceasing, give thanks in all circumstances" (5:16–18).

Paul's call to constant prayer has been taken seriously in the Christian spiritual tradition, for as John Calvin reminds us, God "promises that 'he will be near to all who call upon him in truth' (Ps. 145:18). . . . [And] those who 'seek him with all their heart will find him' (Jer. 29:13–14)."[8]

There are a number of ways Christians throughout the centuries have attempted to find God in constant prayer. All these strategies recognize that there is an intimate and inseparable relationship between prayer as a way of life and the process of bringing the injunction to pray without ceasing to fruition.

One strategy in answer to Paul's call to pray constantly and without ceasing has involved looking to Paul himself. Paul's answer seems simple: In all things and in all ways, give prayers of thanksgiving to God. Yet it is instructive, if not simply astounding, that the man who suffered trials,

hardships, jail, and setbacks in unending succession is the same man
who suggests that the prayer of thanksgiving should be prayed without
ceasing. Yet in 1 Corinthians 1:4, he says, "I give thanks to my God always for you." To the Ephesians he writes, "I do not cease to give thanks
for you as I remember you in my prayers" (1:16). In Colossians 1:3, we
read, "In our prayers for you we always thank God." First Thessalonians
1:2 says, "We always give thanks to God for all of you and mention you
in our prayers, constantly." To the Philippians he sends the greeting, "I
thank my God every time I remember you, constantly praying with joy
in every one of my prayers for all of you" (1:3–4). Constant prayer for
Paul, then, is constant thanksgiving.

Another strategy for constant prayer is the divine office or praying
the liturgy of the hours. Originally codified in the monastic rule drawn
up by St. Benedict of Nursia in the sixth century, the "hours" comprised
an eightfold pattern of monastic prayer intended to provide a frame-
work for constant prayer. In Benedictine monasticism, the hours are
called the *opus Dei*, work of God.[9] Together with personal prayer (*lectio
divina*) and manual labor, the hours addressed the issue of constant
prayer by becoming "pillars of a bridge thrown across the stream of
time." The regularly prayed divine hours, as the work of God, together
with personal prayer and manual labor, provided stability, place, and
community, considered essential for constant prayer. Over the years, the
rule has been modified and adapted in many forms. Today, its original
intention of fostering constant prayer is finding new applications in both
monastic and "secular" settings.[10] Through this work of God, many are
finding new ways in the midst of the often-frenetic pace of contemporary life to be with God in prayer in the "evening and morning and at
noon" (Ps. 55:17).

Another path of constant prayer, which will be discussed further in
later chapters, is through complete participation in, imitation of, or
union with Christ. In this path to constant prayer, Christ's life is a model
of blessedness, holiness, and constant prayer.

In yet another way, constant prayer is equated with constant consciousness or awareness of the presence of God. This strategy often uses
metaphors of conversation or expressions of desire as a way of penetrat-
ing the enigma of constant prayer. Augustine provides an example of this
form of constant prayer centered on the desire for constant awareness of
the presence of God. He doubts, for instance, that constant prayer can
mean anything like ceaselessly bending our knees or ceaselessly lifting
our eyes and hands to God. Instead, he concludes that if we wish to pray
without ceasing, we must not cease to desire. There is for Augustine an
interior kind of prayer without ceasing, recollecting constantly the true
desire of the heart as determined by faith, hope, and charity:

When we cherish uninterrupted desire along with the exercise of faith and hope and charity, we "pray always." . . . What else is intended by the words of the apostle: "Pray without ceasing," than, "desire without intermission, from Him who alone can give it, a happy life, which no life can be but that which is eternal"? . . . "Let your requests be made known to God" [is] not to be understood as if thereby they become known to God [but] that they be made known to ourselves in the presence of God by patient waiting upon God.[11]

Related to the practice of the presence of God is the concept of discipline in prayer, which results in an ongoing habit, a *habitus* or "recollection" of God, that is the unceasing center of our day-to-day existence and actions. In this form of constant prayer, how we act and how we live contribute to the formation of an ongoing habit of godly recollection. The basis for this idea goes back at least to Aristotle and is intimately related to moral virtue. For Aristotle, "moral virtue involves the formation of character; that is, a person develops or has a virtue by forming a habit of acting in a particular way when it is appropriate. We form these habits by practicing good actions just as a person learns a craft by practice."[12] Thus, the *habitus* of this strategy for constant prayer is formed by repeated acts of recollection and virtue. The name for the clothing of monks and nuns, the habit, is intended as an outward reminder of the inward habit of constant prayer. Origen, the third-century Greek theologian, provides an excellent example of encouraging a link between constant prayer and virtue:

He prays "constantly" (deeds of virtue or fulfilling the commandments are included as part of prayer) who unites prayer with the deeds required and right deeds with prayer. For the only way we can accept the command to "pray constantly" (1 Thess. 5:17) as referring to a real possibility is by saying that the entire life of the saint taken as a whole is a single great prayer.[13]

Perhaps one of the most famous routes to constant prayer is found in the Greek Orthodox tradition. This form of prayer, variously known as Hesychasm (meaning stillness or quiet), the Jesus Prayer, or the Prayer of the Heart, takes the imperative to pray without ceasing seriously. It takes it, in fact, literally to heart. Hesychasm means to pray with conscious awareness at every moment of every hour, day and night. The practice takes Paul's call to constant prayer in a literal sense. Other biblical material is also interpreted literally, such as "I will bless the LORD at all times; his praise shall continually be in my mouth" (Ps. 34:1), and "I slept, but my heart was awake" (Song of Songs 5:2). For the Hesychast, the solution to the problem of constant prayer is breath, something we do without ceasing, whether asleep or awake. By linking a short prayer to breath, one is in constant prayer. This form of prayer, though ultimately quite simple, is based on a few precise techniques that we will look at in more detail below.

Finally, some take Paul's injunction to pray without ceasing in a global, communal, and ecclesial context. As members of the body of Christ, the global church *is* in constant prayer at all times. In some place in the world, at any given time, a godly community is in prayer. Connected as we are through the body of Christ, each of us is, in a very real sense, enmeshed in this community of constant prayer.

All these strategies are valid responses to Paul's call to constant prayer. Realistically, however, for most of us, our prayer life is in constant flux. In fact, most of us could say that what is most constant in our prayer life is our constant *failure* to pray. We can soften the blow of this reality, however, by interpreting Paul's statements not as commands but as guidelines for optimizing our awareness of God moment by moment. In this sense, Paul's words are an offer, even an invitation. Constant prayer in this sense becomes the amen by which we go about our business of living in Christ, remembering God, and inclining ourselves to God's will.

At this point it is instructive to look at a few teachers and writers on Christian prayer who take seriously both ideas of constant prayer and of inclining ourselves to God. The thirteenth-century Franciscan Bonaventure, in his *Soul's Journey into God*, writes that "prayer is the mother and source of the ascent."[14] Bonaventure's insight is that prayer as mother and source of our journey recognizes normal human patterns of nurture, separation, progression, growth, loss, transformation, and love that serve, ultimately, to guide us toward God, who is the source of our desires.

Prayer is mother, source, father, and goal. These metaphors, which suggest that prayer resides at the very core of our humanity, are also exemplified in the work of the twentieth-century Catholic theologian Hans Urs von Balthasar. He approaches prayer through the human condition by means of a Christology that emphasizes our essential, personal union with Christ. We inhere in Christ "constantly and essentially," he writes, linked to Christ, who is God's answered prayer to us:

> The fact that, together with all other creatures, we are created in the Word implies not only that we are related to him as our origin, but also that we inhere in him, constantly and essentially. We see this relationship of inherence manifestly and visibly perfected in that God the Son "unites all things" in himself, the Word made man, "things in heaven and things on

earth" (Eph. 1:10), and incorporates all who are willing into his Mystical Body, infusing all the branches of the mystical vine with his blood.[15]

As we inhere in Christ, we are in constant communion with God. This passage has eucharistic overtones: We are engrafted into the mystical vine with Christ's blood. It is that mystical union through Christ's blood that fashions a tree of life sprouting as source and resource for constant prayer. In a sense, through the mutual interconnectedness of all things in Christ, we are freed from constant prayer as an obligation; we are freed to encounter constant prayer as the potential for unceasing encounter with the mystery of God. Concerning this mystery, von Balthasar adds that "[the being of God] is the unique marvel, ever new. No seraph, no saint in all eternity could 'get used' to it; in fact, the longer one gazes into this mystery, the more one longs to go on gazing, glimpsing the fulfillment of that to which our entire creaturely nature aspires."[16] This is a freedom and a claim of constant prayer: We will never get used to it. Ingrafted into Christ, we will long to go on gazing into the mystery of God.

Karl Barth has written that "the Reformation appears to us as a great whole: a labor of research, thinking, preaching, discussion, polemic, and organization. But it was more than all that. From what we know, it was also an act of continuous prayer."[17] Martin Luther, the sixteenth-century Protestant Reformer, gives his own perspective on what Barth might have meant by "continuous prayer." The biblical injunction to pray without ceasing is framed as an imperative. But seldom if ever does Scripture invite, strongly suggest, or even demand that we do a thing that is not possible to do. The command may be difficult, but between our own obedience and the abiding aid of grace, the imperative is never the impossible. For Luther, then, unceasing prayer is not the impossibility that it may at first appear to be. Despite the imperative, constant prayer is, for Luther, more a matter of divine grace given than a matter of human will achieved. Luther frames the freedom of constant prayer in terms of what he calls "spiritual" prayer:

> There is no Christian who does not have time to pray without ceasing.
> But I mean the spiritual prayer, that is: no one is so heavily burdened
> with labor, but that if they will they can, while working, speak with God
> in their heart, lay before God their need and that of others, ask for help,
> make petition, and in all this exercise and strengthen one's faith.[18]

The belief that prayer will be answered is an exercise in faith; faith is by grace alone. Grace, according to Luther, makes of the imperative a gift.

John Calvin, another early leader of Protestant reform, frames the issue of constant prayer in terms of the uncertainties of life:

> For however much after our heart's desire affairs may prosperously flow and occasion for happiness surround us on all sides, still there is no point of time when our need does not urge us to pray. . . . Now if we should consider how many dangers at every moment threaten, fear itself will teach us that we at no single time may leave off praying.[19]

Calvin realizes, however, that the fact that we may at times leave off praying teaches us something. It teaches us that the imperative to pray without ceasing is beyond human effort alone. We cannot will it into being. Therefore, according to Calvin, we are given two aids for the "spiritual" task of constant prayer. The first gift is the Holy Spirit, who both constantly intercedes on our behalf and helps us focus our mind and heart on God. The second gift to aid in constant prayer is the desire or zeal for God that results from that same focus:

> Moreover, zeal for the kingdom of God and his glory ought so to lay hold on us, not intermittently but constantly, that the same opportunity [to pray constantly] may ever remain ours. It is therefore not in vain that constancy in prayer is enjoined upon us.[20]

As with Simon Tugwell, Calvin also recognizes that if we are to pray constantly, not all prayers will be perfect. Yet Calvin assures us that God will "hearken even to perverted prayer." Scripture, he says:

> relates that God has granted fulfillment of certain prayers, despite the fact that they have burst forth from a heart not at all peaceful or composed. . . . Jotham had vowed the inhabitants of Shechem to the destruction that later overtook them. . . . God granted the petition. From this, it seems, we may infer that, although prayers are not framed to the rule of the Word, they obtain their effect.[21]

Our prayers need not be perfect, driven by love or even goodwill. Trivial prayers, prayers of anger, prayers composed in states of disease and sadness, even prayers that do not conform to the core values or rule of Scripture are, according to Calvin, heard by God and have their effect.

St. Francis of Assisi, thirteenth-century founder of the Franciscan order, modeled constant prayer in another way: by identifying completely in body, mind, and spirit with the life and work of Christ. St. Bonaventure, in his *Life of St. Francis,* writes that through constant prayer complete participation in Christ is possible:

The servant of Christ Francis strove to keep his spirit in the presence of God *by praying without ceasing* so that he might not be without the comfort of his *Beloved*. Prayer was a delight to this contemplative who had already become a fellow citizen of the angels; . . . for in everything which he did, distrusting his own effort and trusting in God's loving concern, *he cast his care* completely *upon the Lord* in urgent prayers to him. For whether walking or sitting, inside or outside, working or resting, he was intent on prayer.[22]

Francis exemplified the spirit of service, poverty, and humility through this process of *imitatio Christi*. He *lived* unceasing prayer.

All these writers understand that a *life* of constant prayer must at times include a prayer life of triviality, struggle, lack of composure, even darkness and a sense of abandonment. In the language of the thirteenth century, Bonaventure reports that Francis "used to go to deserted areas and abandoned churches to pray at night. There he often endured horrible struggles with devils who fought him physically."[23]

That the devil physically fought Francis's effort to pray hints of the body. What we might call "constant prayer in the spirit" is deeply integrated in Francis with "constant prayer in the body." Both are essential in the journey toward full participation in Christ. While withdrawing to Mount La Verna, seeking a place of peace and prayer, "Francis received a vision of a winged Seraph in the form of the crucified."[24] There he received the stigmata (an exact replication of the five wounds of Christ received on the cross) as a "testimony of truth by the *seal of the likeness* of the living God, namely of *Christ crucified*, which was imprinted on his body not by natural forces or human skill but by the wondrous power of *the Spirit of the living* God."[25] The stigmata, as a "seal of likeness" imprinted on Francis's body, was an outward sign of inward, constant prayer.

Brother Lawrence of the Resurrection, a late-seventeenth-century cook and sandal maker of the Discalced Carmelite Monastery in Paris, takes a slightly different road to constant prayer. Brother Lawrence focuses on the presence of God in *all* things: cooking, making shoes, mental prayer, reciting the daily office, sleep, correspondence, giving spiritual advice. As he practices the presence of God in prayer, Brother Lawrence finds constant love of God in simple tasks and simple conversation:

He [Brother Lawrence] told me that what matters is renouncing once and for all everything that we recognize does not lead to God, in order to become accustomed to a continual conversation with him, without mystery or finesse. . . . During this continual conversation we are thus taken up in praising, adoring, and ceaselessly loving God for his infinite goodness and perfection.[26]

Hesychasm serves as a final example of constant prayer. *Hesychia* is a Greek term meaning inner stillness, quietness, tranquility. Practiced by monks in Egypt, Syria, Palestine, and Greece, Hesychasm was given theological structure and legitimacy in the fourteenth century by St. Gregory of Palamos and was made accessible to even the most humble of laypersons in the anonymous nineteenth-century classic *The Way of the Pilgrim*. Additional teaching on Hesychasm from the fathers can be found in the five volumes of *The Philokalia,* meaning love of beauty.

Few prayer practices from the Christian tradition reveal such an explicit awareness of the fact that prayer permeates all of life. In this simple prayer, to pray is as essential as breathing; in fact, the prayer is connected with breath. Practitioners of Hesychasm asked a simple question: Is there something we naturally do without ceasing? They found an answer: breathe. The next step was simple: connect prayer to breathing. In this way, the breath of life becomes the breath of constant prayer. Even while the body sleeps, the "breath of the heart" is awake. The "pilgrim" of *The Way of the Pilgrim* describes how a teacher explains it:

> The elder invited me to visit his cell. When we entered, the elder said, "The ceaseless Jesus Prayer is a continuous, uninterrupted call on the holy name of Jesus Christ with the lips, mind, and heart; and in the awareness of His abiding presence it is a plea for His blessing in all undertakings, in all places, at all times, even in sleep. The words of the Prayer are: 'Lord Jesus Christ, Son of God, have mercy on me, a sinner.' Anyone who becomes accustomed to this Prayer will experience great comfort as well as the need to say it continuously." The elder opened the *Philokalia* to the account of St. Simeon the New Theologian and began reading: "Sit alone and in silence; bow your head and close your eyes; relax your breathing and with your imagination look into your heart; direct your thoughts from your head into your heart. And while inhaling say, 'Lord Jesus Christ, have mercy on me,' either softly with your lips or in your mind. Endeavor to fight distractions but be patient and peaceful and repeat this process frequently."[27]

Through additional training and constant repetition of the prayer tied to inhaling and exhaling, the pilgrim eventually learns the prayer as it descends into the mind, the body, and the spirit.

The Christian tradition of prayer is obviously rich with responses to Paul's injunction that we "pray without ceasing." But all the examples we have explored raise an important question: How can busy, modern men and women realistically engage in, much less completely practice, constant prayer? Though some of the illustrations suggested above may seem attainable—such as prayer being constant when the entire body of Christ, the church, is considered, or that what is really meant

by constant prayer is regular liturgical worship—the question actually
assumes an understanding of prayer that rests on a false premise: that
prayer is separate from other areas of life. We pray, for instance, and
we work, we pray and we play, we pray and we sleep.

But what should be apparent by now is that to pray does not mean
to think about God in contrast to thinking about other things, or to
spend time with God in contrast to spending time with family, work, or
friends. Rather, to pray is to think and to live our entire life as it truly is:
in the presence of God. What is really at stake here is that in constant
prayer, regardless of the strategy, we become aware of our desires and
we conform those desires to Christ through service to and love of God,
neighbor, and world. Concerning prayer and this desire, Karl Barth has
said something strange yet really quite wonderful:

> Let us approach the subject from the given fact that God answers. God
> is not deaf, but listens; more than that, he acts. God does not act in the
> same way whether we pray or not. *Prayer exerts an influence upon God's
> action, even upon his existence.* This is what the word "answer" means. In
> Question 129 of the Heidelberg Catechism it is stated that the answer to
> prayer is more certain than our awareness of the things that we request.
> It seems there is nothing more sure than the feelings of our desires.[28]

Constant prayer, beyond anything else, seems to involve becoming aware
of who we are in relation to God. What is strange and wonderful and
beyond our control is that prayer exerts an influence on God's action,
even his existence. Paul calls us to constant prayer so that we may be
in God and God in us.

Darkness and Prayer

> Those who walk in light sing hymns of light; those who walk in darkness
> sing hymns of darkness. All must sing the tune allotted to them by God.
> Fear itself, suspense, desolation, are verses in the hymns of night.
>
>   Jean-Pierre de Caussade, "The Dark Night of Faith"

If prayer is to become a way of life, dark places in life must be not
only acknowledged but also prayed through. Darkness includes many
things and is expressed in many ways. It includes loss, grief, pain, and
suffering. Darkness refers to a felt sense of God's complete absence
rather than comforting presence. Darkness shows itself as anger, envy,
or hatred. It can be expressed as a condition of our relationship with

God. It is experienced in terms of demonic powers or of sin. It inflicts the psychological, social, and cultural aspects of our lives.

In Christian prayer, there are established ways to name and confront, even incorporate, darkness and pain: confession, for instance, or practicing forgiveness, or simply waiting in faith. These are all good, but sometimes we have no patience, we cannot forgive, pain lingers too long, death and grief overwhelm, faith seems a fading memory. So what are we to do? Pray. Enter the darkness. Let the darkness rise. Anger can be prayer. Extreme lament and screaming at God are prayer. As shown in the Psalms and the book of Job,[29] giving up, submission, dejection, and depression can become prayer. As we will see throughout this book, Christian masters of the life of prayer teach us to enter the darkness, not to run from it.

John of the Cross, Teresa of Avila, John Bunyan, and Dorothy Day are but a handful of Christians who have entered the darkness in prayer. These same people also testify to the fact that, as contemporary writer Thomas Green contends, "darkness is really excessive light." Light can be too bright for us to see. It blinds us, and we see nothing. John of the Cross teaches that darkness is really illumination. Thomas Green concurs, writing that at a turning point of his life, "I began to be at home in the darkness and prayer has had a positive and ever deeper meaning for me since." Explaining John of the Cross's famous dark night of the soul, Green goes on to say:

> The darkness is not really darkness, God is not really absent, but we lack the eyes to see, the tongue to taste what is really there. That is precisely the point. God is not absent; God is closer than ever, but we are blind. It is this dark contemplation which is in us, working our healing.[30]

All the models of prayer outlined in this book are streaked with the accents of the powers that interfere with our finest intentions in prayer. Though we are told that the Holy Spirit prays for us with sighs too deep for words (Rom. 8:26), often we cannot hear. In conversational prayer, there is darkness in silence and in word. Relationship can retreat to nothing but brokenness, shattered hope, scraps of forgiveness, sulfur whiffs of reconciliation. Scorpions, deserts, and desolation can suck energy from each step of our journey. Forgiveness and hospitality seem to fly away. No longer energizing forces, they become mocking memories of what was and is no more; they become fences of isolation. Prayer can become as barbed wire, holding in death. We can encounter an angel of death hovering around us in the same moment we are transformed into a new creation. Transformation is not all union and light; much of transformation is steeped in darkness. It is fleeting, *and* it is slow, hard, intermittent, and sporadic. The darkness of God's felt absence and abandonment sums up all the darkness above and more. God is gone. Consciousness of the presence of God can become a memory that mocks.

These are dark periods in prayer. To stand before God during these times is to stand before a cold, empty hearth. No fire burns with necessary warmth. At times, darkness, as much as light, must become a way of life and prayer.

The Active Life and the Contemplative Life

> We are the temple of the living God.
>
> 2 Corinthians 6:16

The story of Christ's visit to the house of Mary and Martha is found in two places in the Gospels. In the better-known account in Luke 10:39–42, we read that Jesus entered a certain town and was received into the house of Martha:

> She had a sister named Mary, who sat at the Lord's feet and listened to what he was saying. But Martha was distracted by her many tasks; so she came to him and asked, "Lord, do you not care that my sister has left me to do all the work by myself? Tell her then to help me." But the Lord answered her, "Martha, Martha, you are worried and distracted by many things; there is need of only one thing. Mary has chosen the better part, which will not be taken away from her."

From earliest Western Christian times, this passage has been interpreted allegorically as indicating Jesus' preference for the contemplative life over the active life.[31] Martha, representing the active life, scurries around, seemingly anxious, serving Jesus, and troubled by her sister. Mary, representing the contemplative life, sits at Jesus' feet, simply dwelling in his presence and listening to his word. Given this allegory, it seems quite obvious that Jesus prefers and recommends the contemplative over the active life: Mary (the contemplative) does the "one thing necessary"; she has "chosen the better part." In the Old Testament, Rachel (contemplative) and Leah (active) have also been similarly interpreted allegorically.

The "one thing necessary" (*unum necessarium* in the Latin Vulgate) and the "best part [*optima pars*], which will not be taken away," have both been interpreted in many ways. The *unum necessarium* has been taken to mean contemplation itself, divine unity, the Trinity, eternal life, the vision of God, the reward of contemplation, and love for and commitment to Christ or God. According to Guibert of Nogent, for example, the "one thing necessary" is that "every saint [will] come to knowledge of divinity only by faith and by love of humanity." Joachim of Fiore interpreted the "one thing" as a call "to look constantly at the living God," while for Thomas à Kempis and John of the Cross, "the essence of the one necessary thing was self denial."[32] Meister Eckhart, surprisingly, reverses the order, giving Martha the "better part." He concludes that Christ's repetition of her name, "Martha, Martha," indicates that *Martha* had all good things, *both* temporal *and* eternal, and that her action was the better part because it had first been grounded in contemplation.

Overall, however, as rich as the tradition of interpretation is, it has created an unfortunate dichotomy for the life of prayer. At its best, it encourages a life of prayer, but it often does so at the expense of ethics or compassionate service. At its worst, it tends to set two classes of people in opposition and to give one priority over the other. In other words, there is the contemplative life or the active life but not both, and the contemplative life is counted as superior. The dichotomy easily leads to spiritual elitism.

But both ways of life, when integrated, *can* be exemplary. The problems arise when the active life and the contemplative life are held in contrast. As we look at the models of prayer in this book, we will be doing so with an explicit understanding that the so-called active life and contemplative life are reciprocal and dialogical. As a part of our baptismal heritage, we are all called to a life containing both active and contemplative elements.

One way to make the integrative quality of the active life and the contemplative life clearer is to look at another venerable Christian tradition of prayer. This way of looking at Christian prayer is an integrated approach that functions as a mutually enhancing circle between action and contemplation rather than as an either/or decision. This tradition has Greek roots and is composed of *praktikē*, which is roughly equivalent to the active life, and two forms of contemplation: *physikē* and *theōria*. *Physikē* generally refers to indirect contemplation of God. *Theōria* generally refers to direct contemplation of God. *Praktikē, physikē,* and *theōria* all have such a long history in the Christian prayer tradition that complete accuracy as to their various meanings is impossible short of an extended treatment of each. Different writers throughout history have given them different shades and nuances of meaning. The following outline, however, does show the importance of a necessary integration of the active life and the contemplative life for all Christians.

Praktikē, the active life, generally consists of three steps: (1) repentance or conversion, (2) development of virtue or human excellence, and

(3) love of neighbor.[33] In *praktikē*, says Evagrios Ponticos, "we practice the virtues in order to achieve contemplation of the inner essences of created things."[34] This stage involves putting into practice advice on how to overcome evil actions, thoughts, and intentions.

The second stage is actually the first stage of contemplation. This is *physikē*, in which we focus on the indirect contemplation or love of God, that is, contemplation of God through contemplation of the created world and the soul. Through regular and not episodic contemplation of the world about us, we are increasingly able to experience all creation (including our own life) as a gift and to discern God's presence in the entire created world. We begin to "read" the "book of nature" and the "book of experience." As we are transformed through this form of contemplation, we begin to recognize the image of God imprinted in creation and present within our soul.

Theōria, the second stage of contemplation, is not just cold, intellectual knowledge but a passionate, contemplative insight involving loving and sharing. It is direct contemplation through both intellect and love of God. Thomas Keating defines *theōria*:

> The Greek Fathers, especially Clement of Alexandria, Origen and Gregory of Nyssa, borrowed from the Neo-Platonist the term *theōria*. This originally meant the intellectual vision of truth, which the Greek philosophers regarded as the supreme activity of the person of wisdom. To this technical term the Fathers added the meaning of the Hebrew *da'ath*, that is, the kind of experiential knowledge that comes through love. It was with this expanded understanding of the term that *theōria* was translated into the Latin *contemplatio*. . . . This tradition was summed up by Gregory the Great when he described contemplation as the knowledge of God that is impregnated with love.[35]

Thus, in the practice of *theōria*, through grace, we are in direct and loving contemplation or union with God without mediation.

In Greek philosophy, *theōria* and *praxis*, or "action," "originally signified two modes of activity at the basis of two forms of life, what we would call the philosophical and the political pursuits."[36] In the Christian prayer tradition, *praktikē* replaced the Greek *praxis* and made an explicit connection between *theōria* (watching) and *praktikē* (doing). For our purposes, it is most important to note that the two are inseparable. In fact, the ascent to perfect union with God was thought to be composed, as Vladimir Lossky has noted, of "two stages achieved simultaneously on two separate but closely interrelated levels." Lossky adds:

> Action (πρᾶξις [*praxis*]) and contemplation (θεωρία [*theōria*]) are inseparable in Christian knowledge. . . . According to St. Maximus, contempla-

tion without action, theory which is not applied in practice, differs in no way from imagination, from fantasy without any real substance. . . . Similarly, action, if it is not inspired by contemplation, is as sterile and rigid as a statue.[37]

For Plato, but especially for Aristotle, the fundamental form of reasoning was *theōria*, the contemplation of a *thing* as it really is. Not only are things known directly, but also in contemplation, the apprehending subject and the object that is known are identical. Thus, in *theōria* it may be said that a mind and a heart in knowing and affection conform to the object; in Christian terms, the contemplative is conformed to God. Thomas Aquinas takes up this Aristotelian argument in the context of happiness, arguing that happiness consists in this very *theōria*. Put another way, God-conforming prayer *constitutes* happiness. By involving conformity to God through contemplation of the "thing as it really is," *theōria* includes but moves beyond the ordinary sciences to the possibility of union with God (*theōsis*) to happiness expressed as compassion in the world.

Obviously, there is room for confusion with regard to the Christian concept of *theōria*. It can mean both a contemplative vision of God in itself and a contemplative vision of God that also includes *praktikē* lived out in the form of virtue.[38] This virtue in turn is also shaped by *theōria*. Theology, then, taken in its broadest sense as *theōria*—the vision of God—is also critical reflection on the experience of virtue. The primary confusion with regard to *theōria* is that it has both a meaning referring only to contemplation of God and also a meaning that is only complete in the context of its partnership with *praktikē*.

Further, as a final contemplative stage, *theōria* can take many forms, including ecstatic or beatific visions (in Clement of Alexandria, for instance, the vision of God is *theōria theou*), intellectual visions of Christ or the Trinity, intuitive union with God described metaphorically in many ways, or various forms of love. Enfolded as it is in *praktikē, theōria* points to a life of humility, poverty, compassion, and hospitality. Though the language and the history of these terms are complex, the essential message is that the so-called active life and contemplative life are mutually enhancing aspects of prayer.

Regardless of the model of prayer, this active/contemplative component of prayer must be seen as integrative and available to all Christians depending on God's goodwill and grace. Today, there is a large body of writing on the relationship between Christian practice and belief. The terms are really not so different from those of the active and the contemplative life or of *theōria, praktikē,* or *physikē,* though they are framed with contemporary concerns of integration and egalitarianism.

Practices in the context of Christian belief are often placed in the context of community cooperation, life together, formation, and regularity over time. One definition of practice, for instance, says:

> [Practices are] patterns of cooperative human activity in and through which life together takes shape over time in response to and in light of God as known in Jesus Christ. Focusing on practices invites theological reflection on the ordinary, concrete activities of actual people—and also on the knowledge of God that shapes, infuses, and arises from these activities.[39]

Christian prayer, both active and contemplative, comprises patterns of cooperative human activity over time in response to God, known in Jesus Christ.

Prayer, Meditation, and Contemplation

> You cannot in one glance survey this most vast and beautiful system of the universe, in its wide expanse, without being completely overwhelmed by the boundless force of its brightness. . . . This skillful ordering of the universe is for us a sort of mirror in which we can contemplate God. . . . The reason why the prophet attributes to the heavenly creatures a language known to every nation is that therein lies an attestation of divinity.
>
> John Calvin, Institutes, 1.5.1

Throughout this book, the word *prayer* is used in an inclusive sense to indicate verbal prayer as well as meditation and contemplation. *Meditation* and *contemplation* are also used interchangeably. At times, however, a fairly precise meaning is intended for a particular use of prayer, meditation, or contemplation. This practice is maintained not because of a lack of clarity but rather for two intentional reasons: (1) The terms themselves have been used interchangeably and without consistency within the Christian spiritual tradition itself, and (2) when talking about prayer as a way of life, the terms, regardless of any initial definitional content, overlap and even at times merge. One might say that there is no "essence" of prayer, meditation, or contemplation. This is amply illustrated in the following quotation from Friedrich Heiler in a chapter titled "The Essence of Prayer":

> Prayer appears in history in an astonishing multiplicity of forms; as the calm collectedness of a devout individual soul, and as the ceremonial liturgy of a great congregation; as an original creation of a religious genius, and as an imitation on the part of a simple, average religious person; as

the spontaneous expression of up-springing religious experiences, and as the mechanical recitation of an incomprehensible formula; as bliss and ecstasy of heart, and as painful fulfillment of the law; as the involuntary discharge of an overwhelming emotion, and as the voluntary concentration on a religious object; as loud shouting and crying, and as still, silent absorption as artistic poetry, and as stammering speech; as the flight of the spirit to the supreme Light, and as a cry out of the deep distress of the heart; . . . as a childlike entreaty for life, health, and happiness, and as an earnest desire for power in the moral struggle of existence; as a simple petition for daily bread, and as an all-consuming yearning for God Himself; . . . as swelling phrases of politeness and flattery before an unapproachable King, and as a free outpouring in the presence of a friend who cares; as the humble petition of a servant to a powerful master, and as the ecstatic converse of the bride with the heavenly Bridegroom.[40]

As we change and grow in our life of prayer, a wide variety of prayer, meditation, and contemplation is there to meet us along the way. At times, we will spend years with one unchanging prayer practice, burrowing deeper into the riches of the practice as we go. At other times, we find ourselves aided and entranced by the flexibility of the wide range and variation in prayer. Irrespective of how we practice or identify it, prayer is legitimate regardless of whether we call it verbal prayer, meditation, contemplation, or something else entirely. We do ourselves no good by being anxious about "getting definitions right."[41]

In many contexts, it is sufficient to remember that teachers of Christian prayer have used the terms interchangeably. Various definitions of prayer have emphasized the use of images, while others insist on the emptying of images, thoughts, sensations, or any interruption that passes into our awareness. A tendency within the tradition is to relegate contemplation to an intuitive, silent, imageless resting in God. Meditation is seen as a process of integrating one's personal story with the divine story narrated in Scripture or in the "book of nature" through the use of reflection, in which imagination, memory, intellect, senses, perceptions, and all human attributes are brought to bear in reflection on an object, person, occurrence, or story. Prayer would then refer to verbal manifestations covering a wide range of options and formulas.

To give some symbolic clarity to these modes of prayer, one might parallel each to a particular flight of birds. In prayer, the mind and the heart are active. One may compare prayer of this sort to the flight of birds that is seemingly random as they flit from one branch to the next. In such prayer, one brings before God one idea or feeling after another. Other prayer is straight and linear as reason is applied to, say, a need, a confession, or thanksgiving in prayer. This is like the flight of a dove: direct, strong, and to the point. Meditation is generally silent or verbal reflection, imagination, experience, memory, or perception applied to Scripture, nature, the soul, others, a place, science, Jesus Christ, doctrine, art, or any other aspect of God-reflecting life. Meditation tends to encircle an object, discerning its God qualities and seeking strategies for compassion based on meditative insights. One can see this in the slow, methodical circular or spiral soaring of birds as they focus ever more precisely on an object or simply soar for the pure joy of it. Contemplation is generally silent, devoid of images. It involves resting in wonder, awe, or worship of the various manifestations of God's wisdom, being, works, or love. One can see this in the flight of birds that is called stilling, often seen in hawks during migration. A bird will rest in the air by stilling itself through barely perceptible adjustments in muscle and feather. In this flight, effort is put to the service of resting.

Prayer, whether linear or random, is "directing time," meditation is "soaring time," and contemplation is "stilling time." However, the grace of prayer is exactly that: a gift of God. Ultimately, we cannot limit or time grace.

The Body in Prayer: Gestures, Postures, Positions

In her book *Praying with Body and Soul,* Jane Vennard recalls her early memories of prayer. With the words "Let us pray," she recalls "a collective silence as we bow our heads. Sometimes hands come together in laps, sometimes folded in front of chests, sometimes with palms open on knees." Urging us to let our bodies teach us to pray, she remembers "Please bow your heads in prayer" being accompanied by a "Shhh! Be quiet! Bow your head"[42] whispered by a parent.

The Christian prayer tradition has not always been so "crimped and pinched" when it comes to gestures and the body in prayer. Today, many people's experiences of the body in prayer are similar to Vennard's as a young girl. In past centuries, and as we are beginning to discover today, the body and the senses are as important to prayer as are mind, heart, imagination, and soul. This book will not treat posture and gesture explicitly, but as is the case with all habitats of prayer, the body is present everywhere in any discussion of prayer.

As early as the third century, Christian writers on prayer were paying close attention to the body. At the end of his long work *On Prayer,* the theologian and spiritual writer Origen speculates:

> It does not seem to me out of place after these discussions to finish this treatise on prayer by speaking in an introductory way about the disposition and the posture one ought to have in praying, the place where one

ought to pray, the direction in which one ought to look barring any chance
circumstance, the suitable and special time for prayer, and anything else
similar. The question of disposition must be referred to the soul, that of
posture to the body.[43]

Origen goes on to say that there are many different postures for the body
in prayer, but the "position with outstretched hands and the eyes lifted
up is to be preferred before all others, because it bears in prayer the
image of characteristics befitting the soul and applies it to the body."[44]
Concerning place, Origen says tellingly, "Every place is suitable for prayer
if a person prays well."[45]

It was said of St. Francis of Assisi that "he made of his whole body
a tongue; more than someone who prayed, he became prayer."[46] In
other words, Francis's body, his movements, his words, his touch, his
senses—all these and more conveyed prayer. It is difficult to imagine
St. Francis of Assisi bowing his head and obediently closing his eyes; it
is no doubt more true to the life of St. Francis that he prayed with eyes
wide open, his face square to the world.

Just a few decades before St. Francis initiated the movement that
became the Franciscan order, an illustrated prayer manual attributed
to Peter the Chanter appeared. It survives in many manuscript forms.[47]
Along with descriptions of the meaning, method, intention, and effects
of prayer, the manual in its various forms contains fifty-eight pictures
of seven distinct postures or "modes" of prayer. Each picture is accompanied by a detailed description of the posture. To a modern reader, the
prayer postures may seem a bit unusual, but they are intended to instill
a sense of reverence for and attentiveness toward God.

In the first mode or posture, the person at prayer stands, with feet
together, eyes open and toward heaven, arms lifted up. In some illustrations and descriptions, the arms are fully extended with palms upward;
in others, the arms are extended with palms together over the head.

The second mode is an obvious imitation of the cross. The person
at prayer stands with arms outstretched, in some cases with eyes open
and face turned upward.

In the third mode, the one at prayer stands, with the hands in front
of the face, palms slightly apart and directed toward the face, as if the
person is reading. In this stance of "reading," one prays as if the Word
is present.

The fourth mode is a posture of kneeling with hands variously posi-
tioned. Sometimes the hands are folded together with head bowed or are
before the face, again in a gesture of apparent reading. At other times
the arms are held out straight with palms upward and open. While the

body from the knees is usually upright, in a few instances, the body is bent at the waist, again with arms outstretched.

The fifth mode of prayer involves forms of prostration in which one prays face down on the ground. The prostrant may lie flat on the floor with head up and hands open and receptive or on his or her knees with head bowed to the floor. In other forms of prostration, ankles, knees, chest, and lips are in contact with the ground, and the arms are extended so that the body forms a cross.

The sixth mode is genuflection in a variety of forms: standing, bent at the waist; or kneeling, with a slight bend at the waist and arms open in a receptive posture; or bent fully at the waist, torso parallel to the ground, with arms hanging straight down and palms held together.

The seventh mode is a combination of prostration and genuflection. One posture in this mode illustrates the person at prayer on his knees, with waist bent parallel to the ground, and supported by the elbows. The hands are then once again open before the face. Another approaches a fetal position. The person is supported by the lower legs, with knees, waist, and shoulders bent, elbows touching the knees. The face is turned either downward into the hands or upward in an attitude of supplication.

Peter the Chanter's work reflects a long tradition of "conditioning" the body for prayer and the actual engagement of the body in prayer. In the Eastern Orthodox Hesychast tradition, for instance, St. Peter of Damaskos writes of "Seven Forms of Bodily Discipline" that either precede or accompany prayer. St. Peter's seven forms of discipline used to integrate the body in prayer include (1) stillness, (2) moderate fasting, (3) moderate vigils, (4) recital of psalms ("prayer expressed in a bodily way through psalms with prostrations"), (5) spiritual prayer in which the intellect is freed from all thoughts, (6) reading the lives of the fathers and the mothers of the church ("for prayer is helped by reading in stillness and reading is helped by pure prayer"), and (7) questioning those with experience about all one's thoughts and actions.[48] The final three may seem at first glance outside the purview of "bodily" disciplines. But the fifth is intended to purify the senses so that they are acute, accurate, and pure. The sixth shows us our own spiritual poverty whenever we view reading as an activity of mind alone. For Peter of Damaskos, in this tradition of prayer, the body is engaged on equal footing with the mind. The seventh, a reference to spiritual direction, indicates the need to explore all areas of one's life in prayer as they relate to God, including and perhaps especially the body.

Shortly after the death of St. Dominic, founder of the Dominican tradition in the thirteenth century, an anonymous writer set down *The Nine Ways of Prayer of St. Dominic*.[49] Claiming to be descriptions of how the founder prayed, these nine ways of prayer quickly caught on within the order and are revered (if not always practiced exactly!) by Domini-cans and other interested Christians today. The nine ways of Dominican prayer are especially interesting because, in addition to describing and illustrating gesture and posture in prayer, they represent particular at-titudes and relations to God in prayer.

Serving as evidence that discounts the claim of Gnostic and Man-ichaean separation of body from spirit in Christianity, *The Nine Ways* begins by saying that "such a method [of prayer] serves to enkindle devotion by the alternate action of soul upon body and body upon soul." Each of the postures is accompanied by short verses from Scripture that either describe the posture or justify Dominic's reasons for practicing this particular way of praying. For example, the first way of prayer, which is a prayer of humility, is accompanied by Psalm 118:107 (numbered and translated from the Latin Vulgate): "I have been humbled before you exceedingly, O LORD."

The Nine Ways also mentions how Dominic shed copious tears when practicing each of these forms of prayer. Tears themselves are long-held signs of true devotion in prayer and spring from and in a sense cleanse the body. The way of tears in devotion and prayer is well established in the Christian prayer tradition and thought of as a sign of grace.[50]

As mentioned, Dominic's first way of prayer symbolizes and fosters humility. In this form of prayer, Dominic humbles himself before the altar of Christ, where "Christ was thought to be personally present, not in symbol alone." Here Dominic stands erect, bowing and profoundly inclining his head toward the altar.

Remorse for sins is the purpose and shaping influence of the second way of prayer, in which Dominic throws himself outstretched on the ground, resting slightly on his elbows, his hands fronting his face.

The third way of prayer is no doubt the most difficult for us to un-derstand today. It is very much a prayer of the body, but as an action of penitence it has the effect of abusing the body. In this way of prayer, Dominic goes to his knees and "gives himself the discipline with an iron chain, saying 'Thy discipline has corrected me unto the end' (Ps. 17:36)."

As a form of petitionary prayer, the fourth way finds Dominic in an active bodily prayer of genuflection. With his gaze fixed on the cross, he bows deeply from the knees, "now rising [to his feet], now kneeling again." Dominic would practice it along the wayside as he traveled, in an inn after a long journey, and often at home "for hours after com-pline, till midnight." The movement of the body in this way is actually very strenuous and must have combined great physical exercise with attention on God.

The fifth way of prayer is done while standing with "hands extended before the breast in the manner of reading a book." The posture of "reading" imaginatively focuses wonder and awe toward the Word from the "book of creation."

In the sixth way, Dominic stands erect with his arms outstretched in the form of a cross. In this intentional imitation of Christ on the cross, Dominic seeks to intercede for those in need and asks for miracles of healing.

The seventh way of prayer finds Dominic "reaching toward heaven like an arrow which has been shot from a taut bow straight upwards into the sky." In this posture for the reception of grace, he stands with hands outstretched above his head and joined together or at times slightly separated as if about to receive the gifts of God. This prayer fosters an attitude of thanksgiving and gratitude and is described in *The Nine Ways* as though it were an ecstatic form of prayer.

While the first seven types of prayer are practiced with or within community, in the eighth way, Dominic withdraws to a solitary place to recollect, listen, and wait upon the Lord. After recollecting himself in the presence of God, Dominic "would sit quietly, and after the sign of the cross, begin to read from a book opened before him." In this way, he would pass from reading to prayer, from prayer to meditation, and from meditation to contemplation. After contemplation, Dominic venerates the book, bows to it, kisses it, and sometimes for a short while prays with his face in his hands. Then he returns to the book "refreshed and in great interior peace."

The ninth way of prayer is walking prayer. As Dominic walks and prays, he enters what would have been considered, during Dominic's lifetime, the apex of Christian life and prayer: the fire of charity and love. Of this form of prayer, the anonymous writer of *The Nine Ways* reports:

> The brethren thought that it was while praying in this way that the saint obtained his extensive penetration of Sacred Scripture and profound understanding of the divine words, and the power to preach so fervently and courageously, and the intimate acquaintance with the Holy Spirit by which he came to know the hidden things of God.[51]

Once again, the meaning of prayer, Scripture, and acquaintanceship with God is encoded in the body. In all these postures of prayer, the eyes of the person at prayer are open wide to the world and to God.

Because most of these postures of prayer from the medieval period are static and still, it is significant that in the ninth and final way Dominic walks as he prays. Many practices of prayer do require quiet and still-ness. In certain established forms of prayer, such as Hesychasm, the body, mind, heart, and breath together activate stillness. But if prayer is to become a way of life, it must also be experienced and expressed in and through the body. Today, in addition to a revival of quiet and still meditative prayer, people at prayer dance, run, skip, walk, swing, sing, and praise God through the sight, touch, taste, feel, and sound of the sun, the moon and stars, wind, water, fire, earth and, in the words of St. Francis of Assisi, "all God's creatures."

Doctrine as Devotion

> The first and basic act of theological work is prayer.
>
> Karl Barth, *Evangelical Theology*

If prayer is a way of life, the study and practice of theology or doctrine, like any aspect of life, can be a way of prayer. For patristic and medieval theologians and contemplatives, doctrine as a form of devotion would have been self-evident and assumed. In the Christian centuries, to the time at least of the rise of humanism in the late fifteenth and early sixteenth century, virtue, theology, liturgy, manual labor, service to neighbor, and reading and interpretation of Scripture were wedded intimately to prayer and contemplation. Equating knowledge and intellect with contemplation, Evagrios of Ponticos, for instance, writes, "Prayer is the ascent of the intellect to God."[52] St. Mark the Ascetic assumes the link between prayer and virtue, saying in fact that "prayer is called a virtue, but in reality it is the mother of the virtues: for it gives birth to them through union with Christ."[53] Evagrios of Ponticos also confirms the link between prayer and theology in his famous aphorism: "If you are a theologian, you will pray truly. And if you pray truly, you are a theologian."[54]

Today, theologians are striving to infuse doctrine, its study and its application, with life-shaping qualities that will have a profound influence on an understanding of prayer. Realignment and correction of the tradition have always been essential tasks of doctrine. One contemporary theologian involved in this realignment is Ellen Charry. Her continuing thesis is that "the classic theologians based their understanding of human excellence on knowing and loving God, the imitation of or assimilation to whom brings proper human dignity and flourishing."[55] Charry focuses on the virtue-shaping function of doctrine. Thus, doctrine teaches and forms virtue. Borrowing Charry's insight about doctrine, we can speak of the virtue-shaping function of the divine pedagogy of prayer that was so essential to the Christian tradition through at least the medieval period. In Charry's words, there is more than just a faint echo of Hugh of St. Victor's dictum that "there are two things that re-store divine likeness to humanity: contemplation of truth and practice of virtue."[56] Her words in fact justify a slight paraphrase of Evagrios: "To be a theologian you must pursue virtue through prayer as a way of life." Theory is never a substitute for practice. "Prayer," as another con-temporary theologian reminds us, "is the first act that links doctrine to practice, and all the other [spiritual] exercises are simply elaborations of this primal act."[57]

Simone Weil, in another context, has written that prayer is "absolutely unmixed attention."[58] For Weil, school studies lead through attention not only to love of God but also to a way of life in this world. They lead to love, attention, and compassion for the needs of others. Likewise, the study of theology can lead through prayer to love, attention, and com-passion for the needs of others. Theology is not only an accent of prayer. It is also a partner in the cycle of practice, belief, and compassion.

The partnership of particular doctrines with the various models of prayer warrants further study. Each of the models grounds itself more particularly in some doctrines than in others. For some, the correla-tion is quite easily made: Prayer as conversation ought somehow to be informed by Logos Christology and the incarnation; prayer as journey obviously has to do with sanctification, grace, and the Holy Spirit; prayer as relationship has to do with the doctrines of Scripture, ecclesiology, and the *imago Dei*; prayer as transformation is related to pneumatology and theological anthropology; prayer as presence has to do with the doctrine of God, creation, and *theōsis*. Some doctrines permeate each model: The Trinity certainly cuts across all five, as do the doctrines of Scripture, soteriology, and ecclesiology. Each doctrine is living and breathing in its own right; it is part of a tradition, part of the present, and will extend into the future. As is prayer, so too is theology, seen in its best light, a way of life. Further work on models of prayer in relation to various doctrines will breathe new life into both.

Personal Prayer and Common Prayer

> Liturgy and contemplation are expressions of the same basic attitude and movement of the Spirit.
>
> M. Basil Pennington, *A Place Apart*

Common prayer refers to corporate prayer in worship or liturgy, but it also includes any form of prayer practiced in community. These may include, for instance, sacramental prayer, liturgy of the hours, silent meditation in a group setting, or prayers offered by informal prayer gatherings held around the world. Common prayer could also be described over against personal prayer. That is, common prayer is any prayer involving more than one person, while personal prayer is the prayer of an individual.

The term "personal" prayer will be used in this book in preference to "private" prayer. As one contemporary writer, Kenneth Leech, puts it:

> Prayer needs always to be seen within this social context, for there is no such thing as *private* prayer. The word *private* comes from the Latin *privatio*, which means robbery. To the Christian, nothing is private, least of all prayer. God is not private but personal and social, Being in relationship.[59]

Margaret Guenther reinforces Leech's idea when she adds that "whether we pray together in the liturgy or in solitude in a private space, we are always praying in company: there is no such thing as *private* prayer. After all, when in the Lord's Prayer we address God as *our* Father, we are acknowledging that there are other children in the family."[60]

Neither common nor personal prayer functions in isolation or in opposition. An individual in prayer is joined by and connected to the whole church, while the church in prayer is a community of individual Christians. The twentieth-century theologian Karl Barth, commenting on the Reformed catechisms, is firm and insistent on the interrelationship between personal and common prayer:

> One fact needs to be stressed: these texts do not mention any differences between individual prayer and corporate prayer. For the authors of the various catechisms one thing is clear: they see the church, *us*, that is to say, the members of a community forming a whole. But they distinguish also among the individuals who constitute this whole. One cannot ask whether it is the Christians who pray, or the church. There is no alternative, for when the Christians pray, it is the church; and when the church prays, it is the Christians. Between these two there can be no opposition.[61]

When we pray in solitude, we do, in a real sense, pray with the blessing of and within the community of all the saints. Similarly, a common prayer is filled with the aroma of personal prayer from individuals who comprise the community. Moving from Barth's Protestant perspective to the Roman Catholic perspective, we find the same insistence on the mutual relationship between personal prayer and corporate prayer. The Benedictine monk Columba Stewart writes:

> The liturgical prayer for which Benedictine monasticism is best known is the ecclesial and communal side of each individual's *lectio divina* [personal prayer]. Common prayer is nurtured and deepened by private prayer, just

as private prayer is energized by corporate experience of the Word in liturgy. To see *lectio* as fundamental to all Benedictine prayer does not downplay the communal liturgy but points to its heart, the unifying Word.[62]

Yet the distinction between common prayer and personal prayer is still useful. After all, we are present in space and time with others or alone. While a number of taxonomies of personal and corporate prayer exist, Paul Bradshaw, in his book *Two Ways of Praying*, does a good job of distinguishing and comparing the two.[63] Bradshaw calls personal prayer "monastic prayer"[64] and common prayer "cathedral prayer." He then suggests five characteristics that distinguish cathedral prayer and monastic prayer. First, cathedral prayer is "something that the whole congregation does"; it is essentially communal, or ecclesial, "for this is not just a prayer group, it is the church at prayer." Monastic prayer, on the other hand, is "fundamentally an individual activity." Second, in cathedral prayer, worship is led by ordained ministers of the church. In monastic prayer, there are no "permanently designated ministries, but each individual in community [or in solitude] has the right and obligation to pray." Bradshaw claims that a third contrast involves the contents of the prayer. Cathedral prayer, he says, is composed chiefly of praise and intercession and tends to have an intrinsically outward-looking orientation. On the other hand, the heart of monastic prayer is meditation and is directed toward an individual's formation and sanctification. Following Barth, however, common prayer is also formational at the deepest personal level, while monastic prayer is not Christian prayer if it is not in some way outwardly directed.

A fourth distinction must also be viewed with caution. Bradshaw claims that cathedral prayer and monastic prayer differ in their inward and outward orientation. He says, rightfully, that "the externals of worship are vitally important to cathedral prayer." In distinction to this, Bradshaw claims that in monastic prayer "externals are ultimately dispensable" and that real monastic prayer "is interior and goes on inside the heart and mind of the worshiper." Exterior action may be an aid early on in monastic prayer, Bradshaw says, but it can be dispensed with once the prayer is thoroughly internalized. Again, however, no prayer is internal only.

Bradshaw's final distinction is based on Paul's injunction to pray without ceasing. People engaged in monastic prayer tend to interpret this literally, seeking to spend as much time in prayer as possible. People engaged in cathedral prayer certainly pray as they can, but they attempt to fulfill Paul's injunction not by praying without stopping but by making their lives a prayer.

Though these distinctions are legitimate to a point, there can really be no opposition between personal and common prayer. Bradshaw, too, admits that "a form of prayer may look 'monastic,' but be understood by those praying it as fulfilling a 'cathedral' function; conversely, something that has the external characteristics of a 'cathedral' pattern of prayer may be used for a 'monastic' purpose."[65]

Not to be forgotten are the books of common prayer and other breviaries and books of liturgical rites that serve to catch the personal up in the community. Such prayer books are structured according to the liturgical seasons of the church and holy days. These seasons of common prayer arranged according to the liturgical calendar engage a worshiper in a cycle of common prayer that unites community and individuals. The usual liturgical seasons of prayer include Advent; Nativity; Epiphany; Ash Wednesday; Lent; Holy Week, with Good Friday and Easter; Ascension Day; Pentecost; and the Sundays that form the season after Pentecost, or Ordinary Time. Various Christian traditions include a variety of feast and saint days for special remembrance. Each season, as it cycles through continuous repetition, is a new time for fresh prayer, both common and personal.

Basil Pennington gives just the right touch to the question of personal and common prayer.

> Many years ago a controversy raged concerning the primacy of liturgy or of contemplation. There were eminent theologians on both sides of the issue. Happily it petered out and these men of learning went on to devote their time and talents to better ends. In fact, both liturgy and contemplation are expressions of the same basic attitude and movement of the Spirit.[66]

In summary, the idea that there is a *distinction* between personal prayer and common prayer is sometimes useful, but the idea that there is an *opposition* between them is not. The necessary balance between common prayer and personal prayer is a matter of individual (and corporate) personality, temperament, and taste. Yet it is also helpful to stretch one's temperament and to imagine the common elements in all personal prayer as well as the personal elements in all common prayer.

Prayer and Personality

> As a fully mature person, Jesus was both Extravert and Introvert, both Sensing and Intuitive, both Thinking and Feeling, both Judging and Perceiving, depending on the situation.
>
> Chester Michael and Marie Norrisey, *Prayer and Temperament*

We all bring different gifts, temperaments, and personalities to prayer. Experienced spiritual directors have known for centuries that certain individuals or communities thrive while using a form of prayer that for others serves only to deaden the spirit. Recently, using a variety of assessment tools, researchers have been studying the correlation between personality types and preferences in prayer. The studies have not only noted differences among individuals and communities but also documented individual changes in temperament and preferences in prayer over time.[67] It should come as no surprise, then, that personality and current life situations have an effect on preferences for the various models of prayer suggested in this book.

One example of how personality and temperament affect prayer can be seen in the different ways people experience prayer as relationship and God as present in prayer. In his book *Blessed and Broken*, Ralph Keifer articulates a concern that not all Christians experience a personal presence of God, nor do they think of themselves as necessarily needing to be present to God in return. Keifer approaches the presence of God primarily through the Eucharist, giving his book the subtitle *An Exploration of the Contemporary Experience of God in Eucharistic Celebration*. Keifer frankly states:

> For many people, one of the most disconcerting features of the Christian spiritual life has become the convention of speaking of God, Jesus Christ, or the Holy Spirit primarily as though they were persons who are somehow to be intimately known as lover, companion, friend, or parent. . . . The conventional Christian "personalism" is also at times a major deterrent to the embracing of the Christian faith. People undergoing religious and spiritual conversion, yet not in any way experiencing what they could identify as a "personal" presence, assume that whatever else might be involved, it could not be the God of the Christian faith.[68]

Keifer admits that there is some truth to the language of presence and what he calls "personalism" and that his aim is not to do away with such language, since for many it obviously reflects an experience of God in both the Eucharist and prayer. What he intends is simply to make room for the Christians for whom the language of relationship and presence is a problem. Essentially, for Keifer, divine presence is simply a matter of the creative imagination, and many people either lack imagination or have an overabundance of active imagination:

> It also must be acknowledged that the ability to feel that God is present as friend, lover, companion, or parent is essentially an imaginative ability that has nothing necessarily to do with the reality of things. Given the appropriate direction of my imagination, I can be brought to feel that Hitler

is in my dining room or that leprechauns are dancing on my bedpost, but the ability to imagine such things as so, and feel them, has nothing to do with their reality. To be able to feel that God is present as friend, lover, companion, or parent only speaks for a certain power of the imagination, not for everyone's spiritual condition.[69]

Keifer's suspicion of imagination as a mechanism for interacting with and interpreting the world and communicating that world to others is unfortunate. For some people, imagination renders reality as well as does reason. For these people, imagination clarifies and gives shape to life just as any of several other God-given human capacities. To imply that the presence of God is "just" imagination is like saying that something is "just" myth. Both imagination and myth are valid means of confronting and evoking the "really real" as well as the "mystery behind the real." The imagination is employed more often as a *response* to divine presence than as a means to conjure it up. In fact, Keifer's rendering of the function of imagination shifts imagination from a vehicle of understanding to a tool of the magician; it places imagination in the realm of theurgy. Both Scripture and the Christian spiritual tradition point to divine presence as first and foremost an ontological reality of God. It is a reality whether we experience or imagine it or not. But mostly it is Immanuel, the fact that God *is* with us. Images such as friend or lover or relationship or presence are used to evoke the mystery of that fundamental reality. They return us, as Dionysius the Areopagite observed, to that point where God dwells. They do not take us there initially, and they are not themselves God.[70] But images and the imagination, just as well as reason and feeling, are tools to share God with one another.

Though Keifer also fails to capture the sense of the community's presence to God in prayer, and though he somewhat misstates the personal nature of God, he is correct that there are degrees of apprehension of divine presence among the many ways Christians have come to know and experience God. He also is probably more than half right when he encourages us to approach "God as mystery, not as friend." But his *primary* point is a good one: Given the legitimate range of personalities and therefore of possible responses to the presence of God, liturgical prayer is at once a blessed antidote and a relief to personal prayer that is wilting with desolation and bafflement or overinflated by imagination. Keifer is correct that "forms of ritual prayer are a saving grace. There is a certain comfortable 'impersonality' about sharing a rite." He adds that, in the rite of the Lord's Supper:

one can act piously without feeling so, and the gestures are of such modesty that this can be done without feeling inauthentic. The careful doing of action in cooperation with others relieves the worshipper of the strain to cultivate an intimate style of prayer. . . . God is addressed as present person, yet through the medium of fixed texts and inherited rites. Thus rite articulates and focuses the ambiguity of the experience of divine presence/ absence. . . . [It] is both personal and impersonal at the same time.[71]

Keifer's comments remind us that divine presence in prayer is not our doing; it is the doing of grace. The ambiguity of God's simultaneous presence and absence can perhaps be addressed only in a healthy balance of personal prayer and common prayer and in the understanding that in both there are individuals and communities blessed with differing temperaments, personalities, needs, and gifts.

Models as Habitats and the "Problem" of Prayer

Models are a kind of habitat for prayer. They can aid us in practicing, assessing, and evaluating prayer. Before moving to the models of prayer themselves, it is helpful to explore how they function as habitats for prayer and to suggest criteria for assessing the validity of models as habitats.

The "problem" referred to in the heading of this section is a conscious allusion to Avery Dulles's seminal work *Models of Revelation*, which opens with a chapter titled the "Problem of Revelation."[72] The "problem" of prayer is that prayer, as with revelation, is by its nature a process and an act that break down boundaries, establish new ways of knowing and being, and lead us into love of neighbor and God in unpredictable ways. Like revelation, the divine gift of prayer is mysterious, ever changing, elusive, and challenging. In fact, in another book, *Models of the Church*, Dulles cites "mystery" as the "problem" that renders models problematic. He writes that "because their correspondence with the mystery of the Church is only partial and functional, models are necessarily inadequate."[73] Nonetheless, Dulles justifies the use of typologies or models "to sharpen issues between different tendencies in the theology of revelation."[74] In that sense, models of prayer help to sharpen distinctions between different tendencies of belief and the practice of prayer.

Models can therefore serve a heuristic function. They give us a starting point that initiates a path through the forest of prayer. Once the path is established, prayer begins to show us new clearings, each of which opens into new paths of prayer. Yet the "old" paths never become obsolete. In fact, they deepen and are polished with age and use. This reminds us again of the word *habitat*, derived from the Latin word *habitus*. As we have seen, the word is venerated and appreciated in many ways within the Christian prayer tradition. A *habitus* is a cluster of habits that form a devotional way of life. Similarly, a way of prayer becomes a "habit": comfortable, needful, and reassuring even as new paths are forged. Like prayer, the tree of life stretches out and grows, explores new territory, takes on new dimensions and shapes. But as with prayer, the new is possible only within the context of a protective, stable, reliable, and forgiving habitat.

Dulles, as do many writers working with models, relies on the work of Ian Barbour, who is trained in both physics and theology.[75] For Barbour, a model maintains "an 'organizing image' which gives a particular emphasis, enabling one to notice and interpret certain aspects of experience."[76] Barbour makes a distinction between experimental models, which in science bear some physical resemblance to the realities they depict, and theological models, which do not claim to provide a literal picture but are used to "develop a theory which in some sense explains the phenomena."[77] Models of prayer do not claim to offer a literal picture; they are not scale-model reproductions.

Prayer does not remain long in confinement, even if boundaries are established with the best of intentions. No description of prayer bears a physical resemblance to what it depicts. A carefully crafted description of prayer can present prayer, but not all that prayer is. Dulles again urges caution in the use and the application of his models. His words apply equally to the use of models of prayer:

> Each model suggests a possible and consistent way of thinking about a certain set of problems, but it in no way guarantees the validity of the hypotheses it suggests. . . . Every effort to say what revelation is must rely on inadequate metaphors, and therefore falls short of the reality.[78]

As with revelation, so too with prayer: Every effort to say what prayer is falls short of the reality of prayer. Nonetheless, the practice of prayer and critical thinking on that practice can be illuminated through the use of models. They help us see and experience the innumerable ways God wishes for and succeeds in making connections with all who pray.

While for Christians the practice of prayer remains a valid and essential component of faith, ethics, and belief, this is of course not the case for many contemporary men and women. Contemporary objections to the idea of models of prayer, let alone the practice of prayer itself, abound.[79] For the most part, however, contemporary objections to prayer can actually serve as cautionary reminders, even guides, in an exploration of prayer. As cautionary warnings or guides, they give added value to Christian prayer practiced in the context of contemporary "secular" and "sacred" knowledge, beliefs, practices, and attitudes. In forcing us to clarify spiritual practice and prayer, they often help us expand our otherwise insular and codified notions of prayer. In the wise words of Dulles, "We assess models and theories by living out the consequences to which they point."[80]

Models as habitats of prayer are valid only to the extent that they help us live out the consequences to which they point. The following criteria for assessing the validity of models serve as markers that enable us to live out the consequences of Christian prayer as conversation, relationship, journey, transformation, and presence.

Karl Barth presents a narrow but helpful set of criteria for true prayer, including the fact that prayer finds its basis in the command of the gracious God, not in human need. Barth notes that true prayer is also sure of a hearing. Though the "we" of the "Our Father" are those who belong to Christ, we nonetheless pray not only for ourselves but also for the world.[81] This is especially important in an increasingly confused and fragmenting world.

A wider range of possible criteria to evaluate models of prayer include the following:[82] Models of prayer illustrate ways and means of response to God, who first calls us. They are based in Scripture. They exhibit faithfulness to Christian tradition and doctrine. They knit the body of Christ together in worship. They tend to foster virtues and values generally upheld by Christians. They are based in experience and witnessed in service and social justice. They are grounded in participation in the humanity of Christ and identify with the risen Lord. They correspond to contemporary religious experience. They enable successful relations and ecumenical and interreligious dialogue. They foster stillness based in attachment to the things of God and detachment from indifferent things of the world. They initiate a habit of personal and social formation and transformation. They promote consciousness of the presence of God. They result in deepening connections among self, others, creation, and God. They draw one ever deeper into the love of God. They enhance a growing sense of the holy in all things.

These are not tests of prayer. In prayer, there is no orthopraxy. Taken as a whole, these criteria are simply guidelines to help us recognize when, how, and where we are living out the consequences of prayer.

Conclusion

Perhaps not all of our elemental practices and experiences of prayer are explicitly mentioned here as habitats. For example, healing prayer may be added, since it intersects with the models of conversation, relationship, transformation, or presence. Forms of liturgy or common prayer not explicitly named may also be cited as examples of habitats of prayer. These may include charismatic and Pentecostal forms of worship, gospel singing, spontaneous prayer, and delivery-and-response preaching of African American congregations. High Anglican or Russian Orthodox liturgies also inject nuance and even inspiration into any list of habitats of prayer. More ritualistic devotions such as the veneration of the cross, walking the stations of the cross, the application of sacred oils, rites of initiation, rites of penance or reconciliation, reciting the rosary, and anointing the sick also carry potential for inclusion in a survey of liturgical or personal prayer. Christian marriage and funeral rites are potentially habitats of prayer, as are the integration of body, mind, and spirit through liturgical dance. Praying with icons can enhance prayer as conversation, journey, relationship, and presence. Finally, eucharistic prayer is of ongoing importance throughout all Christian traditions as the essential habitat for nurturing prayer and life.

Each Christian believer's prayer experience, whether mentioned explicitly in this account or not, brings rich, new prayer habitats to the prayers that form the tree of life. Therefore, readers will benefit from approaching each of the following models of Christian prayer through the lens of his or her own experience with prayer. It is my hope that, with God's grace, not only will your lens be polished and magnified by what follows, but you will also find new, exciting, meaningful, and God-directed lenses through which to view, practice, and share a life of prayer.

May the living God "teach us to pray" (Luke 11:1).

Part 2

Models of Prayer

The Tree of Life

Prayer as Conversation

The Deep Roots of Prayer

To be a Christian and to pray are one and the same thing.

Karl Barth, *Prayer*

The Father spoke one Word, which was His Son, and this Word He always speaks in eternal silence, and in silence must be heard by the soul.

John of the Cross, *Maxims on Love*

In the Beginning Was the Conversation

In the years preceding the Protestant Reformation, the early humanist scholar Desiderius Erasmus of Rotterdam was deeply engaged in a project of translation that would be published just two years after Luther drew up his famous Ninety-five Theses and nailed them to the door of the Schlosskirche at Wittenberg. Following a fundamental tenet of the humanist movement to return to original sources, Erasmus had undertaken a systematic examination and new Latin translation of Greek manuscripts of the New Testament.[1] The translation was destined to update and replace the more than one-thousand-year-old Vulgate of St.

Jerome. Arriving at the Gospel of John, Erasmus made an unconventional but telling translation of the opening words of John's first chapter. Instead of the conventional translation of John's Greek into the Latin *In principio erat Verbum,* Erasmus translated instead *In principio erat Sermo.*[2] John's Gospel, according to Erasmus, thus opens not with "In the beginning was the Word" but rather with "In the beginning was the Conversation." The shift was subtle and yet modified centuries of traditional assumptions and consequent theology. It also had profound implications not only for the process of the "coming into being" of the world but also for prayer.

Erasmus's translation makes the act of creation not a unific spoken word, which in its singular and isolated way brings the universe into being, but rather a communitarian event based on a process of dialogue. The implication of Erasmus's translation is that the act of creation was, and in a real sense continues to be, an ongoing conversation. This chapter explores prayer as an essential partner in this creative conversation.

Words and speech are critical components of prayer. But prayer, as a relationship among God, God's creation, and God's people, is multidimensional. It is not simply words spoken at or to God. Erasmus's opening translation of the Gospel of John touches on a richer, dialogical meaning of prayer. Prayer is discourse more than simply "word"; it is a conversation that includes not only words but also silences, not only listening but also hearing, not only times of resting in God but also times of responding to God. Prayerful conversation is spoken as well as silent. This chapter looks at both verbal prayer as it is commonly known and practiced and silence in prayer. Word and silence are both a part of conversation with God.

John Calvin and Brother Lawrence on Prayer as Familiar Conversation

Many people are surprised to learn that the longest chapter in John Calvin's *Institutes of the Christian Religion* is the one on prayer.[3] In these pages, Calvin emphasizes the essential nature of prayer as "intimate" or "familiar conversation." To enter into "familiar conversation" with God, the mind and the heart, according to Calvin, must be properly disposed. In language reminiscent of patristic and medieval teachers on contemplation, Calvin describes this proper disposition:[4]

> Now for framing prayer duly and properly, let this be the first rule: that we be disposed in mind and heart as befits those who enter [familiar] conversation with God. This we shall indeed attain with respect to the

mind if it is freed from carnal cares and thoughts by which it can be called or led away from right and pure contemplation of God, and then not only devotes itself completely to prayer but also, in so far as this is possible, is lifted and carried beyond itself.[5]

The Latin word *colloquium*, which in Calvin's *Institutes* is translated as "conversation," also means a sharing of words, a discourse, or a simple talk together. The deeper meaning, then, of "familiar" conversation connotes acquaintanceship, intimacy, friendship, and ultimately, the safe, shared, and loving conversation one might find within a family.[6] Conversation, as Calvin employs the term, thus implies two related ideas: (1) to turn around and toward a person or thing, and (2) to abide, live, or dwell with someone, to pass one's life together with another.[7] Thus, when we turn in prayer toward God in conversation, we turn *from* something false in ourselves *to* something true in God. This is not to say that we abandon ourselves. Prayer as conversation with God is the primary speech of the true self to the true God. In prayer, we bring our *full self* to God. Such prayerful conversation means that we come to live and dwell in a familiar, intimate, and loving way with God.

In Brother Lawrence, a seventeenth-century French Discalced Carmelite, we find an example similar to Calvin's own heartfelt sense of prayer. Brother Lawrence advocated lifelong familiar conversation with God as a spiritual practice of the full self turned toward God. For Brother Lawrence, conversation with God is of a particular quality.

> The holiest, most ordinary, and most necessary practice of the spiritual life is that of the presence of God. It is to take delight in and become accustomed to his divine company, *speaking humbly and conversing lovingly with him* all the time, at every moment.[8] . . . It is important, however, to realize that this conversation with God takes place in the depths and center of the soul. It is there that the soul speaks to God heart to heart, and always in a deep and profound peace the soul enjoys God.[9]

His is not a fleeting moment of divine awareness or revelation but a constant, simple conversation reflected in action and flowing from the center of the soul. Calvin would no doubt agree. In a concise statement on the intimate relations among prayer as conversation, prayer as daily activity, and prayer as awareness of the presence of God, Brother Lawrence echoes Calvin.

> We do not always have to be in church to be with God. We can make of our hearts an oratory where we can withdraw from time to time to converse with him there. Everyone is capable of these *familiar conversations* with God.[10]

Familiar conversation is a daily, even constant, devotion of a soul turned toward God. Such prayer serves to destroy the false perception of an impregnable wall between the sacred and the secular world. As the seventeenth-century spiritual director Jean-Pierre de Caussade put it, "We don't even realize that God is *speaking*. . . . Each moment is a revelation of God."[11]

Word and Silence in Prayerful Conversation

While conversation involves elements of listening, waiting, attention, hearing, connection, communication, presence, and response, the two primary modes of prayerful conversation are word and silence. As has been stated, word and silence are not oppositional but rather relational and dialogical. They are partners in the play of conversation. A seventeenth-century German Pietist, Philipp Jakob Spener, captures this partnership well:

> Prayer always occurs before those to whom the basis of our heart is open. Prayer is not only heard by those to whom we speak with our mouths, but also those to whom we open our hearts (Ps. 19:15). . . . Whenever we pray with our mouths God looks at the same time not only upon our tongues but also on the base of our hearts out of which the tongue speaks.[12]

In the context of prayer, silence and word have many shades and nuances of meaning. Silence, for instance, can be "heard" in a number of ways: as the silence of God, as the silence of the one praying, as a referent of mystery, as the real inability to find words for the divine reality in its fullness. It can be "heard," as well, as an unfortunate reality of men, women, and communities who, through economic disadvantage or political repression or pathological, physical, or emotional challenges, have no voice. The silence of speech is the fundamental form of silence, but there are other silences as well. There is silence in the beauty of nature, in the kinetic body, and in the beam of a loving gaze. Silence comforts and refines the will and the senses. It gives wing to imagination, illuminates the memory, tempers judgment, and ignites longing and desire.

In a similar manner, word and language, in their own way, give compass to conversation in prayer. As language, word can be oral, written, spoken, signed, sung, and danced. It is most often sought by the ear and voiced by the mouth, but it can be seen with the eye, felt by a touch, or implied in a smell. In the same manner that silence can represent a form of oppression to the voiceless of the world, word too can oppress, control, abuse, confine, prejudice, even destroy. But words can also build up, free, empower, transform, guide, and give. They can bestow empathy, compassion, or love.

In prayer, word and silence are like partners in a dance. Scripture is full of images that evoke this necessary partnership between silence and word. Jesus' disciples, for example, beg him to teach them how to pray, and he does so in words so keen and sharp that his Lord's Prayer has penetrated into our very bones and marrow to this day. Jesus teaches his disciples by giving them words to pray. Yet at the same time Jesus models long periods of silence, solitude, and listening. The Old Testament is full of prophets, priests, and kings praying verbally to God; the Psalms are themselves 150 verbal prayers. Yet at the same time, the Old Testament also instructs us in silence, stillness, and waiting. We are urged, "Be still, and know that I am God!" (Ps. 46:10); while the Lord is in his holy temple, Habakkuk proclaims, "let all the earth keep silence before him!" (2:20); and the voice of wisdom from Ecclesiastes says sagely, "[There is] a time to keep silence and a time to speak" (3:7).

The fact that silence by its very nature is immune to verbal representation has not stopped Christian writers from attempting to "communicate" its essence to the world. It seems that nothing loosens the tongue or sharpens the quill quite as much as an encounter with silence. Volumes and volumes, words upon words have been devoted to the look, feel, taste, smell, sensuality, or experience of that which is wordless or ineffable. Simone Weil comes close to capturing silence in these words:

> Everything happens as though, by a miraculous favor, our very senses themselves had been made aware that silence is not the absence of sounds, but something infinitely more real than sounds and the center of a harmony more perfect than anything which a combination of sounds can produce. Furthermore there are degrees of silence. There is a silence in the beauty of the universe which is like a noise when compared with the silence of God.[13]

But silence cannot be completely captured; it is not the absence of sounds. There are instead "degrees of silence"—what this book refers to as "spectrums of silence." Even the beauty of the universe is "like a noise when compared to the silence of God." Through her words, Weil invites us to absorb silence, to hear it with all our senses, and through its degrees to give praise to God.

Thomas Merton said that Scripture is like a lake that has no bottom. The same can be said of Christian prayer. Today, in addition to the richness of Christian verbal prayer,[14] many have been blessed by the retrieval of various "communities of conversation" within the Christian contemplative tradition. Those involved in the Christian contemplative tradition rely on body, gesture, posture, mind, heart, and spirit to practice and maintain an attitude of silence, just as those using the verbal tradition rely on the same to maintain an attitude of speech with God. This essential complementarity of verbal prayer and contemplative silence form a circle of conversation—a circle of intimate conversation with God.

It is no coincidence that paradox and mystery are in conversational prayer just as paradox and mystery are in Christian doctrine. In their refusal to fall completely to the ax of reason, both function in Christian formation by compelling us in experiential, sapiential ways to know ourselves in relation to God and the world.[15] The formational function of prayer is predicated not on human effort alone but also on the gift of divine grace, itself a deep mystery. As it conjoins human effort and divine gift, formational prayer also encounters mystery; it enters into "the secret places of divine incomprehensibility,"[16] where prayer moves easily and naturally from lofty pinnacles beyond our knowing to simple conversation between intimate friends.

Prayer as conversation can be understood as depth (with God), width (for others), and breadth (within ourselves). At times, the conversation of prayer is dreary, dark, and dead. At other times, prayer is rich, soulful, and connecting. When the conversation of prayer turns dead, it dries up life. Yet in silence and in word, we learn to enter into and trust the dark. With Christ, even the darkness becomes familiar. After all, prayer is "familiar" conversation. A contemporary writer on prayer and the life of faith, Renita Weems, puts it this way:

> It never occurred to me, because no one ever told me, that I would one day as a minister stop believing [in God in the way she once had]. . . . Had I been warned that this day was coming, . . . I could have taken care to tend more assiduously to the nicks and scrapes a praying heart endures over the years—the unanswered prayers, the weeks of not being able to pray, the contradictions, the hypocrisy in the church, the *months of living with the silence of God.* . . . I was trying to learn how to pray over the noise of a full life. I decided to take my chances with the silence. *I learned to trust the silence* after years of fighting against it. . . . *I learned to trust the winter months of faith,* when it's difficult to remember why one ever bothered to believe.[17]

Familiar conversation helps us learn to embrace the silence as well as the word, the darkness as well as the light.

The Christian prayer tradition has given the dangerous and alienating side of conversational prayer various names: lament, dark night of the soul, dryness, desolation, and more. Yet such prayer begins to heal us through confession, forgiveness, reconciliation, and acknowledging change and loss. It is expressed through slow and painful processes of self-understanding, accepting change, finding voice, and making peace with silence.

Word and silence define the road of prayer like the double helix of DNA. Like the four codes that make the infinite combinations of DNA strands possible, faith, hope, love, and grace are the codes of prayerful conversation. The possible combinations of faith, hope, love, and grace are endless. Combining and recombining with this code, word and silence open prayer into the boundlessness that is God.

What does it mean, then, that prayer is *familiar* conversation with God? It means that prayer is in fact an act of friendship and intimacy. Prayer is confidential; it is safe and a matter of trust and faith between friends. What does it mean that prayer is familiar *conversation* with God? As conversation, prayer implies a turning around; it is an act of turning toward God. Conversation means in part that we turn *from* ourselves *to* something else. In the conversation that is prayer, we turn toward God. More precisely, it means that we turn *with* ourselves toward something other: We turn our eyes, our body, our attention toward our family, our neighbor, our God.

Perhaps most importantly, in familiar conversation, we live and dwell with God. In familiar conversation, we speak, we listen in silence, we act, and we respond. In conversational prayer, we plot and walk a path, we form a relationship, we are changed, we are with God. We enter a circle of "turning toward" and "dwelling with." The essential complementarity of verbal prayer and contemplative silence are, from beginning to end, a circle of familiar conversation.

The sections that follow look closer at this circle of familiar conversation by discussing first verbal prayer and then silence in prayer.

Word in Prayerful Conversation

Forms of Verbal Prayer

For what better gift can a rational being offer up to God than the fragrant word of prayer?

Origen, *On Prayer*

If the heart is not in it, what then? Nothing! All prayers offered solely by the lips are not only superfluous, but they are also displeasing to God.

Karl Barth, *Prayer*

A brother asked Abba Poemen, "Is it better to speak or to be silent?" The old man said to him, "The man who speaks for God's sake does well; but he who is silent for God's sake also does well."[18] On another occasion, Abba Isidore said, "To live without speaking is better than to speak without living. . . . [But] when words and life correspond to one another they are together the whole of philosophy."[19] Both word and silence are integral components of conversational prayer.

Though prayer as familiar conversation is uttered *ex silentii* and from eloquence too deep for words, most of us are more familiar, perhaps even more comfortable, with prayers that are spoken. This is natural. Verbal prayer, for the most part, is all we were taught as children or what we heard in church. Verbal prayer can be a fragrant offering to God, vibrant and alive, or it can be a meaningless jumble detached from the heart, offensive and dead. We turn to verbal prayer with caution and with joy—caution because our conversation is often empty, joy because we are invited nonetheless to converse continuously with God.

Many Christians are familiar with forms of verbal prayer that include adoration, confession, thanksgiving, and supplication (the well-known acronym ACTS). Also traditionally included in verbal prayer are petition, praise, lament, and intercession.[20] Even if we were not taught prayer in a formal way, these forms of prayer have been modeled for us in countless ways and have been handed down to us from generation to generation. They are a part of our personal life of prayer as well as our corporate life of prayer. These forms of verbal prayer have served and will continue to serve communities, families, and individuals well. At various times and places in the Christian spiritual tradition, types of verbal prayer were assumed to form a seamless web with silent prayer and contemplation.

Verbal Prayer in Scripture

In Scripture, verbal prayer is modeled in a variety of ways.[21] Within the Old Testament during the patriarchal period, prayer involved calling on the name of God and was closely associated with sacrifice. In the preexilic period, prayer expanded to other verbal forms, including intercession, thanksgiving, and supplication. The Psalms, blending pattern and spontaneity in prayer, include prayers for pardon, communion, protection, healing, and vindication and prayers of lament and praise. The postexilic period emphasized the social aspects of worship as well as the spiritual aspects of devotion and prayer.

The New Testament contains a number of clearly defined teachings on prayer. The genesis of all instruction on prayer, however, is Christ's own teaching and practice. In the parables alone, Christ set out principles of prayer, including persistence, humility, penitence, charity, simplicity, watchfulness, and expectancy, all of which are grounded in faith. Christ taught that prayer is offered to God in Christ's own name. Modeling prayer himself, Christ sought out places of solitude and prayed in secret, in times of spiritual conflict, in surrender, and in the midst of pain. He offered thanksgiving and praise to the Father, asked for guidance, and interceded for others.

In Acts, the church was born in an atmosphere of prayer. In answer to prayer and in fulfillment of Christ's promise, the Spirit was poured out on the church. Acts also reveals church leaders who urged other Christians to pray and were themselves men and women of prayer. Paul is throughout a person of prayer, continuing the ministry of prayer initiated and modeled by Christ. Perhaps his greatest contribution to an understanding of prayer is establishing its connection to the Holy Spirit and showing that prayer is in fact a gift of the Spirit. Thus, prayer for Paul is presented to the Father in the name of the Son through the inspiration and indwelling of the Holy Spirit. Paul seeks to know God's will in prayer, and he emphasizes that prayer is essential for a Christian. Paul's prayers include intercession; thanksgiving; prayers that others may receive the Spirit, through whom comes knowledge and illumination; and prayers that Christians may receive knowledge and power, through which individuals and the church may grow in perfection.

The Our Father: The Lord's Teaching on Verbal Prayer

"Lord, teach us to pray, as John taught his disciples." He said to them, "When you pray, say . . ."

Luke 11:1–2

As we pray the Lord's Prayer, in private or as a congregation in worship, we enter into words and phrases carrying the authoritative teaching of Jesus and the history of countless repetitions from the lips of apostles, saints, sinners, and friends. In Matthew 6:9–13 and in a shorter version found in Luke 11:2–4, we encounter what must be the closest equivalent in words to the sigh uttered by the Spirit that is a prayer "too deep for words" (Rom. 8:26). The Lord's Prayer stands as a rock of ages pliable enough to conform to the needs of any moment. In Luke, it comes as a response to the disciples' request, itself a prayer: "Lord, teach us to pray." In that sense, it is both an answer to prayer and Jesus' teaching on prayer.

Luke contains hints of a "genealogy" of the prayer: The disciples ask Jesus to teach them to pray as "John taught his disciples [to pray]." Jesus instructs the disciples in a method of prayer passed from master to disciple, a kind of "school of prayer" that was to be imitated in numerous religious communities and movements. Luke also chooses to describe his version of the prayer as a kind of shared secret with the Father. He records Jesus' advice to "go into your room and shut the door and pray to your Father who is in secret; and your Father who sees in secret will reward you" (Matt. 6:6). This advice, too, has served as a model of how to pray: Countless individuals and communities have sought their "secret" places in which to pray.

In Matthew, Jesus warns the disciples not to "heap up empty phrases" in prayer as others do who think they will be "heard because of their many words" (Matt. 6:7–8). The prayer Jesus teaches is spare; it is but a spark. It lights a fire in the world, but of itself it is not a bonfire of heaped up words and phrases, a fire hoping to catch the attention of a nearly blind God. The God of Abraham knows what we need before we ask. Our needs are so great, the words are so spare. They are but small sparks. But what sparks! As we pray the Lord's Prayer, we pray God's answer to our need, a need already known. The prayer seems to us a question, an asking, a petition, and it is; yet in the truest sense, the answer issues from the words that leave our lips as a question. "Your Father knows what you need before you ask him." The Lord's Prayer, uttered innumerable times, is like the first words born to silence.

Augustine says of this gift of the Lord's teaching, "For whatever other words we may say, if we pray rightly, and as becomes our wants, we say nothing but what is already contained in the Lord's Prayer."[22] The initial invocation in the Lord's Prayer is followed by seven petitions, of which the first three refer to God's name, kingdom, and will, and the last four to humanity's need of bread, forgiveness, deliverance from temptation, and victory. The prayer then closes with a doxology that contains a threefold declaration concerning God's kingdom, power, and glory.[23]

The tree of life is supported by the roots of conversational prayer, which is composed of silence and word. The foundation of word is the Lord's Prayer. A commentary on all other types of verbal prayer will always remain refined commentary on the way Jesus taught us to pray.

Types of Verbal Prayer

ADORATION

The prayer of adoration exists on a kind of borderland between silence and word. Because of the mystery that is God, the prayer of adoration can either rest in silent love or give verbal expression to wonder and awe. Further, adoration flows toward the God of creation who is beyond all created things yet also known, to the extent we are capable of knowing, through all things. Before the transcendence of God, we can be still or offer words of praise; before the immanence of God, we can remain silent or speak our wonder. The prayer of adoration recognizes at once both the God of mystery and the God of creation. Rather than being mutually exclusive, these transcendent and immanent aspects of God are complementary. In a real sense, mystery draws us into creation, while creation guides and points us toward mystery. Prayers of adoration are appropriate in both cases.

The essential complementarity between mystery and creation in the prayer of adoration is often missed or slightly askew in the writings of even the best teachers of prayer. Richard Foster, one of the most skillful and accessible contemporary teachers on prayer, focuses primarily on the God of creation. Foster opens his chapter on adoration in his typically eloquent fashion:

> Prayer is the human *response* to the perpetual outpouring of love by which God lays siege to every soul. When our reply to God is most direct of all, it is called *adoration*. Adoration is the spontaneous yearning of the heart to worship, honor, magnify, and bless God.[24]

Foster goes on to say that something of adoration is present in all prayer: "All true prayer is saturated with it. It is the air that prayer breathes."[25] Foster then suggests a practice of using five small stepping-stones to enter into the prayer of adoration. The practice includes (1) paying attention to the small things of creation without studying or analyzing them; (2) entering our "grateful center," where we are free of all grasping, all grabbing; (3) practicing gratitude; (4) magnifying God; and (5) full, joyous, even hilarious celebration of God.[26] While Foster gives a nod to mystery, his primary focus is the practice of adoration through creation. He says, for instance, "We learn about the goodness of God not by contemplating the goodness of God but by watching a butterfly."[27]

Other writers on the prayer of adoration would disagree. For these writers, we *do* learn about the goodness of God by contemplating the goodness of God. Dionysius the Areopagite's *Divine Names*[28] is an ancient example of this approach. The contemporary theologian John Macquarrie also takes this approach:

> God is unique in his absoluteness, and so he is different from everything created and finite. That is why adoration may be offered to God alone. . . . To adore any finite being [i.e., a stepping-stone of Foster's] would be to mistake that being for the absolute, and this would be idolatry.[29]

For Macquarrie, the other side of adoration of God's absolute goodness is not adoration of creation but rather adoration based on our absolute dependence. This absolute dependence is not oppressive but lets us, in prayers of adoration, be truly ourselves as creatures before God.

One of the best integrations of these two avenues of approach is Bonaventure's *Soul's Journey into God*. In the first two chapters, following St. Francis, Bonaventure gives adoration to God through God's vestiges in creation. In the fifth and sixth chapters, following Dionysius, he gives adoration to God by meditating on God's "Being" and "Goodness." We can contemplate something of God's goodness in the butterfly and something of the butterfly in God's goodness. Perhaps Margaret Guenther put it best, writing simply that "in prayers of adoration, God's majesty takes our breath away."[30]

PRAISE

Praise also lies on a continuum that includes all forms of conversation with God. Whether done as a worshiping community, in informal gatherings, or in solitude behind closed doors, praise implies confession of who we are before God as much as adoration of the majesty of God. This fundamental continuum is highlighted even as we attempt to make distinctions between types of verbal prayer. The more we focus on what is different, the more we simultaneously understand the intimate connectedness of most forms of verbal prayer.

Given this continuum, it is not surprising that attempts at distinguishing praise from thanksgiving are particularly difficult. The Christian prayer tradition recognizes four basic formulas for defining and practicing praise and thanksgiving. The formulas serve both to highlight the unique nature of prayers of praise and prayers of thanksgiving and to place praise within the comprehensive arc of verbal prayer.

Friedrich Heiler serves as an advocate of the first formula, noting that, especially in the liturgical context, the early church saw praise and thanksgiving as the first two topics of Christian prayer. Whether in common worship or in personal prayer, praise and thanksgiving have a distinctly contemplative character: Both keep us attentive to the power, wisdom, goodness, and holiness of God.[31] This formulation associates both forms of prayer with God's acts in history. Heiler distinguishes praise and thanksgiving by linking thanksgiving to God's salvation, bestowed upon us, and praise to the greatness and power of God, as witnessed in and through creation. Prayers of thanksgiving are thus given for God's deeds in the history of redemption, while prayers of praise are grounded in God's work in the history of creation.[32]

A second formula distinguishes praise and thanksgiving for abundance from petition and intercession grounded in need. This formulation places prayer in the context of a human response to a God who first addresses us. In this scheme, praise and thanksgiving represent a response to what God has already done for us, while petition and intercession represent a response in view of what we would like God to do for us in light of his promise to hear and respond to prayer.[33] Praise as a response to abundance recognizes simultaneously our ongoing needs (petition and intercession) and our relationship with and dependence on God (confession). It also opens our eyes to God's goodness, mystery, and holiness (adoration).

In both liturgy and personal prayer, praise is full of joy. It is celebratory. It is connective and relational. It is prayer in dance, in song, and with harp and lyre. A contemporary writer notes:

> When I give thanks, my thoughts still circle about myself to some extent. But in praise my soul ascends to self-forgetting adoration, seeing and praising only the majesty and power of God, God's grace and redemption.[34]

This instinct to regard praise as first among equals in verbal prayer also has its basis in patristic writers. Origen, in his treatise *On Prayer*, orders the types of prayers by means of his interpretation of 1 Timothy 2:1: "First of all, then, I urge that supplications, prayers, intercessions, and thanksgivings be made for everyone." Origen interprets "prayers" as "praise." He writes of such prayer that, when placed alongside other types of prayer, it "is something nobler offered by a person with praise and for greater objects."[35] Thanksgiving, confession (supplications in 1 Timothy), and intercession (in that order) follow praise. But "in the beginning and preface of prayer," says Origen, "something having the force of praise should be said."[36]

The fourth formula is the pervasive nature of praise in all of Scripture. Indeed, praise is the fulfillment of a God-appointed vocation, and calls in Scripture to praise God are many and varied. Through prayers of praise, we conform ourselves to God's will; declare the unique nature of God; acknowledge divine mercy, majesty, kindness, constancy, and love; and declare that God's commands are just. Scripture also encourages praise of God's law, praise of God's incomprehensible mystery as well as the goodness and power God displays through creation, and God's kingship, shepherding, and saving works. We are called to praise God's name. The Psalms build to a crescendo of praise (Pss. 145–50) in which all creatures, stars, planets, heavens, saints, and angels are called to praise God. With shouts, musical instruments, dancing, song, and palm waving, public and private jubilant expressions of praise raise prayer to the level of blessing. "Enter [God's] gates with thanksgiving, and [God's] courts with praise. Give thanks to [God]. Bless [God's] name" (Ps. 100:4).

THANKSGIVING

Thanksgiving, adoration, praise, and blessing are brothers and sisters in the familiar conversation of Christian prayer. In speech or listening, in silence or song, each hears something of the other. The Old Testament promotes this family of prayer by implication: It does not have a vocabulary of thanksgiving distinct from that of praise. Though the Hebrew verb *yadah* is generally translated as "thank," the verb *hallal* as "praise," and the noun *todah* as "gratitude" or "thanksgiving," these terms are often used synonymously, and the distinctions are difficult to identify. Still, thanksgiving does have certain characteristics that are gleaned from the Hebrew, clarified in the New Testament, and identified and practiced in the early church. Thanksgiving is a response to what God has done for us: the goodness of creation, the blessing of restoration and healing, the mystery of justification and forgiveness. Thanksgiving is a human response to the abundance given by God; it is gratitude for gifts given out of God's bountiful love.

In the New Testament, thanksgiving is tightly woven into the Gospel narratives, becoming at once nuanced and sharply defined. It reaches a kind of apotheosis in the thanksgiving of Jesus in connection with the bread and the wine of the Last Supper. The word *Eucharist* (from the verb *eucharisteō* and its cognate noun *eucharistia*), meaning thanksgiving, from an early date is used to describe the sacramental quality of the Supper. Thanksgiving, exemplified most concretely in the Lord's Supper, becomes in the New Testament a motive for life and conduct, a general attitude toward life's blessings and trials, and an essential component of prayer.

In the Gospels, as modeled by the life and words of Christ, thanksgiving and praise to God become key elements of Christian life and faith. In John, identity and union of the believer with Christ through the Holy Spirit both enkindle thanksgiving and transform the life of those united to Christ into an offering of thanksgiving. In this sense, thanksgiving is the attitude of prayer equivalent to the life of faith; thanksgiving is a prayerful way of being in Christ.

Paul turns thanksgiving into a way of life: It should, he says, be given at all times and for all things (Phil. 4:6; 1 Thess. 5:18; 2 Thess. 2:13). As recognized in chapter 1, thanksgiving, more than any other form of prayer, is Paul's answer to the question of how to pray without ceasing.[37] Paul urges his listeners in all things to "give thanks." All things, according to Paul, are good if used, with thanksgiving, to the glory of

God (Rom. 14:1–6; 1 Cor. 10:30–31). But prayers of thanksgiving are difficult. To be truly grateful requires that we acknowledge our personal helplessness at the same time that we acknowledge our absolute debt to God. Paul was aware of this difficulty. He lived it. Nonetheless, he knew that God's presence and action in a life invite gratitude leading to thanksgiving.

"Prayer," as Evagrios Ponticos said, "is the fruit of joy and thanksgiving."[38] As with Brother Lawrence, who found thanksgiving in small, everyday blessings, or Gregory of Nyssa, who found thanksgiving in a dark cloud beyond thought and mind, "the last thing that is necessary for prayer is that we give it in thanksgiving."[39]

Thanksgiving, as in the Eucharist, as union with Christ, as a way of life, and as a form of constant prayer is also a prayer of confession. To give thanksgiving to God is to confess God's sovereignty, redemptive power, eternal wisdom, and holy mystery. Equally, to give thanksgiving to God is to confess our own servanthood, powerlessness, wandering, and mortality. As with adoration, praise, and blessing, the circular network of prayer that passes through thanksgiving also runs through confession.

CONFESSION

In the prayer of confession, we acknowledge who God is before us and who we are before God. God is Creator, holy, sovereign, our guide, our strength, our Redeemer. We are God's good creation, yet we are broken. We dwell in self-delusion and darkness. The self-delusion is so deep that even the light by which God illumines our understanding is not sufficient to render it complete. Augustine confesses this dilemma perfectly:

> Therefore, I shall confess what I know of myself, I shall confess also what I do not know of myself, since what I know of myself I know by means of your light shining upon me, and what I do not know remains unknown to me until in your countenance "my darkness be made as the noonday" (Isa. 58:10).[40]

Augustine's confession probes the depths of our darkness, a darkness capable only of reflecting light from an exterior source, a darkness so deep that even the most enlightened self-examination can reveal only truths seen in a glass darkly, one of which is that our very existence is a gift.

Our misunderstandings are numerous. We are caught, for instance, in a complex of systemic brokenness. We are engaged in a web of social, cultural, familial, personal, economic, environmental, and political systems. Each of these systems is, at its core, broken and in constant need of healing. Self-understanding and confessional prayer are grounded not only in our individual natures but also—perhaps even more fundamentally—in the many systems in which we participate.

In confession, we recognize the deep divide between what we can be as beloved creatures of God and what we in fact are. To bring sins, shortcomings, deception, failures, and shattered dreams to God is to acknowledge who we are in relation to God: fully dependent. The irony is that radical dependence on God is the ground of two different but equally legitimate kinds of prayer: confession and thanksgiving. They are different, yet each defines and validates the other. Prayers of thanksgiving swell in praise and adoration yet at the same time convict us of the reality that there is no sense in which we deserve God's gifts. We thank God for our infinite gifts, yet that thanksgiving is at the same time a confession that these gifts are not ours. It is simultaneously a confession that we receive and use these gifts selfishly, as though they were for our glory, not God's.

Two traditional and related forms of prayer aid in self-understanding and help prepare us for confession. In one, the *examen of consciousness*, we take account of how and where God has been present or absent to us during the day and the manner of our response to God's presence in our life. In another, the *examen of conscience*, we invite God to search our heart to uncover areas that need purification and healing. One of the wisest writers on these prayers of examination is William Law, the early eighteenth-century English divine. Law's *Serious Call to a Devout and Holy Life* is written in a plain and pleasing style and is full of practical wisdom concerning the Christian life. As he opens one chapter, it is precisely six o'clock in the evening. This is the time most proper, he says, for examination of sin and confession. His precision does not stop with his timing. His advice on self-examination and confession is equally precise and particular. Of examination, he says, "The necessity of this examination is founded upon the necessity of repentance. . . . It is necessary not only that all our sins but particular circumstances and aggravations of them be known and recollected and brought to repentance." Citing Scripture, he says, "If we confess our sins, he who is faithful and just will forgive us our sins and cleanse us from all unrighteousness" (1 John 1:9). "There seems therefore," Law goes on, "to be the greatest necessity that all our daily actions be constantly observed and brought to account. . . . [Confession] loses all its chief benefit unless it be particular confession and repentance of the sins of that day."[41] In plain style and repeatedly, Law lays down this principle of examination of "particular" sin. General, formulaic prayers will not do. We must see and confess our individual and systemic offenses against God with careful precision:

An examination thus managed will in a little time make you as different from yourself as a wise man is different from an idiot. It will give you such a newness of mind, such a spirit of wisdom, and desire of perfection, [as if you were] an entire stranger to who you were before.[42]

Precise and particular self-examination and confession are nuanced in a variety of ways in the Christian tradition of prayer. For instance, at times "penance" is used in its stead, or "contrition." Penance is usually associated with the actions one takes after having been convicted through the prayer of confession. At its best, penance is an act of reconciliation aimed at renewing bonds between God and the world. Contrition helps us to move deeper, to examine the roots of our sin, not to add them to a growing weight of guilt but to present them to the light of God and his true forgiveness.

There are, however, many ways the soul deceives itself in confession. The retreat director and writer Anthony de Mello reminds us of the dangers lurking behind the seemingly benign and healthy practice of confession: "When repentance is wrongly understood, when there is an overemphasis on guilt and fear of punishment and self-hatred, then repentance becomes a very dangerous thing. All good things are dangerous and the grace of repentance is no exception."[43]

De Mello cautions against three primary dangers associated with the prayer of confession. The first is the refusal to forgive oneself. God is only too willing to forgive us, but many people refuse to believe that forgiveness is unconditional. This danger results in a false sense of unworthiness. De Mello adds that he "knows no greater obstacle to progress in the spiritual life than this false sense of unworthiness."[44] Hate sin, but if you have sinned and repented, then you have reason to rejoice. There is greater joy in heaven over one who repents than over ninety-nine who believe they have no reason to repent.

A second danger associated with confession is an excessive fear of God. This danger comes to those who repent but, living under the burden of the law, maintain a fear of God, especially of God's punishments. This danger is grounded in the law as a breeder of fear, binding and rendering us incapable of serving God freely. The antidote to this excessive fear is a better understanding of God's unconditional love for us, a love surpassing understanding.

A final potential danger related to the prayer of confession is that of experiencing God as the lawgiver long before experiencing Christ as a gift. Confession can heighten the misunderstanding that Christ is always asking for more, insatiable, never satisfied. De Mello ends this section on mistaken apprehension of Christ's demands by saying, "God never demands of you more than what the love you feel for God in your heart demands."[45]

With these cautions in mind, we can read George Buttrick's important distinctions concerning the prayer of confession with greater understanding:

> True confession is neither self-excoriation—to be merciless with anyone, even ourselves, is no virtue—nor casual evasion. Over conscientiousness becomes morbid: under conscientiousness becomes indifference and decay. Confession to those we have wronged is sometimes, not always, wise: there are circumstances in which such confession would spread and aggravate hurt. But confession to God, whom we have more deeply wronged, is always wise: God has understanding and love.[46]

In contemporary culture, there has been a steady decline in simple and honest prayers of personal confession, along with a decline in liturgical prayers of confession. A number of factors have contributed to this decline. One is that it is difficult for a culture committed to "self" to admit anything negative in confession. In addition, popular culture and self-help trends promise reconciliation, wholeness, and self-actualization without confession. The decline in prayers of confession may also be due to moral confusion and ambiguity. Without clear moral categories, it is unclear what to confess or how to make a confession. Confession seems unnecessary. A final contribution to the decline in confession is the weakening of the sense of sin. It is, as one contemporary writer has said, "one thing to learn to 'accept' one's humanity." It is quite another to repent of its misuse before God. "It is one thing to be freed from the compulsion of unconscious complexes; it is another thing to use that freedom for God's glory."[47]

One antidote to this decline in prayers of confession is suggested by Martin Luther. His practice combines direction and discernment concerning moral authority with a clear means of evaluating the nature of sin. Luther suggests meditation on the Ten Commandments and the Beatitudes. For Luther, they are a body of teaching based on the moral authority of God and guides for faithful living based on the reality of sinful nature. As guides and precepts, they invite thankfulness, help reveal our true self, and in effect empower us to ask for and to do what is good. Luther writes, "I take each commandment [and beatitude], in the first place, as a teaching, which in fact it is, and I imagine what in that commandment [or beatitude] our Lord God asks so gravely of me; in the second place, I thank God; thirdly, I make confession; fourthly, a prayer of petition."[48]

Confession, repentance, and forgiveness are core values of the good news of the gospel. Repentance is from the Greek word *metanoia*, which indicates a total change of mind and heart and a turning toward God. The practice of self-examination is itself a God-ward turning act. *Metanoia* introduces other characteristics of confession: relief, joy, and peace. Tears of sorrow coexist with tears of joy; contrition guides body, mind, and spirit into thanksgiving and praise. But the forgiveness of God is, again, costly. *Metanoia* and forgiveness never mean that sin does not matter. Forgiveness is "rather an act which affirms the divine hatred of sin and invites us to share in that hatred at the moment when God's compassion flows to us."[49]

INTERCESSION

Intercession is prayer for or on behalf of a community, event, person, or group. From its Latin root *intercedere,* intercessory prayer means that we go between or intervene on behalf of another. It is a prayer in which we "exist between" God and another, calling God's attention to another and, no doubt, calling another's attention to God. It can be as simple and spontaneous as the soft utterance of a single name or as complex, ritualized, and familiar as ancient prayers from the *Book of Common Prayer.* Like petitionary prayer, intercessory prayer focuses on the particular. George Buttrick counsels that "intercession should be specific, it is pondered: it requires us to bear on our heart the burden of those for whom we pray. . . . Genuine love sees faces, not a mass."[50]

As with other forms of verbal conversation with God, intercession is inextricably linked to other forms of verbal prayer. Intercessory prayer on behalf of another is, at the same time, a prayer of thanksgiving, recognizing in faith that ours is a God who answers prayer. Intercessory conversation with God is likewise confession of God's wisdom, power, and goodness. It is praise that remembers God's interceding acts of the past and hopes for God's promise to heal suffering and brokenness in the future. Always, intercession is a prayer of relinquishment: Results are not always known, and all intercession implies "not my will but yours be done" (Luke 22:42). Intercession, perhaps more than any other form of verbal prayer, has its efficacious silent side: A name of a person in distress remembered, a thought for another in need, even silent intercession for health and well-being for people unknown often shock intercession into grace-filled silence.

Based on the mediating model of Jesus Christ, intercession draws us out of ourselves, transforming self-absorption into attention to others and isolation into community. Margaret Guenther has written that intercession is "a small experience of watching at the foot of the cross." Through intercessory prayers, Guenther continues, "we grow in awareness of the suffering of others. We grow in awareness of our own complicity and power to hurt. We grow in our awareness of the need to support our prayer with action."[51] Intercessory prayer requires attentiveness. Simone Weil writes that "prayer consists of attention" and that the "capacity to give one's attention to a sufferer is a very rare and difficult thing; it is almost a miracle; it *is* a miracle."[52]

Prayers of intercession are seen in the Old Testament, where, for instance, Abraham pleads for Sodom (Gen. 18:22–23), Moses frequently mediates and intercedes on behalf of the Hebrew people (Exod. 5:22–23; 15:25; 17:4–7; 31:11–14; 33:12–16), Nehemiah prays for God to be attentive to the people's needs (Neh. 1:4–11), and even the sailors pray to Jonah's God to save them from the storm and from taking an innocent life (Jon. 1:14). In the New Testament, Jesus' life is in many ways a ministry of intercession. He models intercessory prayer by teaching Peter about forgiveness as the guiding principle of the church (Matt. 18:21–22; Luke 17:4), by praying for the sanctification and protection of his disciples and future believers (John 17:6–26), and by praying from the cross for the forgiveness of all people (Luke 23:34). Paul, in his letters to the Christian communities, instructed them to pray for their needs and the needs of others. During the medieval period, the church prayed not only through Christ but also in the name of angels, Mary, and the saints, who were seen to exist between believers and God. Reformation leaders such as Luther and Calvin insisted that intercessory prayer be addressed only to God or to Christ. Nonetheless, without denying that Christ is the sole mediator, Roman Catholics have prayed as a body with the communion of saints and to Mary. Prayers to saints are commonly given at shrines or places of pilgrimage, where the faithful pray for themselves and others in need.

At its core, intercessory prayer is a response to the God who promises to attend to us in our weakness. Intercession is conversation with God that clarifies that we desire for others far more than we are able to give them ourselves. In that sense, it is a way of loving others. It is an act of compassion and of obligation. Our prayers are grounded in love, but they are backed up and supported by Love, our eternal intercessor: "Christ Jesus, who died, yes, who was raised, who is at the right hand of God, who indeed intercedes for us" (Rom. 8:34). The writer of Hebrews reminds us that Jesus is the eternal priest who "always lives to make intercession" (7:25). Richard Foster asks what it is about Jesus' going to the Father that so radically changes our prayer life. Struggling with the difference Jesus makes, Foster says:

The new dimension is this: Jesus is entering his eternal work as Intercessor before the throne of God, and, as a result, we are enabled to pray for others with an entirely new authority. . . . Our ministry of intercession is made possible only because of Christ's continuing ministry of intercession.[53]

William Law considers intercession to be an exercise of universal love in Christ and that such intercession amends and reforms the hearts of those who use it. It is thus efficacious for the pray-er, the one prayed for, and the world. After observing that the first followers of Christ supported one another in love and ministry by mutual prayers for one another, Law goes on to say:

A frequent intercession with God, earnestly beseeching him to forgive the sins of all mankind, to bless them with his providence, enlighten them with his spirit, and bring them to everlasting happiness, is the divinest exercise that the heart of man can be engaged in. . . . There is nothing that makes us love a man so much as praying for him; and when you can once do this sincerely for any man, you have fitted your soul for the performance of everything that is kind and civil toward him.[54]

Intercessory conversation softens the heart. Through it we learn the great value of others by appearing before God as an intercessor for them. Intercessory prayer teaches attentive compassion and perseverance. We learn compassion as we turn to God with care for the earth and for others. Perseverance is enhanced by the often sad but seemingly essential reality of unanswered prayer. There is no antidote or quick-fix explanation for unanswered intercession. As John Calvin reminds us, there is only perseverance: "We must repeat the same supplications not twice or three times only, but as often as we need a hundred and a thousand times. . . . We must never be weary in waiting for God's help."[55]

Petition

The best way to distinguish the prayer of petition from the prayer of intercession is that in prayers of petition we boldly ask God to tend to ourselves, while in prayers of intercession we boldly ask God to tend to others. The distinction is valid only if we keep in mind that, in a real sense, when we pray for our needs, we pray for the needs of the world, and when we pray for the needs of the world, we also pray for ourselves. Nowhere is this more simply and graphically illustrated than in the Lord's Prayer. The petitions of the Lord's Prayer use what may be called "self-implicating" plural pronouns. When we pray the Lord's Prayer, either in seclusion or within community, we make petitions for others even as we make petitions for ourselves: "Give *us* this day *our* daily bread," "forgive *us our* sins," "deliver *us* from evil."

How do we dare petition God? We dare because we have been invited to do so: "If you then, who are evil, know how to give good gifts to your children, how much more will your Father in heaven give good things to those who ask him!" (Matt. 7:11; cf. Luke 11:13). More important, we are known so deeply that even when we cannot name what we so desperately need and want, God knows: "We do not know how to pray as we ought, but that very Spirit intercedes with sighs too deep for words. And God, who searches the hearts, knows what is the mind of the Spirit, because the Spirit intercedes for the saints according to the will of God" (Rom. 8:26–27).

For what then ought we to pray? God invites us to pray for what we need. God invites us to search ourselves and to declare our needs. If we are confused and hard-pressed to name or acknowledge our needs, the Spirit prays for us. Many have noted the contradiction in asking God for what he already knows we need.[56] This suggestion, however, implies something about God that falls short of his desire for authentic conversation, in which God listens.[57] Even if the contradiction holds, God not only invites but also delights in our asking. As a matter of divine will, we may not always receive the gift we ask for in the way we expect it to come, but God listens. The important point is the prayer itself, the dialogue, even if what we ask for is already in God's plans. As P. T. Forsyth notes, "Love loves to be told what it already knows."[58]

Jesus' teaching on prayer points to persistence, boldness, even unremitting supplication as models of petitionary prayer. Scripture advises that we not be afraid to ask and that we keep at it, as did the woman who wanted justice (Luke 18:1–6). We may, for example, continually petition God for the fruits of the Spirit, "love, joy, peace, patience, kindness, generosity, faithfulness, gentleness, and self control" (Gal. 5:22–23), or that the "spirit of the LORD" may rest upon us, giving wisdom and understanding, counsel and might, knowledge and fear of the LORD (Isa. 11:2), or simply for wisdom to know how to pray. "If any of you is lacking in wisdom, ask God, who gives to all generously" (James 1:5).

Yet Christian spiritual writers have often noted the vicissitudes of petitionary prayer. There are times when boldness in prayer falls short. Scripture becomes a support in prayer, as in faith and life. Hugh of St. Victor expresses how the life of prayer is upheld by the reading of Scripture, what he calls a "descent," in order that the believer may once again "ascend" to God.

> The man who is vigorous in his practice prays lest he grow weak; the man who is constant in his prayers meditates on what would be prayed for, lest

he offend in prayer; and the man who sometimes feels less confidence in his own counsel seeks advice in his reading. And thus it turns out that though we always have the will to ascend, nevertheless we are sometimes forced by necessity to descend. That we ascend is our goal; that we descend is for the sake of the goal.[59]

A person prays to remain strong, meditates on what should be prayed for, reads Scripture for those times when confidence slackens, and ascends to God only through "descent" into a true knowledge of self and needs. If we cease to ask in petitionary prayer, we cease to unite the gift and the Giver. If we do not engage God in conversation, asking for what we need, we do not ask for God.

LAMENT

"Eli, Eli, lema sabachthani?"—"My God, my God, why have you forsaken me?" (Matt. 27:46). "O my God, I cry by day, but you do not answer; and by night, but find no rest" (Ps. 22:2). These are prayers of lament.

Lament is a point of transition between word and silence. From the silence of suffering on the cross, Jesus uses his final breath to shape the words, "My God, my God, why have you forsaken me?" The words then die away into silence. The prayer of lament thus connects the circle of verbal and silent prayer. In abandonment, dryness, and desolation, the prayer of lament often has the effect of transforming our relationship with God. The prayer emerges from a time of testing, a period of trial. Dryness and aridity often drive us deeper into spectrums of silence: We begin to wait (what else can we do?), we listen (often only to silence), we strain to hear, we long to respond, we struggle to find new ways to wed compassion to prayer, we live in silence again, often our last remaining hope to dwell with God. Our memory is fine: Psalms of lament often weave memory of God's past blessings with present suffering. But loss and remembrance intertwine like a vine, following each other as they do in Psalm 22 verse by verse: "O my God, I cry by day, but you do not answer; and by night, but find no rest. Yet you are holy, enthroned on the praises of Israel. In you our ancestors trusted; they trusted, and you delivered them" (vv. 2–4). Rising from the ashes of silence and dying again to ash, lament closes the circle of dialogue. Adoration, praise, and thanksgiving close in on lament and are drowned in its tears. But then the tears water new seeds of hope as adoration dares to push up one new green shoot. For the moment, however, lament compels, even demands, silence.

Suffering and a sense of abandonment form a doorway for the forsaken, the desolate, those trapped in darkness, and those shattered by a sense of the absence of God. The soul walks through this door into a passageway that systematically shatters all personal sense of control and incinerates every idol. Here, God refuses to be who the soul believes it needs God to be. Here, only faint bread crumbs of desire linger to guide—if the soul is lucky. In this passageway, one encounters lament and a dark night of the soul—two columns supporting an archway leading to desolation.

In the lament on the cross, Jesus is speaking directly to God. He is engaged in a complex conversation with God involving words, breath, silence, waiting, listening, responding, and struggle. Likewise, the psalmist, though he receives no answer, continues to speak directly to God. "O my God, I cry by day, but you do not answer" (22:2). The individual and communal psalms of lament, Job, Lamentations, and Christ's final words on the cross are all spoken out of suffering, loss, and pain. Yet in each case, though at present God is obviously not the consoling God of memory, the speaker finds a slim trail of faith, reason enough to talk with God. Anger, loss, denial, grief, and mental and physical suffering are the content of the conversation. The conversation seems to be only one way—from the pray-er to God—but the conversation of prayer still continues.

There is a distinction between lament and the dark night of the soul. In John of the Cross's dark night of the senses, spirit, and soul, or in Teresa's wilted and dying garden of flowers, conversation has simply broken down. Abandoned, forsaken, and lost, the soul no longer has recourse even to the consolation of silence. In the dark night of the soul, a person simply abandons prayer as conversation altogether. The soul in the throes of the dark night *cannot* pray. But what of Jesus' words? He is abandoned. He is dying. He is lost. But he *is* praying to a God he believes is there. Christ, Job, and David in the Psalms, unlike the writers of the dark night of the soul, bring abandonment itself into prayer. They talk about their loss—or yell or scream or mutter it. Such conversation focuses pain into prayer. It is bold to ask God, "Why?" Yet a thin strand of conversation remains. Such prayers address God, even *Deus absconditus,* the absent God.

A final way of noting the distinction between the dark night and lament is to return to the idea that lament, as with all forms of verbal prayer, is not an independent form of conversation. To pray a prayer of lament is to enter into prayer as confession. To lament is to confess one's own helplessness in the face of overwhelming events yet also to confess a faith in God's redemptive power. The prayer of lament is a prayer of petition, though the pray-er seeks, asks, and knocks loudly. It is a prayer of intercession that pleads with God to act on behalf of others as he has in the past. Perhaps most difficult to grasp is the fact that, as modeled over and over again in the Psalms, the prayer of lament merges into, blends with, and issues forth in prayers of adoration, thanksgiving, and praise. As if faith were a fulcrum that balances God's absence and his presence, our certainty and our doubt, our hopes and our fears, lament can be lifted only so high before it is necessarily balanced by adoration, . . . or we are broken. In this sense, the song of abandonment carries a refrain of memory, hope, promise, and transformation.

In the very psalm that cries out:

> My God, my God, why have you
> forsaken me? . . .
> O my God, I cry by day, but you do
> not answer. . . .
> I am a worm, and not human. . . .
> I am poured out like water,
> and all my bones are out of joint;
> my heart is like wax;
> it is melted within my breast;
> my mouth is dried up like a potsherd,
> and my tongue sticks to my jaws;
> you lay me in the dust of death.

we also find doxology, adoration, thanksgiving, and praise:

> To him, indeed, shall all who sleep in the earth bow down;
> before him shall bow all who go down to the dust,
> and I shall live for him.
> Posterity will serve him;
> future generations will be told about the Lord,
> and proclaim his deliverance to a people yet unborn,
> saying that he has done it.
>
> Psalm 22

Recollection: A Midpoint between Verbal and Silent Prayer

Recollection, in its many forms, is practiced in verbal form, in silence, or in the midst of the rhythm of both. Thus, recollection serves as a midpoint or transition between classic forms of verbal prayer and prayers of silence.

As an integral part of contemplation and prayer, recollection is typically taught and practiced according to three guiding principles. The first principle is recollection as collectedness, in which the scattered and fragmented soul is collected and gathered around a unifying center. A second principle focuses on recollection as a form of constant prayer lived in habitual consciousness of the presence of God. The third principle is based on a stream within the Christian spiritual tradition that relies on the symbolic imagination, perception, and senses to relive Gospel stories, experiences of sacred places, and even personal history. None of these three forms of recollection is independent of another; the practice of one reinforces the practice of each of the others.

In the first instance, collectedness is the opposite of wandering. Recollection in this sense finds a unifying center, a home within the self where we find unity and wholeness. This form of recollected prayer is known by a variety of names, including centering prayer, the prayer of presence, and centering down.[60] The key to this form of prayer is not to suppress inner turmoil or pain but to let it go, not to press it down in order to ignore it but to release it. Ultimately, the process is one of self-abandonment to divine presence. This form of prayer is often frustrating because it is foreign to our normal ways of being in the world. But teachers of recollection as connectedness stress that even if we at first achieve no more than an understanding of what we lack in inner unity, we have made progress in inner unity.

Historically, various church writers have explored this "gathering in" aspect of recollection. Athanasius portrays Anthony of Egypt as recollecting his spirit by imitating Christ to prepare for renouncing the world.[61] John Climacus focuses on distractions to recollection: "Fight always with your thoughts and call them back when they wander."[62] Augustine confesses that God is the one who "brings together what is scattered" within himself.[63]

The second principle of recollection seeks to fulfill Paul's injunction to pray without ceasing, with the result that a habitual recollection of God's presence is maintained in every aspect of one's life. Even the smallest details or chores become means for recalling to memory the active presence of God. Two of the most distinctive practitioners of this form of ongoing prayer are Jean-Pierre de Caussade (*The Sacrament of the Present Moment*) and Brother Lawrence (his collection of writings and letters is known collectively as *The Practice of the Presence of God*). For Brother Lawrence, recollection is the holiest and most necessary practice in the spiritual life. It consists of accustoming oneself to God's company at any moment without measure.[64]

A third and final principle can be called symbolic recollection. Here, the imagination, the senses, the body, the mind, the heart, the perceptions, and the intuition are all used to remember, enter into, and relive an event. The recollected event may involve a Gospel story, a sacred place, or an event in one's personal history.

Examples of the use of symbolic recollection are numerous. Richard of St. Victor, for instance, uses Jacob, his wives, and his children in a personification allegory that is intended to stimulate recollection and to aid the soul in contemplation of God. Rachel's maid Bilhah, in fact, represents imagination. It is through imagination that "[Scripture] describes invisible things through the forms of visible things and impresses the memory of them upon our minds through beauty."[65] Julian of Norwich also uses symbolic imagination but uses it to inform, as it were, not her mind, as in Richard, but her body. It is "as a gift and a grace from our Lord, that my body might be filled full of recollection and feeling of his blessed passion."[66] The classic disciplines of *examen of conscience* (recollection used to uncover areas in our life in need of cleansing and purification) and *examen of consciousness* (recollection of God's presence throughout the day and our response to God's presence) are also examples of this form of recollection. Both are important, for example, in Ignatian spiritual formation and are present concretely in William Law's integration of devotion and virtue. The rise of devotion to the humanity of Christ, beginning in the twelfth century and lasting in many forms even today, is also dependent on symbolic recollection, to "recall" the stories of Scripture and of Christ and to apply them to our life.

Recollection is a varied and flexible form of prayer. Its intent is not to suppress the turmoil and pain of this world but rather to let them go. In its active and passive forms, it is a self-abandonment to divine providence and unifying grace. It is a way of life attentive to God's presence in the world that can lead to both active memory and attentive silence.

Silence in Prayerful Conversation

> The music of silence,
> the sound of solitude,
> the supper that renews love.
>
> John of the Cross,
> "Spiritual Canticle"

Conversation in prayer is as much a matter of silence as it is a matter of words. Perhaps the easiest way to think of the language of silence is by imagining a spectrum of silence. The word *spectrum* comes from the Latin verb *specio*, meaning to look at carefully. But *specio* also has other important meanings that seem to speak as much to the heart of silence as they do to the eyes of the heart. The word can also mean to contemplate, to observe, and to watch. Prayer is like a spectrum, something that can be contemplated with the eyes of silence. We can begin to see that the broad and varied range of silence is analogous to the spectrum of light. Light, in and of itself, is invisible. We can see it in reflected or absorbed form, emanating or radiating form, but on its own, it is invisible. Yet it defines what we see. Light itself is the invisible element that defines the visible. In the same way, silence is that paradoxical element that gives birth to sound.

What we know of light alters when we look at it more closely through a prism. Light bent through a prism produces a visible rainbow but also invisible bands. If we could listen to silence more closely through something like a prism, what would we hear? We might hear a broad, delightful, and varied band of meanings of the "sounds of silence." If we could design such a thing as a prism for silence, we might encounter auditory bands beyond even the sounds of silence. Just as light requires equipment more sensitive than our eyes through which to see it, the full scope of silence may require equipment more sensitive than our ears to hear it in its fullness. The Christian tradition has handed down something like a prism of silence: prayer. Through this prism, we may, as it were, hear a spectrum of silence. Ironically, we must use words to communicate silence. This makes silence all the more difficult to hear.

There are exterior and interior forms of silence. Exterior silence involves a peaceful setting and a general absence of noise that, as one contemporary writer has put it, "can set up the conditions for interior silence, but they do not create it. At best, exterior silence serves as a facilitating condition for the deeper, more valuable experience of interior silence."[67]

John Teehan has further characterized internal and external silence as shallow and deep. Shallow silence (exterior) characterizes tranquility and passivity. In deep silence (interior), "a person temporarily transcends awareness of self."[68] In addition to these two kinds of silence, Teehan notes three other types of silence that he associates with various spiritual traditions: (1) Public or ritual silence in community fosters solemnity, reverence, recollection, and a sense of mystery. (2) Ascetical silence is the deliberate practice of keeping silent in order to eliminate chatter and to foster patience, charity, and detachment. (3) Meditational silence directs attention from everyday concerns, fosters calm, and helps the person in meditation become more aware of his or her innermost self as the heart of divine residence. All these forms of silence help us to become aware of both the mystery of our own presence and the all-encompassing mystery of God.[69]

Creation ex Silentii

It [the Eternal Word] was said once, and said in absolute silence. And it is only in silence that we hear it.

John of the Cross, *Maxims on Love*

We and the world around us were created, according to Christian doctrine, *ex nihilo* (from nothing). We can assume then that we were also created *ex silentii* (from silence). Prayer, too, is born from and dies back into silence.

The poet Rainer Maria Rilke writes of the act of creation as a song out of which animals, forests, humans, and the cosmos were "created by silence." In his poem "Sonnet One to Orpheus," Rilke writes, "It turned out the reason they [animals, etc.] were so full of silence / was not cunning, and not terror, / it was listening." The Creator, in the poet's memorable phrase, has created "a temple for creatures deep inside their ears." It is a temple wherein creatures might "hear" their Creator both in word and in silence.[70]

A contemporary writer, Barbara Brown Taylor, gets to the heart of the paradox of silence when she asks, "But how shall I break the silence? What word is more eloquent than the silence itself?" She answers in a tone not unlike Rilke's: "In the moments before a word is spoken, anything is possible."[71] Prayer is born of silence, a silence out of which anything is indeed possible, from expressions of ordinary needs to utterances of beauty and eloquence. Prayer, meditation, and contemplation linger gently in those moments when anything is possible.

Every word is bracketed by silence. Our words are not only born from silence but also die into silence in perpetual rhythm. Having asked her questions about the eloquence of silence, Taylor finds a kind of answer in this very rhythm: "Silence and speech define each other. One is the inhale. The other is the exhale."[72] Prayer as familiar conversation with God is as close as the air we breathe. Living in prayer guides us, over time, into silences out of which all things are possible. William Johnston, in surveying the variety of forms of Christian meditation today, recognizes this guiding hand of prayer that leads us into silence.

> For the fact is that everywhere we see Christians of all ages and cultures sitting quietly in meditation. Some sit before a crucifix or an icon in one-pointed meditation. Others sit and breathe as they look at the tabernacle. Others practice mindfulness, awareness of God in their surroundings. Others recite a mantra to the rhythm of their own breath. Others simply open minds and hearts to the presence of God. Others just talk to God.[73]

Following Augustine, who taught that prayer "consists more in groaning than in speaking, in tears rather than words,"[74] John Calvin is also clear that the best prayers are sometimes silent prayers. What he calls meditation on "God's kindness" and a "right and pure contemplation of God"[75] can lead to a disposition to enter into familiar conversation with

God. This is again, for Calvin, the familiar conversation that integrates mind, heart, word, gesture, and silence in intimate prayer:

> We should hold that the tongue is not even necessary for private prayer.
> . . . [Yet] even though the best prayers are sometimes unspoken, it often
> happens in practice that, when feelings of mind are aroused, unostenta-
> tiously the tongue breaks forth into speech, and the other members into
> gesture.[76]

Conversational prayer is of the heart as well as of the mind and of the body. It is at times spoken, and it is justifiably at times unspoken. In the hospitality of familiar conversation, the whole person prays as words are born from and fall back into silence.

Listening to Silence

> Dreams, angels, prophets—and silence. Our multidimensional God speaks
> in many voices.
>
> Margaret Guenther, *The Practice of Prayer*

Listening is also a key component of the stillness that connects us to the spectrum of silence. Listening reveals the radical reality of two silences: our many forms of silence and the transcendent silences of a present God. In the sixth century, St. Benedict of Nursia established in his rule a life of manual labor, community prayer, and prayerful read-ing of Scripture. The rule is still in active use today.[77] The first word in Benedict's rule is perhaps not unexpected: *Listen*. Benedict begins his guide to a community life centered in God with a word that occupies a central place between word and silence. To listen is to foster an ac-tive attitude of attention. To listen is to await. Listening involves being restful even as the one listening attends to sound. Listening is, in this sense, like *otium*, a Latin word associated with the activity of prayer and connoting "waking sleep." *Otium* is that state between the extremes of busyness and quiet. Listening, too, is a state of attentive rest. One who listens attends to words while resting in silence. We listen in silence as a friend speaks. Just as "waking sleep" describes a paradox, so too is "word and silence" a paradox that combines with listening to form prayer. Both paradoxes, however, help us get to the core of our relation-ship with God in prayer: We listen, and we connect; we are silent, and we connect; we speak, and we connect; we respond, and we connect; we act, and we connect. Then we return to listen once again.

Listening is like a sword used to discern, to cut, to sever the cords of human blindness. Exasperated by the fatigue of "mental prayer," for which she claims she has no skill, Teresa of Avila suggests closing one's eyes, imagining one is blind, and listening imaginatively. Then she suggests "listening" with the other senses, as a person blind from birth might do, to discern that Jesus is present in the room. In imagining blindness, prayer "cures" the blindness; Jesus is "seen" in the silence of listening.

From listening, prayer is born. Yet listening is certainly not easy. Barbara Brown Taylor speaks clearly and simply about this fact:

> Even now, some Christians have trouble listening to God. Many of us prefer to speak. Our corporate prayers are punctuated with phrases such as "Hear us, Lord" or "Lord, hear our prayer," as if the burden to listen were on God and not us. We name our concerns, giving God suggestions on what to do about them. What reversal of power might occur if we turned the process around, naming our concerns and asking God to tell us what to do about them? "Speak, Lord, for your servants are listening."[78]

Listening can also be painful. Renita Weems admits that her formation in listening to silence took place in the fires of loss and disorientation:

> Listening for God focuses on the lessons I have learned in this journey of feeling lost and disoriented. I offer the intimate conversations of listening for God, filled as it is with secret protestations, private doubts, and grateful glimpses of the divine, as proof that even seasoned explorers of the soul can get lost and disconsolate along the way. But no matter how lonely, quiet, and unpredictable the journey, with patient listening holy silence can become music.[79]

Attentive listening may be forged in loss, but when it is, the listener may develop an ear of the heart attuned to the chords of holy silence.

Listening also opens into mystery. Jesus' parables leave spaces of misdirection and expectation that create spaces of silence in which a listener can absorb and interpret the message.[80] Listening in this sense is both concrete and mysterious. It is concrete in the sense that real lives, details, and stories draw the listener in. It is mysterious in the sense that what is heard depends on how and with what part of the self one listens. In this sense, prayer as conversation, like the parables of Christ, remains ambiguous. Yet while the ambiguity is never resolved, it can be fully assimilated and lived as a conversation in that fruitful border between word and silence, listening and action.

In a recent book on the relationship between art and spirituality, Robert Wuthnow makes the observation that an "emphasis on mystery occurs repeatedly in artists' accounts of their work." He adds that "mystery is one of the ways in which artists emphasize the impossibility of fully understanding God."[81] Listening opens into this same impossibility. The real discipline is to be still, to live in the ambiguity, and to accept the silence. If we do so, we begin to live with and savor the fact that God can never be fully known. We accept the mystery behind the real.

Silence: A Colloquy of Love

Imagine standing knee-deep in winter snow before a Douglas fir, bare branches of western oak, sugar maple, alder, and aspen circling and embracing the solitary fir, the wind still, the white broken only by pinches of purple-green needles, blackened branch, gray sky. Silence here is as tangible as a name.

I believe that prayer is like a grove of trees I have visited many times. The trees are masters of silence, sages of quiet. They are trees of life thriving in the spectrum of silence. They are prayers of goodness, beauty, and truth. They each stand firmly rooted in the earth, sharing the intricate web of the forest floor. Their crowns grow through the sky and clouds, up into the heavens. The trees' forest brothers and sisters join in a common prayer of glory to God. In the rain, fog, sun, and wind, the trees vibrate with the prayerful spectrum of silence. The grove is a solid presence throughout the seasons and the centuries, its branches many, its trunk like a living support of love. The fir and its neighbors of western red cedar, alder, bracken fern and sword fern, huckleberry, lichen and moss, scampering creatures and fluttering, and the vast unseen of forest activity, of growth, decay, and death, all form a silent prayer that seeds life.

After opening his rule with the word *listen,* St. Benedict goes on to say that we listen with the ears of the heart to life-giving silence of a Father who loves us.[82] It is no coincidence that he inserts his instruction on silence between lessons on obedience and humility. Benedict says:

> Let us follow the Prophet's counsel: *I said, I have resolved to keep watch over my ways that I may never sin with my tongue. I have put a guard on my mouth. I was silent and was humbled, and I refrained even from good words* (Ps. 39:2–3). Here the Prophet indicates that there are times when good words are to be left unsaid out of esteem for silence. . . . Indeed, so important is silence that permission to speak should seldom be granted even to mature disciples, no matter how good or holy or constructive their talk, because it is written: *In a flood of words you will not avoid sin* (Prov. 10:19); and elsewhere, *The tongue holds the key to life and death* (Prov. 18:21). Speaking and teaching are the master's tasks; the disciple is to be silent and listen.[83]

The trees inhale what we exhale. In a similar way, in prayer we inhale as God breathes upon us. Francis de Sales (1567–1622) speaks of prayer in just this way, as a conversation between lovers exchanging the source of life:

> If prayer be a colloquy, a discourse or a conversation of the soul with God, by it then we speak to God, and he again speaks to us; we aspire to him and breathe in him, and he reciprocally inspires us and breathes upon us.[84]

This language of lovers, according to de Sales, communicates the incommunicable in a language only lovers understand. Where love dwells, sound is not necessary, and prayer is nothing if not a colloquy of love:

> Its conversation is altogether secret, and there is nothing said in it between God and the soul save only from heart to heart. . . . Lovers' language is so peculiar to themselves that none but themselves understand it. . . . Where love reigns, the sound of exterior words is not necessary, nor the help of sense to entertain and to hear one another. Love speaks not only by the tongue but by the eyes, by sighs, and by the play of features; yea, silence and dumbness are words for it. *My heart hath said to thee, my face sought thee: thy face, O LORD, will I still seek* [Ps. 27:8].[85]

One of Augustine's most compelling writings on the power of silence in prayer is his famous "vision at Ostia," in which Augustine and his mother experience an immediate encounter with God through the eyes, touch, and ears of the heart. In it, Augustine uses all his rhetorical skill to, in a sense, give speech to silence and silence to speech. It is an extended prayer, a beatific vision cast in terms of speaking, hearing, and listening. It employs words to evoke a "beatific silence." As Augustine's prayer of praise to silence unfolds, note the melodic use of words related to speaking, hearing, listening, tongue, and silence as he builds to a simple sound. The simple sound is silence in which we "hear God in Godself":

> And while we were speaking and panting for wisdom we did with the whole impulse of the heart slightly touch it. We sighed and left behind "the first fruits of the Spirit" (Rom. 8:23) which were bound there, and returned to the sound of our own tongue where the spoken word has both beginning and ending. How is it like your word, our Lord, "remaining ageless in Itself and renewing all things" (Wis. 7:27)? We said therefore: If to any man the uproar of the flesh grew silent, silent the images of earth and sea and air; and if the heavens also grew silent and the very soul grew silent to itself, and by not thinking of self ascended beyond self; if all dreams and imagined revelations grew silent, and every tongue and every sign and if everything created to pass away were completely silent—since if one hears

them, they all say this: We did not make ourselves, but He who abides made us. Suppose that, having said this and directed our attention to Him who made them, they also were to become hushed and He Himself alone were to speak, not by their voice but in His own [voice], and we were to hear His Word, not through any tongue of flesh or voice of an angel or sound of thunder or involved allegory, but that we might hear Him whom in all these things we love, might hear Him in Himself without them, just as a moment ago we too, as it were rose beyond ourselves and in a flash of thought touched the Eternal Wisdom abiding over all.[86]

Augustine and his mother hear God in hushed and silent tones of love.

Sighs Too Deep for Words

Some of the Pharisees in the crowd said to him, "Teacher, order your disciples to stop." He answered, "I tell you, if these were silent, the very stones would shout out."

Luke 19:39–40

In the conversation of prayer, feelings, needs, sins, experiences, and hopes are often beyond the capacity of words to capture. Much about life is simply beyond the grasp of words. The will and the mind of God are too deep for us, in our own power, to know. Paul says that he knows of someone caught up to the third heaven, where he "heard things that are not to be told, that no mortal is permitted to repeat" (2 Cor. 12:4). But the Spirit intercedes, aiding prayer by helping "us in our weakness; for we do not know how to pray as we ought, but that very Spirit intercedes with sighs too deep for words. And God, who searches the heart, knows what is the mind of the Spirit, because the Spirit intercedes for the saints according to the will of God" (Rom. 8:26–27). We do not know ourselves well enough to pray as we ought. Often our needs are too deep for words. In our silence, the Spirit intercedes at depths beyond even our most profound self-understanding. Through grace, in the silence, God hears a sigh.

If there are parts of ourselves or our self-awareness that are beyond the capacity of words to express, how can words express God? Scripture, reflecting divine revelation through history, narrative, and word, does name and describe God. God the Father, Jesus, and the Holy Spirit are variously described as life, light, wisdom, Lord of lords, King of the ages, Spirit of truth, light of the world, and many more. God is light, it is true, but God is also so much more than we will ever see. We can speak with the God we know through Scripture and experience, but the moment we do, we know we are moving toward the borders of the capacity of language or words to express just who God is. Exodus 3:14, for example, gives a self-description of God: "I AM who I AM." Words describe, but the meaning and the content of these words are difficult to grasp. Beyond this description, words seem to fail us altogether. God certainly is love, but our understanding of love is so limited and flawed that God is more than what we know of love. God dwells with us as love *and* as that love that cannot be spoken. This movement from the concrete to the mysterious has been framed in terms of apophatic and cataphatic prayer. Many Christian theologians, mystics, and teachers of prayer have wrestled with the paradox that God is simultaneously transcendent and immanent. They have struggled with the fact that God is at the same time revealed in Scripture and thus describable and yet also beyond the capacity of any word or words to encompass.[87] Word is essential in prayer with a God who is "with us," while silence is appropriate before a God who is more subtly present than any word is capable of describing.

There is another often more troubling silence in conversational prayer with God. We can see the limits of our language in speaking with God, and thus there are times when the most appropriate posture in prayer is silence. But prayer is a two-way conversation. There are times when *God* is silent. In fact, more times than not, that is simply what God is: silence. These can be dark times, frightening and shattering times. Madeleine L'Engle, with great compassion and understanding, describes the devastating, even hideous, nature of the no of God's silence:

> I have often been told that when one first turns to God, one is greeted with brilliant Yes answers to prayers. For a long time that was true for me. But then, when he has you hooked, he starts to say No. This has been, indeed, my experience. But it has been more than a No answer lately; after all, No is an answer. It is the silence, the withdrawal, which is so devastating. The world is difficult enough with God; without him it is a hideous joke.[88]

As we have seen, teachers of Christian prayer have long known and been familiar with this silence, the desolation that is like a light withdrawn. The silence of God goes by many names and images: the dark night of the soul, the silence of the dark night of faith, the silence of the dark cloud of unknowing. Teresa of Avila speaks of the silence as desolations, while John Bunyan wanders in despair through the slough of despond. All these traditions make it clear, however, that these are common and even essential developmental patterns in the process of maturing in prayer. Many contemporary writers on the spiritual life acknowledge divine silence as well.[89] We will examine these and other examples of how Christians have experienced the silence of God in detail in the context of prayer as journey.

Perhaps it should not be surprising that prayer as honest conversation with God includes God's silence and apparent withdrawal. The narrative of Scripture also seems to tell the story of God's advancing silence. Richard Elliott Friedman chronicles how in the Old Testament God fades away as the narrative moves from Genesis through the Minor Prophets.[90] Barbara Brown Taylor also gives an account of God's retreat into silence:

> After Babel, God was never again made visible to humankind. . . . Once Moses saw God's backside on Mount Sinai, the period of visible, audible, encounters with God began to come to an end. . . . After the delivery of the commandments, God never spoke directly to the people again. . . . The last person to whom God was said to have been "revealed" was Samuel. . . . The last person to whom God was said to have "appeared" was Solomon.

The last public miracle was "the spectacle on Mount Carmel, where Elijah single-handedly whipped the prophets of Baal." After this, "even the angels got scarce. And from Hezekiah on, the world described in the Hebrew Bible was one from which God had largely retired."[91] Such silence is initially, more often than not, an occasion for grieving and loss. But if we trust the scriptural narrative of people of faith and if we can entertain the validity of so many teachers on prayer who have dared to grapple with a silent God, our journeys into the dark nights of silence can lead us into even more intimate, familiar conversations with God. If we are lucky—or more precisely, if we dare explore the very borders of our faith—we will, in the words of T. S. Eliot, "arrive where we started / And know the place for the first time."[92]

Thomas Green, mining the Christian tradition for metaphors of darkness that reverberate with God's silence, suggests the image of "learning to float in the dark." He says:

> I spoke of learning to be at home in the dark. I said that this gradual coming to be at home is perhaps the crucial turning point in the life of contemplative prayer. It means, in terms of floating, that we have learned to be at home in the sea that is God, with no visible means of support except the water whose ebb and flow, whose sudden surging, we cannot predict or control.[93]

In the familiar conversation of prayer, we gradually learn to float in the silence, to be at home in the silent sea of God.

American Elm

A final word on silence is fittingly spoken by Thomas Merton, a contemporary contemplative saint blessed with the gift of silence as well as the gift of words:

> For there is only one language spoken in the City of God. That language is charity. Those who speak it best, speak in silence. For the eternal Word of Truth is uttered in silence. If He is uttered in silence, He must be heard in deepest silence. And His Spirit, the Spirit of Love, is also poured out into our hearts, proceeding from the Father and the Son, in an everlasting silence.[94]

The spectrum of silence is spoken in the city of God. We have already had glimpses of that city. With diligence, practice, and grace, we can learn to speak its language.

Conclusion

The foundational quality of conversational prayer helps sustain our connection to God through joys and sorrows, consolations and desolations, certainty and doubt. The tall, graceful American elm (*Ulmus americana*) on the previous page is a stately beauty that is said to have caused woodsmen to halt their work in reverence and to realize that taking it down would be akin to razing a Gothic cathedral. Yet sadly, since 1930, American elms have struggled against a fungus called Dutch elm disease, carried by the elm bark beetle, and the number of these beautiful trees has dwindled dangerously. Still they survive, and as we can see in this image, the holy beauty of the tree is echoed in the solid, almost intimate intricacy of its searching roots. These roots provide the strong foundation that adapts to water, stone, soil, and weather, growing over the years in concert with their habitat and as essential, living anchors for the tree.

Conversational prayer comprises the roots of the tree of life. They adapt, often largely unseen, to the conditions with which they are presented. They persevere; they reach out and explore; they are a living foundation. The roots of conversational prayer feed the entire tree. They snake their way into the solid trunk of relationship in such a mysterious way that we never know the exact point where conversation ends and relationship begins. Working silently underground, they allow the many branches of our journeys in prayer to take shape. As the roots do their work, new leaves of transformation in prayer are free to color and breathe, to swing with the wind, even to die and be born anew. Perhaps most miraculous of all, in the fragrance of fruit and flower, we see and experience the presence of God extending throughout the tree of life to the deepest, darkest, most daring root.

This chapter explored the natural rhythms in conversational prayer between word and silence. In prayer as conversation, without silence there would be no word. Without word there would be no silence.

Flexibility and rhythm are also apparent in the richness and variety of prayerful listening, waiting, attention, hearing, and responding. These natural rhythms of conversation have been accessed and taught as anchors of prayer by countless Christian masters since the earliest days of the church. Prayer as conversation is not only word and silence but also watchfulness, attentiveness, patience, selfless listening, perseverance in waiting and in listening, and healing response. It is in this rhythmic aspect of conversation that one begins to experience silence as a spectrum containing richness, depth, variation, beauty, and nuance.

Verbal prayer in itself is also flexible and rhythmic, with its tightly interwoven patterns of adoration, praise, thanksgiving, confession, intercession, petition, and lament. While each of these modes of verbal prayer describes a legitimately distinct aspect of conversation, it is not independent. As with the relationship between word and silence, here too distinctiveness is laced with mutuality and interdependence. Conversation in prayer expands, taking on new meaning and dimension, when we realize, for instance, that adoration implies confession of who we are in relation to God and who God is in relation to the world. In a similar way, praise enters conversation with intercession as we begin to see that what we praise God for can become what we ask for on behalf of others. A petitionary prayer becomes a prayer of thanksgiving as we give thanks in faith, believing that what we ask for will be granted. A thanksgiving prayer becomes a petition as our awareness expands to understand that God's gifts are precisely in line with our needs. As modeled in the Psalms, adoration and praise seem to be intimate partners of lament. And as lament makes its painful arc back to adoration, we begin to see verbal prayer not only as rhythmic but also as a continuum on the circle of conversation.

John's Gospel opens by telling us that in the beginning was the Word. In the translation of Erasmus, in the beginning was the Conversation. Prayer is conversation. According to John Calvin, prayer is intimate or familiar conversation. From the beginning, God has invited us to join in this familiar conversation.

Prayer as Relationship

The Solid Trunk of Prayer

Praise be to the God and Father of our Lord Jesus Christ, the Father of compassion and the God of all comfort, who comforts us in all our troubles, so that we can comfort those in any trouble with the comfort we ourselves have received from God.

2 Corinthians 1:3–4 NIV

To Love and to Serve God: Hospitality

In his book *Some Principles of Moral Theology and Their Application,* the late Anglican bishop Kenneth Kirk writes:

The Christian ideal of character is the person of Christ, as manifested in his earthly life. Nothing short of that suffices as a guide. And the simplest summary of this pattern of Christian goodness is to love and to serve God and to love and to serve humanity; this is the essence and the whole of Christian duty—the purpose of life.[1]

97

In the same way, the simplest pattern of Christian goodness is hospitality toward God and hospitality toward humanity, and together they constitute the whole of Christian duty of relational prayer.

This chapter explores relationship as a way of being in prayer. It looks at contemporary writings on relationship that echo prayer and at older writings on the Trinity and prayer that reverberate with the idea of relationship. In tracing prayer as one form of ethical response to another in relationship, the chapter follows prayer as it broadens and deepens from acquaintanceship to love of God. Such a life of prayer entails a lifelong process of loss, grief, and risk as well as connection, reconciliation, and forgiveness. All of us "become" prayer for others, as it were, through relationship. Such relationship in turn shapes hospitality. It shapes an ethic of receptivity toward the world, others, and ourselves. At its core, true, whole prayer is relationship. It is love burning through us; it is a love that reconciles and a love that forgives. It is the solid trunk delivering, supporting, and spreading charity throughout the tree of life.

The Face of Relational Prayer

Several contemporary writers speak of how hospitality, courtesy, and kindness are grounded in relationship in ways that have deep implications for prayer. These concepts will help us make the connection between relationship, reconciliation, forgiveness, and love in prayer.

We do not live without relationship. Any relationship claims our attention; it connects, orients, and gives us meaning. The contemporary thinker George Steiner articulates a vision of an ethic of hospitality that evokes connectedness, relationship, and forgiveness:

> A reflection on or a "thinking of" meetings, of encounters, of communication, itself entails a morality. An analysis of enunciation and signification—that is, any form of signal to the other—entails an ethics.[2]

For Steiner, meetings, signals, any encounter or communication with another enact relationship.

We can think of prayer in a similar way as meetings, signals, encounters, communications that together form a relationship and entail an ethics. As we saw in chapter 1, Simone Weil emphasizes attentiveness as a form of prayer. In a similar manner, Steiner speaks of "any form of signal to the other" as a form of attentiveness. Attentiveness in this sense, for both Weil and Steiner, is prayer in that prayer focuses our attention on the reality and needs of another. Prayer creates relationships of caring.

Steiner also articulates an ethics of receptive hospitality that describes connective encounter through the metaphor of text and interpreter. He says that "a master translator can be defined as a perfect host."[3] To see truly the need of another (that is, to be truly attentive or to truly translate, understand, and respond), we must be the perfect host. The perfect host is alert to any "signal from the other," ready to translate the language of need into a language of hope. Steiner's language, in effect, uses the language of "translating" in a way that the Christian tradition has used the language of "discerning." The practice of hospitality and kindness is a practice of discernment. As Steiner indicates, perfect translation requires perfect hospitality, the ability to ask, "Who are you?" "What do you need?" "Tell me your story." Steiner suggests that a "concept of courtesy" can itself be a way into relationship. It communicates a way of being that demands, fundamentally, a "courtesy of heart" in prayer.

What Steiner says about interpreters and texts is equally true of Scripture and prayer. Parts of Scripture are quite foreign to many of us. Yet with an attitude of hospitality toward Scripture, we begin to accept and feel comfortable even in its "otherness," learning as we do so to translate its truths by opening the home of our heart to its life-giving words. Likewise, in prayer, we come before God on behalf of ourselves or others essentially as strangers. To "translate" the stranger, to truly know the needs of another, to ask the charitable and meaningful questions, there must be an attitude of kindness and an inclination toward courtesy.

Jean-Luc Marion is another contemporary who echoes an ethics of prayerful receptivity. In his book *God without Being*, Marion explores what he calls an ethics of receptivity, courtesy, and hospitality. He suggests that the very act of interpreting the needs of and responding to another in true relationship, or agapic love, requires an ethics of receptivity. Without *agapē*, according to Marion, we cannot gaze upon, let alone interpret or see the true humanity in, the face of another.[4]

Emmanuel Lévinas helps us to see this essential connection between community, ethics, and prayer as relationship. Using the metaphor of the face, Lévinas says that the look or gaze of the face *is* knowledge and perception, but more importantly, "access to the face is straightway ethical."[5] In other words, the very act of coming into close relationship with another (access to the face) is at once both an invitation and a responsibility to respond to another with grace, charity, and justice. Access to relationship is "straightway ethical." If we pray, we are compelled to live ethically; we cannot encounter another only to turn away. Prayer face-to-face is "straightway ethical." To encounter the face of self, God, other, or creation necessitates a master act of hospitality. The very encounter with another calls forth a posture and a visage of courtesy, kindness, *agapē*, justice, hospitality, forgiveness, reconciliation, and relationship.[6]

Prayer carries with it an accompanying ethics of receptivity and hospitality. Meditative prayer done with tact, kindness, reception, and courtesy encounters a God passionately at work in the world who fires our own heart with compassion. Prayer uttered and received with courtesy and an open, hospitable heart helps answer the essential question of prayer once asked by Dietrich Bonhoeffer:

> Has it [prayer] transported him for a few short moments into a spiritual ecstasy that vanishes when every day life returns, or has it lodged the Word of God so soberly and so deeply in his heart that it holds and strengthens him all day, impelling him to active love, to obedience, to good works? Only the day will decide.[7]

Suddenly, There Is the Lord: *Adventus* Prayer

Prayer as relationship grounded in love is in part the art of making space and taking time for others and one's self to grow.[8] The wisdom and the goodness of God are nurtured in this relationship and practiced in charity. In a real sense, through the gift of human relationship, we practice receiving the presence of God. In fact, our very existence is dependent on time and space given us by God. Relationship thus extends from God, engulfs the willing self, and moves outward to creation and others in an ever-expanding connective web. It is like an intricate sphere emerging from and returning to God, all the while creating new space and new time for human flourishing.

But often the hardest space to create for growth in relationship is our own inner space. It is often easier to close and shrink this space than to risk opening it to others. Yet only in welcoming another do we move from simple self-absorption and solipsistic self-translation to expansive hospitality. In opening this inner space of hospitality, we weave an ethic of receptivity, and we practice the art of courtesy. In this sense, prayer is an opportunity to open ourselves and to enter into relationship with God and the world around. It is a way of risking and fully living life.

It is often said that God is closer to us than we are to ourselves. Julian of Norwich, the great fourteenth-century spiritual guide and theologian, puts this much more elegantly:

> For as the body is clothed in cloth, and the flesh in skin, and the bones in flesh, and the heart in the chest, so are we soul and body clad in the goodness of God and enclosed, Yea, and more homely [i.e., closely]. For all these waste away. Yet the goodness of God is ever whole and nearer to us without any likeness [i.e., beyond comparison].[9]

Julian is famous for her image of the hazelnut cupped in the palm of her hand, through which she intuits, in George Steiner's words, "the form of a signal from God." For Julian, the hazelnut is "clad in the gladness of God," and she opens herself fully to it. Gaston Bachelard, the "poet of space," has written that small things and spaces such as nests, shells, corners, seeds, and nuts suggest not only protection and refuge but also potential emerging and new birth. Of the tiny soft-shell crab, he speculates that "we have the impression that, by staying in the motionlessness of its shell, the creature is preparing temporal explosions, not to say whirlwinds, of being."[10] God clothes and protects us more than we are ever fully aware. Yet like the hazelnut and the crab, which emerge as full-grown tree and crab, we are protectively loved and clothed so that we may emerge as "whirlwinds of being" fully and relationally engaged in the world.

But functional relationship necessitates trust, hope, and anticipation that another *will* or *can* enter into our own space and time and grow. It also necessitates a hopeful self with well-defined inner space, a "holding environment" for others where the borders of trust and caring are clear. In the context of both time and space, it requires a willingness to adapt, to be pliable, to conform to the timing and space of others. The theologian Jürgen Moltmann frames the art of relationship in terms of what he calls the "eschatological self." By this he means this same art of creating space for others; it is "self" made pliable, hospitable, and open to authentic relationship because it is open to God and God's future. Prayer encourages this eschatological self. Moltmann's theology of the future is a helpful tool for illuminating how prayer as relationship can create a space for others to grow.

Moltmann points out that there are two possible ways of thinking about the future or eschatological self. These include *futurum*, focused on what *will be*, and *adventus*, focused on what *is coming*.[11] For Moltmann, *futurum* is a dependent future, by which he means that it is dependent on the past and the present. In a sense, it has to happen because its antecedents determine its future shape. Most importantly for Moltmann, it offers no occasion for hope. In the classic formulation that the kingdom of God has already but also not yet come, *futurum* has no *already*. Thus, what we hope for *may* come, but it will also pass away. Moltmann elaborates:

> The process [*futurum*] is irreversible: the future will become the past, but the past will never again be future. The future of becoming certainly offers a reason and occasion for development and planning, prediction and programs; but not for enduring hope.[12]

Development and planning, prediction and programs are part of but fall far short of the full process of enfolding another in relationship or prayer. Development, predictions, and programs do not let us truly attend to another *as* another. *Futurum* thus works against the possibility of truly finding space within for another to dwell and be as he or she is. It excludes being fully open to others in relationship or to God in prayer, because it is open only to the exigencies of history, not hope.

On the other hand, understanding the future as *adventus* means accepting the unexpected future that hope entails. This future does not develop out of the present exclusively, which would be a calculated projection of past and present into the future. Yet it is not altogether unexpected. It is an arrival; it "confronts the present with something new" and is something "that is coming which will never pass away."[13] "Advent" is thus the quintessence of hope, the coming of the completely fresh that will not pass away.

Moltmann goes on to explain *futurum* and *adventus* in ways that help to clarify what they might mean for prayer. In particular, he points toward the possibility of divine inbreaking through *adventus* moments encountered in true relationship. For instance, he makes a distinction between extrapolation and anticipation that has important implications for open relationship and prayer. *Futurum* is associated with ownership and power in relations based on extrapolation:

> There are trends and lines of development in past and present which we can extrapolate into the future. But these extrapolations turn the future into a prolongation of the present. These prolongations of the present are always used to stabilize present conditions of ownership and power.[14]

Extrapolation prolongs the present but allows no space for the growth of others. Our own expectations, sense of ownership, and need for power fossilize relational possibilities. Thus, it does not allow for a real future in which others can claim their own identity, space, or hope. It suppresses alternative possibilities; it suppresses plurality, ethnicity, gender identity. It suppresses mystery. In suppressing mystery, it suppresses full relationship with God. God may come and knock on the door of our extrapolated *futurum,* but that door opens and closes in the same instant; God comes and is gone. Extrapolation does not allow the future to create an open space for others, self, or God to grow.

The understanding of the future as anticipation, on the other hand, helps us attune ourselves to the future. But what that future will be cannot be prepared for, planned for, or extrapolated. The anticipatory self is attuned to the possibility of the unknown much in the way that we might describe prayer as openness to mystery or the unexpected presence of God:

> These foretastes, images, and attunements are part of every perception of the unknown. Without anticipatory awareness we should not discern something that is still in the future at all. But in anticipatory awareness, we always align ourselves to what is last and final—to happiness or unhappiness, life or death. The last thing to penetrate our experience is the first in our expectations. It is in the light of this that we then perceive and judge what can come upon us, and what actually does come.[15]

Moltmann is clear that in actual fact we cannot always separate anticipation and extrapolation. But the eschatological future cannot be reduced to dogma alone, which is a reduction simply to the extrapolary *futurum*. Likewise, the human person cannot be reduced to a single paradigm. But the capacity to believe, coupled with a well-defined inner space opened to true relationship with another, can focus our perspective on an infinite horizon of anticipation and hope. The hopeful self—the self that senses that goodness will arrive, that the world is a safe place, and that people are reliable and can be trusted—is an *adventus* self open to relationship. An *adventus* self is a self in prayer: caring, hospitable, inviting others into intimacy and an open and shared environment. It is a prayer allowing God to break in as well. *Adventus* prayer offers peace in the midst of new ways of being in relationship.

The contemporary writer Margaret Farley captures the essence of *adventus* relationship when she speaks of prayer as "relaxation of the heart." In relaxation of the heart, one relinquishes the kind of ridged expectancy that undermines a capacity for love. It encourages the fearlessness to question unexamined beliefs and the melting of our "icy and forbidden reaches" by the warmth of new insight and new relationship. It infuses prayer with patient endurance and a trustful "letting go" of our desire for mastery.[16]

The advent of God is certainly not *dependent* on prayer; God finds us in one way or another. Writing in the twelfth century, Guerric of Igny described looking for God in all the "right" places. But God finds him only when he relaxes his heart:

> You know how it is, my dear brothers. Some days we go to our *lectio,* and the Lord doesn't seem to show up. We go on to the liturgy, and he is seemingly nowhere around. We approach the tomb of the altar, and it seems completely empty. Then, as we go down the garden path on our way to work, *lo—suddenly there is the Lord.*[17]

This is relational, *adventus* prayer. We are open in anticipation, we believe in the in-breaking of God, we long for relationship. Yet nothing works. Then, lo, suddenly, there is the Lord, seeking, finding, and loving us.

Intimacies: From Friendship to Love in Prayer

God *is* love, which implies that God *is* relationship. Over the centuries, the Christian spiritual tradition has explored the many nuances of this relationship and how these nuances affect prayer. For instance, one aspect of love is intimate friendship. The twelfth-century Cistercian monk Aelred of Rievaulx, in his classic *Spiritual Friendship,* records a dialogue with a friend, Ivo:

> *Ivo.* Shall I say of friendship what John, the friend of Jesus, says of love: "God is friendship"?
> *Aelred.* That would be unusual, to be sure, nor does it have the sanction of the Scriptures. But still what is true of love, I surely do not hesitate to grant to friendship, since "those that abide in friendship, abide in God, and God in them."[18]

Spoken to a friend about what it is to be a friend, Aelred's dialogue reminds us that to be in relationship is to be in God, a God who is in turn both friend and lover.

The deep mystery of relationship with God in prayer is that it has an equally powerful side effect: To be in prayerful relationship with a friend or lover brings us into the presence of God. Aelred writes:

> Friendship is a stage bordering upon that perfection which consists in the love and knowledge of God, so that a person becoming a friend of their fellowman becomes a friend of God.[19]

Relationship establishes a circle. As we are a friend of God, our friendship with others draws us into God. In relationship, this circle only widens. As we learn to befriend ourselves, we learn to befriend others. Creation befriends us with its bounty and beauty as we learn to love with bounty and beauty and grace. As friends of Jesus, John and the other disciples experience God as love. Aelred of Rievaulx's description of friendship reads like a description of prayer:

> But what happiness, what security, what joy to have someone to whom you dare to speak on terms of equality as to another self; one to whom you need have no fear to confess your failings; one to whom you can unblushingly make known what progress you have made in the spiritual

life; one to whom you can entrust all the secrets of your heart and before whom you can place all your plans. Friendship [or prayer] heightens the joys of prosperity and mitigates the sorrows of adversity by dividing and sharing them.[20]

There is something very real about the friendship of God, and in prayer to God, we may "dare to speak on terms of equality as to another self." God is more than simply a friend, and there is much about God that is not equal to us "as to another self." But friendship is one real attribute of God's relationship with us, and therefore, in daring to contemplate God on terms of equality, we may also dare to pray our true self and to present our true self to the world.

Prayer is also relationship that connects us to God as to another self. The contemporary writer on prayer and contemplation, Basil Pennington, chooses to explain the method and the practice of *lectio divina* (from the Latin, meaning sacred reading) using metaphors drawn from relationship.[21] For Pennington, this ancient prayer that plants God's word in Scripture directly into the soil of the heart is fundamentally about relationship. Echoing Aelred of Rievaulx, he speaks of Christ as "this Divine Friend, whom we meet in *lectio,* a Man and a God of infinite self-giving love."[22]

We can speak of four modes of relationship that correspond to the four moments of prayer in *lectio divina.* Just as the four moments of *lectio* take us successively deeper into the heart of God's Word, so these four moments take us deeper into relationship with God and consequently deeper into relationship with ourselves and others.

The first moment of this prayer involves careful reading (*lectio*) of God's Word. In the slow, deliberate reading of Scripture, we begin to listen to and hear the word that God wishes to speak to us. This mode of relationship in prayer is a period of acquaintanceship, a time to get to know God and God's will for our life.

The second moment of *lectio* involves meditation on God's Word, in which we actually place ourselves within the text. One helpful way of approaching meditation is to think of it as prayer in which we become performers enacting the drama or play of Scripture. In this way, prayer becomes performative and is given a ritual or even liturgical meaning, in which we take part. This method of prayer projects us meditatively back into story and narrative. We can also use the text to dramatize current events in our life by using the ideas and persons drawn from Scripture to project God's Word forward into the present. In either case, we are becoming more and more familiar with God's Word. We are making it a part of us. It becomes, in effect, our friend and companion.

Oratio, or verbal prayer, is the third moment of *lectio*. In this phase of the prayer, we take the opportunity to discuss any thoughts, feelings, emotions, hopes, frustrations, or dreams that arise during reading and meditation. This is a close and personal time with God, a time when the power of the Word of God promotes honest and open conversation. Such conversation, as described in chapter 2, can involve any of the forms of verbal prayer, including, for instance, thanksgiving, petition, or lament. Such prayers can range from personal and spontaneous prayer to liturgical, set prayers of worship. Whatever the thoughts or feelings expressed in conversation and prayer, our relationship with God is evolving into areas of trust, safety, and frank honesty that lead us into deeper intimacy with God.

A fourth moment in *lectio* is that of contemplation. There are numerous forms of Christian contemplation, but they all have one thing in common: Our relationship with God has moved into a moment of prayer that consists in deep and abiding love. Here one meets and dwells with God in dark illumination; one closes one's eyes and enters a sea of silence enlivened with connection and truth. We begin to know God. We exist in God's companionship. We share our whole being with God. In this being with God, loving adoration and thanksgiving are sufficient.

But prayer does not cease when reading, meditation, verbal prayer, and contemplation cease. Relationship, likewise, does not cease to grow once we have practiced these various ways of making space for another. Many writers on *lectio*, including Pennington, have expanded our understanding of prayer, helping us to see the continuity between prayer as relationship and the fruits of prayer and to no longer separate the active and the contemplative life. This serves to extend prayer into the work we do and the ministries in which we are engaged. If prayer is a way of life, and our way of life is prayer, the false dichotomy and separation between prayer and action in the world are avoided, and relationship with God and the world can be maintained. Moments in *lectio* that reflect this reach of prayer into our daily life are twofold: One involves compassion, in which we are open to experience the brokenness in the world even as we maintain relationship not only with God but also with all living things. A second moment is action, through which we engage the world in aiding others by participating in God's plan for shalom.[23]

Ministry and active aspects of *lectio* are also most succinctly illustrated through modalities of relationship. The mode of relationship corresponding to compassion is solidarity, in which we are moved to identify with and exist together with all created things. The moment in prayer that is action evokes a mode of relationship best described as covenantal, modeled on God's covenantal relationships and involving mutual trust, support, and peace. A covenantal relationship of charity toward the oppressed of the world, for instance, emerges from compassionate solidarity with the world.

The following chart summarizes the essential, deepening, and patterned correspondence between the ancient practice of prayer as *lectio divina* and what we can call the way of relationship in prayer:

Lectio Divina	Way of Relationship
Reading	Acquaintanceship
Meditation	Friendship
Verbal Prayer	Intimacy
Contemplation	Love
Compassion	Solidarity
Action	Covenant

In the way of relationship, we can say that God, in Christ and through the Holy Spirit, gets into our flesh. Prayer enfleshes and incarnates our relationship with God.

Forgiveness and Reconciliation in Prayer

> Forgive us our debts,
> as we also have forgiven our debtors.
>
> Matthew 6:12

Forgiveness and reconciliation are crucial to the maintenance of relationship. Forgiveness and reconciliation do not simply cover or push aside the pain, loss, and grief we inflict on others or ourselves. In fact, the opposite is the case. To forgive is to shine a light on our participation in and personal responsibility for brokenness and hurt. It means that we confess our participation, whether alone or with others, ask for pardon, and work toward reconciliation. Relationship sustained through forgiveness and reconciliation in prayer is thus a four-step process: (1) finding those places in our life where we have participated in breaking rather than mending relationship, (2) acknowledging and confessing our participation, (3) actively seeking and asking for forgiveness, and (4) working toward true reconciliation.

This section looks at forgiveness and reconciliation in relational prayer from a variety of perspectives, beginning briefly with scriptural perspectives and moving to contemporary writers on relationship and forgiveness.

In Paul's great hymn of reconciliation in 2 Corinthians 5, he says that God is reconciling himself to us and to the world in and through Jesus Christ and has given us the ministry of reconciliation. Though all this has already been and continues to be accomplished for our sakes and for our salvation, Paul nonetheless prays that this very thing that God has done will continue to be enacted. Paul writes, "We entreat you on behalf of Christ, be reconciled to God" (2 Cor. 5:20). In this short petition, Paul reminds us of our own brokenness and sin. He prays that through Christ we might be forgiven and reconciled to God. He prays to God for reconciliation, and he teaches forgiveness and reconciliation as a means of relationship of the saints within the church.

It may seem odd and unnecessary for Paul to pray for what has already been accomplished. Yet regardless of what God has done, God nonetheless covets and urges our prayers.[24] In addition, our relationship with God is tenuous, constantly tested, and in danger of breaking, and so we continue to pray. The fact that our relationship is tenuous is illustrated in Luther's Large Catechism: "For we know that our defense lies in prayer alone. We are too weak to resist the Devil. . . . For what has carried off these great victories . . . if not the prayers of certain pious people who rose up as a rampart to protect us?"[25] Paul confirms that our relationship with God is not only tenuous but tested. As servants of God, we pray for fidelity in the decisive hours, "through great endurance, in afflictions, hardships, calamities, beatings, imprisonments, riots, labors, sleepless nights, hunger; by purity, knowledge, patience, kindness, holiness of spirit, genuine love" (2 Cor. 6:4–6). Luther and Paul both recognize that our relationship with God and our relationships with one another are never complete. Reconciliation and forgiveness are always necessary factors in the equation of relationship.

As Paul makes clear, even the deepest, most harmonious relationships are driven by cycles of intimacy and separation, peace and anger, service and self-centeredness. The Song of Songs is another biblical example of these cycles of relationship, separation, and reconciliation. It is a book of love in which a relationship is expressed in terms of mystic union of flesh and spirit through the image of sexual union between bride and groom. Yet the deeper truth of this story of the lover and the beloved is that intimacy and love contain within them inevitable wounds of separation. In fact, forgiveness and reconciliation are really the power and driving force of the Song of Songs. While the Latin etymology of relationship is a "bringing or carrying back," the real *process* of that "bringing back" of lover to beloved in the Song of Songs is action of mutual forgiveness and reconciliation.

Writing on prayer and reconciliation, the contemporary author Kenneth Leech makes the important point that sin is also social. Individualistic ideas of sin are not only inadequate but also actually harmful. With this social nature of sin in mind, Leech writes:

> Prayer is fellowship with God, the healing of a broken relationship, but it can only occur in Christ and in his great atoning work of prayer. There is therefore a close connection between prayer and the Cross. Christians believe that God has reconciled us to himself in Christ and united things on earth and things in heaven. The purpose of human life is union with God, and this is the purpose of Christian prayer: prayer, life, and the work of Christ on the Cross are a unity.[26]

Paul prays that the saints in Corinth might persevere in reconciliation to God. In the same book, Paul offers telling words: "If we are beside ourselves, it is for God" (2 Cor. 5:13). It is in being reconciled to ourselves (beside ourselves) that we are in relation with ourselves, and it is in relation with ourselves that we disclose our true self before God. Being beside ourselves in this way is another way of expressing the anticipation of Moltmann's *adventus* self. It is the type of open anticipation for God that makes each moment an opportunity for hope, reconciliation, and relational prayer "beside our God" and "beside our neighbors."

In prayer, we can engage in the four operations of forgiveness given at the beginning of this section: shedding light on broken relations, acknowledging them, asking forgiveness, and working toward reconciliation. Such prayer must be both "beside our God" and "beside our neighbors." One without the other is only partial reconciliation, only a temporary patch for our relationships. Prayer itself does not serve to forgive our sins. We are reconciled to God through Christ and forgiven by God. Just as our salvation is not by works, neither does forgiveness come through prayer alone.

Leanne Payne, in her book *Restoring the Christian Soul*, writes of forgiveness in the context of healing prayer. As with a number of other contemporary writers,[27] she equates the prayer of forgiveness with what she calls "healing memories." "Healing of memories," she writes, "means forgiveness of sin, . . . [and] the failure to forgive another is the most formidable barrier to wholeness."[28] The forgiveness of sins, to a large degree, is the healing of memories. For Payne, it is through prayer that those memories are brought to the surface: "We need to look to God for direction in forming prayers of confession and forgiveness. . . . It is through prayer that relationships are mended and our souls are healed of their grievous lacks due to failed relationships of the past."[29] To pray for the healing of someone's memories is to pray for the healing of one's own or another's soul. And the memories themselves are often recoverable only in prayer.

In healing prayer, the power of memory makes the past present and available for healing. God is eternally present where forgiveness and healing are necessary. Prayers of confession, petition, and intercession bring past hurts to the surface through memory where, in an atmosphere of safety and space for growth, the self can confront and seek healing reconciliation.

In Matthew, Jesus reminds us, "If you forgive others their trespasses, your heavenly Father will also forgive you; but if you do not forgive others, neither will your Father forgive your trespasses" (6:14–15). Again, the failure to forgive is a barrier to wholeness. Of course, confession and remembering past events do not immediately heal pain. A history of abandonment, repression of painful emotions, denial, grief, severe loss, the breakdown of normal coping mechanisms, anxiety, the rise of neurotic impulses, or even more schizoid behaviors that split self and relationship at ever deeper psychic levels all work against instantaneous healing of memories and forgiveness. Even when prayers for healing and reconciliation are consistent, deep, and rise from a pure heart, we often find that the wound itself must become a part of the answer to such prayer.

Other strategies are of course needed for wholeness and restoration of relationships. However, these strategies are most effective when they, too, are thought of as prayer. If prayer is a way of life, so too is the process of healing memories. Thus, in addition to formal prayer, touch, transference, bonding, guidance, friendship, perseverance, therapy, and many other healing arts all contribute, with God's grace, to the often-slow movement toward wholeness and reconciliation. In this sense, even medications that address broken bodies and spirits are modern routes to prayer.

Another barrier to renewed relationship in prayer is the failure to receive or accept forgiveness. Leanne Payne describes a number of impediments to receiving forgiveness and entering into new relationships. These include (1) denial, repression, and grief; (2) remaining under the law in such a rigid and unforgiving way that any attempt by another to heal wounds is perceived as a breach of a carefully constructed worldview based on law rather than on forgiveness; (3) the "bad guy within," the very brokenness that needs healing, prevents the forgiveness from reaching the heart of the soul in need of change; (4) a lack of awareness of the need for forgiveness; (5) an inability to name and therefore own the sin; and (6) accepting forgiveness only partially because of the unspoken assumption that we will go out and sin again.[30] Payne ends this discussion with some practical advice:

> The person who has failed to receive forgiveness has most likely confessed
> the same sin over and over. Even so, I ask such a one to confess the sin
> once again, this time while "seeing" Jesus, dying on the cross to take
> sin upon and into Himself. After the person has confessed it, I proclaim
> forgiveness in a way that the penitent can receive it.[31]

Forgiveness and reconciliation run straight through and are pierced
by the cross. Like the "illuminating darkness" of the cross, they restore
relationship from both sides of the bitter divide between brokenness
and healing. From the one side, the more light we can bring to bear
on our brokenness through prayer, memory, and confession, the more
likely we are to receive forgiveness and return it as light to others.
From the other side, the more we enter into the darkness of the cru-
cifixion, the more likely we are to assimilate and live out forgiveness
through the prayer of Christ, "Father, forgive them," even though we
know not what we do.

L. Gregory Jones is another who writes that thinking about forgiveness, let alone finding the courage to practice it, can be difficult. "It may
be easier to understand that forgiveness is the right response than to
be able to give or receive forgiveness, or even want to do so. On paper,
forgiveness is great. The problem comes when we try to take it off the
page and live it out in our actual relations with one another."[32] In this
sense, forgiveness gives us a sense of the true meaning of relationship
as a model of prayer. Forgiveness and relationship each have a kind of
parallel reality: As ways of life, they are often more easily defined in
terms of avoidance than actual practice.

Jones also describes forgiveness in the way that prayer functions: as a
way of life that unites us with God, self, and others: "[The] central goal
[of forgiveness] is to reconcile, to restore communion—with God, with
one another, and with the whole creation. . . . [It is] a way of life that
we live in our relations with one another."[33] Relationship as a model of
prayer restores communion. As we pray with and for one another, we
find that this communion shapes relationship if we are willing to live
in the ambiguity forgiveness demands and the grace by which we are
surprised.

The shape of God's forgiveness begins with God's love, working toward reconciliation amid the sin and evil that mar God's good creation.
As Jones writes, "We are all complicit in sin, whether through loveless
indifference or horrifying evil. In the midst of tragic brokenness, God's
forgiveness aims to heal and re-create communion. . . . Jesus, in his
ministry, gives forgiveness a human, physical form, showing us a way of
life that we are called to imitate. . . . Jesus calls his disciples to embody
forgiveness as a way of life"[34] and to follow him in calling others into

communion with God. On the cross, Jesus prays for forgiveness, even for people unaware of their actions, thoughts, or deeds. In the resurrection, God vindicates the ministry of Jesus, showing that God's forgiving and reconciling love, God's desire for communion, overcome human sin and evil even at their worst.

We are reconciled and in relationship with God because God chooses to be in relationship with us. Jesus Christ is the physical form of forgiveness that makes that relationship possible. The church as the mystical body of Christ also gives shape and form to relationship, reconciliation, and service. The Eucharist, or Lord's Supper, represents the apex of our relational prayer. When we receive the elements of the sacrament, enacted in community, we join in communion with that way of life we are called to imitate.

Whether in the singularly relational prayer of the Eucharist or in a simple prayer of petition, there are stages or typologies of forgiveness and reconciliation that give nuance to prayer as relationship. Those who speak of these stages of forgiveness are careful to insist that the actual process of forgiveness and reconciliation is not always so well defined or clear-cut. William Meninger speaks thus of forgiveness and prayer:

> There are times when we find ourselves in more than one stage [of forgiveness], or we may be in one stage in the forgiveness process for one hurt and in another stage for an entirely different painful experience. Also the progression from one stage to another may not be as precise as theory suggests. It is possible to regress, even on a very temporary basis, and return to an earlier stage for a time before again moving forward.[35]

Jones summarizes Meninger's caution with a simple metaphor of a dance: The "steps" can be identified and practiced separately in rehearsal, but in the performance of the "dance," the steps are integrally interrelated. Jones identifies the steps in the dance of forgiveness in the following way:

- We become willing to speak truthfully and patiently about the conflicts that have arisen.
- We acknowledge both the existence of anger and bitterness and a desire to overcome them.
- We summon up a concern for the well-being of the other as a child of God.
- We recognize our own complicity in conflict, remember that we have been forgiven in the past, and take the step of repentance.

- We make a commitment to struggle to change whatever caused and continues to perpetuate our conflicts.
- We confess our yearning for the possibility of reconciliation.[36]

With his cautions regarding rigid progression in mind, Meninger enumerates five stages of forgiveness, each of which can also be translated into a stage of prayer.[37]

The first stage is claiming the hurt. This can be hard work. Deception or even forgetfulness often seems easier. In claiming the hurt, we must come to terms honestly, precisely, and often painfully with what our injuries are and who inflicted them. Though it is inevitable that our memories and interpretations will be inaccurate or unclear, it is essential for forgiveness and reconciliation that we admit that pain and hurt exist. In prayer, we must identify as clearly as possible whom to forgive and why.

The second stage is grounded in guilt. As we begin to seek an explanation of what has been done to us, it is only natural that we look to ourselves for an answer. Often that answer is self-blame, shame, and guilt. We almost automatically assume that the hurt was, if not directly our responsibility, at least based on something we did. Our internal voice insists that "it must be my fault, maybe even all my fault." In this stage, Meninger advises recognizing the stage for what it is, offering the following advice: If we can recognize how we sabotage ourselves, we can (1) begin to do something about it, (2) find ways to comfort ourselves, and (3) through prayer think and talk over with God our great worth as God's child.[38] Confession and petitionary prayer address this second stage.

Victimhood is the third stage. Meninger says of this stage, "You have accepted the reality of your hurt, have faced its perpetrator, and have accepted the fact that you are not responsible for your wounds. They were unjustly inflicted upon you. Our next 'logical' step is victimhood."[39] In other words, we were hurt, but we did not do it; someone else did it. It was beyond our control. We were helpless, victimized. It is often easy to say in this stage, "It is not our fault. It is someone else's fault. Our hurt and guilt are not our responsibility, and so forgiveness is likewise not our responsibility." In intercessory prayer, we may manage to pray for those who hurt us, but we may feel that to forgive them is going too far. We may say to ourselves that the perpetuator ought to be praying for or approaching us for forgiveness. The victim stage is a cry for help. It allows us to express the sorrow, regret, and opposition we would like to have expressed at the time the wound was inflicted. Moving through the victim stage is a slow process of recognizing our assets, good points, even blessings. It is long, hard work to crawl out of the hole of victimhood. Our prayer at this stage is to accept our past and our pain, remembering that God's will for the future is not a reliving of the past but a new vision stemming from God's promises, love, grace, and helping hand. In a real sense, we are what and who our wounds have made us to be, but as Meninger reminds us, "Always remember that you are more than your wounds."[40]

The fourth stage is anger. Unlike the anger associated with the victim stage, this anger is actually positive and forward looking. It is not focused on getting back at someone but on moving forward. We refuse to be a victim any longer. We use our energy to move us from victimhood to personal responsibility. We even begin to replace self-pity with outrage. This need not be destructive, vengeful, or deceitful. We simply move from anger, guilt, and hurt to a new refusal to be persecuted. Anger is better expressed than suppressed. As we deal with anger in a constructive way, we begin to deal not with the symptoms but with the cause. The cause, rather than triggering anger, now becomes the object of forgiveness and reconciliation in prayer. The cause is usually a combination of self and other. Thus, forgiveness is multidirectional. We forgive ourselves, another, and God. Psalms of lament are prayers that express this anger poetically.

Meninger opens his discussion of the fifth and final stage of forgiveness, wholeness, with a brief recapitulation of each previous stage:

> We begin to deal with our wounds by denying or minimizing them. When we finally do face them surely and recognize the ones who inflicted them, we move on to the next step. This usually involves trying to excuse the perpetrator and blaming ourselves for causing or, at least, not stopping, the original wounds. When we are able to cease the self-blame, we begin to feel sorry for ourselves and to wallow in a mud hole of self-pity, bitterness, and recrimination. The next step is anger. We determine that we will do something about what happened to us and move forward with our lives. We stop rubbing salt in our wounds and we actively seek healing. This leads us to the final stage, wholeness.[41]

At this final stage in the process, we arrive at the place where true forgiveness happens. Here forgiveness is both an initiator and a by-product of our healing. Once more we arrive at that point of irony and ambiguity in forgiveness that echoes the ambiguity of relationship in general and relationship in prayer in particular. We arrive at a place where we can both forgive and accept forgiveness. In that moment of forgiving, healing begins. A helpful prayer is to meditate on our present location in this balance: Are we better able to give or to accept forgiveness? How can we achieve a balance? Reconciliation, forgiveness, and relationship cannot be accomplished prematurely. We must have at least touched on each of the steps in the dance of forgiveness to be open to the possibility of forgiveness, initiate forgiveness, and receive forgiveness as healing. Again, none of these steps is easy. They all must come together to create wholeness.

Prayer is like an arrow of forgiveness. The art of relationship forms a bow to support and provide the tension and kinetic energy for the arrow of recollection and forgiveness. Bow, string, energy, and arrow must all come together for the arrow to soar. The instant the arrow is released, understanding, illumination, transformation, and healing can begin. The fact that more often than not the arrow of prayer simply falls to the ground or manages a few inches of flight before it flops, lost in the undergrowth or woefully off the mark, is simply representative of the fickle nature of relationship as prayer and prayer as relationship. Our aim is seldom true; seldom do we know ourselves well enough to pray or to engage another so as to launch an arrow straight and true. But still, we continue. The moment the arrow of forgiveness is brought close to the bow of relationship, prayer begins, and the arrow can soar. But how the arrow flies, what it strikes, what it misses we cannot always tell or control. Connection through prayer is perhaps the best we can do. The rest is God's work of reconciliation.

Reconciliation without Resolution: Memory and Prayer

Many centuries before contemporary therapeutic insight into the necessity of both asking for and receiving forgiveness, Augustine of Hippo grappled with a similar set of questions. Around the year 420, Augustine was asked by an acquaintance to answer the simple question, How is God to be worshiped? His answer was that God is to be worshiped through faith, hope, and love. Augustine's explanation of faith as a way of worshiping God has particular relevance for relationship as a model of prayer. For Augustine, "faith in the forgiveness of sins," in particular, reestablishes our broken relationship with God and points us in the direction of godly worship and prayer. Augustine understood prayer, worship, and life as an integrated web of relationships.

Augustine begins with the Lord's Prayer, which, if recited daily and faithfully, "cancel[s] tiny daily sins." The same Lord's Prayer also cancels sins "by which the faithful turn away by penance and reform, . . . provided that they truthfully pray *forgive us our sins.*" Augustine adds that, provided that what people say is what they in fact do, those who pray "as we forgive those who sin against us" are also engaged in a work of faith because to "forgive a person who asks for pardon is itself a work of charity."[42] Memory is as important to the prayer of charity and forgiveness as it is to finding ways to enter into and thereby begin to exorcise anger and resentment. Thus, faith as prayer, forgiveness, pardon, memory, and charity together form a circle of reconciliation and renewed relationship between a sinner and God.

Augustine then moves to Luke 11:41, which says in part, give alms, and everything is clean for you. For Augustine, this means that giving alms, as a way of life and a way of remembering, represents a kind of faith involving reconciliation, relationship, and the forgiveness of sins. In Augustine's hands, each component of alms reads like a prayer engendering relationship:

> [Alms] applies to any work of mercy that benefits somebody. Not only somebody who offers food to the hungry, drink to the thirsty, clothing to the naked, hospitality to the traveler, asylum to the refugee, a visit to the sick or the prisoner, redemption to the captive, support to the weak, guidance to the blind, comfort to the sorrowful, medicine to the unwell, a path to the wanderer, advice to the uncertain, or whatever is necessary to a person in need, but also one who offers pardon to the sinner, is giving alms.[43]

Augustine's list is like a summary of prayer in which he equates forgiveness as alms with faith and prayer. Giving alms, like the Lord's Prayer, serves as a petition to God to "forgive us our sins that we may forgive those who sin against us." Relationship through forgiveness, according to Augustine, is the key to giving alms and practicing simple prayers of charity: "[The person who] puts away from his heart that person's sin by which he has been hurt or offended, or prays that it may be forgiven him, is giving alms through forgiveness and prayer."[44]

Two contemporary writers "give alms" through a different means: storytelling and ritual. For Herbert Anderson and Edward Foley, "stories and rituals," like alms, "are both potential agents of reconciliation. . . . [Stories and] rituals have the power to heal broken relationships."[45] Prayer, stories, ritual, and memory help weave together the divine and human relationship. Anderson and Foley suggest what they call a spirituality of reconciliation, which includes the recognition that forgiveness may not, in fact, be received or granted. They call this "reconciliation without resolution."[46] To risk an offer of reconciliation and to experience a refusal to accept it can be a disturbing experience, whether the refusal is from God or another person. But true relationship respects the ambiguity inherent within reconciliation, making of it, as Anderson and Foley say, "a way of living." Thus, the spirituality of reconciliation is a spirituality of uncertainty wherein we find that neither reconciliation nor prayer are entitlements:

Whatever the mode, most of us count on organized religion and its properly designated representatives to deliver comfort and forgiveness when we have done wrong. Ultimately, that is because we expect absolution and forgiveness from God. It is a common way to weave the divine and human narratives: people sin, God forgives, and all is well in the world. Withholding reconciliation challenges our expectations of forgiveness as an entitlement.[47]

As already noted, *offering* reconciliation does not mean that to forgive is to forget. To confess, we must remember; to ask forgiveness of sin and thus reestablish relation, we must also remember. As an exercise in revealing the importance of memory in prayer as relationship, we can substitute the word *prayer* for each use of *memory* or *remember* in the following quotation:

> The whole question of remembering [praying] past pain and forgiving the wrongdoer might better be phrased in this way: in forgiving, we do not forget; we remember [pray] in a different way. We cannot forget what has happened to us. To erase part of our memory [prayer] is to erase part of our very identity as persons. But we can remember [pray] in a different way after we have experienced reconciliation and after we have extended forgiveness. We remember [pray] in a way that does not carry rancor for what has been done. We remember [pray] now from God's perspective, thanks to the grace of reconciliation.[48]

The honest healing work of memory or prayer through story, ritual, and myth moves us toward transformation. Such healing transformation is, in Moltmann's terminology, a healing that again brings forth the *adventus* self, the self that is able to live in an expectant state and open to the necessary ambiguity of relationship.

Trinitarian Contemplation: Sharing and Giving of Great Joy

The theologian Nicholas Lash writes that the trinitarian God initiates the reality of the Christian life, "which consists essentially in the *relationship* between God and us."[49] The contemporary theologian David Cunningham writes of the doctrine of the Trinity in a manner similar to that in which we have spoken of prayer: It is a way of life. For Cunningham, doctrines are not self-referential objects; they affect how we live within and relate to the world. He writes that "doctrines are not formulated as an end in themselves; they draw their meaning from, and are ultimately intended to have some effect on, the practices of the believing community."[50] For Cunningham, the doctrine of the

Trinity, more than any other doctrine, has an effect on how we practice being a community.

The twelfth-century contemplative theologian Richard of St. Victor is especially helpful in understanding how the doctrine of the Trinity illuminates relationship in prayer. Two of his works serve as guides to the relational aspects of the doctrine of the Trinity in the context of prayer. These include *The Mystical Ark,* which suggests the use of the symbolic imagination as a route to prayer, and *On the Trinity,* which, though it functions as a classic treatise on doctrine, is more importantly a work on charity or love as a route to God and prayer.

In *The Mystical Ark,* sometimes known as *Benjamin Major* or *The Grace of Contemplation,* the ark of the covenant is described as a complex symbol to be used to ignite the imagination in contemplation. One means by which Richard of St. Victor emphasizes the relational quality of contemplation is through his commentary on the interrelationships between the various elements of the ark and the cherubim. Using the ark and the cherubim as symbols of the contemplative life, Richard takes us through contemplations that focus on the created world, the soul, and God.

In the ark of the covenant itself, the wood, gilding, and crown of the ark are, for Richard, symbols of the process of outward contemplation of the natural world. The gold of the mercy seat or propitiatory, which forms the top of the ark, represents the process of inward contemplation of the soul. Finally, the two golden cherubim attached atop the ark symbolize the contemplation of God. Contemplation of the first cherubim turns our focus toward the unity or oneness of God. Contemplation of the second cherubim involves the mystery of the trinity of persons within the Godhead. Thus, the two cherubim together form a symbol of the Trinity.

The important point for all these levels of contemplation is the integrative quality of their relationships. The ark itself, with its four levels of contemplation, forms an intimately connected structure. There is a unity to contemplation of creation and of the soul. The cherubim symbolize divinity, but they are connected to the ark, which symbolizes the soul and the natural world. The symbols represent the essential interrelationship among contemplation of nature, soul, and God in prayer.[51] In contemplation, the transcendent and the immanent are represented as two (cherubim), yet they are connected to the whole as one overarching symbol.

Reinforcing the relationship among nature, soul, and God in prayer is the relationship between the two cherubim. As noted, the cherubim represent the Trinity in the complementarity of its opposites; one is unity, another is diversity. Yet Richard is clear that these two aspects of the Trinity gaze upon each other in mutuality, signifying relationship. Relationship is the essential component of the highest levels of contemplation. Richard writes:

> And so those aforementioned cherubim should mutually look at each other and because of mutual consent in harmony, should not turn the eyes of their speculation in a contrary direction. . . . But these two cherubim look at each other mutually because we say that one and the same God is one according to substance and three according to persons. . . . And so cherub looks at cherub.[52]

The passages in Exodus and Leviticus describing the construction of the ark and the cherubim are classic examples of the promise of the presence of God within the biblical narrative. They are theophanies, in which individuals experience direct contact with God. Thus, in Exodus 25:22, after God has given instructions for the construction of the ark of the covenant, he promises, "There I will meet with you, and from above the mercy seat, from between the two cherubim that are on the ark of the covenant, I will deliver to you all my commands for the Israelites." This is a promise of relational presence: Between the cherubim, God (as Christ, according to Richard's christological perspective) will meet the soul. Taking the place of the law, Christ is represented by and dwells on the propitiatory or atonement seat. There God fulfills the promise: God meets and is with us in Christ. This is Richard's journey of contemplation: the use of biblical images to portray the possibility of prayer focused on nature, self, neighbor, and God. That is precisely where Richard of St. Victor sends the contemplative: upon the ark, between the two cherubim. The promise of relationship echoed in the trinitarian God also occurs within the soul. The "two cherubim not only ought to look at each other; they certainly ought to turn their faces toward the propitiatory in looking at one another."[53] As in the book of Hebrews, the ark and the cherubim are now within the human heart. The contemplative has only to turn inward to find the presence of God.

Finally, however, one does not remain within. For Richard, the ark is "an ark of sanctification." Through it we are made holy; through it "we are restored to health," and "whoever is restored to health is restored to health by Wisdom." But such Wisdom does not lock itself within. It is transformed into charity; it lives and works like Christ, as a servant to the world. Thus, Richard writes at the beginning of *The Mystical Ark* that he is teaching a form of contemplation that sanctifies. He is "saying something about the moral sense"[54] of the ark and the cherubim. That is, he is writing about a way of life that orients body, mind, and soul in such a way that they are fully, comtemplatively present to the world.

In his *On the Trinity,* Richard of St. Victor also writes specifically about the Trinity. But again, he does not write about the Trinity as an isolated, objective entity beyond relationship and our way of life but as a meditation on the nature of charity. This is *caritas,* perfect love. It is not "self-less" love, because charity requires self-love that is self-aware. It is "self-full" love that requires another in relationship to become fully true, good, and whole. Richard thus describes charity as a particular form of relationship:

> However, no one is properly said to have charity on the basis of his own private love of himself. And so it is necessary for love to be directed toward another for it to be charity. Therefore, where a plurality of persons is lacking, charity cannot exist.[55]

Where relationship is lacking, the practice of love cannot exist. Where love does not exist, as Richard implies, prayer or contemplation cannot abide. Relationship requires goodness (or goodwill) and, of course, plurality of persons. Thus, using the Trinity as a model, Richard can say, "But fullness of Goodness could not exist without fullness of charity, nor could fullness of charity exist without plurality of divine persons. . . . In mutual love it is absolutely necessary that there be both one who gives love and one who returns love."[56]

But Richard does not stop with a contemplative relationship of two. As he continues to describe the love that exists among the persons of the Trinity and uses that love as an analogy of human relationship, he makes the intriguing claim that perfect charity cannot exist between only two either. Two individuals can share love, but only three individuals can fulfill the requirement of perfect charity: It not only shares but also gives. Richard writes:

> Surely it ought to be noted in the divine persons that the perfection of one demands the addition of another and consequently in a pair of persons the perfection of each requires union with a third. . . . Similarly, as long as the second does not have someone who shares in love for a third, he lacks the giving of excellent joy. . . . Behold how from sharing and giving fellowship with a third person in that Trinity it is argued that concordant charity and consocial love are never found anywhere in an isolated individual.[57]

Richard's trinitarian description of charity makes a difference in how we understand and practice relationship. As the model of perfect charity, the Trinity also makes a difference in how we understand and practice contemplation and prayer. Here "sharing and giving of excellent joy" is a doctrinal description of the model of prayer as relationship.

Julian of Norwich: Solitude Enfolded in Relationship

What does a fourteenth-century anchorite voluntarily enclosed in a cell have to tell us about relationship? Julian of Norwich lived in the solitude of a small cell attached to a cathedral, yet she managed to maintain a profound connection to the world around her. Somehow, even in solitude, or perhaps especially in solitude, the "other" reached into the open cell of her heart. There she learned that, as Julian says, God "is covetous to have us pray continually in God's sight."[58] Her continual prayer somehow managed to be a continual connection, even in solitude.

Julian committed her life to enclosure within a small room attached to the Church of St. Julian in Norwich. There she opened herself to God, received the elements of the mass on occasion, was able to see through a small slit into the cathedral, and, perhaps astonishingly to us today, made deep connections with the natural world outside her cell and the many pilgrims who came to her seeking wisdom and counsel. In her small cell, Julian found a God who is courteous, familiar, and kind, a God of open relationship who "shall make well all that is not well."[59] Alone in her cell, over the years, she gestated love. As her love expanded her soul, her cell also seemed to expand to accommodate her growing soul, her hospitality to pilgrims, and her love of God.

Julian needed space because she found herself enfolded in the ever-growing embrace of God, the Trinity. As the love of that embrace expanded, she found herself "knit and oned" to the Trinity, a "rightful knitting and endless oneing."[60] The "knitting" and the "oneing" occurred through prayer, in which she found herself enclosed in the "cell" of the Trinity itself,

> by the endless assent of the full accord of all the Trinity, . . . out of whom we all come, in whom we be all enclosed, into whom we shall all go. . . . And I saw no difference between God and our substance but as it were all God. . . . For the almighty truth of the Trinity is our Father. For he made us and keeps us in him. And the deep wisdom of the Trinity is our Mother, in whom we are all enclosed. The high goodness of the Trinity is our Lord, and in him we are enclosed and he in us. We are enclosed in the Father. And we are enclosed in the Son. And we are enclosed in the holy Ghost. And the Father is enclosed in us, and the Son is enclosed in us, and the holy Ghost is enclosed in us. All Mightiness, All Wisdom, All Goodness, one God, one Lord.[61]

Julian's enclosures turned out to be doors to opening space. They were doors open to the freedom to pursue and be pursued by relationship in prayer. Such doors were opened by the grace of the Trinity: the almighty truth of the Father, the deep wisdom of the Mother, the high goodness of the Lord.

In this same vision, Julian was shown that this same truth, wisdom, goodness, and one God were the ground of her prayer. Her prayer was pure *adventus* prayer.[62] It was prayer of expectant and unflagging hope, a prayer of openness to relationship, reconciliation, and forgiveness. She awaited the coming of love as one would await a friend. Yet faith being what it is, even *adventus* anticipation can sometimes turn faith to doubt and ash. Julian did not ignore the vicissitudes of faith. She faced them squarely and surrendered even the darkness to prayer: "Pray wholeheartedly, though you feel nothing, though you see nothing, yes, though you think that you cannot." Julian gently encouraged, "Prayer unites us to God. . . . Prayer is a witness that the soul wills as God wills. And so God teaches us to pray and to have firm trust that we shall have it; for God beholds us in love, and wants to make us partners in his good will and work."[63] The image of Julian enclosed in her cell mirrors her image of being, as it were, married in partnership with God, regardless of the feelings of the moment. As her cell enfolded her, so she was enfolded by God.

Grounded in prayer, which itself is grounded in interrelatedness of the Trinity, Julian helps us to correct notions of relationship based on fear or coercion. Contemporary theologian Ellen Charry sees Julian's theology of divine compassion as a healing antidote to forces of punitive piety and disfunctioning relationships:

> Her theology of divine compassion challenges both teachings and popular devotional practices that based piety on God's wrath and thereby encouraged self-hatred, fear of God and the future, or guilt. As she puts it, the church [not God] taught her to see herself as a sinner who sometimes deserves blame and wrath.[64]

As Julian was careful to make clear, her visions were seen "through God's eyes." She understood that by human standards wrath and blame are warranted. Even her famous phrase "shall make well all that is not well" implies that something indeed is *not* well. But through her visions, she saw that in God's redeeming work Jesus took these harsh judgments, and now "God's justice is from his own endless love . . . in which I saw him assign to us no kind of blame."[65] For Julian, wrath and blame are no longer our lot. We have been created for relationship, and we have been created to dwell with another:

> Our soul is made to be God's dwelling place, and the dwelling of our soul is God, who is unmade. A high understanding it is inwardly to see and to

know that God who is our maker dwells in our soul. And a higher understanding it is inwardly to see and to know our soul that is made dwells in
God's substance, of which substance by God, we are who we are.[66]

Julian kept the door of her soul open to the inbreaking of God and
others. With an inner space as deep and wide as a pool of wisdom, she
was also a living testament to the hospitality of boundaries. Proper
boundaries are as essential to defining and maintaining space for others
as are expanding centers of openness and welcome. Only between open
space and boundary can an invitation to others to trust, to care, to enter
hospitality and courtesy be accepted in the expectation that, indeed, all
shall be well. Her living arrangement was an exterior sign of her interior space: definite boundaries surrounding an ever-expanding interior
space of love. She was a "living icon," rendering prayer visible to the
world. A prison to some, Julian's cell swelled as if pregnant with prayer
and devotion drenched in the love of the Trinity. Within the womblike
setting of her cell, she gave birth to the love she found abundant within
the Trinity itself. The boundaries of trinitarian personhood were opened
to the unity of love.

An excellent artistic rendering that illustrates Julian of Norwich's
capacity for relationship and both her inner and outer dwelling space
comes from another century. It is from a mandalic illumination of the
cosmic Christ by Hildegard of Bingen, the twelfth-century mystic, vision-
ary, herbologist, and musician. Hildegard's illumination echoes Julian's
own cell: a boundary that rather than imprisoning gives secure freedom
for the soul to flourish and provides boundaries that, if transgressed,
are transgressed for love.

Hildegard's illumination is bounded by a rectangle. Within the rectangle, Christ's head, hands, and feet are visible, but the rest of his body
is a circular illustration of the cosmos. A circular wheel is visible at
the exact center of the towering figure of Christ. Within the wheel
is Hildegard's vision of the cosmos according to the science of her
day. For instance, the heads of seven animals shine forth, representing the seven planets. Clouds of white and clouds of black represent
what is known and what is hidden. The human figure at the center of
the wheel with arms extended like a cross is like a tree of life at the
center of the world's axis. Of the figure holding the wheel to his chest,
Hildegard says:

> [It is] a wondrously beautiful image within the mystery of God. It had a
> human form, and its countenance was of such beauty and radiance that I
> could have more easily gazed at the sun than at that face. . . . [The figure

is] Love appearing in a human form, the power of the everlasting Godhead,
full of exquisite beauty, marvelous in its mysterious gifts.[67]

The entire cosmos rests within the bosom of this Creator. With the
human figure in the center, the fiery red Christ encircling the cosmos,
and a blue flame just inside the encircling breast of Christ representing
the Holy Spirit, Hildegard expounds the relationship of microcosm and
macrocosm and the moral responsibility we share through participation
in the wheel of Christ.

As pilgrims made the journey to Julian of Norwich's cell, so in Hildegard's vision:

We make the journey within the circle and embrace of the Godhead that
"embraces all." For "in this circle of earthly existence you shine so finely,
it surpasses understanding. God hugs you. You are encircled by the arms
of the mystery of God."[68]

The real humanity of Christ in the illumination is represented by
the depiction of his head, hands, and feet. But of more immediate
import, his body is in the form of a mandala that is the container,
birthplace, and sustainer of all creation. Christ's self dwells in open
relation to creation; all manner of things abide there and are welcome.
In fact, in the illumination, Christ's circular breast pushes the boundaries of the rectangular frame. Emerging out of the top of the head
of Christ is another head, God the Father (in Julian's case, as we will
see, God the Mother). This head extends not only beyond the wheel
of Christ but actually bursts through the rectangular boundary of the
frame to extend even beyond the drawing, representing that which is
beyond the limits of any bounded form. In Hildegard's illumination,
relationship permeates creation, humanity, Creator, beauty, form, the
self, and God. The relationships are illuminated in red to symbolize
the fires of love. In the lower left-hand corner of the illumination is
a very small Hildegard of Bingen, herself envisioning and recording
the illumination.

We can imagine Julian of Norwich with a similar soul. The heart of
her self swells with friendship and hospitality for hazelnuts that reflect
all creation in miniature; she possesses a self that circles and grows
in intimacy with Christ and the Trinity, imaged as mothers of wisdom,
goodness, and nurture, and a self that is open wide to wellness, as she
famously says, "All shall be well, and you shall see it yourself that all
manner of things shall be well."[69] Like Hildegard of Bingen, Julian of
Norwich gives us a model of a soul open as a home inviting in all who
might care to enter the glow of her relationship and prayer.

Prayer Enfolded in Motherhood

The best prayer is the most loving prayer.
The more you love the better you pray; the more you pray the better you love.

Charles de Foucauld, *Meditations of a Hermit*

Julian of Norwich's *Showings* were born out of contemplation and can be seen as an extended prayer directed to God in response to God. A number of recent writers "have speculated that the showings or revelations arose as an extension of the use of imagination in contemplative prayer," especially the practice of *lectio divina*.[70] Julian elaborates on this form of prayer in three parts: first, understanding through reading; second, inward instruction acquired through meditation; and third, contemplation by which the whole of creation is brought to understanding. Thus, through reading, meditation, and contemplation, Julian opens and sustains the nurturing, hospitable self.

Not only do we open inner space for self and others and God, but also in prayer, God opens space for us, drawing us nearer to his own breast than we are to ourselves. Julian uses images drawn from the body, in which we are "enfolded" and "enclosed," to make the point that we are more at home in God than we are to ourselves. She compares the human body to the cell in which she is also "clothed." Starting with the outside of the body, she moves deeper and deeper to that central place of the soul where God finds a home. She then moves outward from the soul into God, where the soul finds its true and closer home. Julian uses the image of the soul and the body being drawn and enfolded into God's goodness as a kind of "home" throughout her *Showings*. She says, for instance, that "in us is his [God's] homeliest home and his endless dwelling." It is as if, as we pray, God prays us home as well. The effect is similar to that of Hildegard of Bingen's mandalic Christ with the fully open center. Pictorially, Hildegard moves us inward to the core of ourselves, where we find our true soul. In turn, the true soul is "clad in the goodness of God and enclosed, Yea, and more closely."[71] Julian uses a similar trajectory as she writes of being enfolded into the motherhood of God.

The two primary points of entry into Julian's relational home of prayer are the passion of Christ and the Trinity. Both serve not as abstract representations of God in a realm outside her own experience but as intensely felt, experienced, and enacted realities in her own life. For Julian, the Trinity can be expressed and experienced in a variety of triads. Through these "economic" trinitarian triads, she finds ways of opening space to God in prayer. But she also focuses on the immanent Trinity, or the inner life and relationship within the Trinity itself. Thus, she sees relationship within the Godhead itself and relationship of God in and through the world, but she does not separate the two poles. As Philip Sheldrake has noted, "The various triads of properties that Julian uses in writing about the Trinity refer outwards to God's active being, that is, God's relationship with creation. For this reason some scholars suggest that Julian concentrates on the 'economic Trinity.' It would be better to say that Julian's approach refuses to separate an economic from an immanent Trinity. For Julian, God is as God does."[72]

Equally important in terms of relationship is Julian's devotion to the humanity of Christ, especially to Christ's passion. Her teaching on God as Trinity and on the creation is always measured by the standard of the cross. Though grounded in suffering, the passion is the ultimate revelatory expression of love as God's ground of being and only true reality. She was heir to the twelfth century's nescient humanism and a new turn to the self. This turn to self coincided with a focus on the human nature of Christ (that nature most closely tied to our own experience), where previously the focus had been on Christ as divine Logos. Other factors included devotional practices that accessed imagination, intuition, feelings, and a more well-rounded conception of the human person. Prayers, visions, and meditations on the personhood of Christ contributed to a new fascination with developing a relationship with the Christ who shared our flesh, heart, and body.[73]

Julian's devotion to the passion is the ground on which she bases both her theology and her prayer. In the passion, she sees and holds suffering and love in redemptive tension. She is acquainted with Christ's suffering:

> And in this suddenly I saw the red blood trickling down from under the Garland, hot and freshly and right plenteously, as it were in the time of his Passion that the garland of thorns was pressed, thrust on his blessed head. Right so, both God and humanity, the same who suffered thus for me.[74]

Yet at the same time that she has the vision of the bleeding head of Jesus, she is given a vision of a hazelnut, "lying in the palm of my hand, as it seemed to me, and it was round as a ball." She wonders what this could be, this littleness that could so suddenly "fall into nothing." And then it comes to her understanding that "it lasts and always will because God loves it; and thus everything has being through the love of God."[75] Julian thus moves from a suffering Christ to an insignificant hazelnut in the palm of her hand to a loving God.

Psychologists today speak of a "holding environment" necessary for an individual to feel safety and trust in order to be open to others and to God. Julian's vision tells us much about this holding environment, boundaries, and the possibilities for opening ourselves to others. In the loving passion, Jesus shatters boundaries; suffering and death are conquered through his own suffering and death. Jesus is able to shatter normal boundaries of space while reconstructing new possibilities for lasting and inviting space. Julian describes this space relationally as the love of God. Love itself is the quintessence of relationship. This same trajectory is echoed in the vision of the hazelnut that comes immediately after one of Julian's meditations on the passion. But now the process is reversed. It is the love of God that keeps the hazelnut from falling into nothing. The literal possibility of disintegration of the nut reminds us of the suffering of Christ. The nut cupped in the palm of Julian's hand (a holding environment of love) is a metaphor of the whole world, a world dependent on love for coherence, continuity, its very existence. Salvation history comes to a point in the cross of Christ, entering as suffering and death, flooding out as love. The hazelnut, in fact, all creation, now reflects this new possibility of redemption and sustaining love. In both cross and nut, Julian sees Love focused, concentrated, then erupting into the world as charity, nurture, and sustenance.

The culminating import for developing relationship in prayer is Julian's unique insight that where Jesus appears, the Trinity is to be understood also. This is of supreme importance in her journey of opening space for God. For Julian, the insight is nearly rapturous and ends in a prayer of blessing to the Lord:

> Suddenly the Trinity fulfilled my heart most of joy, and so I understood it shall be in heaven without end to all who shall come there. For the Trinity is God. God is the Trinity. The Trinity is our Maker and keeper, the Trinity is our everlasting lover, everlasting joy and bliss by our Lord Jesus Christ. And this was showed in the First Showing and in all, *for where Jesus appears the blessed Trinity is understood* as to my sight. And I said, "Benedicte Domine."[76]

This insight has the effect of radically confronting the possibility of finding space and time for God, self, and others. We often concentrate on the agony of isolation and forsakenness in the passion. These are real. Yet as Julian says above, "where Jesus appears the blessed Trinity is understood."

In a bold move that balances the violence and the suffering of the passion with love, Julian also writes that Jesus Christ is our Mother, the one who protects and nurtures:

> Thus, Jesus Christ who does good against evil is our true Mother: We have our being of him where the ground of Motherhood begins with all sweet keeping of love that endlessly follows. . . . And thus is Jesus our true Mother

in nature of our first making. And he is our true Mother in grace, by taking
of our created nature. All the fair working and all the sweet natural offices
of dearworthy Motherhood are proper to the second Person.[77]

More than this, since where Jesus is, the Trinity is to be understood,
the Trinity is also our Mother, our Father, and our Lord:

> For the almighty truth of the Trinity is our Father, for he made us and
> keeps us in him. And the deep wisdom of the Trinity is our Mother, in
> whom we are enclosed. And the high goodness of that Trinity is our Lord,
> and in him we are enclosed and he in us. We are enclosed in the Father,
> and we are enclosed in the Son, and we are enclosed in the Holy Spirit.
> And the Father is enclosed in us, the Son is enclosed in us, and the Holy
> Spirit is enclosed in us, all might, all wisdom and all goodness, one God,
> one Lord.[78]

The image of motherhood, applied to Christ as well as to the whole Trinity,
is a reality of God and of God's relationship with human nature. "Julian
does not suggest that God is *like* a mother, but that God *is* a mother."[79]
Thus, the motherhood of God is the measure of true motherhood, and
motherhood is a reflection of God.

How do Christ and the Trinity as Mother affect our prayer? In terms of
relationship, and especially growth in the capacity to form relationship,
prayer as motherhood is to be in relationship; it is to nurture and make
pliable an opening of love for Love to enter. By first applying the image
of motherhood to Christ, especially Christ on the cross, Julian, while
she does not avoid the issue of suffering and sin in the world, teaches
a prayerful devotion to Christ's humanity, which he shares in common
with us. But by also applying the image of motherhood to the Trinity,
she places in the very heart, the most intimate and immanent center of
God, the relational images of goodness, wisdom, and joy.

Prayer, emerging from "this fair and lovely word 'mother' is so sweet
and kind in itself that it cannot truly be said of anyone except Jesus . . .
the true mother of all things."[80] In a striking passage, Julian compares
the Eucharist to a nursing mother:

> The Mother may give her Child to suck of her milk, but our precious
> Mother Jesus, he may feed us with himself. And does most courteously
> and most tenderly with the blessed Sacrament of his body and blood that
> is the precious food of very life. . . . The Mother may lay the Child tenderly
> to her breast, but our tender Lord Mother Jesus, he may homely lead us
> into his blessed breast by his sweet open side.[81]

Once again, Jesus as Mother leads us home, here in eucharistic prayer.

The relationship of prayer opens us to self, others, and God. It is relationship comparable in terms of safety, care, and sustenance to that of a nursing mother and child. In prayer, we are enclosed within the Trinity as the Trinity is enclosed within us. Julian makes use of the metaphor of motherhood elsewhere when she speaks of prayer as familiarity and acting courteously with God. Since, as she says, what is said of Christ is also true of the holy Trinity, she begins with the image of Christ as Mother, using it to crack open the trinitarian triads: God as Trinity is wisdom, goodness, and strength; maker, protector, and lover; our joy, bliss, and unity; truth, deep wisdom, and high goodness, through which again we are enclosed in God. In a culminating triad, she writes, "To the property of motherhood belong natural love, wisdom, and knowledge, and they are good."[82] In courteous and familiar prayer, God is at home in the soul, and the soul is at home in God. Christ as Mother nurtures and enfolds; the Trinity as Mother enters our heart as love, wisdom, and knowledge. In prayer, Julian "saw that God is present in all things," where "sin itself has no substance,"[83] except to hinder our longing for God and blind us to God's own longing for our heart.

The Trinity itself is relationship, and Julian sees infinite relationship in every vision she has. God is life, love, and light, which are three in one goodness. Each property of God hinges on relationship: "Life is marvelous homeliness, and in love is gentle courtesy, and in light is endless kindness."[84] Home, courtesy, and kindness are three ways of relationship, three ways of prayer. Julian does not ignore darkness, travail, and woe, but for her, faith is light in the midst of these nights. Even in the darkness, God opens space for courtesy and kindness. The greatest space is love: "Love keeps us in faith and in hope, and faith and hope lead us in love. And at the end all shall be love."[85] Prayer enfolds us in this most ecstatic yet humble of all relationships: love.

Conclusion

As prayer is a way of life, relationship is a way of prayer. Prayer is a way of opening ourselves to the broken aspects of relationship as well as a way of healing, binding, and deepening relationship.

The very fact that relationship is fraught with pain, despair, loss, grief, unfulfilled longing, disappointment, and brokenness makes relational prayer honest and true. Rather than hindrances to prayer, these qualities of our humanity are the pith, the sap, the very wood of the solid trunks that support the tree of life. As the *adventus* self develops and grows, as

Used by permission of the Jon Paul Gallery.

Coast Live Oak

we recognize that charity needs two to share and a third to give, and as we find inner and outer space to practice an ethics of kindness, courtesy, and hospitality, we thus begin a healing process in and through prayer that incorporates rather than rejects pain and loss.

The coast live oak (*Quercus agrifolia*) is friend to wind, hill, fog, drought, rocks, grasses, gravity, the trajectory of the sun, and an entire habitat of other flora and fauna that together make up what is often called a coast live oak forest. Thriving but local, these forests extend just inland from the Pacific Ocean along the California coast from Eureka to San Diego. They are forests adapted to microclimates. The coast live oak pictured here, located near Monterey, California, has seen its storms. Its trunk follows the slope of the hill as if for protection; it seems to be sharing intimacies with the grass and the stones around it. It is a bent but solid trunk, a wise tree.

We should not expect the shape of prayer to be any more predictable than the shape of our relationships: The coast live oak seems to bow toward the hill in prayer; the coastal redwoods below stand straight and tall. Both live in forgiving reconciliation with their environments, shaped in relationship to their world.

Used by permission of Fred Voetsch, AcclaimImages.com.

Coastal Redwoods

Sometimes forgiveness, reconciliation, and the interconnected re-lationships in which they thrive are the work of ages. These trees are coastal redwoods (*Sequoia sempervirens*), the tallest conifers and among the oldest living things on earth. The last portion of their Latin name, *sempervirens*, means "ever greening," and so they are. These magnificent trees green in a forest ecology that includes Douglas fir, big leaf maple, California bay laurel, tan oak, California hazel, woodrose, redwood trillium, redwood sorrel, sword fern, bracken fern, and mosses. The redwood forest floor is a thriving and complex mixture of rich soils and forest bedding. These particular trees are from a redwood forest in Del Norte County near Crescent City, California. Like the coast live oak, the coastal redwood is limited to a narrow strip no more than fifty

miles from the Pacific Coast from southern Oregon to central California. Living to ages of over two thousand years, they have a long, steady,
patient, reconciling prayer of growth. Unlike the coast live oaks, the
redwood trunks grow straight, thick, and tall. Their strategy seems to
be to live with the pains and joys of what the forest brings, placing their
faith in the resiliency of years, not the minor perturbations of seasons.
They practice the discipline of *apatheia*: They take in draught, insect
infestation, even fire; they note them, then they set about, slowly, to do
what it takes to pray their way straight toward the sky. As our goal as
Christians is union with God, the coastal redwood's goal is union with
earth and sky and forest. These are ever-greening relationships. The
coast live oak bows down, finding reconciliation with the elements,
and so survives. The coastal redwood invites the years to grow with it,
forgiving fire, welcoming draught or rain. Even in dying, the redwood
contains the nutrients for young redwoods for many centuries to come.
For the coastal redwood, relationship flowers even in death.

Any visitor to an old stand of redwoods is immediately captured by
their stately grandeur and silence, their easy peace. Their trunks are like
the most solid relationships with God in prayer. In the redwood, we see
relationship empowering the roots of conversation and the branches
of journey. Standing in a grove of redwoods connects us to the world,
ourselves, and God; we are connected by something outside ourselves
that is both powerful and compelling. We are small figures brought
together with massive giants in postures of mutual awe and wonder.
The redwood not only reaches to the sky but also connects in common
adoration with anyone who enters its world. To behold these massive
trees is to be drawn close, like a mother to her child, to the mystery of
prayer, God, and relationship.

4

Prayer as Journey

The Many Branches of Prayer

It is the very condition of humanity not to be given, as is the case with angels, to attain immediately to perfection. That is why we must traverse a longer path than that of angels to beatitude.

Thomas Aquinas, *Summa theologiae*, Ia q. 62 a. 5 ad 1

Four Waters

In her autobiography, Teresa of Avila, the seventeenth-century Carmelite nun, writes of how a garden can be watered and how plants and flowers grow or wither depending on how they are watered and tended. She uses the image of watering a garden to illustrate the rhythms of prayer. The image not only evokes the natural rhythms of prayer but also suggests a pattern of the spiritual journey, strategies of discernment, the seasons of faith, and the dynamics of an awakening soul.

In Teresa's metaphor, "the garden is the soul" resolves to practice prayer, "in which the Lord is to take His delight." She continues the analogy by saying that the Lord is the gardener, and we are God's assistants in watering and tending the plants. The water is likened to consolation

133

in prayer. The plants and flowers themselves give fragrance and refreshment to God so that he might come often to the garden and there take delight. Noting that the well-watered flowers do not themselves represent consolation or answer to prayer but rather virtue, she describes four ways in which this garden of prayer may be watered:

> It seems to me that the garden can be watered in four ways: by taking the water from a well, which costs us great labor; or by a water-wheel and buckets, when the water is drawn by a windlass (I have sometimes drawn it in this way: it is less laborious than the other and gives more water); or by a stream or a brook, which waters the ground much better, for it saturates it more thoroughly and there is less need to water it often, so that the gardener's labour is much less; or by heavy rain, when the Lord waters it with no labor of ours, a way incomparably better than any of those which have been described.[1]

Those beginning in prayer are, Teresa says, like those who draw up water from a well. Beginners are in for much tedious labor, annoying distraction, aridity, and trials. In the second water or degree of prayer, the soul experiences some consolation in prayer. Teresa says that "by using the windlass and buckets the gardener draws more water with less labor and is able to take some rest instead of being continually at work."[2] Watering the garden with a river or stream represents the third level of prayer, which irrigates the garden with much less trouble, though a certain amount of effort is still needed to "direct" the water. Teresa names this level of prayer the "sleep of the faculties." This is a state of prayer that is not "ecstatic" but one in which the conscious mind or awareness rests. In this "third water," she says, the "Lord is now pleased to help the gardener, so that God may almost be said to be the gardener Himself."[3] The "fourth water" illustrates what Teresa calls the "passive prayer of union." This level of prayer is wholly dependent on grace. In this state of union, the normal modes of consciousness are "dead to the world" as the soul unites with God. The union is so complete, in fact, that while experiencing the prayer the soul cannot even communicate the fact that it is in prayer: "If it can communicate it," she says, "it is not in union."[4]

For Teresa, this "fourth water" in prayer is essentially wordless. Nothing can be said directly about it; it must be experienced. What she can do, however, is move from description of prayer to doxology and to a prayer of praise. She ends with the words, "O my Lord, how good Thou art! Blessed be Thou forever! Let all things praise Thee."[5]

Teresa of Avila's teaching and sound advice about each level of prayer demonstrate many of the important elements of journey as a model of prayer. For instance, the important issue of divine grace and human effort is addressed and shown, even in this simple form, to have a deep complexity. The utility and gracefulness of metaphor, symbol, and analogy are illustrated by the four waters. Though more complex illustrations of the spiritual journey nuance the developmental character of the life of prayer, the four waters give an account of developmental progression in prayer from beginner, to practiced, to advanced, to proficient. Her depiction of the journey of prayer also shows the many trials, temptations, distractions, and desolations to which the soul in honest prayer may be subject. On the other hand, it also shows the many joys, consolations, assurance, and grace that are encountered by all who undertake a serious journey of prayer.

Teresa's writing also illustrates that we cannot expect consistency with regard to pattern, stages, or shape in the journey of prayer. This is true whether we look for consistency across writers or even within the same writer in different works. Most writers do not cherish consistency in writing about prayer; they cherish truth, love, and compassion. A garden of consistency is good for a season but then withers; a garden of truth, sound teaching, love, and compassion finds a new way to praise God with each turning season.

Most important of all, however, is the fact that Teresa says the water is not for pleasure in prayer; instead, it is for action and virtue in the world. This is the core of prayer for Teresa; it may be the core of the Gospels: "You will know them by their fruits" (Matt. 7:20; cf. Luke 6:44). It is clear that the "fragrance" of the garden is virtue, action, and compassion. As Dietrich Bonhoeffer has written, "Our being Christians today will be limited to two things: prayer and righteous action."[6] This is a garden in which the Lord delights, a garden in which prayer seeds the world.

Follow Me

We are invited to pray.[7] We are invited on an itinerary in search of a hidden God waiting to be found. The invitation to journey into God is an invitation to our whole person—body, mind, and spirit. It is a journey through time and space, through developmental patterns sometimes brilliant with meaning and sometimes dark with despair. It is more a process than a goal, more a series of transitions than discrete steps or stages. It is a symphony played out in chords of wandering, loss, and grief. It is open hospitality, and yet it is also a diminishment of options. We are often lost, sometimes disoriented. If we are lucky, we find a familiar mark of assurance along the way.

As Thomas Merton reminds us, spiritual journeys are fraught with ambiguity, wrong turns, and frustration as well as periods of real growth in self-understanding, compassion, and a sense of the nearness of God. Merton illustrates this ambiguity: On the one hand, in prayer we awaken to a new, more true vision, enabling us to "see things—a tree—for instance, as they truly are, as they are in God." On the other hand, prayer reveals "the terrible secret of faith: a faith which has seen God directly and therefore can no longer be put into words."[8] Or there are times when God is partially absent, and the journey seems at an end. The journey of a life of prayer reflects all these ambiguities. We find ourselves as we truly are, as we are in God, and yet we carry with us other terrible secrets of the faith.

The model of journey allows us to ask a number of questions concerning prayer: What are the developmental components of prayer? What are the patterns of human development and growth? Who is the God to whom we pray? Is it helpful to speak in terms of "stages" of prayer, or ought we to focus on points of "transition"? Is there progress in prayer? If there is progress in prayer, how can we recognize it? Is it teachable? What is the importance and mechanism of integration of early transition points of prayer into later stages? What is the equation in progress in prayer between divine initiative and our response, between human effort and divine grace, between graceful cooperation and human reciprocity? What is the effect of faith on prayer? What is the effect of prayer on faith? How do our actions in the world affect our prayer? Is there a hint or signpost in Jesus' claim that "I am the way, and the truth" (John 14:6)? Responses to these questions have varied over the course of the Christian tradition. The writers and teachers encountered in this chapter address these questions in the context of their own journeys of faith, from their own times and their own cultures.

Many times in the Gospels, Jesus says, "Follow me" (cf. Matt. 4:19; 8:22; 16:24; John 21:19, 22). Interwoven with the joy of companionship is the suffering of the cross; to "follow me" is not an easy journey. As the contemporary writer Renita Weems declares, in our journeys of prayer, we must learn "to trust the winter months of faith, when it's difficult to remember why one ever bothered to believe." She compares the journey of prayer to a continuous cycle:

> Eventually we have to accept that dying and rising, freezing and thawing, resting and rebounding, sleeping and awakening are the necessary conditions for all growth and creativity. The journey of the soul unfolds in a continual cycle, much like the seasons of nature. . . . Winter returns a thousand times, but so does spring.[9]

The pilgrimage of prayer is a process of spiritual and faith formation. The twelfth-century contemplative theologian Hugh of St. Victor writes of five steps of prayer through which the soul is "conformed" to God. These include study, meditation, verbal prayer, charity, and contemplation. In Hugh's depiction of the journey of prayer, we (1) begin to understand God, then (2) seek God's guidance through discernment, (3) ask of God our desires and needs, (4) find God in the face of others, and finally (5) find rest and peace. Then we may begin the cycle once again. The path is not always linear, straight, or narrow. Hugh of St. Victor is aware of this. "To ascend to God is our goal," he says, but in the journey of prayer, we must often "descend for the sake of our goal."[10]

The Jewish rabbi Hillel was once asked, "Why did the thousands assembled not hear the same words that God had spoken directly to Moses?" Hillel's answer was that God is like a mirror in which each sees his or her own way. Like a thousand mirrors, God lets us see ourselves in his presence in different ways. Thus, there are many prayer *ways* to God. Yet there is, in reality, only one mirror. For Hugh of St. Victor, we often must descend in order to ascend; for Renita Weems, the life of prayer is seasonal; for Rabbi Hillel, there is but one mirror. The constant within the spiritual journey of prayer, however, is that every pattern, every theme, every stopping place is an opportunity to acknowledge the companionship of God and Christ's encouraging direction: "Follow me."

Metaphors for the Journey

For God leads souls by many paths.

Teresa of Avila, *Interior Castle*, 6.7.13

The broad swath of the Christian tradition offers a wide and creative variety of metaphors and patterns for our journey of prayer. Though metaphors and patterns as descriptive devices for the journey overlap in many ways, we can determine some important distinctions. Metaphors, images, symbols, allegory, and direct comparisons are used as aids in describing the content of the prayer journey.[11] The content that a metaphor describes may be doctrinal, experiential, relational, imagistic, psychological, and/or transformational. Pattern generally describes a more abstracted structure or outline of the spiritual journey in prayer. For instance, a linear pattern leading from one definite starting point to an end point can be contrasted to a circular or cyclic pattern. The following sections look at metaphors that illuminate the content and patterns that express the shape of journeys that are prayer.

Journey

We should begin by recognizing that journey itself is a metaphor of the life of faith in prayer. A journey generally implies that one leaves one place, encounters transforming experiences, and arrives at another place with new insight or powers. Within this general outline, there is room for nearly infinite variation. Hence, the metaphor of journey is an archetype. Homer's *Iliad* and *Odyssey* touch something true whether we travel to war, to honor, to quests for fame, or to tragic self-awareness. Ovid's *Metamorphoses* is a journey defined by transformations from the malevolent to the kind. The prodigal son embarks on a journey into a kind of "death to self" in which, daring to return home, he finds a parent who both recognizes the old self and unconditionally loves the new (Luke 15). A journey can focus on an individual or a community. The story of the forty-year journey in the desert of Sinai is a story both of Moses and of the Hebrew people. Guides along the journey are many and varied. For instance, Dante, in the *Divine Comedy,* is led in turn by Virgil, Beatrice, and St. Bernard of Clairvaux as he journeys from the fires and frozen ice of hell to a beatific vision of heaven. The journey can be of a soul's journey into God, such as in the work of that name by St. Bonaventure, or of a soul bartered in exchange for power, fame, and fortune, such as Marlowe's, Goethe's, and Mann's treatment of the legend of Faust. The journey can be so focused on a goal in which the failure to attain the goal is equivalent to the failure of the journey, as in the many stories of the quest for the Holy Grail. Or the journey itself can be its own goal. Depending on one's theology of conversion, the journey as goal can be ongoing and necessarily repeatable, as in John Bunyan's *Pilgrim's Progress.* Or it can be intermittently "successful" but never fully so, as in Gregory of Nyssa's *Life of Moses.* Or it can refer to the natural state of the wandering soul (*peregrinatio animae*), restless and lost in a far country until it finds rest in God, as in Augustine's *Confessions.*

The metaphor of journey thus includes all that is encompassed from conception to death and beyond. Within our journey, we are connected in various ways to earth and all creation, to times past and times future, to our philosophies and our stories as told and retold, to time and place, to collective and individual memories, to dreams and to unremembered things, to information and change and technology, to loneliness and isolation that may be transformed into the gentle message of solitude. "LORD, you have been our dwelling place in all generations" (Ps. 90:1). If prayer is a way of life, to journey in prayer is to dwell in God throughout all generations, in all ways, and in all places.

Wandering

Another image similar to journey is that of wandering. The Latin word for wandering, *peregrinatio*, is the etymological source of our name for the peregrine falcon, a bird whose flight pattern, though swift, gives the appearance of an aimless wandering across the sky. Augustine, who was particularly fond of this image, uses it to illustrate how the soul residing here on earth wanders essentially in a foreign land, away from that for which we were intended. We are "doomed," one might say, to wander until, as we learn to "walk by faith and not by sight" (2 Cor. 5:7), we begin to know ourselves as strangers in a strange land. It is only in recollection, prayer, and Scripture that assurance of the "Lord as our dwelling place" begins to dawn on us. Augustine writes to a nun who asked about prayer:

> In the darkness, then, of this world, in which we are pilgrims absent from the Lord, the Christian soul ought to feel itself desolate, and continue in prayer, and learn to fix the eye of faith on the word of the divine sacred Scripture, as "on a light shining in a dark place, until the day dawn, and the day-star arise in our heart" (2 Peter 1:19).[12]

Wandering in this sense has its "benefit" for Augustine in prayer in that it quickens desire for God, awakens the life of faith, and thereby opens the heart and eyes to God's dwelling presence.

The key to Augustine's conception of the spiritual journey and our sojourn here on earth is summed up in a phrase from the *Confessions* in book 8. He says simply, "You never depart from us, yet it is hard for us to return to you."[13] Though in our many wanderings it is impossible to return to God on our own, God "never departs from us." Our journey of wandering serves the function of slowly drawing our attention to the continuing presence of God through compassionate prayer.

Home

Another metaphor of the spiritual journey is that of home. Much contemporary spiritual writing has reemphasized the place of home in the life of prayer and the spirit. One such writer sees the spiritual journey as essentially a search for heaven. Heaven *is* our home in this scenario. Sin makes us nomads, while Christ becomes our path to heaven, the church our threshold to heaven, and communion with the saints our earthly glimpse of heaven.[14] Another writer places the locus of home in the self. In this case, to come home is to reconnect with the self by going deeper within, entering darkness, searching, confronting grief, transforming, and entering fully into the "garden of the soul."[15] A third finds that the home coincides with what we mean by environment. Our home is the recognition of and participation with God, others, animals, plants, and the earth itself.[16] Another writer uses the metaphor to explore a more traditional meaning of home and includes the spirituality of the domestic life, family practices that nurture contemplation, and finding sacred spaces, rituals, and stories that serve as building materials of home and family.[17] As these authors indicate, home is not only a metaphor but often a real place of safety, security, and comfort from the center of which the soul cocreates inner and outer space freely explored and shared.

In some sense, home may seem to be the antithesis of journey. On our journey of prayer, we remember home as a kind of ideal paradise, and we look toward home as a final goal. While it is true that home has many deep connotations for all of us, it is not so much a static, idealized beginning or ending location as it is a dynamic holding environment in which we are secure, safe, and free to grow, change, and evolve into the person God longs for us to be. In this sense, it is subtly linked to prayer as journey. Our memories and our dreams of home combine with our present journey to fill out and make complete Augustine's famous saying: "Our hearts are restless till they find rest in You." Prayer accompanies us in our restlessness and in our rest, in our journey and in our home. Augustine's "You" teaches us the way of prayer that makes our very journey a home for God and our home itself a way of journeying toward rest in God.

Pilgrimage

In most religions, the custom of pilgrimage is an important aspect in the life of prayer and journey. Paul Elie, in his excellent book *The Life You Save May Be Your Own*, follows what he calls the pilgrimage of four recent Roman Catholic saints. He writes:

> A pilgrimage is a journey undertaken in the light of a story. A great event has happened; the pilgrim hears the reports and goes in search of the evidence, aspiring to be an eyewitness. The pilgrim seeks not only to confirm the experience of others firsthand but to be changed by the experience. Pilgrims often make the journey in company, but each must be changed individually; they must see for themselves, each with his or her own eyes. And as they return to ordinary life the pilgrims must tell others what they saw, recasting the story in their own terms.[18]

Elie here focuses on the transformative experience of pilgrimage, the "individualistic" nature of that experience, and the need to communicate that experience in terms of the pilgrim's own life story. Later, he describes pilgrimage in the language of "seeking and finding": "A place of pilgrimage [is] a home, and a destination, where the self encounters the other, where personal experience and the testimony of the ages can be reconciled."[19] In this sense, the pilgrimage—its process, goals, and witness—bears the pilgrim toward and into a numinous, transcendent power where miracles, healing, transformation, and new insight and direction are gained.

As Peter Brown has observed, "Inevitably pilgrimage has been seen as an allegory of the Christian life, from Abraham going out by faith, the wilderness wanderings of old Israel, the return from Babylonian captivity, through Bonaventure's *Soul's Journey into God* to Bunyan's *Pilgrim's Progress*."[20] Pilgrimages to Jerusalem and the surrounding areas are seen as journeys to the country in which Jesus himself taught, healed, and enacted divine redemption. Starting with Anselm in the later eleventh century and continuing in the writings, spirituality, and prayers of Bernard of Clairvaux, St. Dominic, and especially St. Francis of Assisi, Jesus himself becomes literally the "Way." Later Protestant and Catholic piety also reclaimed and added depth to this basic biblical motif from Acts and from the early Christians' self-identification as "people of the way." In this form of prayer, the pilgrims identify their own story with the story of Christ in a new and radical way. The journey becomes the devotional following in the footsteps of the humanity of Christ. For these pilgrims, devotional prayer on the life of Christ becomes the source of the journey. As St. Bonaventure so thoughtfully puts it:

> Divine aid is available
> to those who seek it from their hearts,
> humbly and devoutly;
> and this means to sigh for it
> in this valley of tears, though fervent prayer.
> *Prayer, then, is the mother and source*
> *of the ascent.*[21]

As pilgrimage winds its way through new physical space and through interior space, both leave their transformational mark. Margery Kempe, a late-fourteenth- and early fifteenth-century English woman, for instance, undertakes pilgrimages to specific places: to the Holy Land, Assisi, Rome, and Santiago de Compostela in Galicia. These physical holy places in turn spark inner visions and meditations. In one meditation, she imagines herself present at the place of the Virgin's birth and inwardly imagines herself lending a hand with the practical necessities of housewifery:

"Jesus, what should I think about?" Our Lord Jesus answered in her mind, "Daughter, think of my mother, for she is the cause of all the grace that you have." And then at once she [Margery speaks of herself in the third person] saw St. Anne, great with child, and then she prayed [for] St. Anne to let her be her maid and her servant. And presently our Lady was born, and then she busied herself to take the child to herself and look after her until she was twelve years of age, with good food and drink, with fair white clothing and white kerchiefs. And then she said to the blessed child, "My lady, you shall be the mother of God."[22]

Through her trials, her tears, and her many meditations, Margery undertakes a pilgrimage that is, in its essential parts, a prayerful journey into the times and life of Christ.

The anonymously written *Way of the Pilgrim* contains an illustration of pilgrimage as an effort to fulfill the biblical injunction to "pray without ceasing" (1 Thess. 5:17 KJV). Like the pilgrimage type exemplified by Margery Kempe, this pilgrim is also on a journey to a destination and on a journey within in search of wisdom about prayer. The pilgrim begins the log of his journey by saying:

By the grace of God, I am a Christian, by my deeds a great sinner, and by my calling a homeless wanderer of humblest origin, roaming from place to place. My possessions consist of a knapsack with dry crusts of bread on my back and in my bosom the Holy Bible. That is all![23]

Unlike the metaphors of home, this pilgrim remains purposefully "homeless," a "wanderer . . . roaming from place to place." His "home" is on his back and in his prayer. The pilgrim ends his narrative, in fact, with a blessing from one of his teachers that suggests the pilgrimage itself is a form of heaven. In the pilgrim's spiritual journey to constant prayer, the blessing of God "overshadows his path." In this sense, he has found his home: a pilgrimage overshadowed by God.

Sacred Space, Gardens, and Deserts

Place and space serve as metaphors of the soul and provide images on which can be projected trials, transitions, and transformations of our journey in prayer. From soaring cathedrals to intimate forest groves to solitary hermitages, place and space give physical orientation to our inward journey.

In the summer of 1965, Thomas Merton began to live in the hermitage and found himself with a porch that faced the monastery he had left behind. Behind the hermitage building was a wild area of tangled brush with a rumored hidden stream. He came to associate the "structured" life of the monastery with his increasingly dissatisfied conscious prayer and the "wild" life of bush and spring with the possibilities then welling up from his unconscious and leading him toward a life of solitude. Between the two, providing both refuge and a holding place for his ambivalence concerning prayer, was the "sacred dwelling" of his hermitage. For Merton, this sacred space became a taproot for his new connection to the world around him, and it sheltered the flowering of a new and more comprehensive way of prayer.[24]

Another popular spatial metaphor of the journey is that of the garden. Due in large part to the second account of creation in Genesis (2–3), the garden also has great symbolic power for all Christians. The Genesis garden is a place of safety, security, and bounty. Yet the garden is also the very place where the gifts of connection to God, freedom, and desire are manipulated and separation and loss are introduced.

As a symbol, the garden in Christian prayer and journey is archetypical. In Augustine's *Confessions*, the garden is the setting whenever he experiences a major transformation of consciousness. It is in a garden that he, like Adam and Eve before him, first exhibits secrecy, confusion of desires, and the societal aspects of sin. He says:

> In a garden nearby our vineyard there was a pear tree, loaded with fruit that was attractive neither to look at nor to taste. Late one night a band of ruffians, myself included, went off to shake down the fruit and carry it away. . . . We took away an enormous quantity of pears, not to eat them ourselves, but simply to throw them to the pigs. . . . Look into my heart, Oh God. . . . Let my heart now tell you what prompted me to do wrong for no purpose.[25]

Augustine ruminates on this senseless waste that places him, again like Adam and Eve, into that "region of unlikeness"—the region uninhabited by God. The remainder of the *Confessions* recounts the obstacles and blessings facing Augustine in his journey back to "paradise." After an agonizing struggle, he experiences another major transformation in a garden—his conversion. Overwhelmed by doubts, ambivalence, anxiety, and tears, he "takes refuge in this garden, . . . going out to the garden; . . . Alypius [my friend] followed at my heels." Later, he rushes back into the garden, and "somehow I fling myself beneath a fig tree and give way to tears which now filled my eyes." It is at this point, within the garden, that Augustine "hears" the voice of a child singing: "Take it and read, take it and read." He picks up his Bible, opens it randomly to Romans 13, reads aloud to Alypius, and within the garden he experiences what he describes "as though the light of confidence flooded into my heart and all the darkness of doubt was dispelled."[26]

A final major transformation for Augustine occurs again in a garden. This is the famous "vision at Ostia" reported in his *Confessions* (9.10.23–25). Augustine and his mother, jointly in prayer, have an experience of momentary unifying contact with God. The garden, though seemingly at first glance static, is a rich metaphor for the dynamic life of prayer. It provides images of tending plants and gardening, cyclic patterns of death and renewal, opportunities for partnership with God, an environment suitable to struggle as well as to rest, temptation as well as consolation, and a goal that promises beauty, peacefulness, and home.

The desert would seem at first glance to represent the opposite of all that gardens have to offer, and in many ways it is the opposite. Yet the desert has also etched an indelible landscape on the consciousness of the Christian at prayer. Christian Scripture is full of desert journeys and retreats, from the forty years of purification and testing of the Hebrew people during their desert exodus, to John the Baptist's "deserty edge" in his prophesying and teaching, to Jesus himself, who sought solitude, fought battles, and found refreshment in more than one desert journey into prayer.

Today the tradition continues, with many pilgrims seeking the simplicity, beauty, and purity of the desert as an antidote to contemporary life. The desert has even reached cyberspace! According to the Carmelite monk Elisha Emery, "The sapiential holding environment that is monasticism is not disappearing so much as shifting shape and locus as it incorporates a vision of stability that [was] always valued [in] the heart-centered solitude of the desert: the postmodern networks of cyberspace."[27]

Whether we are truly witnessing the birth of a new desert of cyberspace remains to be seen. What we do know as established and reliable teaching in the many routes and ways of Christian prayer based in desert spirituality comes to us most famously from the lives and teachings of the fathers and mothers of the fourth and fifth centuries who journeyed into the desert to form various desert communities or hermitages in Egypt, Nitrea, Syria, Asia Minor, and Palestine. Of their sayings (collected in the *Apophthegmata patrum*), a contemporary scholar writes that "the essence of the spirituality of the desert is that it was not taught but caught; it was a whole way of life. . . . Prayer was not an activity undertaken for a few hours each day, it was a life continually turned toward God."[28] To discipline themselves to a "life continually turned toward God," the desert pilgrims sought solitude, obedience under a spiritual guide, radical simplicity, charity, and prayer. In contrast to the image of the garden, desert space is wild, open, harsh, unrelenting, exposed, dry, unforgiving, demanding, seemingly empty. But there is something of the desert that draws us. The solitude of the desert is a kind of medium through which an authentic openness and purity of heart can develop. It is a proper medium to communion and communication with the divine. It is harsh. But as Belden Lane suggests from the title of a recent book, there is also a solace in fierce landscapes.[29]

Many other metaphors and images, including narratives and lives from Scripture, ocean journeys, quests, mountains, ladders, wheels, and more, have been used to describe the crucial junctures in our life of prayer. As with those we have briefly examined, they all share something in common: As if to echo the reality of prayer as a way of life, they all confront us head-on. They provide a lens that seems to heighten our perception of what is really real, they work on our conscious and unconscious selves as real archetypes, and they insist again and again that we look deeply into ourselves. These images are thus more than simply metaphors. Gardens, deserts, home—all these are very real. They also point to the mystery within the real as they teach us how to pray.

Patterns of the Journey

> We shall not cease from exploration
> And the end of all our exploring
> Will be to arrive where we started
> And know the place for the first time.
>
> T.S. Eliot, *Four Quartets,* no. 4,
> "Little Gidding," 5

Metaphors illustrate the content of the paths of our journey that brings us into contact with God, self, others, and the world. Patterns of prayer give shape and structure to life and help us put real flesh, blood, and bones onto our journey into God.

Linear and Progressive

Linear and progressive patterns come in a variety of forms but generally follow a path of ascent to God. While ascent is perhaps one of the most common patterns of the Christian journey, a note of caution is appropriate. The idea of ascent is based on a cosmology that understands heaven and God as "above" and earth as "below." But to construe the spiritual journey exclusively as a path from "below" to "above" tends to create chasms—often unbridgeable—between body and soul, the beginner and the adept, the active and the contemplative life, and the powerless and the powerful. Nonetheless, the pattern of progress through ascent to God also shares a history of appropriate and empowering application to the life of prayer. Used with thoughtful understanding, many of the ladders, steps, and mountains to God found in the Christian tradition can serve a valuable function in pursuit of a life of virtue and contemplation of truth.

Most patterns of prayer follow a progressive path. The simplest pattern in this case is a relatively linear movement upward. Here the steepness of the line might indicate the relative nature of grace and human effort; the steeper the line, the heavier the emphasis on grace. A number of writers on prayer have used this rather stiff but plausible pattern, indicating a movement from purgation at the bottom of the line, a state of illumination somewhere midpoint, and the possibility of perfection or union in prayer at the end and highest point.

A pattern in many ways similar to that of the linear pattern is the step pattern. In this pattern, the line moves from beginning to end and also horizontally and vertically forward, but one's advances in prayer from, for example, purgation to illumination to union are indicated as steps rather than as a continuous straight line. The implication in this pattern is that at each vertical step there is an immediate and wholly grace-induced progression in prayer that forms the riser of the step of progress. Others have used a similar step approach, varying it slightly by inserting a dip just before the rise to indicate a period of darkness or brokenness just prior to a vertical step upward. The implication in this pattern is that a form of brokenness or sense of God's absence must precede the transforming step to the next level.

Purgation, Illumination, and Union

Mentioned above, the process of growth in prayer through the interrelated stages of purgation (or purification), illumination (or enlightenment), and union (or perfection) is perhaps the most fundamental pattern in Christian prayer. This pattern is found in various forms and permutations throughout the history and practice of Christian prayer until today. The pattern is first given form in the writings of Dionysius the Areopagite in the late fifth or early sixth century. If the history and practice of prayer as a spiritual journey could be reduced and distilled to one pattern, this would be it. Speaking of the ecclesiastical orders, Dionysius writes:

> Those whom the deacons have purified and the priests have illuminated, the heirarch leads on to an understanding of the sacred things they have beheld, and he does this . . . in proportion to their capacity. Thus he perfects the initiates so that their sanctification may be as complete as is possible for them.[30]

One famous example of the use of this pattern can be found in John of the Cross's dark night of the senses and dark night of the spirit. Thomas Green has written a helpful book using Teresa of Avila and John of the Cross as guides in the life of prayer. For Green, the dry darkness of prayer is first and foremost a process of purgation. Purgation or purification is a necessary point of transition in both Teresa's and John's depiction of prayer and the spiritual life. Green writes of the positive qualities of these "nights of purification": "I began to realize that purgatory is not vengeance but purification and transformation. . . . When I discovered that St. John of the Cross, the great master of prayer, affirms clearly and repeatedly that this dark night is indeed a purgatory for some, I was happy but not surprised."[31]

Green comments further on the stage of illumination:

> John's explanation implies that the darkness is not really darkness, that God is not really absent, but that we lack the eyes to see, the tongue to taste what is really there. That is precisely the point. God is not absent; he is closer than he has ever been, but we are blind. It is the dark contemplation which is in us, working our healing.[32]

Green follows John of the Cross as he moves in prayer from purgation and illumination to union of the soul. As we will see, there are many images or metaphors for describing union with God. Green uses one particularly apt image of John's: Union with God is like a log in the fire. John's dark nights are forms of contemplation, yet in the dark night of the senses, contemplation only "chars and blackens the surface of the [log of] wood." But as the heat penetrates "deeper and deeper into the heart of the log," contemplation in the dark night of the spirit ignites a fire that no longer simply chars the surface. The new fire "now begins to transform the very substance of the wood, until the whole log is incandescent and, in the physics of John's day, the wood becomes fire. The image expresses beautifully the divinization of the soul."[33]

In this one example alone, John of the Cross takes the trajectory of purgation, illumination, and union and has transformed them into a rich vocabulary of transformative prayer.

Hierarchy

Some patterns of the life of prayer contain both a linear or stepped pattern and a circular pattern. These patterns of the spiritual journey can best be defined as hierarchical. Since hierarchy has such a negative connotation today, it might be most helpful to begin by looking at two examples of the positive use of a hierarchical pattern.

The structure of Teresa of Avila's *Interior Castle* is one excellent example. Containing both linear and circular elements, Teresa's mandalic castle image uses a series of seven "interior castles," each with numerous rooms. Her pattern is hierarchical: At any given time in the life of prayer, we may find ourselves in a particular room at the level of one of the seven castles. That particular place best fits our prayer at that moment. Yet as Teresa describes the life of prayer, there is a real sense in which the person or people at prayer are also simultaneously affected by the possibilities of prayer in all the rooms of the castle. In other words, one does not pray in a vacuum; like a hologram in which any portion of the picture contains the whole, in the hierarchical pattern, regardless of where we are in our life of prayer, we are surrounded, protected, and supported by the full castle of prayer. Hierarchy supports the whole *and* the part.

A close relative of Teresa's hierarchical pattern is that of the angelic hierarchy. Traditionally, the various orders of angels are centered around God in progressive order, much like the levels of Teresa's castles. Usually nine orders of angels are proposed in medieval and early Renaissance texts. Those circling closest to God are the seraphim, who represent the path of love. Those circling farthest from God—though still within the hierarchy—are the angels. Each of the nine angelic orders of the hierarchy represents a particular pathway to God as well as a particular form of prayer and a parallel form of ministry on earth. Thus, the route that brings one closest to God is the path of love (represented by the seraphim), the corresponding form of prayer is contemplation, and the ministry is compassion. In the second order are the cherubim, representing the path of the mind. In this path, the study of Scripture and doctrine is prayer, and the ministry is that of teaching. With five orders intervening, the eighth order after the seraphim and cherubim are the archangels, familiar to selected humans in Scripture as protectors and messengers of good news. The ninth order are those angels who, according to Scripture and tradition, have most to do with humanity, guarding, guiding, and also witnessing to the good news of God.[34] As with Teresa's castles, each of the angelic orders has its particular way of prayer and ministry yet also participates in each of the others. The angels, for instance, announce the good news through love and can call others to God by turning them toward an understanding of Scripture.

Teresa of Avila's interior castles and the angelic orders are just two patterns of prayer that rely on the concept of hierarchical arrangement. As mentioned, today many people are uneasy with the idea of hierarchy. It is often thought to be stiff and rigid, not to mention oppressive. It is true that hierarchy as a social or political structure has been used to subjugate, control, and oppress. But the metaphysical and cosmological worldview that developed the concept of hierarchy understood it in a different, life-affirming way. Grounded in Neoplatonic speculation on the metaphysical path of mediation between the human person and the pure realm of ideas, hierarchy originally was simply the sacred or holy (*hiera*) source or first principle (*archē*). As such, it was a structure or process grounded in divine reality. With regard to prayer, it meant simply that, regardless of pattern or metaphor, prayer was grounded in our source and first principle: God.

One of the first uses of the word *hierarchy* in Christian writings is also by Dionysius the Areopagite. Dionysius uses it to mean more than just rank or order. For Dionysius, all creation, including plants, animals, humans, and angels, participate in a sacred order that makes knowledge and activity possible, and that is precisely what hierarchy is:

> In my opinion a hierarchy is a sacred *order*, a state of *understanding* and *activity* approximating as closely as possible to the divine. . . . The goal of a hierarchy, then, is to enable beings to be as like as possible to God and to be at one with God.[35]

Whether patterned in terms of steps or stages on a ladder, as a spiraling movement toward a center, or as a series of concentric circles, prayer as hierarchy is simply participation in the order and unity that is God, thereby making knowledge of God and activity directed toward God possible. Each stage or step or circle maintains its unique identity while participating simultaneously in the originating and sacred divine reality. Thus, the particular and the whole are bound together. The concept of hierarchy in prayer allows individual personality, community identity, and cultural diversity to flourish in the context of the order, knowledge, and activity of the whole.

Circular and Spiral Patterns

Common to all these patterns of the life of prayer is that, though we may return to a point that appears as if it were the exact place we started, this starting point is radically different. We arrive at the starting place, knowing it only now for the first time.

Patterns that repeat the journey yet allow us to arrive home in a new way are many. The most obvious of these is the circle that remains at all times equidistant from its central point and arrives precisely where it left off. In this pattern, prayer progresses, moving through a circular pattern only to return home. Certain medieval writers write of this pattern that prayer is a circle whose circumference is everywhere and whose center is nowhere.

Yet the spiral, more often than the circle, is a pattern of the spiritual journey that reflects the life of prayer. In the spiral, the form of the circle is maintained, but the return is never to the same space as the point of departure. The return may touch close to the start, but the starting point is only glimpsed, as it were, in passing. The spiral that winds inward toward the center is generally a life of prayer finding peace at the center. A spiral radiating outward finds new material and wonder to add to the life of prayer, moving into the depth of creation. The former is a kind of internal or immanent prayer to God within us, the latter a kind of external or transcendent prayer to the God of the universe.

Another pattern that resembles a circle but never quite closes in on itself is suggested by Gregory of Nyssa in his *Life of Moses.* Gregory of Nyssa employs the idea of "eternal progress," or *epektasis,* to emphasize that there is no "goal" in a static sense, as in Platonic philosophy and Christian followers of that philosophy, such as Origen. Making progress itself is the goal. For Gregory, the boundless nature of God implies the boundless nature of the good and the possibility of eternal progress of the soul in prayer to enter into that good. He uses the same language to describe the infinity of God as he does to describe prayer: "How then would one arrive at the sought-for boundary when he can find no boundary. . . . The one limit of perfection is that there is no limit."[36] In our spiritual journey, he adds, "no limit would interrupt growth in the ascent to God, since no limit to the good can be found nor in the increasing of desire for the good brought to an end because it is satisfied. . . . Moses always found a step higher than the one he had attained."[37] There is always more, there is always progress to be made in understanding, dwelling in, and contemplation of God. Gregory's pattern of prayer would thus be something like a spiraling and circular cone returning but ever progressing upward into a boundless God.

Other circular patterns that have guided the journey of prayer include the seasons of the year, concentric circles, and the labyrinth. All these circular patterns suggest patterns of the mandala. *Mandala,* a Sanskrit word, is translated as "circle" or "center" or "that which surrounds." It "denotes the ritual or magic circle used as an aid to contemplation. By meditation on the mandala symbol or by participating in a mandala ritual, one seeks to effect an inner transformation and advance toward a goal in the spiritual journey."[38] The mandala can have a circular or square pattern (or a combination of both) and spatially might be a garden, a drawing, or a sacred dwelling space such as a temple or a church. Teresa of Avila's concentric circles also function as a mandala that moves the contemplative on her spiritual journey toward a transformative encounter with God. The cross itself, with its four directionals emanating from a center point, is also a mandalic form. The form is heightened by the Celtic cross, which incorporates a circle around the center arms of the cross.

The labyrinth is a popular contemporary form of prayer in the spiritual journey that incorporates many of the patterns discussed above. The labyrinth was rediscovered during a restoration of the cathedral at Chartres. The pattern was found on the floor of the cathedral and since that time has been reconstructed both indoors and out as a permanent or portable structure. The pattern of the labyrinth incorporates elements of the circle, spiral, linear path, and mandala. It is a prayer meant to be walked, a prayer that one begins by entering an opening in the outer circle. By a circuitous, labyrinthine route, one arrives at a center and then returns to the starting point of entry. Lauren Artress, a contemporary writer, comments on the labyrinth:

> To walk a sacred path [the labyrinth] is to discover our inner sacred space: that core of feeling that is waiting to have life breathed back into it through symbols, archetypal forms like the labyrinth, rituals, stories, and myths. . . . [Hildegard of Bingen] described the Holy Spirit as the Greening Power of God. Just as plants are greened, so we are as well. As we grow up, our spark of life continually shines forth. If we ignore this spark, we become thirsty and shriveled. And if we respond to the spark, our flower grows.[39]

Artress admits that coming to flower is a different idea than we get in most churches today. The effect of journey in prayer toward a true center or true sacred space is effected in walking the labyrinth. One does not arrive at either the center or the exit of the journey in the same frame of mind and spirit as one entered it: Responding to the spark that is God, we are "greened" and "flower."

Narrative and Sequence in Scripture

Extremely important in the spiritual journey is the use of narrative and/or sequence in Scripture to model a pattern and a way of life for prayer. In this sense, individuals or stories within Scripture become paradigms for patterns in the life of prayer. The scriptural sequence can be followed in either a literal or an allegorical way that becomes normative to and formational for the life of prayer.[40] Thus, for instance, Gregory of Nyssa commends the life of Moses as a worthy model for imitation. Gregory counts Moses as a model of both virtue and contemplation:

> We have briefly written for you, tracing in outline like a pattern of beauty the life of the great Moses so that each one of us might copy the image of the beauty which has been shown to us by imitating his way of life.[41]

As we have seen, Richard of St. Victor also uses Scripture; sequences of events; and personification allegories of Abraham, Sarah, Leah, their handmaids, and their children to depict growth in virtue. His *Mystical Ark* continues the sequencing by looking at the order in which the ark of the covenant was constructed and by assigning different levels of contemplation to each sequence. The result is an internalization of the symbol of the ark as a pattern "reconstructed" from Scripture that gives structure to the contemplative life, leading to the birth of God's presence within. The soul itself thus becomes "holy space."[42]

But in a real sense, it is not so much that we tell and recast the story as that in our journey of prayer Scripture retells and shapes us. Practices that allow us to internalize the Word—Bible study, preaching, *lectio divina,* Scripture memorization, daily devotions, scholarly work, reading and rereading the text—shape and direct our prayer. The biblical scholar and keen student of Christian spirituality Sandra Schneiders comments on the end of John's Gospel: The purpose of encountering John's text is "that you may believe" (John 20:31 RSV). In advocating an informed, contemporary blend of the formational and the transformational reading, Schneiders observes that the noun *faith* never occurs in the Gospel of John, which

> always uses the verb "to believe," because the interaction between Jesus the teacher and his disciples is never something acquired, achieved, possessed. It is an ongoing relationship that either incessantly deepens or ceases. It is a friendship, a love relationship, which cannot remain stagnant without stagnating. . . . The Gospel is a means to mediate, facilitate, nourish this relationship, and therefore reading it must be an ongoing activity. As friends and lovers we do not cease to talk.[43]

For patristic and medieval writers, the encounter with Scripture was always more formational and transformational than simply informational. Schneiders follows suit here, adding her own command of modern and postmodern ways of reading to argue for a dynamic encounter with God's Word that is both transformational and relational. As we encounter the biblical stories again and again, we enter a world in which the biblical narrative becomes our own journey that "incessantly deepens," shapes, nurtures, and enlivens friendship, relationship, love, and thus prayer.

Typologies of Meditation

> Praised be you, my Lord, with all your creatures,
> Especially Sir Brother Sun. . . .
> Praised be you, my Lord, for Sister Moon and the Stars. . . .
> Praised be you, my Lord, for Brother Wind. . . .
> Praised be you, my Lord, for Sister Water. . . .
> Praised be you, my Lord, for our sister Mother Earth.
>
> St. Francis of Assisi, *Canticle of Creatures*

This section explores prayer as a potential encounter with the sacred and the holy in every area of life. Typologies of meditation lead us in our journey of prayer to the transcendent, incomprehensible God as well as to the immanent God of small, mundane things. Seeing with the eyes of St. Francis, we see connection and relation in prayer and in life: We see the face, the mystery, and the glory of God. As the tree of life that is prayer grows within us through our journey of prayer, its fruit begins to reflect the face of a faceless but loving God, while its trunk, branches, and leaves declare God's glory.

The Journey of Meditation on Nature

Meditation on creation "reads" God through the book of nature. In meditating on nature, the arc of the spiritual journey of prayer takes us through the natural, created world into God. God is immanent in the world, but God is not nature and nature is not God. Still, through the senses, the created world shows forth the glory of God. The natural, created world has a symbolic or sacramental quality by which we rightly enjoy God as Creator.

A few reminders are helpful in our practices of meditation on nature. A first reminder is that nature is both concrete and real in itself as well as inherently symbolic of the holy. Hence, we can meditate on creation just as it truly is. The natural world is particular. A cedar clothed with moss, aqueous and gray-green, floored with bracken and sword ferns, smelling of earth and mushroom, dripping condensed fog in stillness is still a tree. We can touch, see, smell, hear, even taste the tree and its community. Yet it is also holy, sacred, and standing as a prayer in itself. It stands as an object through which we can praise God. It serves as an icon of the holy, even as we do it the supreme honor of seeing it just as it is.

A second reminder is the use of a simple preposition. It makes a difference whether we say God is *in* nature or God is perceptible and can be praised *through* nature. The first panentheistically implies that nature is divine, the second that a vestige of God—a kind of theophanic nature mysticism—is discernable in the created world. An example of the careful use of prepositions is St. Francis's famous "Canticle of Brother Sun" (or "Canticle of Creatures" or "Praise of the Creatures") cited at the beginning of this section. In this song of praise, the continuous repetition of the word *per,* which means through or by means of, indicates that God is praised through or by means of God's creatures. The creature—brother sun, sister moon—is not praised as God. Rather, God is praised *through* creation. The created world is a kind of vestige or footprint of God. Again, God is praised through creatures, not in them.[44]

Bonaventure's *Soul's Journey into God* contains a common medieval strategy for contemplating God in both the material and the sense world—both aspects of the natural world for Bonaventure. Bonaventure contemplates creatures and the created world as vestiges of the Trinity, reflecting God's power, wisdom, and goodness. Through these vestiges, God in "power, presence and essence exists uncircumscribed in all things."[45] Augustine finds the image and the likeness of the Trinity in the human person, reflecting the memory, intellect, and love of his divine origin. Bonaventure does something similar, using the vestiges of the Trinity in nature as they reflect God.[46]

In contrast to Francis's simple directness, Bonaventure incorporates speculative theology from Pseudo-Dionysius, Augustine, and Anselm. Bonaventure was enthralled by the intelligible structure of the universe, Francis with the simple joy of the created world and the connection in unity he experienced with God through creatures. Both approaches are valuable road maps for contemporary Christians as we struggle to redefine a balanced and integrated relationship through prayer with the created world.

The Journey of Meditation on the Soul

The Christian spiritual journey inevitably leads to an encounter with our own soul. It is in the very core of our being, deep within our selves, that God is closer to us than we are to ourselves. If we could enter and dwell within our own soul, we would find ourselves connected to God. This is not to say that we, our soul, or any part of us *is* God. It simply means that we are created in the image and likeness of God and that the image and likeness of God within contain a spark of the Creator. Thus, in soul prayer, there is a sense in which we "descend" into the core of our humanity in order to "ascend" into God. Soul prayer involves watchfulness and healing; it is care of the soul. In fact, God invites us to care for ourselves through prayer that leads us into our true selves; the result is an invitation to become ever more connected to God. We are invited to come, through prayer and contemplation, as close to ourselves as God already is to us.

Teresa of Avila's journey through the interior rooms in her treatise *The Interior Castle* is simultaneously a journey of prayer, a journey to the center of the soul, and a journey into God, there to receive an imaginative vision and unity with Christ and an intellective vision and union with God. Many metaphors have been used to explore both the similarity and the difference one finds within the heart of the self between the soul and God. Meditation on the soul is an opportunity for and process of continued self-understanding, continued ministry and witness, ongoing self-nurture, and renewing consciousness of the presence of God. Soul meditation is a form of care of the soul.

The Christian understanding that God is present and lives within, at the core of the soul, is suggested by numerous passages in Scripture.[47] This fact alone is the basis of many forms of Christian prayer, meditation, and contemplation. It is the basis of how we live our lives and how we are in relation with others as we cherish the image of the living God within them. Many of these forms of prayer instill ways of being with God that are generally counter to the ways of surviving in today's world. Contrary to a world of business and consumerism, these forms of prayer nurture centering, stillness, hospitality, and silence. As we saw in the model of prayer as conversation, these forms of prayer tend to open our heart and soul, making them receptive to God's work within.

The theological justification for soul meditation that draws us inward as a way into God is the *imago Dei,* the image of God. In Genesis 1:26–27, we find that we are made in the image and likeness of God. There is something like a vestige or imprint of God's being in our soul, and to journey inward is a journey into divine image and likeness. Augustine is our progenitor of this "inner way." Exploring the possibilities of what it might mean that humanity is formed in God's image and likeness, he assumes that the divine "stamp" must be something like the trinitarian nature of God, since the Trinity describes the essence of God's being. What, Augustine asks, is present within the human person that reflects this essential nature of God? Augustine draws on his Neoplatonic background, especially Plotinus, to formulate a parallel between divine unity and human integration. Augustine then reflects on what he knows of human anthropology and concludes that the trinitarian image or likeness of God common to all humanity involves the human powers of memory, intellect, and will (or love). Memory, he says, is a reflection of the eternity of the Father. Intellect is a reflection of the Son as truth. The will or love is a reflection of the goodness of the Holy Spirit. Augustine thus initiates the "inner way" as a journey leading to the image and likeness of God. This image is "defaced"; it is "diluted" and thus not capable of complete participation in God in this life, but

> we have asserted that it [the mind] still remains the image of God, although an image occurred and defaced by the loss of its participation in God. This is His image because it is a capacity for God and can participate in God: It has this high destiny only because it is His image. Here, therefore, is the mind remembering itself, understanding itself, loving itself. Perceiving this, we perceive a trinity—a trinity far less than God, but now finally an image of God.[48]

Bonaventure follows a similar path inward, finding God's presence in the soul. Bonaventure, however, makes an important distinction. There are those natural powers "stamped" on the soul, following Augustine, that include the powers of memory, intellect, and will. But there is also a trinity of powers in the image and likeness of God reformed by grace: faith, hope, and love. For Bonaventure, the "eye of reason" leads us through the natural powers, while the "eye of the heart," in imitation of Christ, leads us into those powers reformed by grace. Clouded by cares and distractions, the soul cannot normally find the image of God within—it is a fallen image. But with the coming of Christ, the fallen image is restored, eternal Truth itself takes on human form, and Christ becomes a "ladder, restoring the first ladder that had been broken by Adam."[49]

Through a journey into the core of the soul, the journey of meditation on the soul reflects on a broken image of God but, through the grace of God in Christ, in a restored and uplifting form. The Christian tradition is rich in prayer as well as ascetical practices that chart a course for finding God within.

The Journey of Meditation on Scripture

Christians are people of the Book. In soul prayer, we encounter the book of experience. In nature prayer, we encounter the book of nature. In the Hebrew Bible and the New Testament, we encounter God and his plan for our salvation fully revealed. In each case, there are various ways to read the Book. Each way of reading in turn represents its own disciplines, practices, and journeys of prayer and contemplation.

From the earliest times, meditation on Scripture has represented the apex of the Christian tradition of prayer. From meditation on Scripture in search of the virtuous life, to formal and informal forms of *lectio divina*, to the Puritan divines' search in Scripture for the "sweet core of truth," to the nineteenth-century application of historical-critical methods, to the whole range of contemporary ethical dilemmas, Scripture has provided direction, courage, and comfort to the believing community. When we align our stories with the story of Scripture, we enter into the mysterious prayer that God has made of our lives. Christian Scripture can be seen as a continuous meditation on the presence and nature of God.

Early in the history of the church, the reading of Scripture was generally divided into literal or historical reading and various forms of spiritual reading.[50] Literal or historical exegesis is concerned with what actually happened. It is still with us today in the form of linguistic, grammatical, structural, syntactical, and semantic analysis, in historical-critical methods of interpretation, and in deconstruction.

Spiritual reading is more difficult to define because it changes over time, between writers of a certain time, and even over time in a single writer. Spiritual exegesis usually includes three levels of reading. The first is allegorical meditation, which finds the deepest meaning in Scripture reflected in allegorical or symbolic realities. Often an exegete of the Hebrew Bible would find that a story, person, or event was an allegory of Christ, the church, or progress in virtue. A second spiritual reading involves anagogical meditations. Anagogical readings draw from the text a map, as it were, of the proper means of ascent to God or the best way to read the presence of God in any scriptural event or person. Although God is frequently "present" as a character in the story, still, the anagogical interpretation would "read" God's attributes or characteristics as a map of the spiritual journey, a process that has personal, contemporary value for cultivating the presence of God. A third spiritual meditation is the tropological reading. This final spiritual meditation is concerned with moral action in the world: What is God calling the reader to do and to be?

Each of these readings and the many forms of contemporary hermeneutical engagement with Scripture are opportunities to let our story be shaped by the Story. The journey of meditation on Scripture is through intellect, heart, community, body, history, event, works of mercy, and gifts of the Spirit.

There also are, as we have already seen, ways of reading Scripture, *lectio divina* in particular, that are intentionally prayerful. Madam Guyon, the early eighteenth-century French "quietist," says of this form of meditation:

> Taste it and digest it as you read. . . . "Praying the Scripture" is not judged by how much you read but by the way you read. If you read quickly, it will benefit you little. You will be like a bee that merely skims the surface of a flower. Instead, in this new way of reading the prayer, you become as

the bee that penetrates into the depths of the flower. You plunge deeply within to remove its deepest nectar.[51]

The Journey of Meditation on Christ

Meditation on Christ may at first seem self-evident to any practitioner of the Christian faith. But just what, in particular, about Christ ought to claim our consideration and prayer? Does it mean conforming to Christ by participating in the patterns of activity modeled by Christ? Do we come into the presence of God through meditation that focuses on Christ's divinity or on Christ's humanity? Do we pray in and through Christ's prophetic, priestly, lordly, or teaching ministry? Is the Christ in whom we pray the Christ of poverty, humility, or passion? Is meditation on Christ a prayer of birth and the incarnation, of death and the passion, or of new life and the resurrection? Perhaps our itinerary ought to lead through Christ as the preexistent Second Person of the Trinity or through Jesus the Redeemer.

Indeed, we may meditate on many aspects of the life of Jesus Christ. Christ, as established formally at the Council of Chalcedon in 451, is fully human and fully divine. This, perhaps more than any other fact about Christ, affects meditation on Christ. The council held that Jesus Christ is "one . . . Christ . . . in two natures, without confusion, without change, without division, without separation." The "two natures" have led to different emphases in the areas of prayer. Because of the insistence that the two natures are without confusion, change, division, or separation, the emphases are never wholly distinct but broadly visible: prayer based on devotion to the divinity of Christ and prayer based on devotion to the humanity of Christ. Prayer based on a journey following the trail of the divinity of Christ leans toward eschatological, kingdom, and resurrection motifs. Prayer and devotional practice grounded in the humanity of Christ more often lean toward Gospel values taught or lived by Christ, including humility, hospitality, servanthood, simplicity, compassion, and justice. At its best, just as humanity and divinity commingle without confusion in Christ, so too does prayer integrate the divine and the human emphases of both categories of values and core practices.

Devotion and prayer, grounded in either Christ's humanity or his divinity, both lead to consciousness of the presence of God. Emphasis on the divine nature of Christ, however, involves more often than not a form of deification in the sense that participation in Christ's divinity leads to participative identity with divinity itself. Contemplative prayers in the Eastern church and many in the Western church as well thus focus on *theōsis* (deification) through Christ as their primary goal.

It would be wrong, however, to separate meditation on Christ's divinity from meditation on Christ's humanity. Both are legitimate; in them we face once again the theme in Christian prayer of living with ease in the midst of dialectical paradox. Meditation focused on the divinity of Christ tends to stress that deification is manifested only in the context of the human. Something of the divine present in each of us flowers into deification only in the fullest realization of our humanity as God envisions and sustains that humanity. Divinization is thus equivalent to humanization. This excludes issues of grace and works, but in the journey of prayer, meditation focused on the humanity of Christ tends to assume that only in our full humanization do we fully encounter God.

In the Latin West, beginning in the late eleventh century and flowering in the early thirteenth century, continuing in various forms until today, a new emphasis on meditation on the humanity of Christ developed that emphasized imitation of his life, work, ministry, and values. In this tradition, meditation included not only formal prayers and contemplation but also a lifestyle, a journey modeled on patterns in Christ's life. Identity with Christ in this form initially involved focus on Christ's suffering and passion. These prayers also led to practical and ethical issues such as how to live simply in poverty of spirit, with humility before God, and with compassion for others. To illustrate the routes our meditations can take, even today, it is helpful to look at two examples of meditation on the life of Christ that focus on the passion in radically different ways. In the first, the meditation is carried to a harmful extreme. In the second, it is extended to a healthy, life-affirming pattern.

Early in his life, the fourteenth-century Dominican Henry Suso wrote in his book *The Exemplar* that he sought to imitate Christ through suffering and pain in and of itself. He slept on a bed of nails. He wore a cross in which nails were embedded. When he thought this "penance" too ineffectual, he added to his suffering by purposefully lying on the floor, the better to impale himself with the nails. Fortunately, Suso eventually felt he had gone too far, and by the end of his book, he disavowed and warned others against such extremes of self-induced suffering. He came to believe that they were not in the best interest of the gospel he was committed to preach and so advised a more "sensible" outward life that reflected the "inner" man he was called to be.[52] This may seem extreme today, and it is. But there are elements in Suso's piety that linger even today: devotion driven by shame, fear, and guilt; assumptions that the body is really the root of our problems if not the cause; and simple self-loathing.

The phenomenon of the stigmata is similar but more inspiring than harmful. The stigmata are the mirroring of Christ's passion through reception in the hands, feet, and side of the five wounds of Christ. St.

Francis of Assisi and St. Catherine of Siena are famous examples of stigmatics whose complete identification with Christ's five wounds pushes the boundaries of our own humanity to the extreme outer reaches of prayer and activity patterned on the life of Christ. In the case of St. Francis, the stigmata were received while he was in prayer on Mt. Alverna in Italy. During his prayer, he had a vision of Christ crucified, centered in an angel in the form of a seraphim, which symbolically represented the path of love. This, more clearly, was the pattern of Christ's own passion. In their meditations on Christ, Francis and Catherine encountered love rather than suffering. The stigmata were grounded in love and, ideally, led to a life of compassionate charity. In their cases, through imitation of Christ, charity was prayer.

Ways of meditation on the life of Christ are as numerous as the questions we may have about who Christ was and who Christ is. Thomas à Kempis's *Imitation of Christ*, a book of meditations on the life of Christ, for centuries was second only to the Bible in sales and use. Ignatius of Loyola's retreats are essentially guided meditations on the life of Christ, with the goal of discernment of and commitment to the promptings of God. Meditation on the life of Christ opens our eyes to the "Christ" in others. It has prompted individuals and groups as diverse as liberation theology and the work of Mother Teresa in Calcutta, India. Whether focused on Christ's divinity and deification or Christ's humanity and discernment about how to live a life of charity in the world, meditation on Christ is at the core of the Christian spiritual journey and prayer.

The Journey of Meditation on God

At first glance, meditation on God might also sound obvious, even redundant. Is God not the very reason and source for prayer? The immediate answer is yes. But in the details of that yes lie the many metaphors and patterns of spiritual journey and ultimately how, why, and to whom we pray.

This section necessarily looks at just a few of the many ways that meditation on God may be approached. One approach is to focus meditation on God as Trinity. We have already glimpsed something of trinitarian prayer in both Augustine's approach to meditation on the soul and Bonaventure's treatment of meditation on nature. Augustine sees the human faculties of memory, intellect, and love as trinitarian images within the human soul; thus, one can find the patterns of God within the structures of the human person. Bonaventure points out vestiges of the same trinitarian reality in the natural world. God's power, wisdom, and goodness, according to Bonaventure, are discernable in nature and serve, as do Augustine's images within the soul, as points of entry or access to God's presence in the natural world.

Julian of Norwich is one of the most profound sources for recasting trinitarian theology in the language of prayer. Her claim "Where Jesus appears, the blessed Trinity is understood"[53] has wide-ranging implications for prayer. Not only do the attributes of motherhood—protection, nurture, love—shine forth in the life and work of Jesus, but where Jesus appears, the attributes of the Father and the Holy Spirit appear as well. Thus, again, Christ tells her:

> I am he; that is to say: I am he, the power and goodness of fatherhood; I am he, the wisdom and lovingness of motherhood; I am he, the light and grace which is blessed love; I am he, the Trinity; I am he, the unity; I am he, the supreme goodness of every kind of thing; I am he who makes you to love; I am he who makes you to long; I am he, the endless fulfillment of all true desires.[54]

In Julian's wide-ranging thought, Christ is understood not only as Mother but also as the Trinity. Julian's point of entry into meditation on God is a God who both nurtures us in prayer and gently guides us toward consummation in prayer.

Other writers teach of meditation on God in the context of divine attributes. For these writers, the attributes become present to us through prayer. John Calvin, for instance, writes of a God who becomes wholly present to us in prayer through the divine attributes of providence, power, and goodness:

> Words fail to explain how necessary prayer is, and how many ways the exercise of prayer is profitable. Surely, with good reason the Heavenly Father affirms that the only stronghold of safety is in calling upon his name. By so doing we invoke the presence both of his providence, through which he watches over and guards our affairs, and of his power, through which he sustains us, weak as we are and well-nigh overcome, and of his goodness, through which he receives us, miserably burdened with sins, unto grace; and, in short, it is by prayer that we call him to reveal himself as wholly present to us.[55]

Bonaventure meditates on many divine attributes, but two are of particular importance for meditation on God. In *The Soul's Journey into God*, after meditation on nature and the soul, he moves to meditation on God through the divine attributes of God as Being and God as Good. Especially in his meditation on God as Being, Bonaventure reminds us that meditation on God also places us in the region of dissimilarity where God is beyond our ways of knowing. Bonaventure puts this incomprehensible aspect of prayer in metaphorical terms, using blindness and sight, darkness and light:

> Accustomed to the darkness of beings and images of the things of the senses, when it glimpses the light of the Supreme Being, [the soul] seems to itself to see nothing. It does not realize that this very darkness is the supreme illumination of our mind, just as when the eye sees pure light, it seems to itself to see nothing.[56]

Bonaventure's meditation on Being is influenced by what we have come to know as *apophatic prayer*, which focuses on God's unknowability and mystery beyond words, where "darkness is our illumination."

Gregory of Nyssa, in his *Life of Moses*, is generally given credit for giving outline to the first systematic treatment of God's transcendence "beyond" words and thoughts. As we have already noted, Dionysius the Areopagite produced the definitive model for apophatic prayer. Dionysius writes that God is "beyond all being and knowledge,"[57] but more importantly for prayer, such transcendence plunges us into dark silence:

> There is no speaking of [God], nor name nor knowledge of it. Darkness and light, error and truth—it is none of these. It is beyond assertion and denial. We make assertions and denials of what is next to it but never of it. . . . The fact is that the more we take flight upward, the more our words are confined to the ideas we are capable of forming; so that now as we plunge into that darkness which is beyond intellect, we shall find ourselves not simply running short of words but actually speechless and unknowing.[58]

Significantly, these same two explorers of the spiritual journey are also credited with giving form to the "mirror opposite" of negative or apophatic prayer: image or cataphatic prayer. In this more familiar form of prayer, meditation on God is focused on things that can in fact be known and sensed, usually through revelation in Scripture.

The significance of apophatic and cataphatic prayer as found in both Gregory and Dionysius is in the character of the divine nature that each assumes. As might be expected, the full flavor of meditation on God is available only in the juxtaposition of these two apparently paradoxical characteristics in prayer. Thus, the journey of meditation on God encounters God as both immanent and transcendent, both hidden and revealed, both in history and beyond history, both imaginable and unimaginable, both knowable and unknowable. Both journeys are needed; both are true representations of the presence (and absence) of God in prayer.

Patterns of Spiritual Development: Contemporary Insights

The more we know about human development, the more we understand and can practice prayer as a way of life. Contemporary work in patterns or stages of human and spiritual development give valuable insight into what we may be experiencing at various points in the journey of prayer. Work in the areas of psychological, social, and ethical development as well as in developmental aspects of spiritual formation and spiritual direction also lay the groundwork for discerning progress, development, and journey in prayer.[59]

In his book *Stages of Faith*, James Fowler speaks about the forces that form the pattern of our faith. In the spiritual journey, there are discernable patterns to the life of faith, patterns that shift and shape and re-form over the course of our life and that vary from person to person and culture to culture. Recent work in Christian development in areas as diverse as faith, spiritual direction, discernment, psychology, the social construction of knowledge and gender, and religious experience in general all bring light to the question of prayer and journey. New work focused on the relationship between theology and spirituality also inevitably raises the issue of prayer in Christian development. Questions raised by this work, as Fowler says, "help us to get in touch with the dynamic, patterned process by which we find life meaningful. They aim to help us reflect on the centers of value and power that sustain our lives."[60]

New work in Christian development and faith formation also help us to enter into centers of relationship, connection, intimacy, and transformation. Seen in this light, prayer and the spiritual journey thus address those things in life that have ultimate meaning, transcendent value, transformative power, relational coherence, and connections to community and tradition and that serve to return us to ourselves, to love of neighbor, and to God. Developmental patterns of this kind emphasize transitional or transformational spiritual growth rather than rigidly staged or stepped patterns. Work in the area of women's spirituality, women's ways of being and knowing, and the socially constructed patterns of the "seasons of a woman's life,"[61] as one popular writer has put it, has also awakened new and important implications for patterns and development in prayer.

Work focused on developmental patterns that integrate spirituality and psychology tends to explore the full range of human experience beginning in infancy (and often in prenatal experience) and tracing growth through childhood, adolescence, early adulthood, adulthood, and maturity. In this modern research, writing and practice are not so different from centuries of Christian spiritual wisdom. Both periods teach of the presence of God at every developmental stage and transitional point of life. Modern reflection is in many ways a new and robust flowering of the ancient art of recollection. We can see modern writing, practice, and reflection on developmental psychology as a sustained prayer of examen of consciousness. Recollection and recognition of our deepening awareness of self and world challenge us to find within ourselves a prayerful consciousness of God in every pattern of our life.

Elizabeth Liebert asks some fundamental questions of human development and spiritual patterns when she writes:

> One of the significant problems in understanding human development concerns accounting for both the sameness and differences in a person over time. Why is it that we do not disintegrate when enormous changes happen to us? On the other hand, why do we change at all?[62]

Liebert recognizes two major ways of answering these questions: (1) life-span developmental theories and (2) structural developmental theories. She endorses the second, especially the structural focus on transition and embeddedness over static or stepped stages, but she recognizes the value of the first as well.[63]

Life-span developmental theories as a model are most familiar through the research and extensive writing of Erik Erikson and his followers. Erikson "posited a development based on a series of life crises . . . [that] offers a substantial opportunity to set the stage anew for the future."[64] A successful resolution of a crisis prepares one for the next stage of development. Erikson suggests eight such seasons of the life cycle and the crisis an individual must face in each season. These include (1) infancy (the struggle centers around the establishment of basic trust versus mistrust); (2) early childhood (autonomy versus shame and doubt); (3) play age (initiative versus guilt); (4) school age (industry versus inferiority); (5) adolescence (ego identity versus role confusion); (6) young adulthood (intimacy versus isolation); (7) middle adulthood (generativity versus self-absorption and stagnation); and (8) old age (ego integrity versus despair). Erikson's model helps us to see and resolve life demands and tasks. In addition, he was able to incorporate the significant role culture plays in the process of human development. He has been criticized, however, for "abstracting" culture and thereby paying too little attention to postmodern concerns about cultural particularity, ethnicity, gender,[65] and plurality.

Structural development focuses on the individual within the "structure" of culture, social patterns, psychological stages, and spiritual development. The life-span model, driven by crisis and biology, generally posits that each phase or stage continues to occur whether we have successfully resolved the former stage or not. Concentrating on how and when we resolve these crises, this model formulates a ready-or-not structure in which we must meet the next phase and life trial as it develops. In contrast, the structure or web-of-influences model helps to answer a question that the life-span model does not: Why is it that we do not either disintegrate or metamorphose into different personalities as one developmental crisis after another confronts us? Joann Wolski Conn explains that

> from a structural perspective, development does not happen necessarily or inevitably. A next phase or stage may never happen. We can support or inhibit development, but we cannot directly make it happen. Our own experience, as well as research, surely verifies the fact that we cannot make ourselves grow into selves who are completely loving and full of self-knowledge and generosity. Development is a wonderfully complex process that involves much more than our own effort, although our cooperation is surely necessary.[66]

In an analogy that echoes Teresa of Avila's *Seven Mansions*, Elizabeth Liebert likens this structural approach to a tiered system of rice paddies constructed stepwise up a river bank. During a spring flood, water saturates one level before moving on to the next. As the water rises, each level of the rice paddy continues to be soaked and submerged. Similarly, in the structural model of human development, persons can be at different stages simultaneously or at different stages with respect to different issues. This, Liebert says, "compares to the gradual spread of the water all across one field before it rises to flood the next."[67]

Seminal figures in the evolution of the structural model include Jean Piaget, Lawrence Kohlberg, and William Perry. Piaget focused on how young children solve problems, developing a "genetic epistemology" revealing the development of the complexity of the thinking process. Kohlberg used Piaget's cognitive structural theories to investigate the genesis and development of moral reasoning. Perry added two important contributions. He showed that in young adults and college students there is a fundamental evolution of the structure of intellectual processes just as there was in young children. Perry also recognized an essential point of developmental research that is common to the "hard" sciences as well: "The research method greatly influences, even determines, the results attained."[68] An important implication of this insight is gender bias, first described by Carol Gilligan, "who succeeded in bringing to general awareness the gender bias that unconsciously permeated the theory building of most developmentals up to that time."[69]

In her own seminal and integrative book *Changing Life Patterns: Adult Development in Spiritual Direction,* Liebert develops a structural approach to development, especially interpersonal development as a function of the art of spiritual direction and prayer. She suggests three "patterns" of interpersonal styles related to the process of spiritual direction.[70] Each pattern has important implications for prayer.

Her first pattern is the "interpersonal style of a conformist person." Conformist persons feel trust, security, and safety within a group setting, a group that is "like me." A large, broad, and inclusive worldview is, understandably, developmentally beyond this person. Within the group, love, cheer, and "niceness" are apparent; outside the group is seen with malignant suspicion. The beginning of a transition from the conformist stage often involves a willingness to explore the implications of new and unruly emotions, a painful disorientation of one's worldview, or a deepening sense of the mystery of God as a transcendent value over God's authority alone.

Liebert's second pattern is the interpersonal style of a conscientious person, which allows a broadening and deepening of all relationships. The strengths of this stage include the emergence of adult conscience with concomitant abilities to grasp long-term, self-evaluated, self-chosen goals, and the reflexivity that accompanies a developed and differentiated life. Limitations include the possibility of losing one's moorings over the short term as a consequence of confronting a more relativistic world, and idiosyncratic self-centered confidence in one's own assessments and critical reflections. Virtues of the conscientious person include high moral standards, integrity, truthfulness, understanding, empathy, altruism, and humor.

A final pattern is the interpersonal style of inter-individual persons. This involves a growing sense of personal autonomy and a recognition that autonomy is mutual. It inevitably leads to interdependence in one's relationships and community. The strengths of this style include a vision and a commitment beyond the self, while the self is yet an integrated and valued component of the vision, increased tolerance for the autonomy of others, and recognition of possibilities for integrating one's own unconscious self and God. The weakness of this stage is the inability to change structures and institutions according to one's own values. The virtues of the inter-individual stage include increasing intimacy with self, God, and others, a sense of cocreation with God, a commitment to social concerns unrestricted by the boundaries of one's own social group, integrity resulting from enhanced continuity between inner life and outer actions, and moral principles and behavior.

In a much more detailed account, Liebert compares her "stages of ego development" to Steven Ivy's stages of "spiritual consciousness."[71]

Ivy's stages are based on the work of James Fowler and Robert Kegan. In a table comparing the two stages, Liebert suggests both assessment strategies and stage-specific suggestions for pastoral care for each stage. The suggestions can also serve as guides to the content or type of prayer appropriate to each stage. Stage-specific prayers for all levels of ego development and spiritual consciousness, while not always immediately obvious, can be imagined, created, developed, and practiced based on ego needs, "embeddedness in cultures," and forms of symbolic expression for each level. Careful evaluation and assessment of a person's stage of development will greatly help the process of ascertaining appropriate prayers and prayer styles. Forms of prayer outside a given stage may aid in the process of transition from one stage to another or in allowing the pray-er to gain insight into self-other perspectives of another stage.

As in any structural theory of human development, correlating prayer to a kind of psychologically based development scheme has both advantages and disadvantages. Advantages include insight into appropriate types of prayer for a given time in an individual's life or for a given personal or group personality type. A disadvantage is that spiritual direction and pastoral counseling are not the same thing as prayer. Theory is never the same thing as prayer, especially if theory is divorced from a comprehensive way of life. Spiritual directors and counselors need to be familiar with life patterns and the guidance or therapy appropriate to those patterns. Good spiritual direction can lead a person, for instance, from a form of humility that is destructive, false, and often simply a mask for anger and resentment to true humility grounded (etymologically humility is from *humus*, literally, grounded in the earth or soil) in self-knowledge and awareness, compassion for others, and love of God. Prayer includes these as well; it flows most freely from the ground of our true self. But it is also our response to God and God's response and call to us.

At this point, the direct comparison between human development and prayer may begin to break down. Prayer needs to grow out of the soil of our true self, and so it is a child of our personality, temperament, and stage of development. But prayer is also God's relation and presence to us. As such, it is possible that prayer may also crumble, scramble, or break down developmental structures, stages, patterns, and transitions. Confession, for example, is at its core a petition for change. Such prayer is a confession of our brokenness that simultaneously recognizes our need for healing.

However one interprets the relationship between change or development and prayer, these contemporary patterns of Christian development give added dimension to the process of spiritual journey. Developmental patterns are, as we have said, themselves extended prayers of recollection. To become aware of the structural dynamics of transformation is to enter into prayerful recollection of our own interior and social self as we are being reconstituted psychologically, culturally, institutionally, and ethically. Our patterns of development then become a way of life that teaches us how to pray as they simultaneously lend insight into the precious care of souls.

Progress in Prayer

What are we to make of the fact that there are patterns to our spiritual journey, and yet the beginning, middle, and end can display such variation? We are called to a life of holiness and sanctification. In 2 Corinthians, Paul writes that we journey "from one degree of glory to another" (3:18). Apparently, according to Paul, the Christian life is a life of change.

But do we make progress as we change, and in particular, do we progress through various levels of understanding, consciousness, or compassion as we grow in prayer? The question is of importance because if we do make progress, we are faced with two important potential consequences. If we make progress in prayer, then some individuals and communities ought to be able to serve as mentors and guides to those beginning in prayer or moving through periods of dryness and frustration in prayer. This is certainly beneficial and good. On the other hand, if we journey into deeper realities of prayer, there is always a danger of spiritual elitism. This is not beneficial, especially when it results in marginalizing individuals, groups, or certain kinds of prayer. It also is not beneficial in that, even if it is true that we make progress in prayer, the nature of prayer and the ways in which God chooses to act in our lives are such that the simplest prayer can prove to be the most profound; the last can become the first in the blink of an eye. Given these cautions, however, even potential misunderstandings can be mitigated if prayer is practiced with humility, hospitality, and compassion.

One contemporary writer is certain that there is movement and progress in prayer:

> The way of prayer is a way of progress: progress to and in God; progress in holiness; progress towards the Kingdom; progress in communion, and in penitence; progress through conflict. Prayer is like the church, it is always on the move.[72]

Most of the writers we have encountered have acknowledged that through grace we make progress in the journey of prayer, we experience added dimension and value in our life, and we progress in holiness as we develop in our practice of and understanding of prayer. Awareness of the deep mystery of God is often cited as a first recognizable step in progress. This mystery is sometimes a "fear of God," though it is not a kind of fear that debilitates, lessens the self, or induces shame and guilt. It is holy fear, the acknowledgment of mystery and wonder and awe of God and the world God has created.

Self-knowledge, in the sense of knowledge of true self and knowledge of our true self in relation to God, is often proposed as a second transition point in prayer. Kenneth Leech cites the German fourteenth-century mystic Johann Tauler on the essential dimension of self-understanding in prayer:

> I will tell you the shortest way, the most direct: enter your own depths, find out what it is that most hinders your own progress, and keeps you back. Retire within yourselves for the Kingdom of God is within you. . . . Go back into yourself, enter into yourself, with the knowledge of who you are.

Leech himself continues:

> Self-knowledge and proper self-esteem go together. We must know ourselves in order to love ourselves, yet love itself precedes knowledge and makes it possible. Self-contempt and self-negation will prevent self-knowledge. You do not want to know someone you despise, even if that someone is yourself.[73]

The journey of spiritual progress also draws us toward love of God, which can take many forms. Progress in self-knowledge leads to a detachment, or *apatheia,* in which the turmoil caused by uncontrolled passions is brought under control so that we can obey and love God and work for justice in the world. In the hands of the Greek Stoic philosophers, *apatheia* is detachment from the world. It is a virtue but one that disengages us from action. In the Christian tradition, *apatheia* is practice or prayer in which our normal appetites and thoughts still exist (it is really impossible for them not to exist), but they do not agitate or disturb us. Not being agitated or disturbed leads in turn to purity of heart, leading in turn once again to the constant end point of Christian prayer: love of God and love of neighbor. Other indicators of progress in prayer include what we might call "dispositions" rather than virtues per se: attention, focus, centering, stability of mind, solitude, the practice of fasting, the discipline of listening, contrition, gratitude, thanksgiving, and joy.

Diogenes Allen combines progress in *apatheia* with progress in moving from fear to love of God, using the patristic writer Cassian:

Over the course of our spiritual journey, our motives for undertaking it become increasingly pure. In his eleventh *Conference* Cassian recognizes that many of us are initially moved by a fear of hell and think of God solely in terms of God's power. Such a fear is called *attrition*. Attrition is spiritual sterility—unlike *contrition*, where our fear stems from our belief in God's justice and is accompanied by a hope for mercy and forgiveness. . . . As we progress in our journey, we may obey God increasingly out of attraction rather than fear.[74]

Richard of St. Victor provides an excellent example of the progress of the soul in prayer through transition from fear to attraction to God, or as Paul wrote, "from one degree of glory to another" (2 Cor. 3:18). He develops what Grover Zinn has called a detailed and rich "personification allegory" in which Jacob; Rachel and Leah, his wives; their handmaids, Bilhah and Zilpah; and their children each represent progress in prayer.[75] Each group represents successive, sequential stages of prayer leading toward deeper levels of contemplation and action. The children of Leah are virtues that discipline the will; those of Bilhah govern thought; Zilpah's children control deeds; and Rachel's represent a life of asceticism and signify contemplation. The children are meant to represent the twelve stages of the spiritual life, each forming a map of the spiritual journey, an outline of the soul, a transitional stage, and a new form of prayer. As outlined by Richard, progress is apparent as each stage helps us listen more clearly to God in our heart and mind.[76]

To make progress in prayer is also to begin to recognize the goodness of God's creation, the beauty of creation, and the attractiveness of God's design, even apart from its necessary use. Spiritual progress among the fourth- to sixth-century desert fathers and mothers, masters of prayer and the trials and joys of the spiritual journey, is especially illuminating with regard to the integration of mind, body, spirit, and creation. In general, according to the desert fathers and mothers, we move from obedience to God based on fear to obedience to God based on love. This love translates into love of true self in a positive sense, love of God, and love of neighbor. The journey may take us into solitude as a means of deepening our relationship with God, but that relationship is always exemplified, evaluated, and verified through compassionate love for others.[77]

At various times in its history, the church has been accused of teaching that the soul or spiritual aspects of our personhood are exemplary and supersede in importance the value of the body. This could not be farther from the truth. John Calvin, for instance, was an unrelenting advocate of the goodness of God's creation in all its forms. Calvin wrote that God created food not only to keep us alive but also to give "delight and good cheer." He created clothes for "comeliness" as well as warmth

Used by permission of Alain Briot, Baux Arts Photography.

Plains Cottonwood

and decency. "Did he not, then, render many things attractive to us, apart from their necessary use'"?[78]

Is there progress in prayer? Certainly, there is progress. We journey ever deeper into God as we move more fully into prayer as a way of life. But finally, it is more important what we do with prayer—and what prayer does with us—than how we measure it. Does prayer lead to compassion or to elitism? Does it enhance conversation, relationship, transformation, and a sense of God's presence? Does it connect us to God's good creation, or does it isolate us from God, ourselves, and others? Does progress in prayer prod us into the healthy dispositions or healthy disciplines of the spiritual life?

Progress, as T. S. Eliot suggests, may be arriving where we started and seeing it anew as for the first time. It may result in a concentric spreading out in touching others or a concentric deepening within of the sense of God's presence. It may be a long and hard depression or dark night before a single small step of insight. It may be a single contact with mystery, humbling in its ability to prick our mind and heart, exhilarating in that it prompts us to see what we have not fully seen in the past, and freeing in that it encourages us to travel ever deeper into that divine mystery that at its source reveals ever-new secrets both hidden and afire with degrees of splendor.

Progress? Only time and the many branches of journey in prayer will tell. Finally, perhaps what really matters is the moment: Does the prayer of the moment love the neighbor of the moment as God's love directs the moment?

Conclusion

Our journeys in prayer are as varied and as variable as the branches of a leafless plains cottonwood (*Populus deltoids*) at Zion National Park. The branches spread in every direction, showing both ancient, plodding growth and new, energetic shoots just beginning to search the world around the tree. This chapter explored prayer as a journey in growth toward God. For some, the path of prayer runs straight and true for many years with but slight bends or changes. For others, prayer grows straight and strong, then seems to break off and die, only to branch out yet once again, probing and tentative but alive. For still others, prayer is a series of new and creative directions, fresh occasions, patient longings. Some branches could support a community; others would bend under the weight of a sparrow. Some are intimately entwined in a kind of interdependent harmony; others take a more solitary route. These bare branches give us a chance to see both earth and sky, those elements that the tree of life seeks out for nourishment and brings together as mutually enhancing ecologies. In the spring, new leaves will shelter transformations of growth and in their lushness will present a special invitation to linger in their shade.

Our lives of prayer are journeys that spread out over time like the many branches of this cottonwood. The roots of our prayers provide a stage of ongoing conversation, often hidden, but somehow constant, necessary, and nurturing. The cottonwood is given life and stability by the roots hidden beneath the surface. The trunk binds branches and roots together. Wherever the roots creep and tangle in search of nourishment and however the branches reach out, twist, and gnarl, they are connected to the solid trunk. Conversation and journey begin in relationship, return to relationship, and extend outward once again from relationship. Our journeys in prayer are many branches in one fine tree.

5

Prayer as Transformation

The New Leaves of Prayer

Has prayer transported him for a few short moments into spiritual ecstasy that vanishes when everyday life returns, or has it lodged the Word of God so soberly and so deeply in his heart that it holds and strengthens him all day, impelling him to active love, to obedience, to good works? Only the day will tell.

Dietrich Bonhoeffer, Life Together

Transformative Awakening: The Temple of Prayer

The word *contemplation* comes from the Latin *cum,* meaning with or within, and *templum,* meaning originally a space in the heavens marked off for augural observation or signs. Later, *templum* came to mean any open, sacred space or place of worship or temple. To contemplate is thus simply to be with or within a sacred space or temple.

As we dwell in this "temple" of prayer, we realize something rather odd: After a time, we begin to notice that we are conscious, that we are awake. More than that, we begin to see that we have been awake for some time, often without having known it. Our mornings often start like this. We get out of bed and shuffle off to our routines while our consciousness of "being conscious" only slowly begins to dawn. Something similar happens in the temple of prayer. The more we pray, the more we become conscious that we were, in a real sense, asleep to our true self and the true promptings of God (a first phase in prayer). The more we pray, the more we find that a rising consciousness begins to assert itself that we are newly awake (a second phase in prayer). This is transformation born in the temple of prayer. To paraphrase Paul, in the temple of prayer, we are being transformed from one degree of awakening to another.

St. John of the Cross, in another of his beautifully poetic renderings of the spiritual life, writes of awakening to a world transformed by this dwelling in the temple of prayer:

> This awakening is a movement of the Word in the substance of the soul, containing such grandeur, dominion, and glory, and intimate sweetness that it seems to the soul that all the balsams and fragrant spices and flowers of the world are commingled, stirred, and shaken so as to yield their sweet odor, and that all the kingdoms and dominions of the world and all the powers and virtues of heaven are moved; and not only this, but it also seems that all the virtues and substances and perfections and graces of every created thing glow and make the same movement all at once.[1]

If transformation does not precede awakening, at least, according to John of the Cross, they are overlapping dimensions. As we are transformed in the temple of prayer, we come to see that we are awake. What we see upon awakening is that we have changed. The steps and stages of transformation, just as in prayer as journey, are thus not static. More often than not, throughout our lives, we are changing and altering in any given situation in ways that, as Bonhoeffer reminds us in the opening to this chapter, only the unfolding of the day will tell.

Levels or degrees of prayer are, as Gerald May has written, not intended in writers such as Teresa of Avila "to be understood as occurring in a strictly linear way."[2] Teresa herself writes that in certain forms of prayer "the soul is, as it were, occupied in the active and in the contemplative life at one and the same time."[3] May concludes a study of Teresa and John of the Cross by saying, "I have taken pains to emphasize that the degrees or kinds of prayer Teresa and John describe are not steady states and that they do not necessarily occur in a stepwise progression. They are, instead, experiences that people encounter at different times in the course of prayer."[4]

We can say, then, that prayer, transformation, and awakening are overlapping dimensions of our relationship with God. They are not to be understood in a strictly linear way. They are Martha and Mary at the same time. They are experiences people encounter at different times in the course of their lives. Realizing we are awake itself transforms how we see and know and participate in the world. This, in turn, awakens us once again to new ways of being and fresh transformations. The awakening Martha and the transforming Mary both, simultaneously, serve the Lord.

The overlapping dimensions of awakening and transformation are rooted in Christian prayer traditions. The story of the two disciples on the road to Emmaus is a story of such overlapping dimensions. Before they "see" (Luke 24:31), Jesus "illuminates" them concerning all that was said about him in the Scriptures (24:27). Though they do not yet "see," they are "transformed" in that, out of new compassion, they offer Jesus a place to stay for the night (24:29). After Jesus breaks bread and they do finally "see," they realize that even before they had been thus awakened they were being transformed, for even on the road their hearts were burning within them (24:32). In prayer, awakening and transformation likewise are mutually enhancing. Prayer is *going* somewhere, *from* somewhere, *to* somewhere. As prayer develops, it requires the seed of awakening as well as the many leaves of transformation. As Tom Harpur writes, "Prayer is ultimately about growing into an intimate relationship with the One in whose image we have been created. It is about enlightenment, about finally awakening to who we really are and to our total unity with God, with other living beings, and with the seemingly inanimate parts of the cosmos as well—the sky, the seas, lakes, rivers, mountains, and winds."[5]

The model of transformation begins to illustrate the organic unity of all the models, the tree of life in its completeness. Transformation is conversation, it is a journey, it is relationship, and as we explore in the next chapter, it is participation in the esteeming love of the divine presence. But with regard to transformation in prayer, major questions arise: Who is in control? Who is transforming whom, and how? Is God alone the agent of transformation, or do we aid in shaping transformation through receptivity, discipline, and practice? As we look at both contemporary writers and writers from the Christian spiritual tradition as a whole, we see a wide range of answers to these questions. Some teach of divine initiative and human response. Divine initiative can take many forms, and human response as well can range from harsh ascetical practices of quietism or resignation to more gentle practices of receptivity to God's will and presence. Others suggest that transformation through prayer is the process and the result of a more simultaneous participation between God and humanity.

True prayer is constant awakening to God's presence. Each awakening is a new transformation. It is impossible to pray today as we prayed yesterday, even if nothing has changed. Even the "Our Father," each time it is prayed, is never the same. The balance point between God's initiative is mystery wrapped in reciprocity and mutual enhancement. Yes, we cede all transformative power to God. Yes, we can receive the grace of transformation. As we explore the transformative temple of prayer, we give thanks for awakening, praise God for the gift of prayer, and in transformation find new expression for the privilege of adoration.

Transformation: Effort and Consent

Thomas Keating has written that "the chief act of the will is not effort but consent. The secret of getting through the difficulties of contemplative prayer is to accept them."[6] After praying so hard that he is said to have sweated blood, Jesus walked out of the Garden of Gethsemane with a deep sense of consent to God's will. Something similar happens to us in prayer. Through the efforts of our prayers, a kind of progressive understanding occurs in which we gradually consent to the reality of our adoption by God.

The tradition also states the concept of consent in another way, that of detachment, letting go of control. We lose our life in order to gain it. For example, if after working through the stages of grief we are able to abandon the grip that grief had over us, an uncanny transformation begins to take place in which we consent to recognize and tend to the crisis, loss, and grief we see in others. Divine initiative in the transformative nature of prayer is, of course, always out of our control. But the very practice of prayer is in itself recognition of God's initiative and our consent. Transformation in fact may be thought of as opening and enlarging our capacity to consent to God and his world. Throughout the centuries, Christian writers have suggested methods and practices that help us be receptive in our response to God, thereby being receptive in our response to others as well as ourselves.

The concept and practices of asceticism were often borrowed from early Greek philosophy and reconfigured by early Christian writers. The spiritual exercises that resulted were designed not only for moral value but, as Pierre Hadot writes, "the transformation of our vision of the world, and the metamorphosis of our being."[7] By incorporating but moving beyond the Greek use of the exercises for their simple ethical value, these early writers considered them to be a way of being that would ease the process of transformation in prayer from our control to God's. A brief look at the structure, content, and vocabulary of early Christian ascetical practice will help shed light on the divine/human relationship in prayers of transformation.

Asceticism in the modern sense is different from that of the early Christian tradition. Rather than complete abstinence and world-denying lifestyle, asceticism, or *askēsis,* denotes those practices of exercise and training that are life affirming, having as their goal transformation of our vision and metamorphosis of our being. Early Christian exercises were *paideia,* meaning education that "teaches us to conduct ourselves so that we may resemble God, and to accept the divine plan as the guiding principle of all our education."[8] This, of course, was a philosophy leading to exercises intended to help us follow in the way of Christ.

As discussed above, one must be awake in order for transformation of consciousness to occur at all. The fundamental attitudes arising from *paideia* are wakefulness and attentiveness (*prosochē*). The person who is awake is always perfectly conscious not only of what he or she *does* but also of what he or she *is.* In other words, a person is aware of his or her place in the universe and his or her relationship with God. Being thus watchful (*nēphalios*) is itself a transformation of consciousness that in turn heightens the soul's awareness of the balance of grace and work in prayer. Thus, attention to oneself awakens the rational, spiritual, and imaginative principles of contemplation and action that God has placed in the soul. Such an awakening naturally leads to *apatheia,* or detachment, essential to letting go of what is not truly important in contemplative prayer.

Letting go in prayer seems to be a kind of paradox, and in many ways it is. It is a way of being that provides training (*paideia*), shaping, forming, and educating the body, mind, and spirit to attentive awakening and watchfulness of the self so that the soul can enter a way of being that allows detachment and letting go (*apatheia*). The soul, in effect, awakens, looks within, finds its attention drawn from itself, and then loses itself to find itself in God. The soul remembers itself in order to remember God. By paying attention to self with continuous concentration on the present moment, one maintains attention to the present, control of one's thoughts, and acceptance of the divine will. Vigilant watchfulness of the heart instills a "remembrance of God" that centers contemplation and remembers all transformations as originating in a God who wants conversation and relationship to be present and to transform.

Attentive awakening implies self-mastery in the sense of control over distraction, dispersion, and dissipation of the soul. It is "remembrance" that was formulated in many ways within the Christian tradition, including the prayer of recollection, meditation on death and birth, and contemplation on the life of Christ. The desert father Dorotheus of Gaza advises examination and remembrance as a way of enhancing vigilant watchfulness and detachment:

We ought not only to examine ourselves every day but also every season, every month, and every week, and ask ourselves: "What stage am I at now with regards to the passion by which I was overcome last week?" Similarly every year: "Last year I was overcome by such and such a passion. What about now?" The Fathers have told us how useful it is for each of us to purify himself in turn, by examining, every evening, how we have spent the day, and every morning, how we have spent the night.[9]

The remembrance of God is the very essence of attentive awakening. In it, a balance is struck between the contemplative and God that can lead to moral and existential transformation. The link between divine initiative and human response becomes a reciprocating bond. As repentance and conversion turn us toward a God who first turns to us, so our sleeping soul can awaken to God only as God awakens us. Letting go in the temple of prayer to let God transform us is a kind of dance. We enter ourselves to find the transforming presence of God very near. God and the depth of the human soul can participate in this dance only as prayer becomes a way of life and being.

This way of life and being has its roots in Scripture as well. Attentive awakening was transformed into the watch of the heart under the influence of Proverbs 4:23: "Above all else, guard your heart" (NIV). Remembrance and the examination of one's conscience and consciousness found justification in 2 Corinthians 13:5: "Examine yourselves. . . . Test yourselves." Meditation on death as a way to be present to God in life was recommended on the basis of 1 Corinthians 15:31. It is also possible to imagine that Jesus, while praying in the Garden of Gethsemane, was engaged in many of these ascetical practices: wakefulness, watchfulness, attentiveness, shaping by God's will, remembering his ministry to that date, and being so present to God that Jesus understood God's will without it being spoken.

In the early Protestant period, the Lutheran doctrine of the sinfulness of human nature and justification by faith alone tended to undermine the theological foundations of the ascetical writers and practices. In many ways, theirs was a response to an overemphasis on practice to the neglect of grace. Other periods in spiritual history have gone the opposite direction, emphasizing grace to the neglect of practice. But not all the Reformers were of the same mind. Though sharing Luther's doctrinal underpinnings, Calvin, for instance, maintained a piety that more than allowed for continuance of many of these practices, especially in the context of prayer. In his "Rules of Right Prayer" in the *Institutes*, Calvin thus lists "devout detachment required for conversation with God; that we be properly disposed in mind and heart"; that we guard "against undisciplined and irreverent prayer," that we be "freed from earthly cares and affections," and that "we apply our minds and hearts zealously to prayer"; that "we pray with a sincere sense of want, and with penitence"; that prayer is not dependent on a passing mood, and that we should be constant in prayer since "the more harshly troubles, discomforts, fears, and trials of other sorts press us, the freer is our access to him, as if God were summoning us to himself"; and that we "yield all confidence in ourselves."[10] It is clear that Calvin maintains the necessity of discipline and piety as essential to the true practice of prayer. Humanity and God work in concert in the most fundamental ways. Since the time of the Reformation, the ascetical ideal has been upheld in various ways. It is currently enjoying a new revival as men and women begin to realize the life-affirming and life-transforming capacities of the spiritual disciplines.

With regard, then, to our consent or lack of it in transformation within the temple of prayer, we must acknowledge that we cede all control to God, and yet we can help to shape our growth in prayer through discipline and practice. Chapter 6 discusses some contemporary writers who suggest a simultaneous participation between God and the person at prayer. But even here in transformation, and looking mostly at the wisdom of writers from the Christian spiritual tradition, God initiates, and we turn to God in faith. The rest is a mysterious balance of reciprocity and mutual enhancement.

Divine Will and Human Desire

Lectio divina, the ancient practice of praying Scripture, intentionally moves from a model of information to a model of transformation. Speaking in another context about revelation, Avery Dulles defines new awareness or transformation as "a transcendent fulfillment of the inner drive of the human spirit toward fuller consciousness . . . an experience of participation in divine life."[11] Paul sees the life of those who are in Christ as a life of transformation: "If anyone is in Christ, there is a new creation: everything old has passed away; see, everything has become new!" (2 Cor. 5:17). Prayer places us directly into this living stream in which the Lord of glory is transforming us from one degree of glory to another (2 Cor. 3:18).

We have been imagining prayer as a tree of life. Trees grow variously as a rule of drought, fire, disease, pollution, and floods. Deforestation shapes, forms, and sometimes even ends the process of their growth. But within their ecosystem, their connection to organic and inorganic elements of the environment signals their potential for renewal. They sprout gingerly from seeds; inevitably, they die. At other times, they thrive for centuries, transforming as they grow. A gentle rain of God's grace—to alter just slightly Teresa of Avila's beautiful metaphor of four degrees of prayer—waters the tree of life generously and thoroughly. The tree's thirst is slacked as it receives the rain of grace, and the roots of conversational prayer send the nourishing moisture up the trunk of relational prayer, along the branches of our journey of prayer, into the leaves of transforming prayer, feeding the flowers and fruits of prayer of divine presence. All the while the tree grows and is transformed.

Each part of the tree of life changes through degrees of security, loss, grief, sin, hope, faith, and love. But the leaves—in spring, summer, fall, winter—present the leitmotif of transformation. A single leaf is unique in all its parts, yet each leaf is connected and essential to the life of the whole tree. Each leaf is defined as much by the positive shape and space it occupies as by the negative space surrounding the leaf. In transformation, as with the leaves of the tree of life, we are defined in shape and function by our connection to the tree and the sustaining environment. Is it any wonder that our prayers take such unique patterns as well?

All transformation in prayer is dependent on the water of divine grace, God's initiative. All of us, says Paul, are being transformed. Paul puts this in the passive voice. We are "being transformed" by God. Yet in the mystery of transformational prayer, a mystery best described in metaphor, symbol, paradox, and story, our response to grace is equally important in the equation of transformative prayer. How we respond is a matter of discernment, and to discern God's will is often contingent on sorting out our own desires. Desires properly ordered are the best means we have to assess God's will. God places his will in our heart. We sense God's will and come to know it as a deep and abiding desire of our heart.

How precisely to state the relationship and balance between what is essentially God's grace and our work is not easy. With regard to prayer, how one defines the symmetry between grace and practice (or works and desire) is just as difficult. Most classic and some contemporary writers try, in one way or another, to strike a balance, perhaps the clearest distillation of which is divine initiative and human response. Teresa of Avila's example of watering a garden presents a metaphor that, in addition to illustrating types of prayer, also portrays four possible relationships between divine initiative and human response. Even though Teresa writes a delicate and experienced account, none of the four strikes the perfect balance. It is common to interpret classic writers on prayer and contemplation as either too passive (too strong on the side of grace) or too practice oriented (too strong on our work in prayer at the expense of God's gift of transforming grace). Given the "human" equation based on a "divine" formula, this should not be surprising.

Every explanation of how transformation occurs includes the essential human quality of desire. Our foundational desire for transformation, as it echoes through the tradition, is grounded in our desire for God. In the first paragraph of his autobiography, Augustine gives what is no doubt the most well-known formulation of our desire for God, a desire that leads eventually to transformed consciousness and prayer. Augustine's discussion of desire is formulated in this context of praise and peace:

> Can any praise be worthy of the Lord's majesty? How magnificent his strength! How inscrutable his wisdom! Humanity is one of your creatures, Lord, and our instinct is to praise you. We bear about ourselves the mark of death, the sign of our own sin, to remind us that you thwart the proud. But still, since we are a part of your creation, we wish to praise you. The thought of you stirs us so deeply that we cannot be content unless we praise you, because you made us for yourself and our hearts find no peace till they find peace in you.[12]

To paraphrase the contemporary writer on prayer and spirituality, Ronald Rolheiser, prayer and transformation concern what we do with desire.[13] That God-given inner drive toward holiness, peace, rest, relationship, and transformation is rooted in all of us, a desire placed in us by God. It is a desire not unlike that which drives the seed to become a tree of life.

As we look at the leaves of the tree of life, we see the mystery of transformation in prayer as an ever-deepening integration and union of God's will and human desire. This reflects the integration of Augustine's realization that we will find no peace until we find peace in God. It reflects as well Jesus' promise that the kingdom of God is within. It is evidenced in the virtues of compassion, charity, and justice and fed by the spring of divine grace. All these integrations express the mystery of divine will and human desire in transformation.

Separation, Liminality, and Reintegration

Victor Turner suggests in his work on pilgrimage and rites of passage that Christian transformation in prayer is often a threefold pattern of human transformation. Turner's pattern is a helpful template for understanding both the relationship between human desire and divine will and the anthropological shift explored below. The three stages are (1) separation from one's ordinary life routine; (2) liminality, which is entry into and dwelling in a sphere of uncertainty, ambiguity, and unpredictability; and (3) reintegration leading to the discovery of a new configuration and meaning for one's life.[14]

According to Turner, transformation begins with a ritual act of pilgrimage "in which there is a necessary separation from the dominant structures of a given society." There is a necessary dimension of pilgrimage in every experience of leaving the home one has known, and the movement from home to the world mirrors the significance of the emerging and "critical inner journey."[15]

The second stage, or liminality, comes from the Latin word *limen*, meaning threshold. Belden Lane writes that liminality

> locates the pilgrim in a state and process of mid-transition. Having been launched on pilgrimage, the initiate finds themselves "betwixt and between," passing through a doorway from a former structured life to a new pattern of being. In this transitional state, all sorts of alternative selves can be imagined.[16]

In the liminal period, we are free to "play" with prayer in a new way. Though often fraught with uncertainty, liminality is also a time that invites playful questions, new answers, and alternative selves. It is a time that can include periods of painful doubts, deep struggle with faith, and sharp questions concerning God's active presence in the world. But all these possibilities are important junctures in the pilgrim's quest for true identity and integrity. With its enticements of freedom from commitment and the ability to imagine and enact alternative selves, there is a temptation to remain in this liminal state. Exploring liminality in all its various guises can be beguiling. Yet the freedoms of this liminal state are eventually experienced as ephemeral and not ultimately satisfying or self-transcending.

Turner's final state, that of reintegration, eventually begins to beckon from the midst of liminality. Even in the cacophony of alternative selves, a still small voice rings clear. Reintegration then occurs at a higher level with a lifestyle more concurrent with the Beatitudes than with secular, consumerist values. The transformation is in no way complete: It is a life process. But in a sense, the pilgrim arrives at a new home with a renewed appreciation of self; the power of place, God, and others; and perhaps a sacramental sense of the simplicity, holiness, and goodness of all things.

These stages are not discrete; they tend to overlap more than they follow one another in sequential order. There is always a sense in which we are "in a space between" in relation to prayer; we are seldom home or stable. Certainly, peace and a certain amount of tranquility are primary characteristics, even necessities, of prayer, yet transformation and reintegration separate us from what is most comfortable, which in turn restarts Turner's cycle.

This is an appropriate place to introduce the important concept of stability and its relationship to transformation. To this point, we have focused on the transformation that prayer brings, how prayer shapes and changes us. But as with Turner's period of reintegration, an important corollary to transformation is stability and place. Place, space, and geography affect prayer. In the midst of change, stability is an important component of transformation: Even though our prayer today is not yesterday's prayer, there is something essential about us and about God that lends continuity and stability even to transformation. Stability, in fact, is one of the conditions St. Benedict saw as essential to the proper regulation of the Christian monastic life. It is a central theme of his rule. By a vow or a promise of stability, the monks took upon themselves the obligation of remaining within the physical boundaries of the monastery that had accepted their professions of religious commitment. Such stability was to effect community well-being as well as prayer.

Stability implies stasis; transformation implies change. Are these then incompatible? The answer, with regard to the temple of prayer, is certainly no. Stability provides a sense of home, which is soil for growth and change. Transformation provides the wisdom to see growth as stabilizing crisis. Both are necessary. We have recourse once again to the tree of life: roots (stability) are as necessary as the leaves (transformation). Stability provides the environment and the nurture in the midst of which our prayer can continue to change and grow.

Christ: The Media of Transforming Prayer

The Catholic theologian Hans Urs von Balthasar suggests a way of understanding the temple of prayer as transformation through Christ. According to von Balthasar, there are three media through which Christ transforms the world. These include (1) life itself, (2) new life in Christ, and (3) the church. Each medium and the transformations Christ works within it have corresponding and appropriate types of prayer, meditation, and contemplation.

In the first medium, God's Word in Christ transforms normal human existence between life and death. In this dimension, the possibilities are limited only by the vast range of transformational qualities and journeys of life itself. Here meditation and contemplation on the life of Jesus are the perfect forms of prayer for interpreting meaning and engaging in the drama of God's transforming work in our life. Von Balthasar writes that in the life of Jesus "scene by scene as each stage of [his] life unfolds, [the contemplative] is shown the meaning of life as God sees it and desires us to see it."[17] In this first medium, "the person at prayer need only let himself be carried from one picture [of Jesus in the Gospels] to the next: in the humanity which [the pray-er] encounters in each picture he will see a revelation of eternal, triune love."[18] In other words, in the richness of Christ's life rests an eternal, interpretive mirror that, in prayer, can reflect and guide our own life. Von Balthasar sums up this first medium by commenting on the inexhaustible nature of Christ's story within the Gospels:

> Anyone at all versed in contemplation will surely have had this experience. Every gospel scene seems new and fresh each day; it does not seem threatened by the dust, pallor and obsolescence of history. Every day the eyes of faith witness the miracle: the gospel is the only factor within history which is superior to the laws of history. "Heaven and earth may pass away; but my words will never pass away."[19]

The Christ who comes to be present with us also returns to God. Without revoking the incarnation, Jesus Christ rises from the dead and returns to God. This is the second medium, that of history and time. This second medium of transformation, from the old to the new, from death to new life, is "so radical that the One being transformed cannot in any way control the process himself: he must let it be accomplished in him by the omnipotent Father."[20] Through the second model of contemplation, we thus learn that there are certain things we can do in prayer, but ultimately, we do not control the process. Death transformed through resurrection signals that the contemplative can only let go of life, wait, be still, and know that God is God. Through the medium of Christ's transformation of death, we learn that only in dying are we reborn. Translated into prayer, this means that we accept the darkness of death for the promise of the light of new life.

Von Balthasar's third medium is contingent on the first two. In this medium, "through the Holy Spirit, heaven causes Christ's fullness of transformation to be 'distributed' and poured out into history in the immeasurable richness of the Church." It is in this dimension that the contemplative "finds the church as the medium designed and prepared to exhibit and develop the fullness of Christ through all the ages, to the end of the world and beyond, into eternity."[21] It is only in this third dimension of transformation that the church opens all the doors of contemplation. Here the contemplative confronts the unique and ecclesial truth of Christ. The community contemplates as the bride of Christ and is transformed into the image and likeness of God.

Within each of the three media, von Balthasar finds corresponding interdependent forms. The medium of "being" corresponds to the first medium of life itself; the medium of "knowledge" corresponds to new life or new awareness; the medium of "love" corresponds to the church. Thus, through these media, prayer transforms all that we are: being, mind, and heart. The greatest of these, love born of the heart, is communicated by the Holy Spirit and is the last of Christ's transformations poured out for the church. Here von Balthasar echoes the images and revelations of the Christian prayer tradition, especially the relationship in prayer between love and transformation.

Love necessarily flows from contemplation. If the contemplation is of Christ's transformation, then the eyes of contemplation see the light of love. Von Balthasar concludes that the church provides the core and source of that love. In it, our contemplation will be boundless; we will discover that no "higher studies" are needed. According to von Balthasar, as we pray, we enter into the various dimensions of love. Our engrafting into the risen Lord and the church function as formational guides in prayer. They water and nourish the tree of life; their sustenance functions continuously as the organic basis for the cycling new leaves of transformation.

The Potency of Disorder

Honest prayer changes. This is true in both senses: Over time we change the ways we pray, and over time prayer changes us. Conversation, journey, relationship, presence—all these models of prayer are transformative. Spiritual disciplines of any kind, especially prayer, undertaken in the context of faith, change us. At times, however, our moments of transformation bring us into crisis.

In the latter portion of the twentieth century, a number of developmental theorists, in describing human growth and transformation, pointed to the potency of crisis. Writers such as Piaget, Kohlberg, Loevinger, Erikson, Maslow, and Fowler mapped the transformational dynamics of cognitive, moral, social, psychosocial, self-actualization, and faith developmental patterns respectively. One contemporary writer concludes, "By and large, these theorists suggested that life is made up of a succession of stages characterized by relative stability which are succeeded by periods of crisis."[22] Growth is thus often a consequence of grief or loss, and all these researchers "would agree that growth is more likely to occur during periods of instability than during times of stability."[23] Erikson thus speaks of the "potency of disorder." Life crises can be evaluated in a positive way, "not as a threat or a catastrophe, but as a turning point, a crucial period of increased vulnerability and heightened potential."[24]

James Loder, another contemporary writer on development, looks to both Christian theology and the human sciences for insights into human transformation. He sifts through not only theological and clinical approaches but also what he calls "transforming moments" in their own right. "Transforming moments," Loder declares, "need to be recognized as sources of new knowledge about God, self, and the world, and as generating the quality and strength of life that can deal creatively with the sense of nothingness shrouding the extremities and pervading the mainstream of modern life."[25] His work explores what he calls "convictional experiences" that manage to find potency in the equally formative moments of pervasive, shrouding doubt and despair. Loder's larger project is to bring such convictional experiences arising from transforming moments into contemporary relevance and interpretation, with an eye to informing our response to God. But for Loder, our response is only transformative to the extent that it moves *through* negation *to* love. His route is through convictional experiences that transcend reason, that incorporate but ultimately bypass the classical stage approach to human development, and that finally approach holiness through an analogy of the Holy Spirit to the human person. His is an ambitious, complex project but one that would not sound unfamiliar to many Christian mystics who preceded him, mystics who discovered love through the cross. We are driven, sustained, and renewed by "transforming moments" that distill the potency of disorder into a potion of love.

A Threefold Transformation

To set the stage for the potency of disorder in prayer, we will look once more at a pattern of prayer that may at first glance seem to be free of crisis or trial. This kind of baseline prayer will help calibrate the transformational quality of crisis.

On the surface, the simple, elegant, and classic three-stage transformational process of purification (sometimes called purgation), illumination, and union (called perfection by some authors) appears to be fairly smooth. But though seemingly smooth on the surface, this pattern contains subtleties of transformation. Purgation is certainly an active process of change. Illumination is perhaps the primary transformative stage. Union with God or perfection is the final goal, and it too is transformative. Between each phase or stage are points of transition; since we hardly ever travel this path in a predictable linear pattern, we are also changed in the transitions as we move from stage to stage.

In his *Celestial Hierarchy*, Dionysius the Areopagite glimpses God's transforming power at each level of the threefold way:

> Therefore when the [celestial] hierarchic order lays it on some to be puri-
> fied and on others to do the purifying, on some to receive illumination
> and others to do the illumination, on some to be perfected and on others
> to bring about perfection, each will actually imitate God in the way suit-
> able to whatever role it has.[26]

Here Dionysius is talking about human enlightenment as much as about
angelic enlightenment, but the important point is that at each stage, in
the temple of prayer, we are being transformed from one degree of glory
to another. For Dionysius, God actively transforms. But more importantly,
God *is* transformation. Prayer orients us toward and draws into purification because God *is* purification. Conversation and relationship with
God renew, illuminate, and enlighten because God *is* enlightenment. In
the presence of God, prayer shows us a vision of perfection and helps
us surrender to the process of perfection because God *is* perfection.

"This Darkness Is My Illumination"

We have seen the many branches and paths of our journey through
prayer, and so it should not be surprising that another master teacher
of Christian prayer can take the same threefold formula and utilize it
with a different emphasis. Where Dionysius focuses on a hierarchical,
staged, and basically progressive process of transformation, St. John
of the Cross emphasizes the transition periods between purgation and
illumination and illumination and perfection, those periods during which
the potency of crises intervenes and change occurs. These transition
periods are his famous "dark nights," periods of painful though maximal
transformation. St. John of the Cross describes two dark nights of the
soul, one of the senses and one of the spirit. Though he uses the pattern
of purgation, illumination, and union, it is really these two transitional
points of crisis in contemplative transformation that focus his attention.
John explains that the dark night of the senses is a transitional period
between purgation and illumination; the dark night of the spirit is a
transitional period between illumination and union/perfection.

St. John of the Cross insists that these nights, these points of transition sometimes lasting years, are potential points instituted by God in
prayer for our growth and transformation. He says that the dark night
of the senses is much more common; the second, "horrible and frightful
to the spirit," is very rare:

> Hence the one night or purgation will be sensory, by which the senses are
> purged and accommodated to the spirit; and the other night or purgation
> will be spiritual, by which the spirit is purged and denuded as well as ac-

commodated and prepared for union with God through love. The sensory night is common and happens to many; these are the beginners of whom we shall treat first. The spiritual night is the lot of very few.[27]

Dark illumination may seem odd at first, but as John is aware, it is something many experience and seems to be essential for the transforming worth of prayer during the desolate periods of our life. Both dark nights are, in fact, "horrible and frightful" if we are not prepared for them or if we see the darkness as divine abandonment. Thomas Green writes that "the peculiar problem in prayer is that we cannot see God as we see a spouse or a friend. Even if we have become convinced of our need for him and of the transforming value of the hard times, how do we "read the face of God"?[28] How, indeed, do we read the face of God in the darkness?

St. John of the Cross describes this bleak state as a prelude to illumination and insight. He says that God desires to use the dark night of the senses "to lead them on to a higher degree of divine love, . . . in which they become capable of a communion with God. . . . It is at the time they are going about their spiritual exercises with delight and satisfaction, when in their opinion the sun of divine favor is shining most brightly on them, that God darkens all this light and closes the door."[29]

The dark nights are painful but natural and often given by God, not as a test but as moments that force us, before we move on, to learn to awaken and see once more, as if we were asleep or blind. While St. John would not offer consolation where consolation is not due—the night *is* a night, a sunny disposition simply does not cut through this kind of darkness—he does suggest three signs by which we may come to know that we are really treading this path of sensory night. The signs are not a cure. They are simply indicators that one still dwells, though harshly, in the temple of prayer.

The first sign is that souls undergoing the dark night of the senses "do not get satisfaction or consolation from the things of God, they do not get any out of creatures either. . . . [God] does not allow it [the soul] to find sweetness or delight in anything."[30] No longer do either the things of God or the things of the world give one pleasure. The second sign for discernment of this night is that "the memory ordinarily turns to God solicitously and with painful care, and the soul thinks it is not serving God but turning back, because it is aware of this distaste for the things of God." In this second sign, then, one who is not undergoing the dark night normally has "no solicitude about serving God." However, one who is in the darkness of the senses is concerned and pained about not serving God. Thus, if the symptoms of the dark night are obvious, but those symptoms drive the person away from seeking God, the diagnosis is something other than the dark night. But if the symptoms actually increase a longing and desire to serve God, the dark night is from God. The third and final sign is that the "senses are powerless, in spite of one's efforts to meditate and make use of the imagination. . . . At this point God does not communicate through the senses." Thus, meditative techniques that formerly were effective simply no longer work. From this third sign we can discern whether the darkness is from what John calls "bad humor," what we would call depression, grief, or loss.

The dark nights of the senses and of the spirit are formational elements in the life of faith. They serve as transitional periods during which one's prayer and contemplative life undergo transformation. The transformation results in a deeper longing for God. The dark nights wound—the experience of grief and loss remain—but the soul now experiences this as a wound of love. The soul now sees more clearly the wounds that pierce the world, and for those likewise wounded, it seeks to care.

Transformation in a Crystal Castle

In her treatise *The Interior Castle,* Teresa of Avila also describes the power of disorder in the dark night of prayer as a hidden process of transformation, yet she does so in the context of an image of a well-ordered crystal castle. The disorder of the dark night or dark and hidden contemplation represents the unconscious dimension of the spiritual life. For transformation to occur, there must be some way in which real disorder is safely contained in an equally real system of order. As psychologist Gerald May has written regarding both Teresa of Avila and St. John of the Cross, darkness in prayer exists and moves us toward transformation because "if we really know what we were called to relinquish on this journey, our defenses would never allow us to take the first step. . . . Thus God darkens our awareness in order to keep us safe."[31] In a similar manner, Teresa of Avila writes of chaos, darkness, and transformation in prayer within the "safety" of her ordered, crystal castle.

Teresa thus writes that there is a kind of guiding order or quality of discernment even in the dark of prayer. Often, just at that point where we cannot seem to find our own way in prayer, we become open to God's protection, and the darkness becomes, according to John of the Cross, a "guiding night," a "night more kindly than the dawn."[32] Due to our complex system of defenses, denial, and deceptions, we would never accomplish this "dawn" on our own. What brings the dawn of transformation is a mystical coparticipation between God and person. In her *Interior Castle,* Teresa makes clear that entering the castle itself means entering the temple of prayer to find, at the very core of the castle (the symbol for the human soul), mystical coparticipation with

God. God, the goal of all our desires—which for Teresa is love—can be reached in no other way than through this transforming coparticipation between God and the soul.

Teresa's *Interior Castle* itself is a map of contemplative transformation from one degree of glory to another. In an earlier work, *The Way of Perfection,* Teresa recalls that Augustine looked for God in many places and finally found him within himself. Teresa too looks for God within. She says, "However quietly we speak [that is, pray], God is so near that God will hear us. We need no wings to go in search of God, but have only to find a place where we can be alone and look upon God present within us."[33] Teresa's own map of transformation takes the form of a beautiful, ordered, and imaginative image: She "considers our soul to be like a castle made entirely out of diamond or of very clear crystal, in which there are many rooms."[34] She describes the castle as a series of seven concentric "soul circles," each containing many rooms. The diamond castle of clear crystal is given beauty, radiance, and shape by the God who abides at the center of each of these many rooms. The outer wall of the castle is represented by our body. Teresa's story is that of a soul awakening from a deep sleep to find itself fully transformed and awake to the loving presence of God within:

> All our attention is taken up with the plainness of the diamond's setting or the outer wall of the castle; that is, with these bodies of ours. Well, let us consider that this castle has, as I said, many dwelling places: some are up above, others down below, others to the sides; and in the center and middle is the main dwelling place where the very secret exchanges between God and the soul take place.[35]

Prayer is the "gate and entry to this castle," she says, the route from outer wall of the body, through all our crisis and hurts, into our central, essential love and union with God.[36]

The castle does not represent order as linear progress. It is a beautiful crystal, not a ladder, and what is more, there are many dwelling places above, below, to the sides, and at the center. While it is true that God dwells at the center of the soul, God also surrounds and permeates the soul, allowing transformation and "very secret exchanges between God and the soul" at any level, in any room. The castle functions as a fortress that provides a holding environment in which we can safely encounter the potency of disorder. Teresa's interior castle is not an antidote to crisis; it is a place to come face-to-face with pain and darkness. She is honest enough to admit that the closer she gets to the light at the center of her soul, the darker the journey becomes. The more we awaken to who we are, acknowledge what we are, and accept distress and loss, the more rooms we find. In faith, Teresa knows and has experienced that the many rooms of the castle lead her on a path toward God because God is the Creator, source, and beauty of the castle-soul. The soul is like a crystal, reflecting and refracting the light of God with every tilt and sparkle. To do this it must reflect and refract as well the shadows and the planes of darkness.

It is in the fifth dwelling place that Teresa first introduces her famous image of the silkworm and the little white butterfly, a quintessential image of transformation and renewal. But once again, the other side of transformation is death within the self; something must die in order for the new and transformed to be born. Teresa's image of the butterfly is thus as much about care as it is about cure. In her care of souls, the old self (the silkworm) dies, and the new self (the butterfly) is born. Here Teresa describes the worm, cocoon, and butterfly:

> The worms nourish themselves on the mulberry leaves until, having grown to full size, they settle on some twigs. There with their little mouths they themselves go about spinning the silk and making some very thick little cocoons in which they enclose themselves. The silkworm, which is fat and ugly, then dies, and a little white butterfly, which is very pretty, comes forth from the cocoon.[37]

It is somewhat surprising that in this extended allegory the butterfly is not Christ or God. Rather, as Teresa says, "the silkworm . . . begins to spin the silk and build the house wherein it will die. I would like to point out here that the house is Christ." She adds, "I have read or heard that our life is hidden in Christ or in God, or that our life is Christ."[38] In Teresa's allegory, Christ is the cocoon. The butterfly is the soul.

In this prayer of union, enfolded in Christ, the soul dies, not to be transformed into Christ or God but to have experienced union with God and Christ within the cocoon:

> When the soul is, in this prayer, truly dead to the world, a little white butterfly comes forth. O greatness of God! How transformed the soul is when it comes out of this prayer after having been placed within the greatness of God and so closely joined with God for a little while.[39]

The soul has experienced union (Teresa says for a short time, never more than half an hour) and emerges a little white butterfly. But now there is a problem. Teresa continues: "See the restlessness of the butterfly, even though it had never been quieter and calmer in its life. . . . The difficulty is that it doesn't know where to alight and rest. Since it has experienced such wonderful rest, all that it sees on earth displeases it."[40]

In such a state, the soul-butterfly makes the difficult transition into the sixth dwelling and the prayer of spiritual union. The difficulty lies in the fact that it has tasted the sweetness of communion with Christ yet is still restless; it alights here and there as, in comparison to Christ, nothing pleases it for long. These rooms harbor periods of intense spiritual joy and clear periods of discernment. Some rooms even provide space for what Teresa calls intellectual visions of the divinity of Christ and visions of the humanity of Christ. But with greater favors from the Lord come greater trials and pains.

Transformation and contemplation in these six dwellings of the castle of the soul have many consolations, yet desolations that are treacherous to memory, intellect, and will reside here as well. In these dwellings are Teresa's analysis and encouragement concerning the dark night of the soul. The soul has experienced union, briefly, but mostly that is exactly the problem. "Consolations" are less frequent, but their memory, at least, remains fresh. The soul, having once felt the fiery presence of God, is now out from God's light and recognizes how far it is from God and how inadequate are its own efforts.

Teresa uses her own experience to guide souls into and through this dark night. After an apparent experience of union of the type she describes using the image of the silkworm, Teresa confesses her own darkness. Having once "touched" Christ, the beloved, he is now no longer anywhere to be found; naturally, she believes that God and Christ have forsaken her.

In short, new awareness and transformation do not move from charring and blackening the log to flame, to use John's image, without pain and darkness and trials. Once again, Teresa warns her sisters, "You will think that these souls to whom the Lord communicates Himself in this unusual way will already be so sure of enjoying Him forever that they will have nothing to fear nor sins to weep over, . . . [but that is] a great mistake because suffering over one's sins increases the more one receives from our God."[41] Teresa is also concerned that the memory and practice of sins once thought "purged" come back to haunt. Here she uses a memorable image: "These favors [consolations from God] are like waves of a large river in that they come and go; but the memory these souls have of their sins cling like thick mire. It always seems these sins are alive in the memory and this is a heavy cross."[42]

Finally, the transformed soul, having experienced something of the brilliance and peace of the divine light, "retraces" its steps, returning in humility to the humanity of Christ as model and guide. Wedding our soul and, more importantly, our actions to Christ is Teresa's "strategy" for the potency of disorder. She says, "It will also seem to you that anyone who enjoys such lofty things [as contemplative union] will no longer meditate on the mysteries of the most sacred humanity of our Lord Jesus Christ."[43] But that is exactly the direction we should turn: toward the life and humanity of Christ, the life of healing and the life of the cross. "I believe," she counsels, "I've explained that it is fitting for souls, however spiritual, to take care not to flee from corporeal things to the extent of thinking that even the most sacred humanity causes harm. . . . I cannot imagine what such souls are talking about. To be always withdrawn from corporeal things and enkindled in love is the trait of angelic spirits, not of those who live in mortal bodies."[44]

In the seventh place of dwelling in the crystal castle of the soul, Teresa experiences the final, most profound, and most ineffable transformation: Her soul in prayer "marries" this shining Christ. But with her pleasing metaphors, engaging style of writing, and gentle way of placing herself in the story of her journey, it is easy to forget that Teresa is all the while speaking of prayer. For all her talk of soul, union with Christ, visions of the Trinity, heaven within, butterflies, and charity, she is still describing what she calls "this way of prayer."[45] Though she repeatedly laments the impossibility of justly describing these innermost rooms, the transformations that allow her to dwell there are driven by, consummated in, and sustained by prayer. It is in prayer that she walks—fully wedded to Christ in mind, body, and spirit—into that light, the light that she calls love.

The seventh chapter of Teresa's *Interior Castle* is sprinkled with delightful and compelling metaphors of the "experience" of entering these endlessly enchanting dwelling places at the center and core of the soul. She describes the soul as a second heaven. Scales fall from the "eyes of her heart," and she beholds a vision of the Trinity. She marries her bridegroom Christ with a kiss. From divine breasts flow streams of milk, bringing comfort to all people throughout the castle. Two flames from two candles unite, and the soul as a drop of rain falls into the ocean of God. Light streams through colored panes of cathedral windows. She laughs at her insufficient descriptions and yet tries again and again for just one more.

But these wonderful images aside, what we are finding, especially in prayer's transitional and transformative aspects, is that in some way the purpose of prayer surpasses its practice in importance. Teresa explains that the purpose of prayer is ultimately God's purpose, and the practice of prayer is essential to discern that purpose. For Teresa of Avila, the purpose of prayer is to "join Martha and Mary together." It is to wed prayer and compassion, to unite contemplation and charity, and to find that shalom and service in the world are intimate lovers. By the end of her *Interior Castle*, Teresa has undergone a lasting and ever-deepening transformation of consciousness. She has walked through chaos and potency of disorder into love and ministry. The darkness remains, but it is tempered by tenderness, trust, courtesy, and the openness of a glorious and inviting crystal castle of faith, hope, and love. There the transformed and transforming soul residing in the seventh mansion dwells in the "soul's heaven" of prayer with God while simultaneously rendering a ministry of service to the world.

"Thy Whole Body Shall Be Full of Light"

> The light of the body is the eye:
> if therefore thine eye be single, thy whole body shall be full of light.
>
> Matthew 6:22 KJV

Prayer as transformation is not transformation only from one degree of disorder to another. It is also a process of transformation from one degree of glory, splendor, or light to another (2 Cor. 3:18). "Glory" implies light. Though dark nights and crisis are a normal part of development, transformative contemplation is also a process of entering into the light of Christ, who said, "I am the light of the world" (John 8:12).

Several passages from Scripture point to the light of the world. First John 1:5 puts it most plainly by saying that "God is light." Moses, after encountering God on Mt. Sinai, returned to the people "radiant" with light. His face was so full of light from the Lord that the people could not look upon his face (Exod. 34:29–35). Jesus is spoken of as "the true light that gives light" (John 1:9 NIV).

Spiritual writers on prayer naturally turn to light to express their experience of the glory of God in the temple of prayer. From the desert tradition, we hear that one of the brothers went to see Abba Sisoes on Abba Anthony's mountain. While they were talking, the brother said to Abba Sisoes, "Have you already reached Abba Anthony's stature, Father?" The old man said to him, "If I had one of Abba Anthony's thoughts, I should become all light."[46] Abba Anthony's thoughts are not themselves the light; the rather cryptic saying simply asserts that Abba Anthony had been purified and cleansed in such a way that his thoughts served as a perfect mirror for reflecting the glory of divine thought to others. In writing of the deep mystery of the Trinity, Catherine of Siena also longs for light to see God's light: "You are insatiable; you in whose depth the soul is sated yet remains always hungry for you, thirsty for you, eternal Trinity, longing to see you with the light in your light."[47] Angela of Foligno compares an encounter with God to fire, with the soul burning for Christ. For Angela, the light of God saves, promotes progress, and brings to perfection, but only through prayer and meditation on the life of Christ:

> Divine light causes us to begin and to make progress, and it leads us to the summit of perfection. Therefore if you want to begin and to receive this divine light, pray. If you have begun to make progress and want this light to be intensified within you, pray. And if you have reached the summit of perfection, and want to be superilluminated so as to remain in that state, pray. . . . And pray in this fashion, namely, always reading the Book of Life, that is, the life of the God-man Jesus Christ.[48]

Throughout the centuries, prayer, light, and transformation have been closely integrated in Christian writings. Prayer is a form of illumination, a light held to the world. Through the eyes of prayer, God's glory is refracted as though through a prism into a spectrum of light that reaches into the darkest corners, adding shades and hues of compassion as we give witness to that light.

Richard of St. Victor: Contemplative Transformation

Richard of St. Victor's great work on contemplation, *The Mystical Ark,* describes six degrees or transitions in the practice of contemplation. These six degrees form the practical basis of prayer and lead to the goal of meeting with, speaking with, and finally becoming an image of the glory of the Lord. Richard draws his images for contemplation from Scripture.

In the patristic and medieval periods, there were a variety of ways to interpret Scripture. The first was the historical or literal sense of Scripture, which attempted to interpret what really happened. In addition, spiritual senses included the allegorical sense, in which Christ was generally understood as underlying all Scripture, and thus all Scripture understood in an allegorical sense referred to a particular dimension of Christ. A second spiritual sense was the anagogical sense, used to uncover how God is present in the world and how we might, through the wisdom of Scripture, ascend to God. A third spiritual sense was the tropological, or moral, sense. This sense involved the ethical interpretation of Scripture, reading Scripture to ascertain how one should live one's life. One might expect Richard, as he directs his own attention to Scripture and contemplative transformation, to base his exegesis on the anagogical (ascent) interpretation or perhaps even on the allegorical (Christ) interpretation. Instead, Richard chooses the tropological (moral) interpretation, which directs ethical behavior as the true guide and sign of transformation, as the proper interpretation on which to base his contemplative methods and teaching.

Richard of St. Victor defines contemplation as "the free, sharp-sighted gaze of the mind suspended in awe and wonder in the visible showings of divine wisdom."[49] He has a complex notion of the mind and its capacities, with wisdom—determined and verified in how we live and practice charity—being the apex of his understanding of how we can be in relation to God, self, and others. Since God created everything, Richard identifies any object of creation as a potential revelation of God's wisdom. As such, it is worthy of our awe and wonder.[50] It is just that very process of holding an object or idea in an attentive gaze of wonder and awe that, for Richard, comprises prayer. All of God's good creation is thus potentially material for such contemplative prayer: nature, worship, beauty, others, birds, the human mind, the soul, friends, a walk, trees. All these, as visible showings of God's wisdom, are times and objects for prayer.

Richard of St. Victor thus enters into the world of biblical symbols and mystical theology, making of them vehicles of spiritual instruction and transformation. He looks at levels of contemplation keyed to various parts of the ark of the covenant described in Exodus 25. As an integrated whole, these parts direct the contemplative inward, outward, upward, and in the direction of any object, inspiring "awe and wonder in the visible showings of God's Wisdom." The narrative surrounding the construction of the ark and cherubim in Exodus 25 depicts a theophany. Here is a place where God's manifestation of wisdom is manifest. God promises to be present with and to speak to his people atop the ark and between the two cherubim. Richard uses this text of divine presence to teach a contemplative method whereby the contemplative moves progressively deeper into conversation—or silence in wonder and awe—with the manifest wisdom of God present on the ark and by "degrees" theophanically present wherever we can turn our gaze in awe and wonder.

As with Teresa, God permeates Richard's entire image. The first three forms of contemplation are grounded in the visible manifestations of God's wisdom as they are observed in the natural world and the human body. Symbolized first by the wood, second by the wood gilded with gold, and third by the gold crown of the ark, the transitions between these three forms allow real transformations of contemplative awareness while remaining crucially dependent on one another. Richard makes use of the materials themselves to represent progressive assimilation of divine wisdom. The materials move from the strong but rough character of wood, to wood lined with a thin gilding of gold, to the more refined gold of the crown of the ark. Eventually, in the fifth and sixth levels of contemplation, the material representing the highest form of prayer is the pure "angelic gold" of the cherubim.

Taken together, Richard's first three levels depict contemplation as a kind of "theophanic nature mysticism." Here, the soul begins to grasp the invisible things of God through the use of imagination and reason, as well as through the use of the visible things of the world. As such, it engages a process of purgation leading to growth in humility, a new sense of self-worth, and self-understanding.

Transition into the fourth level of contemplative awareness, also accessible to reason and imagination, has for its object of wonder the human spirit rather than the natural world. This fourth level represents a kind of "theophanic soul mysticism," in which knowledge of the true, inner self can lead to an initial understanding of divinity. This level of mystical consciousness guides the human spirit once again to the core of the soul, wherein God dwells:

> Therefore, the first thing in this consideration is that you should return to yourself, you should enter your heart. . . . This is the gate. This is the ladder. This is the entrance. This is the ascent. By this we enter into the inmost parts, by this we are raised to the heights, . . . and in this way we rise up through a consideration of your spirit to contemplation of spiritual things.[51]

The fifth and sixth levels of contemplation, totally dependent on grace, are symbolized by the two cherubim of pure gold attached to and covering the ark, with their wings seeming to provide protective shade. The first cherubim is "above" reason but not contrary to it; the second is "beyond" reason and, as Richard says, seemingly contrary to reason. The cherubim have two primary objects of contemplation: Christ and the Trinity. With Christ as the object of contemplation, the first angel provides material for contemplation of the humanity of Christ; the second angel contemplates the divinity of Christ. With the Trinity as the object of contemplation, the first angel contemplates the unity of God, the second the three persons of God. The contemplation that is symbolized by the cherubim is connected to and grounded in the ark. The angels are attached to the ark, yet they symbolize flight. Transformation is nurtured in the natural world and occurs in the soul. If transformation is occurring through meditation on Christ and the living Trinity, it is transformation that is "grounded flight."

For Richard, then, any prayer, personal or common, fractured or whole, desolate or consoled, desperate or at peace, minuscule or complex, liturgically rich or plain, dark or light, in action or in rest, in service or being served, upholds at least a strand of glory from God's wisdom.

The book of Hebrews speaks of the first covenant, the first tabernacle, the first ark, the first cherubim, and the first "Holy Place," into which only the high priest could enter (9:25). This was the earthly tabernacle made of human hands. But there was a new covenant, "when Christ came as high priest of the good things that are already here, he went through the greater and more perfect tabernacle [not made by hands], . . . not a part of this creation. . . . He entered heaven itself, now to appear for us in God's presence" (9:11, 24 NIV). Now, "all who keep [Christ's] commandments abide in him, and [Christ] in them" (1 John 3:24 RSV). The tabernacle not made by human hands resides within us. God dwells within us, at the center of our soul, and it is within and through that contemplative center that manifestations of divine wisdom can be discerned as such. The ark and the cherubim of the first covenant become, as it were, an internal icon of the new covenant. With this image of the holy of holies thus internalized, we have potential access to Christ at any moment, at any place. In prayer, we gaze in wonder and awe at the manifestation of God's wisdom within. Turning within, we turn outward as well, participating with Christ in love and care for one another. Love as charity is the manifestation of God's wisdom within and without.

Transformation is the result of attuning the eyes, heart, and mind in wonder and awe to the various manifestations of God's wisdom. As we enter this temple of prayer, we begin to see that there is nothing that is not in some basic and essential way a showing or a manifestation of God's wisdom. Once we begin to contemplate God's universe, that universe becomes God's milieu, through which we, as pilgrims of prayer, are privileged to witness the mundane being transformed into the holy, the commonplace into manifestations of divine wisdom.

The Role of Common and Corporate Prayer in Transformation

The pattern of transformation in prayer is often a loop between personal, transforming experience and living out that experience in community. But transformation can also move in the opposite direction. Common prayer, liturgy, and witness can transform personal lives. Both directions within this pattern are essential for living out the Christian call to service and transformative living. Individuals express their experiences of transformation by writing a memoir, preaching a sermon, or engaging in acts of kindness, compassion, or hospitality. Communities express their experiences of transformation often by communal action or communal witness.

Thus, it is important to highlight the role of liturgical or common prayer in transformation. Once again we can recall, from chapter 1, that the division between personal prayer and corporate prayer in worship is entirely arbitrary and unwarranted. Karl Barth, with reference to the catechisms of the Reformation, decried this artificial division unequivocally:

> One fact needs to be stressed: these texts do not mention any differences between individual prayer and corporate prayer. For the authors of the various catechisms one thing is clear: they see the church, us, that is to say, the members of a community forming a whole. But they distinguish also among the individuals who constitute this whole. One cannot ask whether it is the Christians who pray or the church. There is no alternative, for when the Christians pray, it is the church; and when the church prays, it is the Christians. Between these two there can be no opposition.[52]

The seeming imbalance in favor of the transformative prayer of the "Christians" involves the tendency of individuals to define, explain, and offer their experience of prayer through spiritual autobiography, memoir, biography, and other forms of written communication. The church as a whole tends not to write its autobiography of prayer. If it did, "autobiography" would not name the genre well. Perhaps "ecclesiography" would do, but again, coauthored memories of transformation are rare. What the church does have is witness, service, mission, and liturgy. These forms of "ecclesiography" could be considered the church's memory of transformation. They are similar to autobiography in that they tell a story, but they are different in a very important way. The church's "autobiography" is a biography that is lived and ritualized, not written. This is similar to the Word of Scripture (the story of transformation) and the Word made flesh (the life in transformation). Witness, stewardship, hospitality, charity, and evangelism all enflesh the reality of transformation in a bodily way to the world. The church's transformational prayer is lived. It is transformational prayer that is seen.

Another way of reclaiming common or corporate prayer as transformative is to look toward monastic communities. Though monastic lifestyles and practices are varied, most if not all devote large portions of the day (and even the night, in some cases) to prayer in community. In addition to giving praise to God, common prayer in this sense is intended to give shape both to the community and to individuals, while personal prayer in turn helps form community. In a book appropriately titled *Prayer and Community*, a contemporary commentator on Benedictine monasticism echoes Barth in his insistence on the reciprocity of personal and common prayer: "Common prayer is nurtured and deepened by private prayer, just as private prayer is energized by corporate experience of the Word in liturgy."[53] St. Benedict himself, who early in the sixth century wrote the rule that forms this community in prayer, lays out a simple theology of prayer that recognizes the transformative nature of common prayer:

"We believe that the divine presence is everywhere. . . . We should believe this all the more, without any doubt whatsoever, when we attend to the divine work."[54] This "divine work" is common, community prayer transforming the Christian, the church, and the world.

The Role of Verbal Prayer in Transformation

As with common or corporate prayer, verbal prayer is underrepresented in the literature on the process of transformation. Meditation and contemplation, like personal prayer, often make for the most striking examples of transformation, while verbal prayer seems almost mundane by comparison to the sometimes lofty claims of contemplative transformation. Yet verbal prayer is transformative. Though we are not as apt to hear reports of radical transformation through simple, persistent verbal prayer, those who pray primarily in the verbal style are just as likely to experience transformation as those deeply engaged in silent, contemplative prayer.[55]

Verbal confession cleanses the heart and mind, rendering a soul pliable, humble, and receptive to the work of the Holy Spirit. Like confession, all the various types of verbal prayer have transformation as their purpose and their core. Petition requires self-honesty and clarity of soul as it separates obsessions, narcissism, restlessness, and unfocused desire from self-knowledge, critical assessment of one's true needs, and areas in need of healing from the scars of crisis, grief, and loss. To know oneself is a vital element to transformation in petitionary prayer.

Intercessory prayer flings us into the world. Intercessory prayer is prayer for the transformation of injustice, poverty, neglect, disease, and loss of hope. In the process, it transforms our hopes and dreams and aligns our longings with the purposes of God. In a sense, it projects our selves into the world in an active way for the healing consolation of the world. Intercessory prayer is always a prelude to action and compassion, which in turn are, by God's grace, transformative.

Prayers of thanksgiving and praise transform our heart and mind and our perceptions of the world as God has created and adorned it. Thanksgiving and praise stand like a tree rooted in the good soil, with branches and leaves held high. They allow us simply to stand in wonder and awe before the creation God has provided, the care God gives, and the beauty, truth, and love God bestows.

Taken in all their forms, verbal prayer utilizes our imagination, our creative intuition, our intellect, our will, and our love. In effect, it is the equal of contemplation in terms of transformation. Both are fed by the sunlight of compassion and grow in the rich and fragrant soil of charity.

In Love with Prayer

As trees cycle from seed to full growth, then in death to new seed, so too are we in a constant cycle of death to self and renewal in God. Jesus says, "Unless a grain of wheat falls into the earth and dies, it remains just a single grain; but if it dies, it bears much fruit" (John 12:24). Paul tells us, "Set your affection on things above, not on things on the earth. For you are dead, and your life is hid with Christ in God" (Col. 3:4–5 KJV). In a passage that echoes the image of death and birth through replanting of the seed, he says, "Do you not know that all of us who have been baptized into Christ Jesus were baptized into his death? Therefore we have been buried with him by baptism into death, so that, just as Christ was raised from the dead by the glory of the Father, so we too might walk in newness of life" (Rom. 6:3–4).

In prayer, we are in a constant cycle of dying and being reborn. It is clear from Scripture, tradition, and contemporary insight that as we die and are buried with Christ (Col. 3:3), we are reborn and released to love. In 1 John, for instance, we read this admonition: "Beloved, let us love one another, because love is from God; everyone who loves is born of God and knows God. Whoever does not love does not know God, for God is love" (4:7–8). As we have already seen, we "are being transformed into [that] same image" (2 Cor. 3:18). We are being transformed into love. We are being transformed into a love that is grounded in a healthy and open sense of self and incarnated in the capacity for compassionate love for others. When that time arrives, when we will know God *fully*, what we will know is love: "For now we see in a mirror, dimly, but then we will see face to face. Now I know only in part; then I will know fully, even as I have been fully known. And now faith, hope, and love abide, these three; and the greatest of these is love" (1 Cor. 13:12–13). To see and to know is to pray. Love is what we come to see and to know in the temple of prayer.

In the Christian prayer tradition, prayer at a fundamental level involves the process of transformation into love. Prayers of supplication, petition, intercession, and thanksgiving, from the first time they are uttered until they are whispered with our last breath, are prayed in faith, hope, and love. Faith and hope and love transform. To pray these prayers, to pray simple short prayers of confession, to be adept at centering prayer or using Richard of St. Victor's complex system of contemplation, to practice opening our very self to others in hospitality, to pray the Book of Common Prayer in community—all these prayers change us. They change us toward love.

St. Diadochos of Photiki's writes of what he considers to be the deepest secrets of the virtue of prayer. Diadochos opens one of his most important works with the words, "All contemplation should be governed by faith, hope and love, but most of all by love." This same work concludes that the transformative property of prayer is that we are reborn from one degree of love to another:

> He who loves God consciously in his heart is known by God, for to the degree that he receives the love of God consciously in his soul, he truly enters into God's love. From that time on, such a man never loses an intense longing for the illumination of spiritual knowledge, until he senses its strength in his bones and no longer knows himself, but is completely transformed by the love of God.[56]

We have already encountered a number of classical writers who speak of the spiritual path of love. All these writers make their comments in the context of prayer. Gregory the Great writes that love itself is a way of understanding. In the twelfth century, during the great revival of love in secular and religious culture, William of St. Thierry echoed Gregory by saying, "Love is itself a [highest] form of knowledge." Throughout the twelfth century, Christian writers on prayer and contemplation sought to live a life of charity in both prayer and service through the order of love, showing how Christians ought to live.

Catherine of Siena, writing in the fourteenth century, opens her *Dialogues* with a prologue on transformation through which, in a common metaphor of her day, she seeks to clothe herself in love. The route to this newly clothed and transformed self is, Catherine says, through prayer. It is only in prayer that the soul is fashioned into the image of Christ. As Catherine puts it, Christ "makes of her another himself":

> But there is no way she can so savor and be enlightened by this truth except in continual humble prayer, grounded in the knowledge of herself and of God. For by such prayer the soul is united with God, following in the footsteps of Christ crucified, and through desire and affection and the union of love he makes of her another himself.[57]

Catherine of Siena gets at the heart of what death and rebirth in Christ mean and how they lead to the transformation of love. In dialogue form, God speaks to Catherine:

> But beyond the beauty I have given the soul by creating her in my image and likeness, look at those who are clothed in the wedding garment of

charity, adorned with many true virtues: They are united with me through love. So I say, if you should ask me who they are, I would answer, "the gentle loving Word"; they are another me; for they have lost and drowned their own will and have clothed themselves and united themselves and conformed themselves with mine.[58]

For Catherine, transformation of the soul in prayer leads one to become "the gentle loving Word."

Contemporary writers on prayer also focus on the transformative quality of prayer. While they may not speak so often of stages, preferring rather more overlapping patterns of transition and openness, they use images of transformation that inevitably speak of renewal, regeneration, integration, and growth. Often these categories reformulate classic categories of prayer, transformation, and love.

Gerald May, the psychologist and writer on spirituality, is one contemporary example of a writer who makes explicit connections among transformation, love, and prayer. He asks, in effect, "Do we pray because we love, or do we love because we pray?"

When desire for love is felt, owned and intended, some kind of prayer happens. In one form or another, prayer is the beginning and the way of being in love. If we say yes to love's intention, to whom do we say it? . . . Desire in itself can be prayer when it turns us toward the source of love. . . . At times . . . it is clear that the source of love is everywhere; our very life becomes prayer.[59]

For May, a "desire for love" leads to and in some way *is* prayer. It could be argued that May is saying only that the *desire* for love, not love itself, turns us toward prayer. But he does present a compelling reversal or, perhaps more properly, a compelling reminder that love itself, in some sense, permeates the world; in doing so, love draws us to prayer, just as prayer draws us to love and makes of "our very life" a prayer.

Love also opens our eyes to the holy, not only to the holiness of God but also to the holiness of all creation. The Old Testament is concerned not only with the holiness of God but also with a corresponding responsive holiness from men and women: "Be holy, because I am holy" (Lev. 11:45 NIV). But in the Old Testament, the world was divided into things holy and things common. So Aaron was told to "distinguish between the holy and the common" (Lev. 10:10), and Ezekiel, when measuring the temple, is instructed to "make a separation between the holy and the common" (Ezek. 42:20). The New Testament writers are equally concerned with holiness. The word *holy* (*hagios*) is used 227 times in the New Testament; 93 are references to the Holy Spirit, and 61 refer to Christians themselves. In his book *True Prayer*, Kenneth

Leech points out that the New Testament gives us a radical new picture of holiness: "To be holy is not to be separate but to be close. And the holy and the common are one. Christians are called to a life of holiness."[60] Prayer as a way of life, as a way of transformation, allows us to see the common as holy. In Nicholas Lash's memorable phrase, prayer transforms our awareness so that in all things that surround us we find "Easter in ordinary."[61]

Love and prayer make connections: Prayer connects the common and the holy; it draws together the mundane human and the holy divine. As Catherine of Siena says, in the house of prayer, God makes of us another himself. On the other side of that mysteriously balanced equation between grace and consent, as Angela of Foligno says just as artfully and simply, "It is in prayer that one finds God."[62] Angela concludes that through these simple truths we are being transformed into the body of Christ:

> The more one knows, the more one loves; the more one loves, the more one desires; the more one desires, the more one grows in the capacity to act accordingly. How one acts is the sign and measure of love. And the test of pure, true, and upright love is whether one loves and acts in accordance with the love and action of the loved one, Christ, the Beloved.[63]

Strongest in the Broken Places

Ultimately, transformation in the temple of prayer is a mystery. We can imagine media through which God may work the mystery, but the essential mystery remains. Transformation sets us on a road that, finally, has no name. But as Hans Urs von Balthasar reminds us, the mystery of this process need not "confuse the contemplative."[64] In prayer and contemplation, mystery need not end in anxiety or confusion; we can find a certain comfort in mystery. We are like Jeremiah's clay in the hands of the potter. Mystery in prayer is a kind of holy waiting in which we learn that the potter's face we never see is as trustworthy and kind as the sculpting hands we may always feel.

Like the potter's clay, parts of us are often broken, even discarded. But the potter remains at the wheel, loving our brokenness into being. Peter Hodgson, in his book on the life and work of the nineteenth-century novelist George Eliot, nicely captures the reality of the manner in which brokenness and pain shape our lives. He shifts the metaphor from a potter and clay to what is a rumination on the tree of life:

We human beings for the most part are knotted, misshapen, but noble
trees. The wounds of life damage and disfigure us but need not destroy
us; instead we become stronger in the broken places. We may experience
serene happiness and true love, but these are brief moments in the relent-
less flow of life. We must learn to cherish and remember them, thankful
for the gift of life and the all provident eye of God that redeems us from
our worst moments and saves us for the best.[65]

We are all misshapen trees, strongest in the broken places.

If we are strongest in the broken places, it is through those broken
places that love finds an entry. The Christian spiritual tradition has always
recognized the transformative function of pain, crisis, and darkness in
the journey of prayer. But love finds its way as well. That such love is
present at all is because Love itself has already transformed our lives,
our deaths, our renewals, and our communities of faith.

Conclusion

The path of transformation in prayer is a trail of love that travels
through death on the cross. Such a death rends curtains, shatters stones,
shrouds the sun, wails into the darkness of total abandonment.

Yet even from the cross Christ prays, "Forgive them" (Luke 23:34).
What has he seen that allows him to utter such words at such a time?
We do not know exactly. But we do learn that love, kindness, hospitality,
reconciliation, and compassion are the fruits of love spoken from that
cross. The cross is our most abundant tree of life; it perseveres through
seasons of death and seasons of hope.

Picture the leaves of autumn as Christ on the cross. Every fall the
leaves of deciduous trees die on their branches, on their own wooden
cross. They are beautiful, radiant in their mourning. Set off artistically
against the white, paper-like bark, the leaf cells of the quaking aspen
begin to harden in the early autumn cold. This prevents nutrients from
the roots, trunks, and branches from flowing into the leaves. The produc-
tion of green chlorophyll is thereby halted, and the green of the leaves
begins to fade. No longer masked by the chlorophyll, the other colors
in the leaves—reds, yellows, oranges, purples—are free to erupt into a
cascade of color.[66] The leaves are dying, but in radiant beauty. The leaves
of autumn are like Christ on the cross.

Often mixed among other New England species such as yellow pop-
lar, sassafras, Eastern dogwood, sweet gum, and sugar maple, the red
maple (*Acer rubrum*) sets the autumn forest afire. It has brilliantly hued
yellow leaves and orange ones. But its special genius, its most inspired

Red Maple

display and the true genius of its palate, is how it sets the forest aflame with glorious leaves in blood-red hues. *Brilliant, afire,* and *aflame* are purposefully chosen words because the leaves seem to be glowing with the inner light of their own color. These glorious trees are on fire, incinerating a season. Their bark is lovely, their branches strong. But the winter is more lovely yet in its uncompromising demands and stronger even than the trunk. To persevere, to save the tree so that it may live, the leaves of the red maple fall as great drops of blood. They are like the drops of blood in Gethsemane; they are blood falling from his brow, from the nail wounds in his hands and feet, and from the wound in his side. The falling leaves are a silent prayer. Their prayer is a silent "Forgive them."

In the spring, the red maple is one of the first trees to swell with new buds, to produce new leaves, laying the groundwork for the essential early stages of reviving the forest's other animals and plants.

Transformative prayer is prayer that perseveres; it is prayer that finds a way of renewal, even in the midst of death. There are questions in the seasons of transformation that elude any kind of ready answer: forgiveness in the midst of injustice; beauty in death; pain in healing;

blood that opens the heart to love. But because we are asked by Christ to join him in prayer, we watch and pray. If we fall asleep, we awaken and pray once again.

The cross is the autumn and winter of our prayer; the resurrection is our spring and summer. Transformation is multicolored, accomplished only with the support of many other new leaves and old. The maturity of our prayer becomes a tree of life as it is entwined with the cross of Christ, a cross radiant with beauty and love. This love is like the beauty in the dying leaves of autumn and the joyful hope of the new leaves of spring: It has gazed deep into the face of incarnate Love on the cross. This love "bears all things, believes all things, hopes all things, endures all things" (1 Cor. 13:7).

Prayer as Presence

The Fragrant Fruits of Prayer

The Immanuel Quality of Prayer

God is with us. As prayer becomes a way of life, we become ever more aware of this fundamental fact. Participating with God in his presence, we become present to God. Our companionship in prayer flows out into the world as ethical presence, formational practice, and attentiveness to the world. The reciprocity of prayer as God's presence with us and our presence with God can be captured in the phrase "the Immanuel quality of prayer." This chapter explores the Immanuel quality of prayer as it is lived out in all of Christian life, both personal and communal.

But there is another side to presence. Generations of Christian teachers have guided faithful Christians through the painful reality of God's apparent absence. We often come to know the deep, working depths of God most profoundly as a result of divine absence and withdrawal. Illustrated in the Song of Songs, the truth of how we participate in God's love is reflected in the cycle of union, separation, loss, longing, and reunion of the beloved and the loved. The bride calls out, remembering their last embrace, "Let him kiss me with the kisses of his mouth!" (1:2). Absence sharpens our seeking; it sets the tone and temper of our attentiveness; it sets us on a fine edge of listening expectantly; it hones our heart for hospitality; it opens doors of receptivity. Absence prepares us to share ever more fully in God's promised "kiss" of presence. The beloved, absent from her love, remembers the lover's presence:

> As a lily among brambles,
>   so is my love among maidens.
> As an apple tree among the trees of the wood,
>   so is my beloved among young men.
> With great delight I sat in his shadow,
>   and his fruit was sweet to my taste.
> He brought me to the banqueting house,
>   and his intention toward me was love.
> Sustain me with raisins,
>   refresh me with apples;
>   for I am faint with love.
>
> Song of Songs 2:2–5

God's love, promise, and memory are themselves like a lily of presence among brambles of absence. God's intention toward us is love. Even in the shadow of absence, faint with love, we are blessed.

"Let him kiss me with the kisses of his mouth!" Prayer is like a kiss given and received. Given, it is God's presence to us; received, it is our presence to God. Yet we wander and are absent from God. Our lover is there, beneath the apple tree. Yet as our love becomes faint and the banquet a receding memory, we too are challenged to be present to God. This means being attentive and intentional; it means recognizing that God's love is inescapable; it means sitting in "delight in his shadow." It means that in prayer we sense, however faint, the loving lips of God pressed upon our own.

The kiss of presence is not simply the coming together of a single self and God. It also sustains and refreshes the entire community of the church. The church is also a "lily among brambles." The kiss is as directed toward the liturgy as it is toward the personal. Throughout the liturgical seasons, divine presence and divine absence mingle, weaving a tapestry of our worship and prayer together. The kiss of charity, the kiss of hospitality, the kiss of justice is as often faint and disappointing as it is fulsome and effective. All the while the church and the world faint for love.

Yet as if by some miracle, often when we least expect it, we present ourselves to God in prayer, and our wish is fulfilled: The petition "Let him kiss me with the kisses of his mouth!" is answered. Through prayer, we consent to be taken into the deepest groves of God's presence.

In the models of prayer as conversation, journey, relationship, and transformation, we have been moving toward the Immanuel quality of prayer as a way of life. As in the union and separation of the lover and the beloved in the Song of Songs, at times this Immanuel quality is successive: Absence and presence follow one upon the other like hope and assurance. At other times, the relationship is more simultaneous. God's presence is felt, but only as we confront and accept the deep abyss, darkness, incomprehensibility, and mystery of God. In prayer, entry into the absence and presence of God is made all the more mysterious when we acknowledge the same abyss, darkness, incomprehensibility, and mystery within ourselves, creation, and others.

As we grow in the ability to recognize and to live with these paradoxes within ourselves, we begin to experience that same paradox in the world around us as a reflection of the wondrous mystery of Immanuel. If God is with us, then in regard to others we can do nothing but the same: be with them in service and in love. If God is with us, then in regard to creation we can do nothing but become stewards of the deep and loving connections between all things. If God is with us, then we can do nothing but care for, nurture, and love ourselves. In all these forms, prayer is like a kiss expressing love.

As the contemporary writer on the spiritual life Gerald May has said, "Contemplation happens to everyone. It happens in moments when we are open, undefended, and immediately present. People who are called contemplatives are simply those who seek the expansion of the moments, who desire to live in that quality of presence more fully and continually."[1] "Presence" is our own open presence to each moment. In this sense, presence is the willingness, honesty, and courage to face ourselves, others, and the world just as we—and they—are. In that facing toward another, presence asks a question of another: How is God kissing us now?

Presence in Centering Prayer

But how do we live the quality of presence more fully and continually? How do we notice if God is kissing us now? One practical way is centering prayer. Centering prayer is an effort to renew in contemporary form an ancient Christian practice of contemplative prayer. Such prayer has its roots in the teaching of the early desert fathers and mothers, especially the fourth-century teacher John Cassian and a much later source, the anonymously written fourteenth-century book on contemplative prayer, *The Cloud of Unknowing*.[2] Today, centering prayer has emerged and spread to many parts of the church, encouraging a simple and yet profound form of prayer based on the presence of God.

One of the most insightful teachers on contemplative prayer, Thomas Keating, begins a short essay on centering prayer with Teresa of Avila's comment that all our difficulties in prayer come from a single source: *"Praying as if God were absent.* Many of our difficulties in daily life are probably the result of *living as if God were absent."*[3] Keating himself goes on to describe how God is in fact present to us at all times, if we have the eyes to see:

> The impression is sometimes given in religious instruction that God is outside of us. On the contrary, God is totally present to us all the time: closer than thinking, closer than breathing, closer than choosing, closer than consciousness itself. God could not be any closer. God is so close that, in a sense, he is our true self.[4]

Centering prayer, entering our true self and encountering the presence of God, is simple. A single word is used as a prayer word. One sits quietly, repeating the word silently to oneself a number of times and then gently letting the word dissolve and disappear. Any time a thought or distraction enters the mind, one gently returns to the prayer word, "covering" the thought softly as if a feather were floating down onto a piece of cotton. This is not a prayer of effort; it is imageless and gentle. It is natural that all manner of thoughts and distractions will enter our consciousness. We do not fight these thoughts; we simply return to the prayer word. After sitting twenty to thirty minutes, one spends a brief time accustoming oneself to the surroundings and normal stream of awareness. The Lord's Prayer may be repeated slowly as a way of moving in a seamless manner from the contemplative period of resting in God's presence to extending the effects of the prayer into daily life.

Centering prayer allows us to stop thinking and to enter into the rest of God's presence. We are not conjuring God's presence; instead, the sacred word we use in the prayer is simply a symbol of our intention to consent to God's activity. It is natural that, as we begin this prayer, we like Martha are "distracted by many things" (Luke 10:41). Keating puts it this way:

> When we begin to pray in this way, we observe that our consciousness is like a river that is constantly flowing. On the surface are all kinds of particular ideas, memories, sense perceptions, and emotions that we might compare to boats. Indeed, we are so dominated by the awareness of boats that we rarely see the river itself on which the boats are floating. Beneath the surface of this river of consciousness is the Divine Indwelling, the God who is the source of our being at every level: body, soul, and

spirit. In Centering Prayer, we consent to God's presence and to receive Divine love without self-reflection.[5]

As we become more familiar with centering prayer, we begin to slip beneath the surface of consciousness as if beneath the surface of the flowing river. Just below the surface there may be debris, fish, plants, and rocks that, like the boats at the surface, will distract us. Again, we simply return to the sacred prayer word. As we begin to go deeper and deeper into the flowing stream, we encounter fewer and fewer distracting thoughts. We may reach a state where we notice that there are no distractions and that we have been floating for some time in the presence of God, at a level well beneath our normal stream of consciousness. This is good, but even to *notice* that we have been completely free of distraction while present to God is an interruption of the purity of that presence, and so once again, ever so gently, we return to our sacred prayer word.

Keating describes the practice of centering prayer according to four basic guidelines.[6] The first guideline is to choose a sacred word of one or two syllables as a symbol of our intention to open ourselves and to yield to God's presence and action within. Sample words may include those with explicit religious content such as *God, Abba, Jesus,* or *Mary,* or words with less explicit content such as *peace, shalom, love, stillness,* or *joy.* Once the word is chosen, it should not be changed during the time of prayer. To do so would involve a thought process in itself; eventually, after practicing the prayer for some time, the sacred word becomes deeply embedded in our consciousness, and we begin to return to it as needed almost automatically.

The second guideline is to sit comfortably with eyes closed and to settle briefly. Having settled comfortably and closed our eyes and begun letting go of our surroundings and of our interior occupations, we silently introduce our sacred word as a symbol of our consent to God's presence and action within us. This is done with our mind, not vocally with lips or voice. The word is repeated slowly. It may become vague or even disappear briefly. In the beginning, we normally have to say the sacred word almost constantly. But after the process is established, we need only return to it in order to reaffirm our consent to God's presence.

The third guideline is that when we become aware of thoughts we return ever so gently to the sacred word. Whenever we notice a thought, feeling, impression, memory, or external stimulus that attracts our attention, we gently return to the sacred word as a way of reaffirming our original intention to consent to God's presence and action within us. The sacred word is not meant to overpower the thought; it is to be returned to gently, again as if it were a feather floating softly onto a pillow. The process is an interior discipline of disregarding thoughts by turning our attention to the divine presence within. Using the river analogy, we may be floating downstream beneath the surface and resurfacing a number of times, and at first this can be disconcerting. But a growing habit of consenting to God's presence and action within us is gradually being established. The consent opens us to the divine light, life, and love.

After practicing centering prayer for twenty or thirty minutes, according to the fourth guideline, we take a little time to return to the ordinary awareness of the external senses and the usual flow of thoughts. We do this by keeping our eyes closed for a couple minutes but beginning to think in the usual way. Vocal prayer is helpful at this time. Repeating the Lord's Prayer slowly is especially effective.

In centering prayer, *thoughts* is an umbrella term for every perception, including sense perceptions, feelings, images, memories, reflections, and commentaries. In his book *Open Mind, Open Heart,* Thomas Keating describes the various types of thoughts that may be distinguished: ordinary wanderings of the imagination or memory; thoughts that give rise to attractions or aversions; insights and psychological breakthroughs; self-reflections such as "How am I doing?" or "This peace is great!"; and thoughts that arise from the unloading of the unconscious.[7] Each of these thoughts represents a distraction from our intention to consent to the action and presence of God within us.

Centering prayer opens our body, mind, spirit, and heart to the presence of God. It is a prayer of intention and consent. Praying this prayer does not mean that we abandon other forms of prayer as God calls us to them. In fact, other prayers will be deepened and energized. More importantly, perhaps, while the practice of centering prayer has proscribed times and guidelines, the effect of our consent to God's presence working within us does not end with the practice of the prayer itself. On the contrary, our capacity for God begins to grow as the experience of centering prayer slowly but insistently permeates all phases of our life. As we practice the presence of God in any form, our way of life itself becomes a symbol of our intention to consent to the presence of God as that presence penetrates outward appearances and we begin to perceive divine presence in everyone and everything we encounter.

Ways of Presence: Gifts of God for the People of God

Centering prayer helps us to become more aware of the Immanuel quality of prayer each moment of our life. It is a specific practice that results in a consciousness of the presence of God in events large and small. But as we explore various ways that the presence of God is awakened and illuminated in prayer, we need to acknowledge once again that not all Christians experience God's presence in the same way. The gifts of God come in many and varied forms to the people of God. The models of prayer, taken together, represent various means of receptivity and acceptance of the gifts of divine providence, guidance, and presence that have different meanings for people at different points in their lives.

One way of expressing these gifts is through the language of human perceptions and senses. From Origen in the third century to Karl Rahner in the twentieth century, Christians, by referring to the "spiritual senses," have given witness to being "kissed" by the Immanuel quality of prayer. This does not mean something spiritualized and therefore separate and superior to the body. Rather, the intent is to seek different ways of seeing, different ways of hearing or touching, or a mind and a heart illuminated in such a way as to apprehend God's presence most clearly.

Spiritual sight is one good example. Augustine, for instance, suggests three kinds of vision by which we might "derive life": corporeal vision, spiritual vision, and intellectual or mental vision. By the time of Bonaventure, these types of vision were spoken of as "eyes" by which we contemplate God in various settings. Thus, through the "eye of the flesh," we contemplate God through the natural world. Through the "eye of reason," we contemplate the image of God in the soul. Through the "eye of contemplation," we contemplate and see the presence of God.[8] Approximately one century before Bonaventure, Richard of St. Victor suggested an even more complex system for "seeing" the presence of God in prayer. Along with the eye of the flesh and the eye of reason, Richard suggested the "eye of understanding" for contemplating the invisible things of the soul and the spirit of the angels. In contemplating the unity of God, he teaches that we "see by means of ecstasy of mind." In contemplating the highest things of God, the things that render God's presence not only restorative and a gift but also essential for the very sustenance of life, we can pray only with "the eye of faith."[9]

Other Christians write of the prayer of presence as a kind of transformed awareness. In this form of recognizing the gift of the Immanuel quality of prayer, every moment, no matter how mundane, contains potential for an explosion of holiness. Their experience of divine presence is not so much beyond words as it is an expression of the sacred and holy quality of the small things of daily living. Brother Lawrence thus claims:

> The holiest, most ordinary, and most necessary practice of the spiritual life is that of the presence of God. It is to take delight in and become accustomed to divine company, speaking humbly and conversing lovingly with him all the time, at every moment, without rule or measure.[10]

Brother Lawrence finds that the prayer of divine presence follows him in outward daily activity as well as inward contemplation; God's presence is habitual. For Jean-Pierre de Caussade, God speaks to and is present to every individual in all action, intention, and thought, moment to moment. As a spiritual director, de Caussade was familiar with the various manifestations of the dark nights of faith. But his simple discipline of surrender allowed him to find a God who is eternally present in the shadows of small things as well as the light of the large:

> Thus wide horizons, sure ground, and solid rock can only be found in that vast expanse of the divine will which is eternally present in the shadows of the most ordinary toil and suffering; and it is in these shadows that God hides the hand which upholds and supports us all.[11]

For both writers, God's presence in prayer is not an abstract fantasy but a concrete reality transformed by simple prayer that awakens the awareness of the possibility of glory within the real.

The "original" title of *The Mystical Ark* by Richard of St. Victor, whom Dante said "in contemplation was more than human,"[12] is *De gratia contemplationis* or *The Grace of Contemplation*. Grace is a gift from God, and contemplation is a gift we offer God, at God's bidding and invitation. The more we participate in prayer, the more we begin to realize that what we at first thought was our approach to God is in reality God's approach to us in and through grace. Though we gather up this gift of the grace of prayer as offered and wear it like a robe, like a habit, as a *habitus*—it is at times a priestly garment, at times a kingly robe, at times a beggar's loincloth, at times a worker's tattered woolen coat, at times a coat of many colors, at times brown and coarse and hooded—it never ceases to be a gift. The gift is offered, and we can choose to take it or we can ignore it.

But how do we speak in words or communicate this relationship, participation, or simple presence? As we have seen, one time-honored way is through silence. Yet we long to communicate the prayer of God's presence to others; prayer is not complete unless we share it as a gift with others. Thus, through the centuries, Christian writers and teachers of prayer have sought through words and images to communicate the presence of God.

Thomas Gallus, for example, was a thirteenth-century writer known for his ability to hold the paradox of the presence of God in tension. Gallus is able to join the language of God's ineffable transcendence to concrete metaphors of divine presence, here emphasized in italics:

"My beloved to me and I to him." It would seem that some word of love must have been inserted, for example, *"is fastened," "cemented with glue,"* or *"is joined"* or something similar as in 1 Corinthians 6:17, "He who is fastened to God"; or Jeremiah 13:11, "I have glued to me"; or *Divine Names*, 1, 6, "we are joined to them." But he does not insert any of these, because he has not discovered any word worthy of expressing so sublime a coupling. The union is above mind and thus is ineffable.[13]

Another approach to divine presence in contemplation is through the projection of the threefold process of purgation, illumination, and union upon the human soul. In this approach, the soul encounters divine presence as cleansing, transforming, and enlightening. Purgation involves the acquisition (and gift) of self-understanding, self-knowledge, and God knowledge. Normally, it is quite active and anything but passive, involving the conscious practice of virtues and disciplines. Illumination involves transformation: new seeing, new awareness, new consciousness of the possibility of the presence of God. Perfection or union using these categories involves the soul's complete availability to the presence of God. Each of these three classic stages or transitions recognizes God's presence in different ways. They each reflect contemplation and prayer as a process of knowing, a way of being, and progress in understanding and living in the presence of God.

The metaphors and patterns of prayer explained in the chapter on prayer as journey are also helpful in illuminating different ways in which the presence of God is made known to us. Each also helps us to move toward acknowledging and engaging God's presence more fully. Since Bonaventure has produced one of the most synthetically comprehensive typologies of prayer, we can focus on his *Soul's Journey into God* as a representative example.[14]

As seen in earlier chapters, each of Bonaventure's typologies of prayer focuses on a different object, yet each serves to bring us into the presence of God in new ways. For Bonaventure, divine presence can be contemplated in the natural world both as it is in itself and as it appears through our senses. This is contemplation of the presence of God that is "outside ourselves." In contemplation of the natural world, we are assimilated through analogy into God's presence. God may also be contemplated in the soul that is "stamped" with the natural powers of memory, intellect, and will and in the soul reformed by grace through the virtues of faith, hope, and love. This contemplation of the presence of God is "within ourselves." In contemplation of the soul, we are assimilated through reason into God's presence. Finally, God may be contemplated in Godself. For Bonaventure, God is best contemplated through the attribute of divine Being, which encounters God's presence as unity within the Trinity. God can also best be contemplated through the attribute of divine Goodness, which encounters God's presence as a trinity of persons within divine unity. Finally, for Bonaventure, God can be contemplated in an "ecstasy" of mind, wherein the intellect passes over into love, leaving the soul at rest in the presence of God. These final forms of contemplation encounter divine presence "above ourselves." Bonaventure is careful to point out the importance of the trinitarian character or reality of each of these forms of contemplation. Whether as a vestige in the natural world, as an image in the soul, or as complete likeness to God, the Trinity is the core of each contemplation and thus the core of divine presence in all prayer.

The Immanuel quality of prayer is a gift that comes in many forms. To receive that kiss of love is to be changed forever. From the previous chapter, we recall Teresa of Avila's little white butterfly that had been "kissed" in the cocoon of Christ. Like the bride of the Song of Songs who had received the kiss of the beloved, Teresa's butterfly was restless, flitting from place to place, finding no rest. Only in the seventh castle, where the soul reaches the fragrant fruit of service and charity, does the butterfly begin to receive anything like a permanent embrace. It is likewise with the bride of the Song of Songs: Only in the shade of the bower does she receive the nourishment of the fragrant fruits of charity. In both cases, the Immanuel quality of prayer involves the conscious reception of the gift of divine presence and the equally conscious gift of returning that fragrant fruit to God in the form of charity and compassion toward others. In the sections that follow, we continue to encounter some of the many ways souls kissed by God have expressed the act of prayer as participation in this rhythmic grace of the divine presence.

Presence as Participation

Participation is another comprehensive way of approaching prayer as presence. Although participation implies an active and cooperative engagement with God, participation can be considered a subhead under presence. Presence is always responsive, never passive. Likewise, participation is always reflexive, never dominant. Prayer as presence has the element of participation in it. Although the image of participation is at its heart an image of presence, for the sake of clarity, this section distinguishes prayer as presence and prayer as participation.

Participation is a particularly helpful image as we begin to take seriously the notion of prayer as a way of life. Participation in the work of Christ creates the possibility of the whole arc of our life illuminated by the light of prayer as imitation of Christ. In quiet times of intercession or meditation, hectic times of daily life, or compassionate times of serving bread to the hungry, we share in the life and work of Christ in prayer. Participation implies a partnership; God's initiative and our response become simultaneous, like a dance between loving partners. As a full partner with God, we live our life moment to moment flecked, speckled, and colored by Christ. We are not full partners in the sense that we are equal or equivalent to God. Instead, we are a partner in the sense that we receive the presence of God and we find a way to give it away as a new gift to others. Thus, between the partners in this dance of prayer rests the rhythm of reception and giving. The prayer of participation, we might say, is a prayer of learning and practicing hospitality.

A new movement has recently emerged led by theologians such as John Milbank, Catherine Pickstock, and Graham Ward known as Radical Orthodoxy. With a passionate commitment to classical Christian belief and in conversational critique with postmodern and postsecular thought, this growing movement is often complex but illuminating. Without attempting anything more than a glance at Radical Orthodoxy, we can point out these writers' intense interest in participation and how participation in the sense they use it impinges on prayer.

John Milbank, for example, offers themes of participation in God as Being, Christ as the Word, and the Holy Spirit as an equal exchange of love between the Father and the Son. In the Immanuel quality of prayer, the believer is "present" to this eternal trinitarian exchange through participation in an equally reciprocal exchange of giving, receiving, and accepting. Milbank's project is a series of writings concerning gift. His analysis of gift is also complex but is centered on the idea of reciprocal exchange. The gift is given, but it must also be received. This reciprocal giving and receiving is the basis of overcoming a one-sided personalism; hence, he emphasizes participation as an eternal two-sided reciprocity between God and humanity.

To the question of why concentrate on gift, Milbank answers:

> The primary reason is that gift is a kind of transcendental category in relation to all the topoi of theology, in a similar fashion to "word." Creation and grace are gifts; Incarnation is the supreme gift; the Fall, evil and violence are the refusal of gift; atonement is the renewed and hyperbolic gift that is for-giveness [his most recent book focuses on forgiveness, reconciliation, and pardon]; the supreme name of the Holy Spirit is *donum* (according to Augustine); the Church is the community that is given to humanity and is constituted through the harmonious blending of diverse gifts.[15]

For Milbank, this emphasis on gift is best understood in the sense of participation. He insists that such participation extends into the whole realm of human activity from language to culture to history to personality and prayer. Thus, there is a sense in which we participate in what we might call the "gift of the kiss" of divine presence in all forms of prayer. As a way of life, such participation includes conversation, journey, relationship, and transformation. Teresa of Avila's gift of the experience of the "prayer of union" in the seventh castle casts her back into the world of human activity. Milbank's comprehensive category of gift likewise sets up an exchange wherein to accept the gift of divine presence is, at the same time, to return to ourselves, the created world, and others with at least a remnant of that same gift in hand. This is similar in many ways to centering prayer, which practices intentional openness to divine presence in encounters with all people and all things.

The exchange of the gift is key to participation and presence in prayer. The exchange is like the kiss of the bride and the bridegroom. In Shakespeare's play *Romeo and Juliet,* the two lovers join hands for the first time in an intentional posture of prayer. Romeo says, "Let lips do what hands do" (act 1, scene 5). We know of the tragedy to come, and so there is no more poignant yet true image in literature of the mutual exchange of gift—in this case of love—than this moment of lips brought together in prayer. Milbank refers to the apotheosis of this exchange as "a participation of reciprocal exchanges in an infinite reciprocity within the divine *donum.*"[16] Like the kiss, a gift is not a gift without exchange. A gift is not a gift without reception, which is itself simultaneously an acknowledgment and a renewal of the gift. Thus, true *donum* is gift, gift giving, and gift reception in simultaneous repetition. As with the kiss of Romeo and Juliet, the other can never be a mere object. In participation, the partner in a kiss is always a part of the gift.

Milbank further refines the notion of participation that has implications for prayer in saying that the mark of the giver is always on the gift:

> It is just *because* things as created can only be as gifts, just because their being is freely derived, that one has to speak of creation in terms of participation and of analogical likeness of the gift to the giver—since if this mark is not upon the gift, how else shall we know that it is a gift?[17]

If God's mark is not somehow contained within the gift of prayer, how will we know that it is prayer? God's mark may come in the form of conversation, relationship, journey, transformation, presence, or even absence. But the Immanuel quality of prayer, which is a gift of God, is marked by God.

One of Milbank's primary concerns in *Being Reconciled* is that the gift, even with the mark of the Creator, can be refused and the reciprocity broken. To reject this divine gift is sin. Reconciliation is possible only through participation in the gift via the *habitus* of acceptance. There is thus also a built-in ethical quality to participation and presence. Evil is not simply a privation of the good, nor is it an entity of its own in opposition to the good; both of these possibilities were rejected early in Christian theology. As Milbank formulates them, the questions of evil and sin take place at the level of will. We choose not to accept God's gift. We turn away from the Holy Spirit. Rejection of the gift is sin. Virtue is the free acceptance of the gift and the continuation of exchange.

Participative prayer, in the sense that we have been examining it, can also be practiced as *imitatio Christi,* the imitation of Christ. A case could be made that divine presence in prayer is participation in a dance, the music, rhythm, and steps of which place us in partnership with Jesus Christ. In this sense, imitation, again, implies accepting the gift of our true self and offering that gift to the world. God has gifted us to participate in a dance with Christ; how we do so is our life; it configures our prayer. The Gospels show a Christ who participates with whomever he encounters at whatever moment.

There are many ways of such participation with Christ in the Christian tradition. One way of taking part in Christ is the model offered by St. Francis of Assisi, who participated so perfectly in a dance with Christ that he carried the same wounds of love. Ignatius of Loyola developed meditation retreats intended to assimilate the life of Christ so completely that one becomes a contemplative in action. Thomas à Kempis wrote a book, *The Imitation of Christ,* that became second only to the Bible in readership for centuries. He inspired untold others to begin new movements or new lives dedicated to illuminating the presence of God in Christ. Dorothy Day struggled with her writing, activism, and isolation, in which she heard only the faintest echoes of music yet danced the Catholic Worker movement into being and gave back God's gift in the form of houses of hospitality that model Christ.

John Calvin calls *imitatio Christi* the ideal of participation, sharing, and contemplative "engrafting in Christ." "We do not, therefore, contemplate him outside ourselves from afar, . . . but because we put on Christ and are engrafted into his body—in short because he deigns to make us one with him."[18] Since we participate in Christ, our prayer and contemplation are not with a distant God but with a God who participates with us and is closer to us than we are to our own skin.

How we experience the presence of God in Christ within us is mediated by the place and time in which we live, our language and culture, and our personalities, dreams, and vocations. We would not expect that Francis or Ignatius or Thomas à Kempis or Dorothy Day or John Calvin would dance to the same music we do today. But however we are made aware of and enact the presence of God, Calvin reminds us that the presence of God is a gift and that participation in divine presence is the gift we are gifted to accept.

"Impressed with a Remembrance of God"

We bring all we are to prayer: imagination, hopes, dreams, fears, losses, perceptions, grief, memory, and joy. Or we could say that God captures all that we are in prayer. Whether in solitude or in community, through our journey of prayer, our body, mind, and spirit are caught up in the presence of God. We can recall Brother Lawrence's image of the statue. Slowly, as the stone is chipped away, an emergent human form begins to take on not only the shape of the model but also the image of God. Brother Lawrence's point is that our true self lies buried under unshaped stone. He suggests that there are times when we appear to do the chipping and the chiseling, and there are times when it is apparent that God is the sculptor. By the time the statue begins to take shape, God has but to "impress a remembrance" of God's self, and the statue comes to life:

> When his duties distracted him somewhat from thinking about God, God impressed a remembrance of himself on his soul, giving him so intense an awareness of God, warming and inflaming him so strongly, that he cried out and made exaggerated gestures, singing and jumping about like a fool.[19]

Here God's sculpted remembrance seems to make Lawrence a "fool." But Brother Lawrence's larger point is that the body, the mind, and the spirit cooperate in the spiritual work that forms us into "fools for Christ." As the statue of our true self begins to emerge, in the remembrance of God that God impresses on our soul, we see the outlines of the form and the figure of divine presence itself.

Origen, writing in third-century Alexandria, was the first to interpret the Song of Songs as an allegory not only of a dialogue between Christ and the church but also as the love between Christ and the individual soul. In the prologue to his *Commentary on the Song of Songs*, Origen writes that "this book seems to me an epithalamium, that is, a wedding song, written by Solomon in the form of a play, which he recited in the character of a bride who was being married and burned with heavenly love for her bridegroom who is the Word of God."[20] According to Origen, this heavenly union is achieved in cooperation with God primarily through contemplation employing both mind and heart. With regard to mind, Origen says that divine presence is rendered through "the contemplative discipline defined as that by which we transcend visible things and contemplate something of divine and heavenly things and gaze at them with the mind alone."[21] But we are also led into fellowship or divine presence, according to Origen, through the contemplative path of love:

> He also handed down the subject of contemplation in the book we have in hand, that is, the Song of Songs, in which he urges upon the soul the love of the heavenly and the divine under the figure of the bride and bridegroom, teaching us that we must attain *fellowship* with God by the paths of loving affection and of love.[22]

For Origen, both mind and heart are gifts of and pathways to the presence of God. The mind brings us into the presence of God through a "gaze of heavenly things." Through love, the body, mind, and soul are present to God in a way that goes deeper than a simple "gaze." The writer of the Song of Songs sings, "I am faint with love" (2:5). Origen's anthropology allows him to speak of entering divine presence both through the contemplative gaze (intellectual vision) and through the very real human experience of being faint with love.

In fourth-century Cappadocia, Gregory of Nyssa used biblical theophanies that expressed the remembrance of the presence of God. Using the image of the burning bush, Gregory equates the truth of the presence of God to the truth of the presence of light itself. From this he then moves easily to the Gospels and their enlightening quality of God made visible—and with us—Christ in flesh and in soul:

> And if the flame by which the soul of the prophet was illuminated was kindled from the thorny bush, even this fact will not be useless for our inquiry. For the truth is God and truth is light—the Gospel testifies by these sublime and divine names to the God who made himself visible to us in the flesh—such guidance of virtue leads us to know that light which has reached down even to human nature. Lest one think that the radiance did not come from the material substance, this light did not shine from some luminary among the stars but came from an earthly bush and surpassed the heavenly luminaries in brilliance.[23]

But Gregory of Nyssa is also known for initiating the language of *apophasis*, or the dark way, as another, equally important context for encountering the presence of a transcendent God. If God is present as a wound to the flesh, God is also present, paradoxically, in an incomprehensible way to the mind wherein darkness becomes the means of our illumination. Of this darkness Gregory says:

> When, therefore, Moses grew in knowledge, he declared that he had seen
> God in the darkness, that is, that he had then come to know that what is
> divine is beyond all knowledge and comprehension.[24]

With Gregory, in addition to darkness and light as metaphors of divine
presence, incomprehensibility itself takes on an aura of presence. But
it is this darkness, this incomprehensibility, this mystery that keeps the
soul coming back in prayer for more. As Gregory says, "This truly is the
vision of God: never to be satisfied in the desire to see him."

In the Christian prayer tradition, we are also captured by the remembrance of God through the images of angels. In this tradition, typically
nine orders of angels manifest a unique way of being present to God.[25]
The angelic order of the seraphim, as the path or mystical experience of
love, generally exemplifies the possibility of a direct, pure, simultaneous,
and immediate presence of God. Recalling that each of the orders also
represents a way of prayer or contemplation as well as a corresponding
exemplar of service and ministry for humanity, the writers in angelic
spirituality thus found a ready means for teaching the agency and nature
of divine participation. On the unmediated relationship of the seraphim
with God—and by implication of our own ministries and experience
of God—the twelfth-century theologian Alan of Lille writes that "the
Seraphim are irradiated by God's brilliance, receiving God's radiance
with immediate understanding."[26] Gregory the Great intends that we
take our lesson from the seraphim and imitate them:

> The Seraphim, since they have been so united to God that no other spirit
> may intervene between them and God, burn all the more fiercely as they
> see God more intimately. Their love is truly a flame, since the more they
> look upon the glory of God's divinity, the more savagely they burst into
> flame with God's love.[27]

The seraphim enjoy a relationship with God in which "no other spirit
may intervene." Though we are not seraphim and though Gregory the
Great and all the writers in this tradition are clear that it is only Jesus
Christ who mediates salvation, the clear intention is that through imitation of the various orders of angels, humanity also has the opportunity
to enter the presence of God with or without intervention.

The twelfth-century artist of love Bernard of Clairvaux uses other images to describe the imprint of divine presence through prayer. As might
be expected, he focuses on love as the route to body, mind, and spirit.
In his treatise *On Loving God,* for example, he uses images drawn from
Scripture, personal experience, and imagination to evoke a personal
experience of the presence of God so intense that he writes of becoming

united with God: "When will it [the body] experience this kind of love, so that the mind, drunk with divine love and forgetting itself, making itself like a broken vessel (Ps. 30:13), may throw itself wholly on God and, clinging to God (1 Cor. 6:17), become one with him in spirit and say, 'My body and my heart have fainted, O God of my heart; God, my part in eternity' (Ps. 72:26)?"[28] To lose oneself in this way is, for Bernard, God coming to us so that we might become like God. Such loving presence annihilates the false self in such a way that the true self, enhanced in love, becomes or remembers the divine presence. This can only really be described by using image and metaphor. Bernard employs such images in rapid succession. Some imply the memory of presence as complete loss of false self, others imply God's presence as love, still others imply that in the presence of God the self remains, although it is now transformed as the true self God intended it to be:

> To love in this way is to become like God. As a drop of water seems to disappear completely in a quantity of wine, taking the wine's flavor and color; as red-hot iron becomes indistinguishable from the glow of fire and its own original form disappears; as air suffused with the light of the sun seems transformed into the brightness of the light, as if it were itself light rather than merely lit up; so, in those who are holy, it is necessary for human affection to dissolve in some ineffable way, and be poured into the will of God. How will God be all in all (1 Cor. 15:28), if anything human remains in one? The substance remains, but in another form, with another glory, another power.[29]

For Bernard, it is the "substance" of the self that remains, though, as he says, "in another form." That substance, again, includes the body, the mind, and the spirit. None is annihilated. Rather, they are ecstatic with love, as it were, in a kind of heightened perception of the impress of the remembrance of God.

Teresa of Avila's comprehensive writings on prayer incorporate elements of prayer as journey, relationship, transformation, and also presence. She shares Bernard of Clairvaux's proclivity for images of union that, in the context of prayer, serve as directional signals of the presence of God. Teresa gives one of the simplest yet most profound expressions of presence: "The truth is that the treasure [of divine presence] lies within our very selves."[30]

Along with the Song of Songs, Origen, John of the Cross, and Bernard of Clairvaux, Teresa takes the presence of God as a wound of love; it is shot through with the pain of loss. But precisely through this wound—what we experience as loss, grief, envy, mourning—the presence of God flames white-hot, cauterizing though never completely eradicating the wound.

Accepting and living our wounds, we enter into a new way of presence with God, what Teresa calls "continual companionship":

> The vision is something definitely understood to be a gift from God and human effort would not be sufficient to produce this experience. . . . This *continual companionship* gives rise to a most tender love for His Majesty, to some desires even greater than those mentioned to surrender oneself totally to His service, and to a great purity of conscience because *the presence at its side makes the soul pay attention to everything.* For even though we already know that God is present in all we do, our nature is such that we neglect to think of this. Here the truth cannot be forgotten, for the Lord awakens the soul to His beside it.[31]

Meister Eckhart (1260–1329), perhaps the most-quoted—though also misunderstood—Christian mystic, takes a different approach to the imprint of divine presence in prayer. On the one hand, Eckhart places God beyond Being (in Neoplatonic fashion); on the other, he defines God as Being-as-such (a Thomist position). This combination of influences and Eckhart's own unique formulation of the doctrine of creation allows for the possibility of a sort of "equality" between God and humanity. God is "born" in the soul, and the soul is "born" in God. As with Teresa, this is as much a physical birth as it is a spiritual birth. In one of his sermons, Eckhart even argues that Martha (compassionate in mind and body) actually has the "better part" over Mary (contemplation in spirit and body).[32] In other words, if one is completely present to oneself, one is completely present to God, and if one is completely present to God, one is completely present to others. The implication of this for prayer is that God is as immediately present in the soul as the soul is in God. This allows for Eckhart's famous "birth of the Word in the soul," in which true presence to God is an ongoing cycle of birth-death-rebirth taking place "instantaneously" at every moment in time. In acknowledging and participating in that birth, we find ourselves steeped in the presence of God.

This all sounds abstract, but Eckhart actually preached this doctrine of divine presence to his congregation. He could be abstract, and often was in his Latin treatises, but many of his German sermons urge his listeners to live this "presence beyond all being." In one sermon, his more abstract metaphysical constructions are put in concrete terms of God's will and justice. After dismissing those who want to do only their own will and those who want to do God's will only if it conforms to their own, Eckhart says, "The just have no will at all; what God wills is all the same to them. . . . What is my life? God's being is my life."[33] What could be simpler and yet more profoundly true? God's will, God's justice, and

God's being are one; if we conform to God's will, our being is God's being, God's presence is our existence, God's memory is our memory.

In this same sermon, Eckhart preaches the birth of the Word in the soul. It would be difficult to imagine a sermon today in which we are told that God is within us, simply on the basis of our existing and being alive. We are perhaps more used to hearing that sin is within simply on the basis of our existing and being alive. Without disregarding the reality of sin—and none of these writers, classic or contemporary, do—the implications of God's continual birth and therefore continual presence within us are staggering. Our very being, consciousness, and breath are prayers indistinguishable from the presence of God. Our body, mind, and spirit are prayers that, like the womb, may gestate the birth of God within. While recognizing evil, sin, loss, brokenness, and grief, Eckhart calls us to an awareness of prayer that depends on a simple turn in the direction of God's will; the "turn" may be no more than the blink of new understanding. Preaching on 2 Corinthians 3:18, "We shall be completely transformed and changed into God" (Eckhart's version), Eckhart adds, "What is changed into something else becomes one with it. I am so changed into him that he produces his being in me as one, not just similar. By the living God, this is true! There is no distinction."[34]

Eckhart had more than a little hardship with the church during his own lifetime due to the unusual direction of his theology. But the direction of his thought and sermons breathes new life into our notion of God and prayer. God, in a real sense, gives birth to us without ceasing, and the Word of God is born and imprinted within ourselves, also without end. This is an open, reciprocating relationship. To take hold of that idea, if even for a moment, is to become conscious of the eternal presence of God in our body, mind, and soul; in others; and in the world around us.

The height of mystic consciousness exemplified by Meister Eckhart illustrates God's imprint on our full humanity and our awakening to that imprint as if to a memory of God present with us here and now. The divine presence is also displayed convincingly in the simple presence of Jesus Christ. Christ's presence is our prayer for all time. In taking the bread and the wine, we share in the body and blood of Jesus Christ and remember him until he comes again. True participation in the life of Christ leads us into ministries of service to the poor and the oppressed and hospitality to the broken and the ignored. These acts of compassion are simple prayers of and care for the hurting and the hungry as well as small prayers of divine presence.

The "little way" of the Carmelite nun Thérèse of Lisieux, who was canonized in 1925, also directs us toward a way of divine presence through charity, body and soul, and following the way of Christ and his new commandment that we love one another just as Christ has loved us (John 13:34–35). Thérèse reminds us that this is Christ's own commandment (15:12) and that "it is no longer a question of loving one's neighbor as oneself [Lev. 19:18] but of loving Christ as he, Jesus, has loved *his* neighbor and will love him to the consummation of the ages."[35] The true unity with the presence of Christ is, for Thérèse, the little way of charity. Charity can only be offered in the spirit of abandonment to the presence of God in mind, body, and spirit.

In his *Imitation of Christ*, Thomas à Kempis speaks of prayer as "close friendship with Jesus." He says that "to know how to talk with Jesus is a great skill; to know how to hold fast to Jesus is great wisdom." But above all, it is the presence of Jesus that renders prayer meaningful and life, all of it, worth the time and the risk:

> When Jesus is present, everything seems good and nothing difficult. When Jesus is absent, everything is hard. When Jesus does not speak to us inwardly, we have little comfort. But, let Jesus speak just one word and our sense of satisfaction is great.[36]

From Origen to Bernard of Clairvaux to Meister Eckhart to Thérèse of Lisieux to Thomas à Kempis is a series of great leaps. But each preaches, in his or her own way, a way of life that is imprinted with the memory of God. It is through that memory that each becomes for us a symbol of an intention to consent to the presence of God.

Wonder and Awe in Divine Beauty, Truth, and Goodness

The closer we come to God in prayer, the more God's mystery becomes apparent. Jean-Pierre de Caussade captures some of the wonder of this mystery by comparing it to the weaving of a beautiful, shimmering tapestry:

> All goes well when God is, so to speak, both the author and the object of our faith, the one complementing and augmenting the other. It is like the right side of a beautiful tapestry being worked stitch by stitch on the reverse side. Neither the stitches nor the needle are visible, but, one by one, those stitches make a magnificent pattern that only becomes apparent when the work is completed and the right side exposed to the light of day; although while it is in progress there is no sign of its beauty and wonder. The same applies to self-surrendered souls who see only God. The accomplishment of that [vision] is at each moment one imperceptible stitch added to the tapestry. And yet it is with these stitches that God performs wonders.[37]

Indeed, God performs wonders. As we have noted, one way prayer brings us into the presence of the mystery of God is that through God's sanctifying work we are transformed—from one degree of glory to another—into the image of God. Deification (literally, being made godlike), *theōsis,* and union with God are just some of the ways that the great Christian writers on prayer have expressed this work of mystery. Another way to express this mystery of divine presence is to speak of it in terms of theophany (literally, God sightings) that are akin to Moses' encounter with the burning bush, his entry into the cloud at Mt. Sinai, God's presence within the ark of the covenant or the holy of holies, or the transfiguration. With the advent of Jesus in the New Testament, a whole life is actually lived and revealed as a literal theophany. Imitation of or union with Christ in prayer brings us into intimate contact with the theophany of God.

In the Christian prayer tradition, there are many ways of describing theophany or the process of deification. These run from a transitory and immediate deifying awareness of God to the intentional prayer of godlike action and thought that is carried in body and soul moment to moment. These opposite extremes are not mutually exclusive but often complementary.

One early non-Christian writer has proven particularly influential in the area of providing language and self-definition for deification in prayer. As Bernard McGinn writes, "No other ancient author has portrayed the psychology of mystical [and prayer] states with their complex passages between the consciousness of duality and unity with greater subtlety than Plotinus."[38] Plotinus's (205–70) Neoplatonist categories exerted profound influence on the mystery of presence in Christian prayer. His work focuses on strategies for blending duality (ourselves and God) and unity (God) without collapsing the difference completely. His influence was not only philosophical but also, as McGinn notes, psychological and therefore easily translated into the language of the journey of the soul to union with God. Nine treatises, called the *Enneads,* were collected and published by his pupil Porphyry. In the *Enneads,* Plotinus proposes three transcendent levels of reality that exist beyond the visible universe: the One, the intellect, and the soul. The soul was further divided into the transcendent universal soul and nature, or the material world, in which the human soul is embodied.[39] The system allows for a "vestige" of the One even at those levels of emanation most distant from the One. Plotinus's system has been interpreted in a number of ways. Philosophically, he employs an emanationist metaphysic in which the procession, or emanation, from the higher to the lower stages is reversed (or completed) in the process of conversion or return. The system can also be internalized and seen as a kind of metapsychology that presents

an analysis of the possible fulfillment of human consciousness or desires of the human soul. In other words, one can turn inward in order
to turn upward.

A brief look at Plotinus will help to clarify our own Christian contemplative system of God's descent in Christ, which allows for the possibility of human ascent to God. In this system of procession and return,
even those levels most distant from the One contain an element or a
shadow of that same One or source. In theological terms, this distance
is equivalent to transcendence, while the shadow is equivalent to immanence. In the Christian interpretation of Plotinus's system, the energy
or means of contemplative return from the shadow across the distance
is accomplished in a variety of ways: through beauty, truth, goodness,
desire, longing, human effort, intellect, love, or grace.

Beauty is a particularly appropriate example, since it is seldom used
as a form of prayer today. Yet the beauty of the natural world, of the
human form, of design, of art, of ideas has been an especially powerful
motivating force in the history and practice of Christian prayer. Through
the use of the creative and intuitive imagination, meditation on beauty
has been taught as a form of prayer leading to the presence of God as
beauty. A few examples from Plotinus's own treatise on beauty in the
Enneads help shed light on how presence, mystery, and beauty may be
reformulated in Christian prayer.[40]

The soul is able to participate in the One and abide in its presence,
according to Plotinus, because the "soul, being what it is and related to
the reality above it, is delighted when it sees any signs of kinship" to itself.
In beauty, the soul actually sees a kinship to God. Beauty represents the
similarity of the soul to the goal *and* the driving force of the emanation
and return of the soul to the One. For Plotinus, beauty resides in both
unity (or the One, later interpreted by Christian writers as God) and the
parts (individual souls). Beauty for Plotinus is both transcendent and
immanent. Plotinus is strikingly personal in his metaphysical system:
Porphyry claimed to have been present on four occasions when Plotinus
did in fact come into the presence of the One. This personability is evi-
dent in his description of the soul's gathering the "fragments" of beauty
and cherishing them as means of ascent to participation in the One. The
soul, he says, "draws it [beauty] within oneself to present it there to one's
interior and indivisible oneness as concordant, congenial, a friend" (1.6.3).
Beauty dwells as a kind of connective tissue between the soul and the
One. For Plotinus, "They are sharers of the same idea" (1.6.2).

Plotinus also "heightens" the spiritual intuition of the senses in a way
that influenced Augustine and countless others after him: Only lovers of
beauty are stung by the truth of the presence of the One (God) within and
without and then only through a "seeing [that] is done only with the eye

of the soul" (1.6.4). Beauty thus opens the eye of the soul. Plotinus offers this advice to all at prayer: "That is why one is right in saying that the good and the beauty of the soul consist in its becoming godlike because from the divinity all beauty comes and all the constituents of reality. Beauty is genuine reality; ugliness is its counter" (1.6.6). Beauty of the soul as "genuine reality" in the Christian context consists in becoming "like God" or present to God, since all beauty is from God. In this sense, beauty transforms and is an end product in itself, being in the image of God. This is the basis of prayer as a way of life: that beauty/God is the constituent part of reality to which all prayer is oriented. "We must close our eyes," Plotinus writes, "and invoke a new manner of seeing, a wakefulness that is the birthright of us all, though few put it to use" (1.6.8). But to become like God in the presence of God, we must remain in a state of "wakefulness" in which the soul beholds God by "remaining solely itself" (1.6.7). The paradox of the "genuine reality" is that the soul is imprinted with the presence of God and becomes godlike in prayer by "remaining solely itself."

Another Plotinian element later incorporated by Christian writers on prayer is that virtue is also a prerequisite to the ability to see beauty. Like anyone awakened, he says, "the soul cannot look at bright objects. It must be persuaded to look first at beautiful habits" (1.6.9). Through virtue, the soul journeys to its "authentic self," or a self that grows in its capacity to see. The authentic self is just another way of saying "beautiful soul." That same beautiful soul is the eye that sees God. This process of attaining a vision of the authentic self as beauty through the work of virtue is expressed by Plotinus in an image of a sculptor and a statue:

> If you do not as yet see beauty within you, do as does the sculptor of a statue that is to be beautified: he cuts away here, he smoothes it there, he makes this line lighter, this other one purer, until he disengages beautiful lineaments in the marble. Do you this, too. Cut away all that is excessive, straighten all that is crooked, bring light to all that is overcast, labor to make all one radiance of beauty. . . . Do you see yourself in this state? Then you have become the vision itself. . . . No eye that has not become like unto the sun will ever look upon the sun; nor will any that is not beautiful look upon the beautiful. Let each one therefore become godlike and beautiful who would contemplate the divine and the beautiful. (1.6.9)

Plotinus, especially in this treatise on beauty, had a profound influence on Christian prayer, meditation, and contemplation. The influence can be seen both in the practice of virtue and in contemplative rest as two viable routes of the soul to God. The body is chipped and chiseled until beauty reveals itself and the soul becomes a likeness of God.

There is much of Plotinus that, applied to Christian prayer, would render such prayer unhealthy or even *not* Christian prayer. A few of these elements include the obvious fact that Christ is not present; that the One is not the personal God of Moses, Abraham and Sarah, Isaac and Rebecca, Peter, and Paul; that human effort and sheer will are weighted extremely heavily as paths to the One; that there is no sense of grace or the work of the Holy Spirit. According to Plotinus, there is an "image" of the One in the human soul, but it is nothing like the Christian *imago Dei*. In Plotinus's system, creation is a necessary, not a decisive and divinely initiated, act. Equally at odds with Christian prayer is Plotinus's emphasis on the soul's personal and individualistic ascent to God. He is famous for his soul's journey into God as the "flight of the alone to the alone." Community seems not to be a factor at all.

Nonetheless, much of Plotinus's system proved to be flexible and immensely valuable to Christian prayer, especially the prayer that drew the contemplative, through meditation on truth or beauty and a life of virtue, into the presence of God. Kenneth Leech reports how the Christian tradition assimilated and transformed Plotinus's system of procession from God and return to God with the doctrine of the incarnation. The purpose of the incarnation, Leech declares, "was to raise humanity to share the Divine life." He gives a number of striking examples:

> So Origen (188–254) speaks of our divinization (*theopoiēsis*) through contemplation, while St. Irenaeus (130–200) speaks of our participation (*metochē*) in God. "The Word became man," he says, "in order to make us what he is himself." Again, St. Athanasius (296–373) writes that "he became man that we might become divine." In the seventh century, St. Maximus the Confessor says, "A firm and trustworthy basis for hope of the deification of human nature is God's incarnation which makes of man a god in the same measure as God himself became man." . . . S. Thomas Aquinas repeats it: "The only begotten Son of God, wishing to enable us to share in his divinity, assumed our nature, so that by becoming man, he might make men gods."[41]

In addition to transforming a pagan philosophy into a vibrant doctrine of eschatological hope and transformational prayer, early Christian writers borrowed from Plotinus to claim the seemingly impossible: The goal of prayer grounded in the incarnation is the union of humanity with God.

In our decision to consent to God's presence working within us, we find that in a real sense God "descends," and in our contemplations, God's grace reminds us of our likeness to God. In that memory, most concrete in Scripture and in Christ, we are led back to the presence of God. But in the Christian tradition itself, it is clear that the presence of God is like the presence of a lover beckoning our love in return. In varying ways, God shows a willingness to exhibit love. In prayer as a way of life, in a real sense, we become a presence ourselves. Perhaps the best way to phrase this is that in cooperation with the rhythms of grace we become the presence of God to others. In prayer, the life of formation becomes life as discipleship and witness.

Aquinas: Proofs as Meditations on the Presence of God

How we think about and experience God affects our consciousness of the presence of God in contemplation and prayer. While theological anthropology is especially important for understanding prayer as relationship, both theological anthropology and the doctrine of God are of particular relevance to prayer and divine presence. Thomas Aquinas is one example of the fact that how one thinks about God affects how one prays. Aquinas's philosophical and theological proofs for the existence of God are valuable tools for meditation on the presence of God.

Thomas Aquinas did not claim that the effects of God in the world can help us know God's inner nature or essence, but he did believe that we can establish *that* God exists and characterize God with some degree of accuracy. Using Aristotle and human reason, Aquinas establishes five "proofs" of God from God's effects in the world. The proofs also serve to establish attributes and characteristics of the existing God, characteristics we might experience in the prayer of presence. The conclusion of Aquinas's first proof of God's existence gives us a God who is pure act (here there is no potential; all divine potential is realized in divine action). The second proof shows that God is also the first efficient cause; all other secondary causes and their effects are dependent on this first efficient causality. Third, Aquinas characterizes God as necessary being. All other secondary beings are contingent, dependent on God's necessary being. All secondary beings are contingent because in them essence (what they are) and existence (that they are) can be distinguished. In God, *what* God is cannot be separated from the reality *that* God is. Fourth, God is the source of all limited perfections (such as beauty and truth) that we have in the world. For this fourth proof Aquinas draws more on the Platonic tradition, in which the forms, put into the mind of God, are God's perfections. All created things are exemplars, vestiges, and shadows of the forms in the divine mind. In the fifth and final proof, God is known as the final cause or continuing source of all motion and reality, maintaining order in the movement from potential to active reality.[42] Aquinas's philosophical proofs of God's existence thus lead to five attributes or categories of God that in themselves can serve as meditations on the presence of God: (1) God is pure act; (2) God is the first efficient cause; (3) God is necessary being; (4) God is the source of all perfections; and (5) God is the final cause of all things.

Aquinas's proofs of God and the divine attributes that can be derived from them reveal that how we describe God determines in large measure how we are conscious of God's presence in prayer. For instance, if God is fully realized potential and pure act, our prayer is dynamic and grounded in a constantly reinforcing relationship between our God-given potential (our full humanity) and our act (how we live in the world). To be present to pure act is to be present to the love that moves the sun and the other stars. To be present to God as first efficient cause is to be present to an eternity held within the present. Our cycles of cause and effect are caught up in God's originating cause. Contemplation in the presence of necessary reality or being has, as all these attributes have, a purgative, illuminative, and perfecting quality. In prayer, as contingent beings coming before necessary being as God, we are gracefully humbled. As we understand our contingency in the context of God's necessary reality, we come to see our dependency as necessary in an illuminating way. The insight of our own necessary dependency calls us closer to the perfection of God as our contingent natures begin to glow in the light of divine and necessary perfection. To be present to the source of all perfections is to participate in an ever-deepening way in perfection itself. We do not pray as the source, but through grace we can pray in the light of perfection. Finally, to be present in prayer to the final cause of all things opens the eyes of our heart to the small but essential role each of us has in fulfilling that final cause, the eschatological consummation of all causes and beings. Regardless of the seeming insignificance of that role, if it partakes in the final cause, it is of the quality of the final cause.

Doctrine or laying out divine attributes certainly did not begin or end with Thomas Aquinas. His system merely provides one possible avenue for prayer. Representatives of the many other divine attributes proposed and even insisted on include impassibility, omnipotence, omniscience, divine suffering, kenotic self-limitation, and more. Each of these can be fruitfully applied in the renewal of prayer.

The Divine Names as Ways to Prayerful Presence

A final excursion into the characterization of the presence of a personal God with us in prayer involves divine names as revealed in and through Scripture. This involves what the Bible tells us specifically about God and how we name and characterize God. Deep in both the Jewish and Christian traditions, God cannot be named. The Jewish tradition of not speaking the name of God is strong; God's name is too holy to be spoken. In the book of Exodus, God self-names when he says cryptically but simply, "I AM THAT I AM" (3:14 KJV). In the Christian tradition, God's incomprehensibility is always acknowledged in the awareness that God's names as revealed in Scripture never limit God, never capture God, but always are glimpses of the fullness of God's glory. Language is always partial, never complete. Divine names help us to acknowledge and to pray the reality of God's simultaneous presence *and* absence. To approach the profound but mysterious dilemma of God's simultaneous ability to be named and to be beyond all names and the effect of that reality on God's absence and presence in prayer, we turn once again to Dionysius the Areopagite.

In his short treatise *The Divine Names,* Dionysius says, "Theologians praise [God] by every name—and as the Nameless One."[43] Dionysius then lists over ninety-seven names from Scripture applied to God, Christ, or the Holy Spirit. These include such obvious names as light, truth, good, beautiful, wise, God of gods, and many more. Others may not be quite as obvious but are also all from Scripture. A few include ancient of days, the unaging and unchanging, greatest of all and yet the one in the still breeze, water, bread, wind, and rock. Other words apply human or animal forms to describe divinity: eyes, face, back, and wings. There are many more, all of which Dionysius urges us to "behold in acts of heavenly contemplation."

The divine names can help us enter into the presence of God—and be present ourselves to God—by beholding in heavenly contemplation both what God is and what he is not. The names help both to place necessary boundaries around our experience of God and to open our horizon to ever-expanding possibilities of heavenly contemplation of divine presence.

As mentioned in an earlier chapter, Dionysius links the methods of apophatic and cataphatic theology that help us to undertake new ways of thinking about and being with God. Dionysius makes the link clear: To approach the ineffable One, one must practice both forms of prayer. On the one hand, he emphasizes the truths of cataphatic theology and God's presence:

> In my *Theological Representations,* I have praised the notions which are most appropriate to affirmative theology. . . . In the *Divine Names* I have shown the sense in which God is described as good, existent, life, wisdom, power, and whatever other things pertain to the names of God. In my *Symbolic Theology,* I have discussed analogies of God drawn from what we perceive.[44]

On the other hand, he emphasizes apophatic theology. In prayer that draws us to the throne of God, the more we move toward God, the more analogies, metaphors, or images of any kind falter:

> The fact is that the more we take flight upward, the more our words are confined to the ideas we are capable of forming; so that now as we plunge into that darkness which is beyond intellect, we shall find ourselves not simply running short of words but actually speechless and unknowing. . . . The more language climbs, the more language falters.[45]

"Plunging into darkness" can be translated as plunging into mystery, which Dionysius describes as "beyond assertion and denial. There is no speaking of it, nor name nor knowledge of it. It is beyond assertion and denial. We make assertions and denials only of what is next to it."[46]

A short meditation using the divine names can also help us see the interrelationship of divine presence and absence. This form of meditation is based on the concept of what Dionysius calls "descending affirmations" and "ascending denials." In other words, in saying what God *is*, it is simpler and more precise to begin by affirming the highest names of God (for instance, we can say with some ease that God is love and truth) and then *descend* to lower names of God that are revealed in Scripture but are, at first glance, not so obviously related to divine presence (for example, God as wind or rock). Though God is referred to as both wind and rock in Scripture, it is much easier to begin by affirming that God is love and end by affirming that, in a certain sense, God is also our rock.

Using the *via negativa*, or path of denials, the process is just the opposite. In this case, in saying what God *is not*, it is simpler and more precise to begin by denying the lowest names of God (God is *not* wind or rock). These are fairly easy attributes to deny: Wind and rock, seen from this perspective, seem to limit the transcendent God. We are generally comfortable with this, and therefore our prayer in the path of denial would start by saying that God is not simply the wind or a rock.

But we must, to be honest about our limitations and God's transcendence, also ascend to higher names of God. Denying first that God is rock, we must in honesty deny that, to our limited way of knowing, God is beyond our most informed and cherished conceptions of truth. Therefore, God is not really truth or love as our feeble abilities are able to conceive or experience them. God is always *more* than what we can ever know of truth or experience of love. Thus, using love as an example, it is truth to affirm that God is love, but it is also truth to *deny* that God is love, because human love will forever fall short of God's perfect love and compassion.

To practice this form of Dionysian meditation, one begins with an intuitive meditation on each of the divine names. All human faculties including intellect, memory, and emotion are brought to bear on imagining and focusing on the name of God. In this way, we enter into the full meaning of the divine name in both its biblical context and in our own personal and community experience. The exercise begins by affirming each name of God. It continues by denying each name of God. The purpose of each affirmation is to support and build up devotion. The purpose of each denial is to challenge our inadequate and limited concepts of God, which hinder us from growth. The meditation continues from name to name as in a circle, beginning with love and moving through wisdom, good, and so on in descending order until one reaches, for instance, God is a rock, wherein descending affirmations and ascending denials blend one into the other. Ascending denials then begin, beginning with God is not rock, moving through God is not light, and so on.

The exercise can be done individually or with a group. One particularly useful way to practice this prayer is to form a circle, passing a stone or other object from one to another. Each person takes a turn with the next divine name on the list as the stone is passed to them. The meditation continues around the circle. The emotional and cognitive dissonance that begins to mount as we approach the moment of denying, for instance, that God is love is always palpable. Often the person who is in line to speak "God is not love" will hesitate, even refuse to speak, and pass the stone. Participants are invited to do this if they so choose. Obviously, it is difficult to let go of control over our ideas concerning who and what God is. Often it is a good practice to end the meditation by passing the stone completely around the circle, allowing each person to affirm a positive name of God of their own choosing. Overall, this is an exercise that must be led by a skilled and gracious leader who is able to be pastorally sensitive to participants who may experience some difficulty in the path of negation, a new concept for many people unfamiliar with this practice.

Through both affirmations and denials, the overall effect of this exercise, however, is to increase (rather than decrease) our sense of awe and wonder at the mystery of God. God is present in the large and in the small. This divine-names prayer is a prayer of presence in which our expectations and imaginings about God are realigned, even at times shattered. Throughout, however, God's presence remains particularly strong as we begin to accept God's power, wisdom, and goodness in transformative ways.

"A Treasure in the Earth": A Short Letter on Prayer

In a "Letter on Prayer," by the same anonymous fourteenth-century author of the *Cloud of Unknowing,* we find an endearing explanation of the how and the why of the presence of God in prayer, illustrated by an extended allegory using the tree of life.[47] It is altogether a delightful, wise, and fitting final letter.

Throughout the letter, the author employs an allegory of the tree of life as a metaphor for the presence of God. In the allegory, the soul or church at prayer is the gardener assisting God, who is simultaneously the master gardener and the master to whom the fruits of the garden are offered. Julian of Norwich, a contemporary of the anonymous writer of this letter, also writes of the tree of life and speaks of prayer as a "treasure in the earth which the Lord loved."

The anonymous author of the letter also knows of a "treasure in the earth which the Lord loved." The writer speaks of a "staff of hope" that supports that love with trust, and what the author refers to as "reverent affection" for the presence of God. The author plants his or her own treasure in the earth, the seed of a prayerful tree of life whose fruition culminates in a new consciousness of the presence of God. As the fruit is harvested, it becomes sweet in and of itself and is now suitable as an offering returned to God, as compassion offered to others, as stewardship for the rest of the treasures of the earth, or even for the sweet fruit of self-knowledge. The gardener begins to see the fruit not simply as a gift but as something much sweeter: the presence of God *as* God *for* the world. The fragrant, sweet, colorful, enticing, and ripe fruit is a new treasure grown from the earth for the hand, lips, and mouth in prayer. The ripe fruit has as its source hope and love of God.

But the practical advice of the letter also shows that the author knows the other side of presence: "[Sometimes] you feel this exercise [of prayer] to be hard, heart-constricting, and without consolation." In a vivid image, he writes of this lack of consolation: "The greenness of the fruit [is] still hanging on the tree, or else just plucked, puts your teeth on edge."[48] Nevertheless, he says, "it is profitable." Prayer is beyond our control. One moment we are with God; the next we reach for what we think to be the sweetest fruit only to find it puts our teeth on edge.

Yet for the writer of this short letter, the tree of life grows from a treasure in the earth. Prayer rooted in a healthy fear of the wonder, majesty, and mystery of God, stabilized on a trunk of hope, branching out into service of charity, and coming to ripe fruition in the presence of God is a tree of life buried deep in the soul. It matures into prayer in which "God breaks open the fruit and gives you a part of your own present."[49]

Apples, Voeikovo, near St. Petersburg, Russia. Used by permission of Gennadiy Nikishkov.

Mutsu or Crispin Apples

The "present" here means both gift and presence: a treasure to shock and delight the roots of the soul.

Conclusion

> The single presupposition of a genuine state of prayer is thus the readiness of the whole person for this Presence, simple turned-towardness, unreserved spontaneity.
>
> Martin Buber, *The Eclipse of God*

Writing about prayer in general, Nicholas Lash makes an observation that applies especially to the prayer of presence. Commenting on the difficulty of prayer in contemporary times, he says, "If it is in this time and place that we try to pray, then we should not be surprised if we find it dauntingly difficult to articulate our speech with accuracy and integrity."[50] Articulating prayer, not to mention articulating God's presence in our prayer, is dauntingly difficult. But it is this daunting difficulty that reflects the strength and the integrity of the model of prayer as presence.

First, presence serves to preserve the mystery of God. Divine presence that can be expressed only with great difficulty forces us to turn toward God in wonder and awe and without preconceived expectations. It frees us from any excessive effort to control our experiences of God in prayer. Simply put, this difficulty of presence lets God be God.

The apples on the previous page are Mutsu or Crispin apples developed in the Aomori Research Station, Kurioshi, Japan, in 1937 and popularized in American orchards in the 1960s. Known for their crisp texture and juicy sweetness, they have been tended by a loving orchardist with great care. In early spring, frost was chased away by a few old smudge pots, a wind machine blowing colder air from depressions in the land, and the trick of watering the trees so that a thin frozen layer forms, protecting the new buds and blossoms from damage. The trees have been fertilized, thinned, propped, irrigated, sprayed, and the land around them mowed throughout the season. These are the things the orchardist can control. Others are out of his hands. Perhaps it hailed early in the season and some apples were bruised, making them suitable only as juicers. Or perhaps the cool nights and warm days lasted into October, raising the sugar content to sweet perfection. The orchardist has walked this land many times looking for mildew, bugs, gophers, a thousand little things. The work is dauntingly difficult. The fragrant fruit returns year after year, a mystery, a gift, a consolation, a red orb loading the trees, coaxing the earth, enticing the sky, inviting prayer. The daunting difficulty also reminds us that divine presence in prayer is pure gift. Prayer is a gift that may be received or rejected; it is up to us. Prayer is a gift of presence that, even in the dark night of the dauntingly difficult, God continues to offer for our reception.

Another sense of the daunting difficulty of prayer is apparent in the poverty of language to express the presence of God. Yet Christians throughout the centuries have found ways to communicate the presence of God to others. Thus, though it is dauntingly difficult to express divine presence, we are compelled to try. But equally important as finding ways of communicating the presence of God is the task of living out that presence with integrity. This is the fruit of prayer, how we live out prayer as a way of life. Though prayer, meditation, and contemplation are at times dauntingly difficult, the fruits of prayer have always been the criteria by which we measure the integrity of our prayer as we practice and participate in prayer as a way of life.

Divine presence and our presence to God are the fragrant fruit and flowers of prayer. Yet they are fed by the entire tree: From the root of conversation, to the trunk of relationship, to the branches of our journey, to the leaves of transformation, each of the models of prayer is essentially connected and entrusted to every other element of the tree. Each model represents contemplative practice and compassionate action growing organically from the tree of life within its ecology.

As a final exercise, we will briefly note the reciprocal influence of presence on the other models of prayer. In prayer as verbal conversation, God is present as a trusted partner. Whether in liturgical prayer or personal prayer, verbal prayer is based in part on conversational models from Scripture. Conversation also involves listening and silence as well as words and actions, which are also modeled in Scripture. Augustine models both words and silence in conversational prayer based on an experience of the presence of God. After his shared vision at Ostia, he ruminates on the riches of silence before he and his mother return to conversation as speech. His ruminations (in words) are ruminations on divine presence heard in silence as the voice of love:

> Suppose that the heavens and even [a person's soul] were silent, no longer thinking of itself but passing beyond; suppose . . . every tongue and every sign and all that is transient grew silent—for all these things have the same message to tell: We did not make ourselves, but he who abides forever made us. Suppose after giving us this message, . . . they fell silent and he alone would speak to us . . . in his own voice the voice of the one we love in all of these created things.[51]

Conversation with God forms the roots of our presence to God.

Human relationship is a paradigm for understanding the divine-human relationship. All that comprises our human relationships informs how we are present to God and how God is present to us. Though human relationship does not represent the full spectrum of how God is present to us, from our standpoint, human relationship is the most effective metaphor for understanding God's relationship to us. If prayer is a way of life, then relationship, which in a sense defines our lives, is a way of prayer. Other attempts to reach an understanding of the presence of God become subordinate to such relationships as prayer or contemplative practice. Prayer and contemplative practice discipline our relationships as formational, consensual activities opening our body, heart, mind, and soul to divine presence. Thus, for the tree of life, relationship is the solid trunk, fed by honest conversation, which supports and feeds the fullest flowering of the fruits of presence.

In our journey, both personal and communal, we travel from one degree of consciousness of God's presence to another. Our life of prayer takes us over ever-expanding profusions of branches. Some are green, risky, and new. Others are well worn, strong, trusted, and safe. All have the potential to lead us into the presence of God. There are many branches, but they share a common trunk and common roots that ground us securely in the treasure of the earth even as we risk reaching to the treasure of the sky.

Human transformation through prayer depends on divine initiative, divine participation, and the earthly treasure of divine presence. Fruits, flowers, and seeds pollinate and create new life from the old. The leaves of transformation are so delicate and yet so vital to life, even as they shrivel and die. The grace and effort of their tasks maintain a sublimely calibrated balance between life and death. The tree of life grows in grace as God is present in these transforming moments.

Divine presence creates, redeems, and sustains conversation, journey, relationship, and transformation in prayer. John Calvin urges us to prayer as the means by which God can reveal this presence to us. It is, he says, by calling on God's name in prayer that "we invoke the presence" of God's providence, power, and goodness.[52] Calvin adds that it is because of God's promise to us of ever-present consolation that we can be bold in turning to God's gift of prayer:

> Persevere in prayer and, with desires suspended, patiently wait for the Lord. Then we shall be sure that, even though he does not appear, he is always present to us, and will in his own time declare how he has never had ears deaf to the prayers that in men's eyes he seems to have neglected.[53]

Here Calvin joins the cloud of witnesses to God's enduring presence: Even though God does not appear, God is always present, even when apparent absence brings tears to the eyes and deafness to the ears. Patience, waiting, perseverance, and God's appearing are the simple strengths of God's gift of presence. From a treasure hidden in the earth, it blossoms as a gift of fragrant fruit.

Part 3

The Ecology of Prayer

Sustaining Connections

Gathering and Practice

A nation that destroys its soils destroys itself. Forests are the lungs of our land, purifying the air and giving fresh strength to our people.

Franklin Delano Roosevelt, letter to state governors,
February 26, 1937

Franklin Roosevelt's insights about forests can be adapted to prayer. Prayers are the lungs of our soul. They purify our heart and intentions and give strength for the journey. Taken together, our trees of life comprise a forest ecology. Like the natural forests, this ecology of prayer helps sustain the larger ecology of planet earth. Our earth is but a speck in the ecology of this universe. The lungs of land and the lungs of souls breathe the air of love that flows from the divine ecology. Without prayer, we destroy our true selves and we decimate our communities of faith. God's ecology commands us to pray. But as Martin Luther intuited centuries ago, this is a command based on God's deep care for our survival.[1] Prayer is the air of life and the birthing place of love's breath.

Prayer is as much a way of life as breathing. We are knit together in the ecology of prayer most fully, however, through the practice of prayer in all its forms and in the communities that gather us together. In the ecology of prayer, the practice of prayer provides the vital, interconnected system by which our trees of life flourish and grow. Our interconnected systems of practices give structure to, ensure integrative reconciliation of, and foster freedom for all who gather in prayer. Practices give structure through discipline; they ensure integrative reconciliation among disparate personalities, peoples, and cultures; and they foster the freedom to become the persons, genders, cultures, races, and communities God would have us be. The ecology of prayer thus also includes this vital process of gathering. In prayer, we gather our selves, our communities, and our care for others and stewardship of creation; we gather our fears, our hopes, and our joys.

The models provide templates through which Christian history, theology, and spirituality may be applied to our practice of and our gatherings in prayer. Any gathering in the forest-rich practice of prayer can, in God's graciousness, provide the lungs of the soul with the breath of life until Christ comes again.

The Ecology of Prayer: Practices

> I have to keep reminding myself that it is not enough just to own the book.
>
> Margaret Guenther, *The Practice of Prayer*

The primary habitat of prayer is the *practice* of prayer. The tree of life grows from the soil of faith, hope, love, and persistence in prayer. The ecology of prayer finds sustenance and vitality in the *doing,* the *being,* and the *dwelling* in prayer. But Margaret Guenther is probably correct when she writes that "we do more talking *about* prayer than actual praying."[2] We must pray. A primary theme of this book is that prayer is a way of life. In a real sense, the writing and the reading of this book have been a prayer. But the intention of this book is to point beyond, to the world around us, as holding countless opportunities for practicing and embodying prayer in daily life.

Anthony de Mello writes of a time when his meditations had become nothing but a jumble of distractions. During this time, he had the good fortune of meeting an old Jesuit, Father Calveras, with a reputation for wisdom in prayer. After talking at length, the older Jesuit suggested to de Mello that he use his rosary to pray. De Mello mentions that he was quite taken aback by this: In his mind, he had come to consider the rosary and prayer beads antiquated practices suitable only for simple, uneducated, or naive people. But Father Calveras said even more:

> Possibly, give up your meditation altogether and just pray for all the graces you need. Pray for your fellow retreatants. Pray for those you love. Pray for the world. The fruit of a retreat is not obtained through meditation and deep reflection. It is a pure gift of God and while a certain amount of

reflection is helpful, even necessary, this gift is obtained through asking, through begging. So beg for this gift of prayer and the Lord will give it to you. Ask for the grace to pray. Ask for the grace to be generous with Christ. Ask for the grace of experiencing his love.[3]

De Mello writes that Father Calveras taught him that prayer is good and true in many forms. But in whatever form it is practiced, the fact that we can pray at all is a gracious and pure gift from God.

The five models of prayer presented in this book are linked to the tree of life. They are a part of that very real ecology of prayer that draws us together as a community of faith. The models help us see more clearly the range and modalities of prayer. Conversation, relationship, journey, transformation, and presence can be seen as discrete qualities or aspects of prayer. Our prayers are conversations; they are modeled on relationship; they evolve in ways that form an ongoing journey throughout our life; they awaken and transform us into new ways of seeing, doing, and being. The practice of prayer simultaneously opens us to the presence of God as God becomes present to us. Yet we see the truth of these models only as we begin to see that prayer is larger than any one particular model alone. Alone, prayer configured according to any one of these models would die, just as fruit without the roots soon would shrivel and fall. But together, they are graces of prayer that nourish and sustain something larger than the parts. Gathered together, they participate in a fully formed tree of life.

Today, resources are available that support the ecology of prayer and the desire we have to grow in prayer. Many books serve as excellent resources and guides for the practice of prayer. There are also retreat centers around the country (and around the world) dedicated to study, practice, training, and formation in spirituality, many of which incorporate prayer as a part of their program. Another excellent prayer resource is the contemporary retrieval of the wisdom and teaching of ancient writers from the various Christian traditions. Yet another resource is the lively contemporary interest in the concept of spiritual formation and practice itself. Today, the *practice* of prayer is seen as an essential component in the process of absorbing a tradition, ritualizing changing life patterns, forming community, and disciplining devotional commitments. We practice prayer as a way of knowing and being in the world. Another abundant resource has been with us all along. While it is true that there is a fresh, renewed vitality in prayer today, the church, its liturgy, and its people are a rich resource for the ecology of prayer. The church prays without ceasing. We are all aware of certain men and women of deep and quiet prayer whom we know keep the eyes of their heart open to the needs and care of others and their devotions centered on God.

Finally, in the context of all these resources and more, individuals and communities are feeling empowered to experiment. With regard to prayer, we are in a period that incorporates tradition, transition, and transformation. The use of the imagination, senses, mind, body, heart, and spirit in new and creative ways is constantly creating practices of prayer that plumb the depths of the life of prayer as it has been practiced and handed down from the past while directly addressing contemporary needs and hungers.

In the ecology of the practice of prayer, God guides and directs. Within God's grace of prayer, we are free to pursue our own niche in the ecology of prayer as we discern it. As our formation in the life of prayer continues, we are also free to include elements of prayerful conversation, patterns of prayer as relationship, pilgrimage features of prayer as journey, the formative dynamic of prayer as transformation, and the sacramental nature of divine presence, all of which encourage the tree of life to grow in our heart.

It is my prayer that in your own practice of prayer you will experience, share, and proclaim the generous grace of God's love.

The Ecology of Prayer: Gatherings

> He will feed his flock like a shepherd; he will gather the lambs in his arms, and carry them in his bosom.
>
> Isaiah 40:11

Gathering: The Call of Prayer

God calls, and we gather as communities to worship and to pray. There are many types of gatherings, many communities, many ways of responding. We hear a still, small voice, and we strain all the more to listen. We hear a clear, unmistakable call, and our response is joy and sharing.

At other times, we appear to be doing nothing in prayer. We hear nothing; God is silent; prayer is dry. When drought comes, trees wait, become even more still, and bide their time. Thomas Green writes that in the drought of silence from God prayer continues only as we learn to "waste time gracefully."[4] This we can learn from the trees of the forest; they are masters of survival through wasting time gracefully. At such times, we are right: *We* are indeed doing nothing. Yet something is being done: *God* may be closer than he has ever been but with a light so bright that we are blind, shrouded in darkness and doubt, regret and loss. Still, the tree of life that is the core of our soul waits.

The tree of life is a master at perseverance. In an anonymously written medieval manual on prayer, the life of prayer is organized allegorically on the basis of the six wings and feathers of the angelic seraphim. According to this medieval sage, these six wings and the various feathers help to give flight to seraphic prayer. The fifth wing is love of God, while the sixth and final wing of prayer is love of neighbor. After detailing each of the wings and the feathers of prayer associated with each wing, the author comes to the last feather on the final wing, by which we fly to the heights through love of neighbor. What is the last feather on the final wing of prayer? Perseverance.[5]

Gathering around the call of prayer, we learn through waiting, patience, perseverance, and practice. How we practice prayer as a way of life is an evolutionary process in the ecology of prayer. The Spirit and our spirits shift, change, evolve, and blow where they will many times during our life. But if we are truly to gather around the call of prayer, as we persevere, we inevitably give voice to our way of life as a response to encountering the world as delicate, intricate, interconnected, and hopeful.

In gathered prayer, whether in a spontaneous small group or as a worshiping community, we join our hearts, minds, spirits, eyes, and ears in common anticipation of God's gifting call. In that gathering and in that listening, prayer as a way of life takes root, gives shelter, and fills the lungs with love of neighbor and love of God. Charles de Foucauld writes that "the best prayer is the most loving prayer."[6] Love is the call and dynamism of prayer's ecology.

Gathering Christian Prayer: Tradition and Retrieval

We gather Christian prayer in a literal sense as well. Though the church is always in prayer, and though many unknown saints of the church radiate a life of deep prayer through their faith and their works, for various reasons, much of the Christian prayer tradition has been diluted and in many places nearly forgotten. Today, formation in prayer or contemplation is, for most Christians, spotty at best. For many, it is simply nonexistent. Thus, a major part of prayer includes the literal retrieval of forms and practices long forgotten or ignored, the recovery of the art of prayer formation itself, and creative adaptation of these recovered forms to contemporary needs.

A major part of such a program of retrieval and adaptation involves making available texts on teaching prayer and contemplation that are as uncorrupted and as true to their original intent as possible. Though reconstruction of critical editions of prayer began during the latter part of the nineteenth century, it is only in recent years that breadth, originality, clarity, and integrity of original teaching in spirituality in general and prayer in particular have become widely available. Even well-respected scholars writing in the early years of the twentieth century simply did not have access to accurate editions of early writers on prayer.

Two well-known examples are particularly illuminating. Evelyn Underhill is among the most distinguished and widely known writers on mysticism from the early part of the last century. Her book *Mysticism: The Nature and Development of Spiritual Consciousness*,[7] first published in 1911, surveys her early work on spirituality, mysticism, and religious experiences. The book remains a classic and is still cited and read for its insights into prayer and the spiritual life. But her use of sources, though critically accurate for her day, is often based on corrupt or insufficient texts, resulting in clear gaps or inaccuracies in her understanding of prayer. Another classic work is Friedrich von Hügel's book *The Mystical Element of Religion*, which focuses on Catherine of Genoa and her circle.[8] First published in 1908, it is still considered to be, in the words of one contemporary writer on mysticism, "one of the masterpieces of the modern study of mysticism."[9] Von Hügel continues to be cited even today for his typology of three elements of religion. But as with Underhill, his interpretation of Catherine of Genoa and her friends is often embarrassingly archaic, with the result that his writing on prayer is frequently far off the mark.

This is in no way meant to disparage either Evelyn Underhill or Friedrich von Hügel. Their work lives on. But the fact that, even in authors of this stature, basic errors arise due to a lack of accurate sources only accentuates the need for a careful retrieval of the Christian tradition. And that is being done. Around the year 1965, after the end of Vatican II, more accurate critical editions and translations of classic works on Christian prayer began anew, with no end currently in sight. This is true not only for Roman Catholic traditions but also for Protestant, Orthodox, and other Christian traditions as well. Today, the resources are plentiful, even overwhelming. At times, the abundance is so overwhelming that the original intent can actually be reversed: Faced with such abundance, we can be overwhelmed by a sense of anxiety or confusion. With detailed instructions, we may ask a bit sheepishly, "Am I doing this prayer correctly?" We may give our best effort or constant practice and only wonder why it is not "working." Our mind wanders, our problems remain, God is as distant as ever. There is no quick answer to any of these concerns, only that prayer is seldom what we expect or want it to be. But the process of retrieving the full body of Christian prayer is well on its way to helping us reconnect with the deepest roots of who we are as a praying people. Perseverance is crucial.

Parallel to the process of retrieval is that of adapting or retranslating Christian prayer practice in ways that meet the needs, desires, and expectations of contemporary men and women. A prayer practice such as *lectio divina* retrieved intact and unchanged from its monastic roots would quickly overwhelm many of the most dedicated practitioners. It can still be practiced in its original sequential form by some and with great benefit. But in slightly altered or reshaped forms, and while remaining true to the original focus and intent of the prayer, *lectio* can also evolve into a fluid, flexible, and satisfying form of prayer for many people in today's busy culture. The ecology of prayer thus retrieves and reformulates practices as it gathers the wisdom available to us from our brothers and sisters of past times and places.

Gathering Community: Identity and Plurality

Gathering for the practice of prayer defines and sharpens identity within a community. A community at prayer forms its own values, culture, and self-understanding. Values, culture, and identity are further sharpened as the ecology of prayer opens us to our own community's dependence on and relation to other communities. But true community develops only through the recognition of common identity, which at the same time preserves our essential differences. Failure to honor difference leads to isolation, fear, and suspicion. Failure to participate as full members of a community leads to alienation, separation, and loss. Prayer serves as a kind of bridge between community identity and plurality. The ecology of prayer recognizes the important mechanisms of support present in our immediate environment. It also has the potential to carry us across boundaries of gender, race, nationality, sexuality, culture, denomination, and religion. In the global evolutionary ecology of prayer, hospitality is the core value in identity formation. Invitation and hospitality are in turn the repositories of goodwill toward the "other."

The ecology of prayer allows expressive and imaginative possibilities for a truly global environment of dialogue, understanding, and shared practice in community. One methodology for discussion and understanding across borders is elaborated in the work of John Donne.[10] In Donne's rubric, we engage in the process of crossing over into the culture and community consciousness of the "other" and then return to our own community with an enhanced and deeper understanding of both. One begins the encounter with communities of difference, however, by first participating in and being nurtured by a local, particular habitat. One walks on one's own soil, so to speak. Then, with this self-understanding, provided there is an invitation, one visits other habitats, other locales, other ecosystems. We dwell in the home of another and through hospitality, to the extent to which it is possible, make it our home as well. The process is reciprocal. We open ourselves in hospitality to others. In visitation, dialogue begins, ecologies are shared, and prayer expands. Then one returns home to a native ecology. But we return with new eyes. Or to continue the metaphor of ecology, we return to an environment enriched with new seed, new forms of adapting, new species, and new life in our ecology of prayer.

Gathering Self: Fragmentation and Centering

There is a creative tension embedded within our multiple roles in contemporary culture. Fragmentation of self is the harmful response to this tension. Fragmentation splits allegiances, confuses priorities, and counteracts full participation in community. It thwarts our visions, goals, and hopes. Gathering self in prayer responds to the same tension through the disciplines of integration and centering. Centering the self in prayer does not remove us from the often-chaotic chores and responsibilities that circle around us. Given the fragmenting character of contemporary culture, the ability to hold various tasks and responsibilities together while still functioning in a responsible and responsive manner reflects a truly gathered self, centered in prayer.

Using the image of the ecology of prayer, an eco-environment is itself, by definition, fragmented. Nutrients and water enter the roots of the tree, while high above in the sky, light through photosynthesis is transformed into food. The two tasks are necessarily separated: One takes place underground, deep and dark within the soil; one is accomplished in the light, with leaves reaching ever upward toward the sky. Yet for the survival of the tree, roots and leaves are dependent on each other. The ecology of prayer can be fragmented in this sense. The conversational roots of prayer may seem cut off from the slow process of transformation, symbolized in this book by the new leaves, or cut off from a felt sense of the presence of God, symbolized by the fragrant fruit. Yet ongoing conversation with God is essential to personal or community transformation, and the intimacy of conversation is often an essential first step in the growth leading to the love felt in divine presence. Prayer can sometimes feel fragmented, but the roots of prayer feed the leaves and the fruit in an interdependent structure. At times, growth in prayer is slow or nonexistent; at other times, we grow in prayer in joyful leaps. The self centered in prayer participates in an ecology of mutual determination.

Yet we all experience fragmentation and distraction in prayer. Distractions lead us away from our true self. Fragmentation opens a door to poor discernment. The opposite of fragmentation is not rock-solid walls built up around the self to keep out distraction. If we do build such walls, we experience a third self that is neither fragmented nor centered: We simply become too empty, letting nothing in and nothing out, or too full, hoarding everything and keeping nothing out.

But in being truly centered, we learn to open the soul to the ecology of prayer. The dark, protecting soil and the humbling light of the ecology of prayer help open safe, permeable borders that let others in and our constant grabbing after ego out. In the ecology of prayer, we gather in others and God in gestures of hospitality. Centered in self, place, and time, the soul at prayer, like the tree of life, "is recognized by its fruit" (Matt. 12:33 NIV).

Participation in spiritual practices that are nurtured on one's own soil can expand our understanding and practice of prayer. But fragmentation occurs when one participates in such spiritual practices without a tradition or community to draw these encounters together and give them coherence. An ecology of prayer that is self-centering occurs in the larger ecology of a practicing community.

The centering prayer movement, for instance, teaches a practice of prayer intended to develop this capacity for centering. As centered beings, we begin to find ways of living in a fragmented world with mindfulness and in care for others. If the core spiritual value of gathering community is hospitality, the core spiritual value of gathering self is *habitus,* the development of practices and habits that keep us centered, receptive, and expectant in an ecology that on the surface often appears to be fragmented and broken unless practiced in the larger ecosystem of faith.

Gathering Intimacy and Grace: The Gift of Prayer

Every Christian is called to an intimacy with God that expresses itself through prayer. Yet intimacy is often elusive. Why is this? It may be the result of the nature of intimacy itself. Though intimacy suggests availability, comfort, and reliability, it can also become more like a fire in a windstorm. In the latter case, the closer we get to the center of intimacy, the hotter it burns, the more apt it is to singe and surprise us, or catch us off guard, or even disorient us with abrupt change. On the other hand, the embers of intimacy may smolder for years, then flare up again and even engulf us in a new fire of love. Intimacy is elusive.

Intimacy with God is especially elusive. God comes and goes like the wind. We do not know God's ways or reasons. It is interesting to note that of all God's many names and manifestations in Scripture, no name describes a motionless, static, or inactive God. Even naming God "rock" signifies a firm but *active* foundation on which to build our faith, in the sense that the same rock is the rock of our salvation, a salvation that is in part God's work of sanctification as a lifelong process of actively building up the faithful. No wonder Yahweh could abide no idols. No idol can capture the God of action and mystery. No ritual short of the Eucharist can embody God's elusive essence. Fortunately, capturing essence is not essential to intimacy with God. What is essential is an open wonder at the ever-deepening and loving connection with a God who promises a radical transformation and a new covenant. There is no idol here.

So what of prayer? Prayer too is a new encounter. It is a warm conversation. It is a fresh face to relationship and a dynamic unfolding of our full humanity. It is a journey toward intimacy that lasts a lifetime and more. It is a transformation humbly recognized and boldly embraced. It is a divine revelation that shows itself in mundane details, in daily events, even in ecstatic imaginings. In the ecology of prayer, all is gift. In a real sense, God prays us into life. Prayer is the gift of God for the people of God. We, of course, gather grace only as it is given; it is like manna in the desert. If there is no manna, all our expeditions, regardless of how wide, long, well intentioned, or expertly practiced, will yield nothing. Grace is God's free gift in prayer. And we are free to do with it what we will. We can receive it as manna, or we can disdain it. We can be afraid of it or celebrate it. We can choose not to recognize it, turn our backs on it and walk away, or we can open our eyes and risk a taste. But there is even a gift to the gift. Medieval writers on prayer refer to this added gift of grace as *manuductio*: God's guiding hand. Prayer, as the wondrous dynamism of an ecological system, is a gift guided by a gift. The comprehensible God guides us with faith, hope, and love. The incomprehensible God guides us through mystery, awe, and glory. The gift of prayer is accompanied by the gifts of the Spirit. See and taste the bread and the wine, the gifts of God for the people of God: prayer, faith, hope, love, assurance, wonder.

Conclusion

In an article titled the "Quiet Evolution of Trees," Eric McLamb writes that our wondrous diversity of plant and animal life, including every tree, evolved from the hot blood of the seas. They came via a quiet evolution of twists and turns after land plants had struggled to rise from the oceans. Commenting on the various, unlikely "miracles" that needed to take place for the evolution of trees, McLamb writes:

> To move from the water to land, plants had to adapt systems that would support their weight, provide transport of water and nutrients throughout their system, protect them from drying out, and insulate them from the sun and temperature changes. Obviously if these adaptations were not difficult, plants would have moved on to land much earlier in the geological history of the Earth. Instead plants, and even more so trees, appear rather late in the history of life on this planet.[11]

In the process of their evolution, trees and forests have taken on vital importance for the world's health. They sustain life as we know it in many ways. Trees' powerful roots break up the earth's crust, helping to create soil and habitat for other living things. Globally, trees are essential to the health of ecosystems and their functions, biodiversity, and economic stability. Forests provide essential, life-giving services for our planet, including climate regulation, cycling and distribution of nutrients, and provision of raw material and resources. They cleanse the air and provide oxygen, help soil retain water, shield animals and other plants from the sun and other elements, and provide habitat for animals and other plants. Esthetically as well as practically, they provide shade, solitude, seasonal variation, and beauty.[12]

Prayer too evolves, rising as a primordial gift to meet the often-harsh conditions we face in our often-fierce struggle for spiritual, mental, social, economic, and physical survival. No prayer equals no life. The ecology of prayer echoes the ecology of trees and forests. Prayer too is essential for the health of the soul, the mind, and the body of Christ, the church. It promotes health and diversity. It impacts and gives meaning to other essential environments such as the psychological, the ethical, the economic, the social, and the somatic. Prayer regulates, cycles, distributes, feeds, and provides. It cleanses mind and body, provides air to the soul, retains what is good, shields from what is harmful, and provides habitat and hospitality to others. Prayer connects us to others, aids in keeping us collected and centered, promotes solitude as well as community, guides us through seasonal cycles and variations, adapts and transforms us as needed and as is beneficial. Prayers can be things of beauty, inspiration, and hope in themselves. They orient us toward presence to self, others, creation, and God. As with the ecology of forests, the ecology of prayer is a living, breathing, and evolving thing.

Ecology is not an old word, nor is it foreign to the Christian tradition. At its simplest, the Greek *oikos* means home or the place where we live. Ecology today is thus the science and the art of ascertaining how all living creatures interact within our home. For the ecology of prayer, our home can be our innermost self, our immediate family, friends, church, societal communities, environmental communities, a good book, a fine wine, a friendly conversation, renewed hope. Foundationally, our home is in God.

Yet for Christians, *oikos* has a rich, deep, and multifaceted family of meanings, all of which can be translated in ways that give insight to the metaphor of the ecology of prayer. In the Christian tradition, *oikos* can mean house or home or a place where one dwells. *Oikos* and its cognates take on communitarian overtones in both the Old and the New Testament. It can variously mean one's household, the members of a household, or family. As a verb, it can mean to live, to dwell, or to have one's habitation with another. In regard to members of a household, it came to mean "members of the household of God" (Eph. 2:19) or "those who are of the household of faith" (Gal. 6:10 RSV). Thus, in its cognate forms, it came to be associated with the family of the church itself. Hebrews 3:2–6 draws a contrast between the *oikos* of which Moses was a member and the *oikos* over which Christ presides. In verse 6, in fact, it is Christ himself "whose house[hold] we are" (KJV). Thus, we dwell in the household of Christ, and Christ is himself our household. *Oikos* is also associated with the whole inhabited earth (cf. Luke 4:5; Rom. 10:18).

In Christianity, *oikos* is our home, our dwelling, our community, our church, the earth; it is Christ himself. The ecology of prayer roots us firmly where we belong: at home in self, neighbor, creation, Jesus, Spirit, and God. The ecology of prayer is where we dwell; it is our home. Home is also that place from which we wander, encounter crisis, remain restless, negotiate transitions, and make our way. Yet even as we wander, even as we evolve, we are caught up in the ecology of prayer. In the broadest sense in which trees and forests are the lungs of our land, the ecology of prayer finds deep, life-giving breaths in conversation, relationship, journey, transformation, and presence. The ecology of prayer is our habitat. Prayer is our journey from home, our longed-for return, and the life-giving connections that sustain us along the way.

Notes

Preface

1. Bonaventure, *The Tree of Life*, in *Bonaventure*, trans. Ewert Cousins (New York: Paulist Press, 1978), 120–21.

2. Ibid., 122.

Chapter 1

1. Morton T. Kelsey, *The Other Side of Silence: A Guide to Christian Meditation* (New York: Paulist Press, 1978), 18.

2. Anthony the Great [by attribution], "On the Character of Men," in *The Philokalia: The Complete Text*, trans. and ed. G. E. H. Palmer, Philip Sherrard, and Kallistos Ware, vol. 1 (Boston: Faber & Faber, 1979), 333.

3. Simon Tugwell, *Prayer in Practice* (Springfield, IL: Templegate, 1974), 7.

4. Pierre Hadot, *Philosophy as a Way of Life: Spiritual Exercises from Socrates to Foucault*, trans. Michael Chase (Oxford: Blackwell, 1995).

5. This "uncanny resemblance" is no coincidence. Hadot looks intentionally at the classical philosophical influences on Christian spiritual practice. He finds a direct lineage running from classical philosophy as a quest for wisdom to Christian spiritual practice as a way of life. See especially ibid., part 2, "Spiritual Exercises," 79–144.

6. Ibid., 265.

7. Margaret Guenther, *The Practice of Prayer* (Cambridge, MA: Cowley, 1998), 61–62. For a helpful introduction to methods of prayer suitable to varying personality types, see Chester P. Michael and Marie C. Norrisey, *Prayer and Temperament: Different Prayer Forms for Different Personality Types* (Charlottesville, VA: Open Door, 1991).

8. John Calvin, *Institutes of the Christian Religion*, ed. John T. McNeill, trans. Ford Lewis Battles (Philadelphia: Westminster, 1960), 3.20.7.

9. There were originally eight hours: vigil, laud, rime, terce, sext, none, vespers, and compline.

10. Helpful books for applying Benedict's rule to contemporary ways of life include much of the work of Norvene Vest, as in *Desiring Life: Benedict on Wisdom and the Good Life* (Cambridge, MA: Cowley, 2000); and *No Moment Too Small: Rhythms of Silence, Prayer, and Holy Reading* (Cambridge, MA: Cowley, 1994). See also Esther de Waal, *A Commentary*

on the Rule of St. Benedict (Collegeville, MN: Liturgical Press, 1995); Columba Stewart, O.S.B., *Prayer and Community: The Benedictine Tradition* (Maryknoll, NY: Orbis, 1998); and Suzanne Guthrie, *Praying the Hours* (Cambridge, MA: Cowley, 2000). Much of the work of Kathleen Norris also integrates Benedictine prayer and contemporary life.

11. Augustine of Hippo, *Letter CXXX, to Proba,* in *Nicene and Post-Nicene Fathers of the Christian Church,* vol. 1, ed. Philip Schaff (Grand Rapids: Eerdmans, 1956), 465.

12. Diogenes Allen, *Philosophy for Understanding Theology* (Atlanta: John Knox, 1971), 133. Allen adds the important detail that the idea that "habits" play a large role in spiritual formation must be modified in a number of ways for Christian theology and prayer. For instance, the theological virtues of faith, hope, and love must be infused by grace in Christian moral theology, not by intellect or act alone.

13. Origen, *On Prayer,* in *An Exhortation to Martyrdom, Prayer, [and Selected Works],* trans. Rowan A. Greer (New York: Paulist Press, 1979), 104.

14. Bonaventure, *The Soul's Journey into God,* in *Bonaventure,* trans. Ewert Cousins (New York: Paulist Press, 1978), 60.

15. Hans Urs von Balthasar, *Prayer,* trans. Graham Harrison (San Francisco: Ignatius, 1986), 20.

16. Ibid., 24.

17. Karl Barth, *Prayer,* ed. Don E. Saliers, trans. Sara F. Terrien (Louisville: Westminster John Knox, 2002), 3.

18. Martin Luther, "Treatise on Good Works," in *Devotional Classics,* ed. Richard J. Foster and James Bryan Smith (San Francisco: HarperSanFrancisco, 1993), 133.

19. Calvin, *Institutes,* 3.20.7.

20. Ibid. Citations in text are from the same chapter in the *Institutes.*

21. Ibid., 3.20.15.

22. Bonaventure, *The Life of St. Francis,* in *Bonaventure,* 272–73. Italics refer to biblical phrases cited in the text.

23. Ibid., 274.

24. Ibid., 54.

25. Ibid., 182. Bonaventure models constant prayer not only on christological participation illustrated by the stigmata but also on trinitarian likeness (a kind of literal *imago Dei*) through references in this short passage to God, Christ, and the Spirit.

26. Brother Lawrence of the Resurrection, *Writings and Conversations on the Practice of the Presence of God*, trans. Salvatore Sciurba, O.C.D. (Washington, DC: ICS Publications, 1994), 97.

27. Helen Bocavcin, trans., *The Way of the Pilgrim* [anonymous] (Garden City, NY: Image Books, 1978), 18–19.

28. Barth, *Prayer,* 13, emphasis added.

29. Dark nights of faith are described again and again in Scripture. See Gen. 15, 22—Abraham; Gen. 28—Jacob; Exod. 2—Moses; 2 Sam. 11–12—David; 1 Kings 19—Elijah; Jer. 38—Jeremiah; Hab. 1–2—Habakkuk; Matt. 26—Peter; and Acts 8–9—Paul.

30. Thomas H. Green, S.J., *When the Well Runs Dry: Prayer beyond the Beginnings* (Notre Dame: Ave Maria Press, 1998), 126–27.

31. For one of the most comprehensive surveys of the use of these allegories, see Giles Constable, "The Interpretation of Mary and Martha," in his *Three Studies in Medieval Religious and Social Thought: The Interpretation of Mary and Martha, The Ideal of the Imitation of Christ, The Orders of Society,* 3–144 (Cambridge: Cambridge University Press, 1995).

32. All citations are from ibid., 12.

33. This outline closely follows that of Diogenes Allen, *Spiritual Theology: The Theology of Yesterday for Spiritual Help Today* (Cambridge, MA: Cowley, 1997), 10–14. Allen follows the fourth-century writer Evagrios of Ponticos.

34. Evagrios Ponticos, *On Prayer*, in *Philokalia*, vol. 3 (1984), 61.

35. Thomas Keating, *Open Mind, Open Heart: The Contemplative Dimension of the Gospel* (New York: Continuum, 1986), 19–20.

36. Bernard McGinn, *The Presence of God: Foundations of Mysticism*, vol. 1 (New York: Crossroad, 1991), 106.

37. Vladimir Lossky, *The Mystical Theology of the Eastern Church* (Crestwood, NY: St. Vladimir's Seminary Press, 1976), 202–3.

38. Another potential cause for confusion in the use of *theōria* is its use in exegetical terminology. Thus, in addition to "vision" in contemplation, *theōria* could mean the "spiritual senses" of Scripture as opposed to its "literal interpretation" (or *historia*). To complicate matters even further, the Alexandrian and the Antiochian exegetical tradition each had a different understanding of the meaning of *theōria*. See Gregory of Nyssa, *The Life of Moses*, trans. Abraham J. Malherbe and Everett Ferguson (New York: Paulist Press, 1978), 6–7.

39. Miroslav Volf and Dorothy C. Bass, eds., *Practicing Theology: Beliefs and Practices in Christian Life* (Grand Rapids: Eerdmans, 2002), 3.

40. Friedrich Heiler, *Prayer: A Study in the History and Psychology of Religion* (Oxford: Oneworld Publications, 1932), 353.

41. For those whose anxiety is *relieved* by getting it at least somewhat right, definitions do abound. Many of the writers from the tradition we will encounter in this book are writing specifically about prayer, meditation, and/or contemplation. These writers provide an almost bottomless resource. A few helpful contemporary sources include Michael Downey, ed., *The New Dictionary of Catholic Spirituality* (Collegeville, MN: Liturgical Press, 1993); M. Basil Pennington, *Lectio Divina: Renewing the Ancient Practice of Praying Scriptures* (New York: Crossroad, 1998); William Meninger, O.C.S.O., *1012 Monastery Road: A Spiritual Journey* (Petersham, MA: St. Bede's Publications, 1989), 59, 71; Green, *When the Well Runs Dry*; Keating, *Open Mind, Open Heart*, esp. 1–32; Hans Urs von Balthasar, *Christian Meditation*, trans. Sister Mary Theresilde Skerry (San Francisco: Ignatius, 1989); idem, *Prayer*; Richard J. Foster, *Prayer: Finding the Heart's True Home* (San Francisco: HarperSanFrancisco, 1992); Thelma Hall, R.C., *Too Deep for Words: Rediscovering Lectio Divina* (New York: Paulist Press, 1988), 7–57; Ronald Rolheiser, *Rediscovering a Felt Presence of God* (New York: Crossroad, 2001); and Claudio Naranjo, *On the Psychology of Meditation* (New York: Viking Press, 1971).

42. Jane E. Vennard, *Praying with Body and Soul: A Way to Intimacy with God* (Minneapolis: Augsburg, 1998), 9.

43. Origen, *On Prayer*, 164.

44. Ibid., 165.

45. Ibid., 166.

46. Cited in William Short, O.F.M., *Poverty and Joy: The Franciscan Tradition* (Maryknoll, NY: Orbis, 1999), 31.

47. Richard C. Trexler, ed., *The Christian at Prayer: An Illustrated Prayer Manual Attributed to Peter the Chanter (d. 1197)* (Binghamton, NY: Medieval & Renaissance Texts & Studies, 1987). Trexler's book contains an extensive introduction, illustrations, and the critical edition of the text in Latin. The descriptions of postures in prayer are taken from these sources.

48. St. Peter of Damaskos, "The Seven Forms of Bodily Discipline," in *The Philokalia*, 3:89–93.

49. The short but complete *Nine Ways of Prayer of St. Dominic* can be found at http://www.op.org/domcentral/trad/domdocs/0005.htm (accessed March 24, 2005). Illustrations and citations of the nine ways are taken from this seven-page document.

50. For an excellent survey and interpretation of tears as a legitimate and long-held form of devotion and prayer, see Maggie Ross, *The Fountain and the Furnace: The Way of Tears and Fire* (New York: Paulist Press, 1987).

51. *Nine Ways of Prayer of St. Dominic*, 7.

52. Ponticos, *Chapters on Prayer*, 60.

53. St. Mark the Ascetic, *No Righteousness by Works*, in *Philokalia*, 1:128.

54. Ponticos, *Chapters on Prayer*, 62.

55. Ellen T. Charry, *By the Renewing of Your Minds: The Pastoral Function of Doctrine* (Oxford: Oxford University Press, 1997), 18. Other recent books on the relationship among theology, virtue, and spiritual practice of value for prayer include Volf and Bass, *Practicing Theology*; Allen, *Spiritual Theology*; Simon Chan, *Spiritual Theology: A Systematic Study of the Christian Life* (Downers Grove, IL: InterVarsity, 1998); David S. Cunningham, *These Three Are One: The Practice of Trinitarian Theology* (Oxford: Blackwell, 1998); Mark A. McIntosh, *Mystical Theology: The Integrity of Spirituality and Theology* (Oxford: Blackwell, 1998); and Philip Sheldrake, *Spirituality and Theology: Christian Living and the Doctrine of God* (Maryknoll, NY: Orbis, 1998).

56. Hugh of St. Victor, *The "Didascalicon" of Hugh of St. Victor*, trans. Jerome Taylor (New York: Columbia University Press, 1991), 54–55.

57. Chan, *Spiritual Theology*, 125.

58. Cited in Dorothee Soelle, *Suffering* (Philadelphia: Fortress, 1975), 77. For an extended treatment of the relationship between studies (theology) and attention (prayer), see Simone Weil, "Reflections on the Right Use of School Studies with a View to Love of God," in *The Simone Weil Reader*, ed. George A. Panichas (New York: David McKay, 1977), 44–52.

59. Kenneth Leech, *True Prayer: An Invitation to Christian Spirituality* (San Francisco: HarperSanFrancisco, 1980), 8.

60. Guenther, *Practice of Prayer*, 45.

61. Barth, *Prayer*, 5.

62. Columba Stewart, O.S.B., *Prayer and Community: The Benedictine Tradition* (Maryknoll, NY: Orbis, 1998), 32.

63. The comments that follow are based on Paul F. Bradshaw, *Two Ways of Praying* (New York: Abingdon, 1995), 13–26.

64. Already, because of connotations of isolation in monastic prayer, caution must be exercised not to equate isolation, which separates, with solitude, which rejuvenates and enriches.

65. Bradshaw, *Two Ways of Praying*, 22.

66. M. Basil Pennington, *A Place Apart: Monastic Prayer and Practice for Everyone* (Liguori, MO: Liguori/Triumph, 1998), 70.

67. Helpful books exploring the relationship between prayer and personality include Patricia D. Brown, *Paths to Prayer: Finding Your Own Way to the Presence of God* (San Francisco: Jossey-Bass, 2003); Malcolm Goldsmith, *Knowing Me, Knowing God: Exploring Your Spirituality with Myers-Briggs* (Nashville: Abingdon, 1997); Charles J. Keating, *Who We Are Is How We Pray: Matching Personality and Spirituality* (Mystic, CN: Twenty-Third Publications, 1987); and Michael and Norrisey, *Prayer and Temperament*.

68. Ralph A. Keifer, *Blessed and Broken: An Exploration of the Contemporary Experience of God in Eucharistic Celebration* (Wilmington, DE: Michael Glazier, 1990), 134–35.

69. Ibid., 138–39.

70. See Pseudo-Dionysius, *The Mystical Theology*, in *Pseudo-Dionysius: The Complete Works*, trans. Colm Luibheid (New York: Paulist Press, 1987), 141.

71. Keifer, *Blessed and Broken*, 140.

72. Avery Dulles, S.J., *Models of Revelation* (Maryknoll, NY: Orbis, 1999), 3–35. Dulles's book was first published in 1983. The following have also made substantial contributions

using the methodology of models in various fields: Stephen B. Bevans, S.V.D., *Models of Contextual Theology* (Maryknoll, NY: Orbis, 1997); Max Black, *Models and Metaphors* (Ithaca, NY: Cornell University Press, 1962); Avery Dulles, S.J., *Models of the Church*, expanded ed. (New York: Image Books, 1987); Sallie McFague, *Metaphorical Theology: Models of God in Religious Language* (Philadelphia: Fortress, 1982); David Tracy, *Blessed Rage for Order: The New Pluralism in Theology* (New York: Crossroad, 1978), esp. chap. 2; Ian T. Ramsey, *Models for Divine Activity* (London: SCM, 1973); H. Richard Niebuhr, *Christ and Culture* (New York: Harper Touchstone, 1951); and John Goldingay, *Models for Scripture* (Grand Rapids: Eerdmans, 1994).

73. Dulles, *Models of the Church*, 28.

74. Dulles, *Models of Revelation*, 25. Dulles cites as warrant for his use of typologies Ernst Troeltsch, *Social Teaching of the Christian Churches*, trans. Olive Wyon, 2 vols. (New York: Macmillan, 1931); and Niebuhr, *Christ and Culture*.

75. Ian G. Barbour, *Myths, Models, and Paradigms* (New York: Harper & Row, 1974).

76. Ibid., 16.

77. Ibid., 30.

78. Ibid., 31, 35. See Dulles, *Models of the Church*, 29–33, on the process of a model rising to the status of a paradigm in the sense of Thomas S. Kuhn's use of the term. Geoffrey Wainwright uses Niebuhr's typologies of the relationship between Christ and culture to formulate "types of spirituality," which also shed light on a different approach to thinking about prayer. Though Neibuhr's typologies are no longer held in quite the esteem they once were, his methodology can still provide useful paradigms for considering approaches to prayer. Cf. Geoffrey Wainwright, "Types of Spirituality," in *The Study of Spirituality*, ed. Cheslyn Jones, Geoffrey Wainwright, and Edward Yarnold, S.J., 592–605 (Oxford: Oxford University Press, 1986).

79. Dulles suggests a number of contemporary objections to the Christian doctrine of revelation that can be applied to prayer as well. These include philosophical agnosticism, linguistic analysis, modern and postmodern epistemology, empirical psychology, biblical criticism, and comparative work in religion and spirituality. See Dulles, *Models of Revelation*, 6–7.

80. Dulles, *Models of the Church*, 27.

81. Summarized by I. John Hesselink, "Karl Barth on Prayer," in Barth, *Prayer*, 88–91.

82. Portions of the following list are adapted from Philip Sheldrake, "What Is Spirituality?" (lecture at Dominican Center at Marywood, Grand Rapids, 2001); and Craig Dykstra and Dorothy C. Bass, "Times of Yearning, Practices of Faith," in *Practicing Our Faith*, ed. Dorothy C. Bass, 1–12 (San Francisco: Jossey-Bass, 1997).

Chapter 2

1. The Greek edition and accompanying Latin translation were first published as *Novum instrumentum* by Froben of Basel in 1516. This first edition retained the *Verbum* of John 1:1. The second and much corrected edition, published in 1519 and given the title *Novum testamentum* by Erasmus, contains the opening, *In principio erat Sermo*. Though the John translation caused much controversy, as did several other sections of the translation, Erasmus stayed with *Sermo* in subsequent editions. In polemical commentary on John 1:1, Tertullian also uses *Sermo* in his *Liber adversus Praxean* 31.3 and *Liber adversus Hermogenem* 20.4. The early Calvinist theologian Theodore Beza was also apparently convinced enough by Erasmus's translation that his own Latin translation with commentary, used by the translators of both the Geneva and the King James Version, contains *Sermo*. My thanks to Victor Perry for information on Beza.

2. Erasmus uses *Sermo* to translate the Greek word λόγος.

3. See John Calvin, *Institutes of the Christian Religion*, ed. John T. McNeill, trans. Ford Lewis Battles (Philadelphia: Westminster, 1960), 3.20.1–52.

4. This does not mean, however, that Calvin believes that God listens and responds only to prayers of "pure intention," which theologically and psychologically would account for precious few prayers. Calvin recognizes our fallen nature and yet exhibits his overriding pastoral compassion, noting that God "harkens to perverted prayer" as well. Cf. *Institutes*, 3.20.15.

5. Ibid., 3.20.4. See also ibid., 3.20.5, where through "great kindness" God invites us into "intimate conversation."

6. Of course, family conversation does not always reflect love. It can be self-centered, angry, confused, and full of bile and distrust. But so can prayer. Calvin's essential point remains: Openness and trust implied in the image of prayer as "familiar conversation" is prayer focused not only on self, neighbor, and world but also on God.

7. *Conversatio* has the dual meaning of dwelling and conversation; *conversio* means a turning around or revolution. The verb *conversio* also carries the dual meaning of to turn around and to abide, live, or dwell with someone or to pass one's life with someone.

8. Brother Lawrence, *Spiritual Maxims*, in *Writings and Conversations on the Practice of the Presence of God*, trans. Salvatore Sciurba (Washington, DC: ICS Publications, 1994), 36, emphasis added.

9. Brother Lawrence, *Letter 2*, in *Writings and Conversations*, 53.

10. Brother Lawrence, *Practice of the Presence of God*, in *Writings and Conversations*, 107, emphasis added.

11. Jean-Pierre de Caussade, *The Sacrament of the Present Moment*, trans. Kitty Muggeridge (San Francisco: HarperSanFrancisco, 1989), 68.

12. Philipp Jakob Spener, "God-Pleasing Prayer," in *Pietists: Selected Writings*, ed. Peter C. Erb (New York: Paulist Press, 1983), 90.

13. Simone Weil, "Forms of the Implicit Love of God," in *The Simone Weil Reader*, ed. George A. Panichas (New York: David McKay, 1977), 490.

14. The middle portion of this chapter, "Prayer as Conversation," focuses on verbal prayer as it is commonly practiced, including prayers of adoration, confession, petition, lament, etc.

15. See Ellen T. Charry, *By the Renewing of Your Minds: The Pastoral Function of Doctrine* (Oxford: Oxford University Press, 1997), 19 and elsewhere for an enlightening reassessment of the sapiential and what Charry calls "aretegenic" formational quality of doctrine.

16. Richard of St. Victor, *De arca mystica*, Patrologiae latina, ed. J.-P. Migne, 217 vols. (Paris, 1844–64), 196: 140C. For a discussion of mystery and the role of divine grace in prayer and contemplation, see Steven Chase, *Angelic Wisdom: The Cherubim and the Grace of Contemplation in Richard of St. Victor* (Notre Dame: University of Notre Dame Press, 1995).

17. Renita J. Weems, *Listening for God: A Minister's Journey through Silence and Doubt* (New York: Simon & Schuster, 1999), 36, 38, emphasis added.

18. Ward, *Sayings of the Desert Fathers*, 188.

19. Ibid., 98.

20. The older division of prayer into mental and verbal (sometimes vocal) prayer will not be used in this book. Though interesting historically, it is not as helpful today and is often confused and confusing. Briefly, verbal prayer in this system involves both submission to divine will and recognition of an intimate relationship of every creature with God, who both transcends and is immanent in creation. Mental prayer, based on theology of the incarnation, which sees an identity between the divine and the human (though not an identity of essence), provides the basis of contemplative prayer, which, through grace, has as its goal *theōsis*, or union with God. Friedrich Heiler, in his early twentieth-century

book *Prayer*, used the same distinction, referring to verbal prayer as "prophetic" and mental prayer as "mystical." Also reflecting this split is John of Damascus: "Prayer is either the ascent of the mind to God, or the asking God for things which are fitting" (*On the Orthodox Faith*, in *Saint John of Damascus: Writings*, Fathers of the Church, vol. 37, trans. Frederic H. Chase Jr. [New York: Fathers of the Church, 1958], 328). In this sense, verbal prayer and mental prayer normally correspond roughly to verbal prayer and certain forms of contemplation, but the terms are also used in another sense that confuses rather than clarifies. Some distinguish verbal from mental prayer on the basis of the distinction between set, formulaic prayer and spontaneous prayer.

21. The following discussion relies on J. G. S. S. Thompson, "Prayer," in *New Bible Dictionary*, ed. J. D. Douglas, N. Hillyer, and F. F. Bruce, 2nd ed. (Wheaton: Tyndale, 1982), 958–61, where biblical citations may also be found. See also John H. Wright, S.J., "Prayer," in *The New Dictionary of Catholic Spirituality*, ed. Michael Downey (Collegeville, MN: Liturgical Press, 1993), 764–75. For a more detailed look at prayer in Scripture, see Oscar Cullman, *Prayer in the New Testament* (Minneapolis: Fortress, 1995); Robert J. Karris, *Prayer and the New Testament: Jesus and His Communities at Worship* (New York: Crossroad, 2000); and Patrick D. Miller, *They Cried to the Lord: Forms and Theology of Biblical Prayer* (Minneapolis: Fortress, 1994).

22. Augustine of Hippo, *Letter CXXX, to Proba*, in *Nicene and Post-Nicene Fathers of the Christian Church*, vol. 1, ed. Philip Schaff (Grand Rapids: Eerdmans, 1956), 466.

23. Maximus Confessor, *Commentary on the Our Father*, in *Maximus Confessor: Selected Writings*, trans. George C. Berthold (New York: Paulist Press, 1985), 102–3.

24. Richard Foster, *Prayer: Finding the Heart's True Home* (San Francisco: HarperSanFrancisco, 1992), 81.

25. Ibid.

26. Ibid., 87–90.

27. Ibid., 87.

28. Pseudo-Dionysius, *Divine Names*, in *Pseudo-Dionysius: The Complete Works*, trans. Colm Luibheid (New York: Paulist Press, 1987), 71–76.

29. John Macquarrie, "Prayer, 1. Adoration," in *The Westminster Dictionary of Christian Spirituality*, ed. Gordon S. Wakefield (Philadelphia: Westminster, 1983), 307–8. Interestingly, Macquarrie claims that the prayer of adoration exceeds the boundaries of language and must therefore be silent. He does, however, then reclaim adoration within a model of conversation by recognizing that the language of adoration is most precisely a language of the body: bowing, kneeling, genuflection, and prostration.

30. Margaret Guenther, *The Practice of Prayer* (Cambridge, MA: Cowley, 1998), 46.

31. Heiler's insight reinforces the notion and the validity of prayer as conversation. Praise and thanksgiving move through modalities of conversation that include speaking, listening, response, and contemplative silence. Heiler rather sharply divides prayer into "prophetic" and "mystical," the latter of which he sees as a Neoplatonic accretion and not at its basis Christian. The distinction is archaic, but many of his insights on prayer are helpful and hold up well. See Friedrich Heiler, *Prayer: A Study in the History and Psychology of Religion* (Oxford: Oxford University Press, 1932), 317–23.

32. Ibid., 319.

33. Cf. Wright, "Prayer," 764–75.

34. Ole Hallesby, *Prayer*, trans. Clarence J. Carlsen (Minneapolis: Augsburg, 1959), 34.

35. Origen, *On Prayer*, in *An Exhortation to Martyrdom, Prayer, [and Selected Works]*, trans. Rowan A. Greer (New York: Paulist Press, 1979), 109. Origen also has helpful sections in this treatise on the words of prayer (*proseuchē* and *euchē*), typical objections to prayer, the benefits of prayer, and benefits of "praying as we ought" by using biblical examples.

36. Ibid., 169.

37. First Cor. 1:4; Eph. 1:16; Phil. 1:3–4; Col. 1:3; and 1 Thess. 1:2 all link constant, ceaseless prayer to the prayer of thanksgiving. See chap. 1 for the content of these verses.

38. Evagrios Ponticos, *On Prayer*, in *The Philokalia: The Complete Text*, trans. and ed. G. E. H. Palmer, Philip Sherrard, and Kallistos Ware, vol. 3 (Boston: Faber & Faber, 1984), 58.

39. Spener, "God-Pleasing Prayer," 91.

40. Augustine of Hippo, *Confessions*, in *Augustine of Hippo: Selected Writings*, trans. Mary T. Clark (New York: Paulist Press, 1984), 125.

41. William Law, *A Serious Call to a Devout and Holy Life: The Spirit of Love*, ed. Paul G. Stanwood (New York: Paulist Press, 1978), 328–39.

42. Ibid., 335.

43. Anthony de Mello, *Contact with God: Retreat Conferences* (Chicago: Loyola University Press, 1997), 129. The discussion that follows on the dangers of confession relies on the work of de Mello from the same text, 129–40.

44. Ibid., 130.

45. Ibid., 139.

46. George Buttrick, "Prayer," in *Devotional Classics*, ed. Richard J. Foster and James Bryan Smith (San Francisco: HarperSanFrancisco, 1993), 101. In regard to confession, Buttrick advises, as he did with thanksgiving, that our prayer should be specific: "It should be ruthless, but it should not excuse: it should set hooks into the facts. 'I confess *this* sharp judgment, *this* jealousy, *this* cowardice, *this* bondage of dark habit, *this* part in the world's evil'" (101).

47. Michael Ramsey, *Be Still and Know: A Study in the Life of Prayer* (Cambridge, MA: Cowley, 1993), 93.

48. Martin Luther, *A Simple Way to Pray*, Weimarer Ausgabe, 38, 365, 1–4, cited and translated in Marc Lienhard, "Luther and the Beginnings of the Reformation," in *Christian Spirituality: High Middle Ages and Reformation*, ed. Jill Raitt, Bernard McGinn, and John Meyendorff (New York: Crossroad, 1987), 289.

49. Ramsey, *Be Still and Know*, 92.

50. Buttrick, "Prayer," 102.

51. Guenther, *Practice of Prayer*, 57.

52. Simone Weil, "Reflections on the Right Use of School Studies with a View to Love of God," in *Simone Weil Reader*, 44, 51.

53. Foster, *Prayer*, 193.

54. Law, *Serious Call to a Devout and Holy Life*, 301–2.

55. John Calvin, *Sermons on the Epistle to the Ephesians*, trans. Arthur Golding, Leslie Rawlinson, and S. M. Houghton, rev. ed. (Edinburgh: Banner of Truth Trust, 1973), 683.

56. Augustine suggests that we pray to God, who "before we ask knows what things of which we have need," not so much to inform God of what we need as to increase our desire for the very gifts that God is prepared to bestow. See Augustine, *Letter CXXX*, 464.

57. As Richard Foster has wisely put it, "It seems that God has freely chosen to allow the dynamic of the relationship to determine what we will eventually ask. The fact that God is all-knowing does not preclude his withholding judgment on matters in which the decision depends on the give and take of relationship" (Foster, *Prayer*, 180).

58. P. T. Forsyth, *The Soul of Prayer* (1916; reprint, London: Independent Press, 1949), 38.

59. Hugh of St. Victor, *The "Didascalicon" of Hugh of St. Victor: A Medieval Guide to the Arts*, trans. Jerome Taylor (New York: Columbia University Press, 1991), 133.

60. See Foster, *Prayer*, 161.

61. Athanasius, *Life of Anthony*, trans. H. Ellershaw, in *Nicene and Post-Nicene Fathers*, vol. 4, ed. Philip Schaff (New York: Christian Literature, 1892), 196.

62. See John Climacus, *The Ladder of Divine Ascent*, trans. Colm Luibheid and Norman Russell (New York: Paulist Press, 1982), 112.

63. See Augustine, *Confessions*, 159.

64. See Brother Lawrence, *Spiritual Maxims*, 41–42.

65. Richard of St. Victor, *The Twelve Patriarchs*, in *The Twelve Patriarchs; The Mystical Ark; Book Three of The Trinity*, trans. Grover A. Zinn (New York: Paulist Press, 1979), 67. Richard of St. Victor, emphasizing the role of memory, echoes Plato's myth almost exactly. See *Mystical Ark*, 278.

66. Two translations of Julian's work will be used. The most recent, translated as *Showing of Love*, conflates the so-called short and long texts based on the most recent critical edition of Julian's work by Sister Anna Maria Reynolds, C.P., and Julia Bolton Holloway (Florence: SISMEL, Edizioni del Galluzzo, 2001). This translation is Julian of Norwich, *Showing of Love*, trans. Julia Bolton Holloway (Collegeville, MN: Liturgical Press, 2003). The second, and at this date still better known, is Julian of Norwich, *Showings*, trans. Edmund Colledge, O.S.A., and James Walsh, S.J. (New York: Paulist Press, 1978). The latter contains the "Short Text" (ST) and "Long Text" (LT) and is based on their own critical edition of *A Book of Showings to the Anchoress Julian of Norwich* (Toronto: Pontifical Institute of Medieval Studies, 1978). Though the Holloway edition is generally to be preferred as to accuracy, a vast amount of literature since 1978 has relied on the Colledge and Walsh edition. This book will use both. The citation above is from Julian of Norwich, *Showings* (Long Text), 3, 180.

67. Rameo J. Bonsaint, S.C., "Silence and Transcendent Presence," *Spiritual Life: A Journal of Contemporary Spirituality* 50, no. 2 (Summer 2004): 99–112.

68. John F. Teehan, "The Place of Silence in Thomas Merton's Life and Thought," in *The Message of Thomas Merton*, ed. Patrick Hart (Kalamazoo, MI: Cistercian Publications, 1981), 101.

69. Ibid., 91–114.

70. Rainer Maria Rilke, "Sonnet One to Orpheus," in *Selected Poems of Rainer Maria Rilke*, trans. Robert Bly (New York: Harper & Row, 1981), 195.

71. Barbara Brown Taylor, *When God Is Silent* (Cambridge, MA: Cowley, 1998), 3.

72. Ibid., 96.

73. William Johnston, *Mystical Theology* (London: HarperCollins, 1995), 134.

74. Augustine, *Letter CXXX*, 465: "To use much speaking in prayer is to employ a superfluity of words; but to prolong prayer is to have the heart throbbing with continued pious emotion towards God to whom we pray. For in most cases prayer consists more in groaning than in speaking, in tears rather than words."

75. Calvin, *Institutes*, 3.20.4.

76. Ibid., 3.20.33.

77. Little is known of the life of Benedict of Nursia (c. 480–c. 550). The order he founded, in which the Cistercian and Benedictine orders of today have their roots, was grounded in the vows of stability, obedience, and humility. The Benedictine day is evenly divided between *opus Dei* (the work of God), or liturgy of the hours, and devotional reading, or *lectio divina*. Of particular interest for prayer in Benedict's rule is his "Ladder of Humility." These twelve steps to humility could be conceived of as twelve steps of prayer.

78. Taylor, *When God Is Silent*, 50.

79. Weems, *Listening for God*, 17. Note Weems's phrase for her relationship with God during this time: "intimate conversation."

80. See Taylor, *When God Is Silent*, 114.

81. Robert Wuthnow, *Creative Spirituality: The Way of the Artist* (Berkeley: University of California Press, 2001), 2–3.

82. See St. Benedict, *The Rule of St. Benedict*, trans. Anthony C. Meisel and M. L. del Mastro (New York: Image Books, 1975), 43.

83. Ibid., 6.1.

84. Francis de Sales, *Treatise on the Love of God*, cited in *Light from Light: An Anthology of Christian Mysticism*, ed. Louis Dupré and James A. Wiseman (New York: Paulist Press, 2001), 367.

85. Ibid., 368.

86. Augustine, *Confessions*, 115.

87. As the Christian mystical and contemplative traditions have been retrieved in recent times, much has been written about the reality and the power of a practice of silence before a God "beyond" mere words. We will look at a number of the older writers on this subject in the text. Three excellent places to begin an inquiry into contemporary thought on divine incomprehensibility include Michael A. Sells, who looks at Christian and non-Christian sources of apophatic theology and prayer in *Mystical Languages of Unsaying* (Chicago: University of Chicago Press, 1994); Bernard McGinn, who gives a magisterial and panoramic sweep of the Christian mystical/contemplative tradition in *The Presence of God: A History of Western Christian Mysticism*, vols. 1–5 (New York: Crossroad, 1991); and a series of essays on the subject edited by Oliver Davies and Denys Turner in *Silence and the Word: Negative Theology and Incarnation* (Cambridge: Cambridge University Press, 2002).

88. Madeleine L'Engle, *The Irrational Season*, cited as an epigram in Weems, *Listening for God*, 11.

89. Helpful examples include Taylor, *When God Is Silent*; Morton T. Kelsey, *The Other Side of Silence: A Guide to Christian Meditation* (London: SPCK, 1976); and Thomas H. Green, S.J., *When the Well Runs Dry: Prayer beyond the Beginnings* (Notre Dame: Ave Maria Press, 1998).

90. Richard Elliott Friedman, *The Disappearance of God: A Divine Mystery* (Boston: Little, Brown, 1995). The book was reissued under the title *The Hidden Face of God*.

91. The citations chronicling God's slow fade are from Taylor's summary of Friedman, *Disappearance of God*, in *When God Is Silent*, 53–55.

92. T. S. Eliot, *Four Quartets*, no. 4, "Little Gidding," 5.

93. Green, *When the Well Runs Dry*, 143.

94. Thomas Merton, *Bread in the Wilderness* (New York: New Directions, 1997), 129.

Chapter 3

1. Kenneth Kirk, *Some Principles of Moral Theology and Their Application* (New York: Longmans, Green, 1920), 238.

2. George Steiner, *Real Presences* (Chicago: University of Chicago Press, 1989), 141.

3. Ibid., 146.

4. Jean-Luc Marion, *God without Being: Hors-Texte*, trans. Thomas A. Carlson (Chicago: University of Chicago Press, 1991), 110–11.

5. Emmanuel Lévinas, *Ethics and Infinity*, trans. Richard A. Cohen (Pittsburg: Duquesne University Press, 1985), 85.

6. Ibid., 91.

7. Dietrich Bonhoeffer, *Life Together*, trans. John W. Doberstein (New York: Harper, 1954), 88.

8. This brief definition and paragraph is adapted from James K. Dittes's definition of pastoral care. See James K. Dittes, *Pastoral Care: The Basics* (Louisville: Westminster

John Knox, 1999); and James K. Dittes and Donald Capps, *Re-Calling Ministry* (St. Louis: Chalice, 1999). I am indebted to my colleague Jaco Hamman for the reference.

9. Julian of Norwich, *Showing of Love*, trans. Julia Bolton Holloway (Collegeville, MN: Liturgical Press, 2003), 11. As indicated in the last chapter, the present book uses both the Holloway edition (*Showing of Love*) and the Colledge and Walsh edition (Julian of Norwich, *Showings*, trans. Edmund Colledge and James Walsh [New York: Paulist Press, 1978]) as clarity dictates. The bracketed information in the text is from *Showings*, 186.

10. Gaston Bachelard, *The Poetics of Space*, trans. Maria Jolas (Boston: Beacon Press, 1994), 111.

11. A synopsis of Moltmann's two "futures"can be found in Jürgen Moltmann, *God in Creation: A New Theology of Creation and the Spirit of God*, trans. Margaret Kohl (Minneapolis: Fortress, 1993), 132–39.

12. Ibid., 133.

13. Ibid.

14. Ibid., 135.

15. Ibid., 134–35.

16. Amy Plantinga Pauw describes Farley's ideas of relaxation of the heart in her chapter "Attending to the Gaps between Beliefs and Practices," in *Practicing Theology*, ed. Miroslav Volf and Dorothy C. Bass (Grand Rapids: Eerdmans, 2002), 48.

17. M. Basil Pennington, *Lectio Divina: Renewing the Ancient Practice of Praying the Scriptures* (New York: Crossroad, 1998), 40, emphasis added.

18. Aelred of Rievaulx, *Spiritual Friendship*, trans. Mary Eugenia Laker, S.S.N.D. (Kalamazoo, MI: Cistercian Publications), 65–66. The allusion is to 1 John 4:16.

19. Ibid., 73.

20. Ibid., 72.

21. Pennington suggests four modes of relationship corresponding to the four moments of *lectio* that are slightly different from those suggested here. Corresponding to the four moments of reading, meditation, *oratio* or prayer, and contemplation, Pennington proposes the relational modes of acquaintanceship, friendly companionship, friendship, and union. See Pennington, *Lectio Divina*, chap. 7 and p. 108.

22. Ibid., 80–81.

23. Ibid., 87–90. See also appendix 4, *"Lectio Vere Divina,"* 154–62.

24. Cf. Karl Barth commenting on Luther in *Prayer*, ed. Don E. Saliers, trans. Sara F. Terrien (Louisville: Westminster John Knox, 2002), 24. A useful discussion of prayer in times of trial and conflict can be found in Kenneth Leech, *True Prayer: An Invitation to Christian Spirituality* (San Francisco: HarperSanFrancisco, 1980), 145–72.

25. Cited in Barth, *Prayer*, 24.

26. Leech, *True Prayer*, 127–28. See 126 regarding the harmful nature of individualistic conceptions of sin.

27. Cf. Leanne Payne, *The Healing Presence* (Wheaton: Crossway, 1989); Agnes Sanford, *The Healing Gifts of the Spirit* (New York: Lippincott, 1966); and David Seamands, *Healing of Memories* (Wheaton: Victor, 1985). For a particularly astute and comprehensive look at Christian healing in the context of recent medical and psychological developments, see Morton Kelsey, *Healing and Christianity: A Classic Study* (Minneapolis: Augsburg, 1995).

28. Leanne Payne, *Restoring the Christian Soul: Overcoming Barriers to Completion in Christ through Healing Prayer* (Grand Rapids: Baker, 1991), 68, 81.

29. Ibid., 69.

30. Compiled from ibid., chaps. 7–9.

31. Ibid., 150.

32. J. Gregory Jones, "Forgiveness," in *Practicing Our Faith: A Way of Life for a Searching People*, ed. Dorothy C. Bass (San Francisco: Jossey-Bass, 1997), 134.

33. Ibid., 134–35.

34. Ibid., 140–41.

35. William A. Meninger, O.C.S.O., *The Process of Forgiveness* (New York: Continuum, 1996), 48.

36. Jones, "Forgiveness," 138–39.

37. Meninger's stages outlined here are given in detail in *Process of Forgiveness*, 48–72. Meninger's stages are based on Sidney Simon and Suzanne Simon, *Forgiveness* (New York: Warner Books, 1990); and Beverly Flanagan, *Forgiving the Unforgivable* (New York: Macmillan, 1992). In his book, Meninger also includes five useful prayers and practices that he calls "tools for forgiveness." These helpful tools include scriptural meditation, compassion meditation, centering meditation, the process of focusing, and vulnerability.

38. Meninger, *Process of Forgiveness*, 58.

39. Ibid., 59.

40. Ibid., 62.

41. Ibid., 68.

42. Augustine of Hippo, *The Augustine Catechism: The Enchiridion on Faith, Hope, and Love*, trans. Bruce Herbert (Hyde Park, NY: New City Press, 1999), 94.

43. Ibid., 94–95.

44. Ibid., 95.

45. Herbert Anderson and Edward Foley, *Mighty Stories, Dangerous Rituals: Weaving Together the Human and the Divine* (San Francisco: Jossey-Bass, 1998), 167.

46. Ibid., 168.

47. Ibid., 170.

48. Robert Schreiter, *The Ministry of Reconciliation: Spirituality and Strategies* (Maryknoll, NY: Orbis, 1998), cited in ibid., 172.

49. Nicholas Lash, *Easter in Ordinary: Reflections on Human Experience and the Knowledge of God* (Charlottesville: University Press of Virginia, 1988), 111.

50. David S. Cunningham, *These Three Are One: The Practice of the Doctrine of the Trinity* (Oxford: Blackwell, 1998), 15.

51. For more detail on Richard of St. Victor's relational conception of contemplative prayer, see Steven Chase, *Angelic Wisdom: The Cherubim and the Grace of Contemplation in Richard of St. Victor* (Notre Dame: University of Notre Dame Press, 1995), chap. 3; appendix, table 1.

52. Richard of St. Victor, *The Mystical Ark*, in *The Twelve Patriarchs; The Mystical Ark; Book Three of The Trinity*, trans. Grover A. Zinn (New York: Paulist Press, 1979), 296–97. See also Chase, *Angelic Wisdom*, chap. 4.

53. Richard of St. Victor, *Mystical Ark*, 297.

54. All citations in this paragraph are from ibid., 151–52.

55. Richard of St. Victor, *Book Three of The Trinity*, 374.

56. Ibid., 375–76.

57. Ibid., 388–89, 393.

58. Julian of Norwich, *Showing of Love*, 53.

59. Ibid., 3.

60. Ibid., 79.

61. Ibid., 80–81.

62. See the discussion on *adventus* prayer above.

63. Quotations are from Julian of Norwich, *Showings*, 249–250, 251, 253.

64. Ellen T. Charry, *By the Renewing of Your Minds: The Pastoral Function of Doctrine* (Oxford: Oxford University Press, 1997), 188.

65. Julian of Norwich, *Showings*, 257.

66. Julian of Norwich, *Showing of Love*, 81.

67. The illumination is not from Hildegard's more well-known *Scivias* but from a manuscript written twenty years later, *De operatione Dei (DOD)* or *On the Work of God*. A German translation of the critical edition of this work is Hildegard von Bingen, *Welt und Mensch: Das Bach "De operatione Dei,"* trans. Heinrich Schipperges (Salzburg: Müller, 1965). Translation of brief portions into English with nicely reproduced illuminations can be found in *Illuminations of Hildegard of Bingen*, with commentary by Matthew Fox (Santa Fe: Bear & Company, 1985), 25–26.

68. Hildegard of Bingen, *On the Work of God*, in *Illuminations of Hildegard of Bingen*, 38–41.

69. Julian of Norwich, *Showing of Love*, 95.

70. See Philip Sheldrake, *Spirituality and Theology: Christian Living and the Doctrine of God* (Maryknoll, NY: Orbis, 1998), 101 and 216n1 for a survey of literature on imaginative vision as an extension of meditation, especially on scenes from the Gospels in Julian's case, growing out of the practice of *lectio divina*.

71. Ibid., 11.

72. Sheldrake, *Spirituality and Theology*, 112.

73. On the development of devotion to the humanity of Christ, see ibid., 102–12; and Ewert Cousins, "The Humanity and the Passion of Christ," in *Christian Spirituality: High Middle Ages and Reformation*, ed. Jill Raitt (New York: Crossroad, 1987), 375–91.

74. Julian of Norwich, *Showing of Love*, 7. Though graphic, Julian's description is relatively tame compared to others of her period. One description, however, is especially telling in that it depicts the agony of death engendered by the plague, of which she was all too familiar: "I saw his sweet face as it were dry and bloodless with the pallor of dying, and then deadly pale, languishing, and then the pallor turning blue and then the blue turning brown, as death took more hold upon the flesh" (Julian of Norwich, *Showings*, 206).

75. Julian of Norwich, *Showing of Love*, 9.

76. Ibid., 7, emphasis added.

77. Ibid., 89.

78. Julian of Norwich, *Showings*, 285.

79. Sheldrake, *Spirituality and Theology*, 116.

80. Julian of Norwich, *Showings*, 297.

81. Julian of Norwich, *Showing of Love*, 90–91.

82. Ibid. Triads can be found on 101, 7, 81, 91.

83. Julian of Norwich, *Showings*, (ST) 137, (LT) 225.

84. Julian of Norwich, *Showing of Love*, 122.

85. Ibid., 123.

Chapter 4

1. Teresa of Avila, *The Life of Teresa of Jesus: The Autobiography of Teresa of Avila*, trans. E. Allison Peers (New York: Image Books, 1991), 128.

2. Ibid., 148.

3. Ibid., 163.

4. Ibid., 174.

5. Ibid.

6. Dietrich Bonhoeffer, *Letters and Papers from Prison*, trans. Reginald Fuller, Frank Clark, et al., enlarged ed. (New York: Simon & Schuster, 1997), 300.

7. Karl Barth uses these words to open his commentary on the Lord's Prayer. He notes, of course, that we are also exhorted to pray. See *Prayer*, ed. Don E. Saliers, trans. Sara F. Terrien (Louisville: Westminster John Knox, 2002), 22.

8. From the journals of Thomas Merton, cited in Paul Elie, *The Life You Save May Be Your Own: An American Pilgrimage* (New York: Farrar, Straus & Giroux, 2003), 105, 118.

9. Renita J. Weems, *Listening for God: A Minister's Journey through Silence and Doubt* (New York: Simon & Schuster, 1999), 36–37.

10. Hugh of St. Victor's comments on the steps to contemplation are from *The "Didascalicon" of Hugh of St. Victor*, trans. Jerome Taylor (New York: Columbia University Press, 1991), 132–33.

11. This book will not make distinctions among rhetorical devices such as metaphor, simile, and allegory. The point to be emphasized is that this use of language in all its variance is nearly universally employed by those describing prayer and the spiritual journey.

12. Augustine of Hippo, *Letter CXXX, to Proba*, in *Nicene and Post-Nicene Fathers of the Christian Church*, vol. 1, ed. Philip Schaff (Grand Rapids: Eerdmans, 1956), 460–61.

13. Augustine of Hippo, *Confessions*, trans. R. S. Pine-Coffin (New York: Penguin, 1961), 163.

14. Cf. M. Craig Barnes, *Searching for Home: Spirituality for Restless Souls* (Grand Rapids: Brazos, 2003).

15. Cf. Joyce Rupp, *Dear Heart, Come Home: The Path of Midlife Spirituality* (New York: Crossroad, 1996).

16. Cf. Shannon Jung, *We Are Home: A Spirituality of the Environment* (New York: Paulist Press, 1993).

17. Wendy M. Wright, *Seasons of a Family's Life: Cultivating the Contemplative Spirit at Home* (San Francisco: Jossey-Bass, 2003).

18. Elie, *Life You Save May Be Your Own*, x.

19. Ibid., 29.

20. Peter Brown, "Pilgrimage," in *The Westminster Dictionary of Christian Spirituality*, ed. Gordon S. Wakefield (Philadelphia: Westminster, 1983), 301–2.

21. Bonaventure, *The Soul's Journey into God*, in *Bonaventure*, trans. Ewert Cousins (New York: Paulist Press, 1978), 60, emphasis added.

22. Margery Kempe, *The Book of Margery Kempe*, trans. B. A. Windeatt (New York: Penguin, 1985), 52–53.

23. Helen Bocavcin, trans., *The Way of the Pilgrim* (Garden City, NY: Image Books, 1978), 13.

24. For an excellent rumination on sacred space and Merton's life at this time, see Belden C. Lane, "Merton's Hermitage: Bachelard, Domestic Space, and Spiritual Transformation," *Spiritus* 4, no. 2 (Fall 2004): 123–50.

25. Augustine, *Confessions*, 47.

26. Ibid., 171, 177–78.

27. Elisha Emery Obl. O.S.B. Cam., "The Postmodern Desert: Solitude and Community in Cyberspace," American Benedictine Academy Preconvention Papers, http://www.osb.org/aba/aba2000/every.html (accessed March 20, 2005).

28. Benedicta Ward, S.L.G., trans., *The Sayings of the Desert Fathers* (Kalamazoo, MI: Cistercian Publications, 1975), xxi.

29. Belden C. Lane, *The Solace of Fierce Landscapes: Exploring Desert and Mountain Spirituality* (Oxford: Oxford University Press, 1998).

30. Pseudo-Dionysius, *The Ecclesiastical Hierarchy*, in *Pseudo-Dionysius: The Complete Works*, trans. Colm Luibheid (New York: Paulist Press, 1987), 188. Dionysius uses hierarchy and the dynamic of purification, illumination, and perfection in this treatise, applying the dynamic to orders and offices within the church and to sacraments.

31. Thomas Green, S.J., *When the Well Runs Dry: Prayer beyond the Beginnings* (Notre Dame: Ave Maria Press, 1998), 125.

32. Ibid., 127.

33. Ibid., 128.

34. On the angelic orders, their paths, prayers, and ministries, see Steven Chase, trans., *Angelic Spirituality: Medieval Perspectives on the Ways of Angels* (New York: Paulist Press, 2002).

35. Pseudo-Dionysius, *Celestial Hierarchy*, 153–54, emphasis added.

36. Gregory of Nyssa, *The Life of Moses*, trans. A. Malherbe and E. Ferguson (New York: Paulist Press, 1978), 31.

37. Ibid., 116.

38. Ewert Cousins, *Bonaventure and the Coincidence of Opposites: The Theology of Bonaventure* (Chicago: Franciscan Herald Press, 1977), 178.

39. Lauren Artress, *Walking a Sacred Path: Rediscovering the Labyrinth as a Spiritual Tool* (New York: Riverhead Books, 1995), 15.

40. On the use of the sequence of events in Scripture to develop a pattern of prayer in the spiritual journey, see Steven Chase, "What Happens Next? Biblical Exegesis and the Path of the Soul's Journey in Origen and Gregory of Nyssa," *Patristic and Byzantine Review* 10, nos. 1–2 (1991): 33–45.

41. Gregory of Nyssa, *Life of Moses*, 136. Book 1 of Gregory's *Life of Moses* is "The Life of Moses or Concerning Perfection in Virtue," while book 2 is "Contemplation on the Life of Moses."

42. See Richard of St. Victor, *The Twelve Patriarchs; The Mystical Ark; Book Three of The Trinity*, trans. Grover A. Zinn (New York: Paulist Press, 1979); and Chase, *Angelic Wisdom*, chap. 6.

43. Sandra M. Schneiders, *Written That You May Believe: Encountering Jesus in the Fourth Gospel* (New York: Crossroad, 1999), 10–11.

44. Many versions of the canticle are available. See Cousins, *Bonaventure and the Coincidence of Opposites*, 27–28. For a detailed discussion of the use of this phrase in the canticle, see Bernard McGinn, "Was Francis of Assisi a Mystic?" in *Doors of Understanding: Conversations in Global Spirituality in Honor of Ewert Cousins*, ed. Steven Chase, 145–74 (Quincy, IL: Franciscan Press, 1997).

45. Bonaventure, *Soul's Journey into God*, 65.

46. Bonaventure's justification for doing this is based on a sophisticated metaphysics of emanation, exemplarity, and consummation in which we are "illuminated by spiritual rays and led back to the highest reality," as he says in his *Hexaemeron* 17 (332).

47. Cf. John 14:17; Acts 17:24–28; Rom. 8:9; 1 Cor. 3:16.

48. Augustine of Hippo, *On the Trinity*, in *Light from Light: An Anthology of Christian Mysticism*, ed. Louis Dupré and James A. Wiseman (New York: Paulist Press, 2001), 64.

49. Bonaventure, *Soul's Journey into God*, 88.

50. Though much has been written on this subject, a good place to start is Beryl Smalley, *The Study of the Bible in the Middle Ages*, 3rd rev. ed. (Oxford: Blackwell, 1983).

51. Cited in Patricia D. Brown, *Paths to Prayer: Finding Your Own Way to the Presence of God* (San Francisco: Jossey-Bass, 2003), 53.

52. See Henry Suso, *The Exemplar*, trans. Frank Tobin (New York: Paulist Press, 1989). Note that the title *The Exemplar* echoes the idea of the imitation of Christ. Because Christ is our exemplar, Suso sought to serve as an exemplar to others.

53. Julian of Norwich, *Showing of Love*, trans. Julia Bolton Holloway (Collegeville: Liturgical Press, 2003), 89.

54. Ibid.

55. John Calvin, *Institutes of the Christian Religion*, ed. John T. McNeill, trans. Ford Lewis Battles (Philadelphia: Westminster, 1960), 3.20.2.

56. Bonaventure, *Soul's Journey into God*, 96–97.

57. Pseudo-Dionysius, *Mystical Theology*, 135.

58. Ibid., 141, 139.

59. Most work in the areas of human and spiritual development does not focus specifically on prayer. Two recent and helpful books that do correlate personality and prayer are Chester P. Michael and Marie C. Norrisey, *Prayer and Temperament: Different Prayer Forms for Different Personality Types* (Charlottesville, VA: Open Door, 1991); and Ruth Fowke, *Finding Your Prayer Personality* (Nashville: Abingdon, 2002).

60. James W. Fowler, *Stages of Faith: The Psychology of Human Development and the Quest for Meaning* (San Francisco: Harper & Row, 1981), 3–4.

61. Daniel J. Levinson, *The Seasons of a Woman's Life* (New York: Knopf, 1996).

62. Elizabeth Liebert, S.N.J.M., "Seasons and Stages: Models and Metaphors of Human Development," in *In Her Own Time: Women and Developmental Issues in Pastoral Care,* ed. Jeanne Stevenson-Moessner (Minneapolis: Fortress, 2000), 19.

63. Fowler's well-known work *Stages of Faith* fits this first life-span developmental model and is a good example that this remains a valuable tool for understanding human development. Fowler has seven stages of faith: infancy, where faith is undifferentiated; intuitive-projective; mythic-literal; synthetic-conventional; intuitive-reflective; conjunctive; and universalizing.

64. Liebert, "Seasons and Stages," 21.

65. The issue of the social construction of gender in human development currently enjoys much attention. See Stevenson-Moessner, *In Her Own Time*; Joann Wolski Conn, ed., *Women's Spirituality: Resources for Christian Development,* 2nd ed. (New York: Paulist Press, 1996); Levinson, *Seasons of a Woman's Life*; and idem, *The Seasons of a Man's Life* (New York: Knopf, 1978).

66. Joann Wolski Conn, "A Developmental View of Salesian Spirituality," in *Women's Spirituality*, 315.

67. Elizabeth Liebert, S.N.J.M., *Changing Life Patterns: Adult Development in Spiritual Direction,* 2nd ed. (New York: Paulist Press, 2000), 59. As compelling as the structural developmental approach is, it has its drawbacks. James Fowler has pointed out three important difficulties: (1) its tendency to separate cognition, or knowing, from emotion, or affection; (2) its restrictive role of imagination in knowing, its neglect of symbolic processes generally, and its lack of attention to unconscious structuring processes other than those constituting reasoning; and (3) its related failure to address the process involved in development of the moral self. Cf. Fowler, *Stages of Faith*, 101–5.

68. Liebert, "Seasons and Stages," 26.

69. Cited in ibid., 32. Carol Gilligan's insights can be found in her book *In a Different Voice: Psychological Theory and Women's Development,* rev. ed. (Cambridge: Harvard University Press, 1993).

70. Liebert, *Changing Life Patterns*. The following comments on Liebert's patterns are drawn from the excellent summary in Elizabeth Liebert, "Interpersonal Style of a Conformist Person," in *Women's Spirituality*, 349–61.

71. See tables 1, 2, and 3, "Pastoral Assessment of Symbolic Communication," "Pastoral Assessment of Self-Other Perspectives," and "Delineation of Stage Specific Pastoral Care," in Liebert, *Changing Life Patterns*, 220–25.

72. Kenneth Leech, *True Prayer: An Invitation to Christian Spirituality* (San Francisco: HarperSanFrancisco, 1980), 173.

73. Ibid., 43.

74. Diogenes Allen, *Spiritual Theology: The Theology of Yesterday for Spiritual Help Today* (Cambridge, MA: Cowley, 1997), 89.

75. See Zinn's introduction to Richard of St. Victor, *The Twelve Patriarchs*. The outline that follows is from Steven Chase, *Contemplation and Compassion: The Victorine Spiritual Tradition* (Maryknoll, NY: Orbis, 2003), 50–51.

76. See Chase, *Contemplation and Compassion*, 49–52 for a detailed account of this allegory.

77. Cf. Allen, *Spiritual Theology*, especially "Progress in the Spiritual Life" and "The Eight Deadly Sins," 62–96.

78. Cited in ibid., 71; Calvin, *Institutes*, 3.10.2–3.

Chapter 5

1. John of the Cross, *The Living Flame of Love*, in *The Collected Works of St. John of the Cross*, trans. Kieran Kavanaugh, O.C.D., and Otilio Rodriguez, O.C.D. (Washington DC: ICS Publications, 1973), 644.

2. Gerald G. May, *The Dark Night of the Soul: A Psychiatrist Explores the Connection between Darkness and Spiritual Growth* (San Francisco: HarperSanFrancisco, 2004), 115.

3. Teresa of Avila, *The Life of Teresa of Jesus: The Autobiography of Teresa of Avila*, trans. E. Allison Peers (New York: Image Books, 1991), 170. See May, *Dark Night of the Soul*, 122–24 for some of the apparent ambiguities and puzzlements of this stage of prayer.

4. May, *Dark Night of the Soul*, 127.

5. Tom Harpur, *Prayer: The Hidden Fire* (Kelowna, BC: Northstone Publishing, 1998), 193–94.

6. Thomas Keating, *Open Mind, Open Heart: The Contemplative Dimension of the Gospel* (New York: Continuum, 2000), 71.

7. Pierre Hadot, *Philosophy as a Way of Life: Spiritual Exercises from Socrates to Foucault*, trans. Michael Chase (Oxford: Blackwell, 1995), 127.

8. Clement of Alexandria, *Stromata*, 11.52.3, cited in ibid., 128.

9. Dorotheus of Gaza, *Didaskaliai*, 111.13; 117.7, cited in Hadot, *Philosophy as a Way of Life*, 134–35.

10. John Calvin, *The Institutes of the Christian Religion*, ed. John T. McNeill, trans. Ford Lewis Battles (Philadelphia: Westminster, 1960), 3.20.4–8.

11. Avery Dulles, S.J., *Models of Revelation* (Maryknoll, NY: Orbis, 1999), 98.

12. Augustine of Hippo, *Confessions*, trans. R. S. Pine-Coffin (New York: Penguin, 1961), 21.

13. Ronald Rolheiser, *The Holy Longing: The Search for a Christian Spirituality* (New York: Doubleday, 1999), 7.

14. See Belden C. Lane, "Merton's Hermitage: Bachelard, Domestic Space, and Spiritual Transformation," *Spiritus* 4, no. 2 (Fall 2004): 133–38; and Victor Turner and Edith Turner, *Image and Pilgrimage in Christian Culture: Anthropological Perspectives* (New York: Columbia University Press, 1978), 1–39, 243–555. Lane gives an excellent summary of Turner, on which the following relies.

15. Both citations in this paragraph are from Lane, "Merton's Hermitage," 133.

16. Ibid., 134.

17. Hans Urs von Balthasar, *Prayer*, trans. Graham Harrison (San Francisco: Ignatius, 1986), 199.

18. Ibid., 201.

19. Ibid., 202–3.

20. Ibid., 205.

21. Ibid., 200.

22. Pat Collins, *Prayer in Practice* (Maryknoll, NY: Orbis, 2001), 199.

23. Ibid., 200.

24. Erik Erikson, "Reflections on Dr. Borg's Life Cycle," *Daedalus* 105 (Spring 1976): 1–28.

25. James Loder, *The Transforming Moment*, 2nd ed. (Colorado Springs: Helmers & Howard, 1989), xi.

26. Pseudo-Dionysius, *The Celestial Hierarchy*, in *Pseudo-Dionysius: The Complete Works*, trans. Colm Luibheid (New York: Paulist Press, 1987), 154.

27. John of the Cross, *The Dark Night*, in *Collected Works of St. John of the Cross*, 311.

28. Thomas H. Green, S.J., *When the Well Runs Dry: Prayer beyond the Beginnings* (Notre Dame: Ave Maria Press, 1998), 113.

29. John of the Cross, *Dark Night*, 312.

30. The three signs of the dark night of the senses are explained in ibid., 313–16.

31. May, *Dark Night of the Soul*, 72.

32. John of the Cross, *Dark Night*, "Stanzas of the Soul," 5, p. 296.

33. Teresa of Avila, *The Way of Perfection*, ed. and trans. E. Allison Peers (New York: Image Books, 1991), 184.

34. Teresa of Avila, *The Interior Castle*, trans. Kieran Kavanaugh, O.C.D., and Otilio Rodriguez, O.C.D. (New York: Paulist Press, 1979), 35.

35. Ibid., 36.

36. Ibid., 38.

37. Ibid., 91.

38. Ibid., 92; cf. Col. 3:3–4.

39. Ibid., 93.

40. Ibid., 93–94.

41. Ibid., 143.

42. Ibid., 144.

43. Ibid., 145.

44. Ibid., 149, 145.

45. Ibid., 185.

46. Abba Sisoes, in *The Sayings of the Desert Fathers*, trans. Benedicta Ward, S.L.G. (Kalamazoo, MI: Cistercian Publications, 1984), 214.

47. Catherine of Siena, *The Dialogue*, trans. Suzanne Noffke, O.P. (New York: Paulist Press, 1980), 364.

48. Angela of Foligno, *The Instructions*, in *Angela of Foligno: Complete Works*, trans. Paul Lachance, O.F.M. (New York: Paulist Press, 1993), 234.

49. Richard of St. Victor, *The Mystical Ark*, in *The Twelve Patriarchs; The Mystical Ark; Book Three of The Trinity*, trans. Grover A. Zinn (New York: Paulist Press, 1979), 157.

50. Excluding the obvious physiological advances of today, from an epistemological and even metaphysical standpoint, the medieval "anthropology" of mind relevant to John of the Cross, Teresa of Avila, and Richard of St. Victor includes wonder and wisdom as well as intellect and understanding, and it thus, perhaps surprisingly, is as complex as contemporary models of the mind. *Mens*, the Latin word for "mind," could even justifiably be translated as "soul." See Steven Chase, trans., *Angelic Spirituality: Medieval Perspectives on the Ways of Angels* (New York: Paulist Press, 2002), 240–41.

51. Richard of St. Victor, *Mystical Ark*, 225, 228.

52. Karl Barth, *Prayer*, ed. Don E. Saliers, trans. Sara F. Terrien (Louisville: Westminster John Knox, 2002), 5.

53. Columba Stewart, O.S.B., *Prayer and Community: The Benedictine Tradition* (Maryknoll, NY: Orbis, 1998), 32.

54. *The Rule of St. Benedict*, chap. 19. Benedict's rule is available in a number of editions and translations.

55. One form of verbal prayer that we associate with transformation is healing prayer. For the most part, this is verbal prayer as intercession and supplication.

56. St. Diadochos of Photiki, *On Spiritual Knowledge and Discrimination: One Hundred Texts*, in *The Philokalia: The Complete Text*, trans. and ed. G. E. H. Palmer, Philip Sherrard, and Kallistos Ware (Boston: Faber & Faber, 1979), 1:256.

57. Catherine of Siena, *The Dialogue*, 25, in the prologue.

58. Ibid., 26.

59. Gerald G. May, *The Awakened Heart: Opening Yourself to the Love You Need* (San Francisco: HarperSanFrancisco, 1991), 58–59. Many of the contemporary writers cited in the chapter on prayer as relationship also provide valuable insight into prayer as transformation. Elizabeth Liebert, for example, looks at stages of ego development, evaluates them on the basis of a number of developmental criteria, and provides a pastoral assessment of each that, translated into typologies in prayer, provides insight into the transformative nature of prayer. Her final two stages, in fact, are crucial components of transformative prayer: "[the] search for love and justice; support of universal compassion." See Elizabeth Liebert, S.N.J.M., *Changing Life Patterns: Adult Development in Spiritual Direction*, 2nd ed. (New York: Paulist Press, 2000), 211–25, including tables 1–7.

60. Kenneth Leech, *True Prayer: An Invitation to Christian Spirituality* (San Francisco: HarperSanFrancisco: 1980), 35. The Scripture illustrations that accompany this paragraph are also from Leech. Leech's first example of a model of growth in holiness is from Clement of Alexandria, whose "steps" of perfection also lead from faith to knowledge to love.

61. Nicholas Lash, *Easter in Ordinary: Reflections on Human Experience and the Knowledge of God* (Charlottesville: University Press of Virginia, 1988).

62. Angela of Foligno, *The Instructions*, in *Complete Works*, 286.

63. Ibid., 290.

64. Von Balthasar, *Prayer*, 201.

65. Peter C. Hodgson, *The Mystery beneath the Real: Theology in the Fiction of George Eliot* (Minneapolis: Fortress, 2001), 37.

66. The description of Aspen foliage is adapted from Gilbert King, *Trees: Natural Wonders of North America* (Philadelphia: Courage Books, 2003), 10.

Chapter 6

1. Gerald G. May, *The Awakened Heart: Opening Yourself to the Love You Need* (San Francisco: HarperSanFrancisco, 1991), 193.

2. On the historical roots of centering prayer, see M. Basil Pennington, O.C.S.O., *Centering Prayer: Renewing an Ancient Christian Prayer Form* (Garden City, NY: Image Books, 1982), 25–59; M. Basil Pennington, "Centering Prayer: A Living Tradition," in *The Diversity of Centering Prayer*, ed. Gustave Reninger (New York: Continuum, 1999), 11–16; and Thomas Keating: *Open Mind, Open Heart: The Contemplative Dimension of the Gospel* (New York: Continuum, 2000), 19–32.

3. Thomas Keating, "Practicing Centering Prayer," in *Diversity of Centering Prayer*, 16.

4. Ibid.

5. Ibid., 17.

6. Keating's guidelines are available through a number of sources and books. His organization, Contemplative Outreach, is online at http://www.centeringprayer.com and explains the prayer in detail (accessed March 23, 2005). The guidelines that follow in the text are taken from this source. Another form of centering prayer influenced by Christian sources but also by the Hindu use of mantra is the Christian meditation movement started by John Main.

7. Keating, *Open Mind, Open Heart*, 53–115.

8. See Ewert Cousins, trans., *Bonaventure* (New York: Paulist Press, 1978), 30–34.

9. See Steven Chase, *Angelic Wisdom: The Cherubim and the Grace of Contemplation in Richard of St. Victor* (Notre Dame: University of Notre Dame Press, 1995), 147–49.

10. Brother Lawrence of the Resurrection, *Spiritual Maxims*, in *Writings and Conversations on the Practice of the Presence of God*, trans. Salvatore Sciurba, O.C.D. (Washington, DC: ICS Publications, 1994), 36–37.

11. Jean-Pierre de Caussade, *The Sacrament of the Present Moment*, trans. Kitty Muggeridge (San Francisco: HarperSanFrancisco, 1966), 20.

12. Dante, *Paradiso*, in *The Divine Comedy of Dante Alighieri*, trans. John D. Sinclair (New York: Oxford University Press, 1961), 153.

13. Thomas Gallus, *Commentaires du Cantiques des Cantiques*, ed. Jeanne Barbet (Paris: J. Vrin, 1967), cited in James A. Walsh, S.J., trans., *The Pursuit of Wisdom and Other Works by the Author of the Cloud of Unknowing* (New York: Paulist Press, 1988), 163–64. *Divine Names* is probably from the early sixth-century writer Pseudo-Dionysius. Cf. *Divine Names*, in *Pseudo-Dionysius: The Complete Works*, trans. Colm Luibheid (New York: Paulist Press, 1987), 103.

14. See Bonaventure, *The Soul's Journey into God*, in *Bonaventure*. Each of the seven chapters covers one of the seven contemplations outlined above.

15. John Milbank, *Being Reconciled: Ontology and Pardon* (New York: Routledge, 2003), ix.

16. Ibid., x.

17. Ibid., xi. That this is a form of emanational metaphysics cannot be denied, though Milbank refines classical emanational theory to negate its historical implication of the *necessity* of creation. He is also careful to deny a gift before being as a "pre-ontological *unum*," or a gift beyond the One. Being and gift are coincidental and thus not static.

18. John Calvin, *Institutes of the Christian Religion*, ed. John T. McNeill, trans. Ford Lewis Battles (Philadelphia: Westminster, 1960), 3.11.10. For an excellent book on union with Christ that can be read as a treatise on the presence of Christ as well, see Dennis E. Tamburello, *Union with Christ: John Calvin and the Mysticism of St. Bernard* (Louisville: Westminster John Knox, 1994).

19. Brother Lawrence, "Third Conversation," in *Writings and Conversations*, 93–94.

20. Origen, *An Exhortation to Martyrdom, Prayer, [and Selected Works]*, trans. Rowan A. Greer (New York: Paulist Press, 1979), 217.

21. Ibid., 231.

22. Ibid., 232, emphasis added.

23. Gregory of Nyssa, *The Life of Moses*, trans. Abraham J. Malherbe and Everett Ferguson (New York: Paulist Press, 1978), 59.

24. Ibid., 95.

25. For a more comprehensive overview of angelic ministries, forms of contemplation, and expressions of the various ways God might become present to us, see Steven Chase, trans., *Angelic Spirituality: Medieval Perspectives on the Ways of Angels* (New York: Paulist Press, 2002).

26. Alan of Lille, *Treatise on the Angelic Hierarchy*, in *Angelic Spirituality*, 210.

27. Gregory the Great, *Homily 34*, sec. 10, in *Angelic Spirituality*, 100.

28. Bernard of Clairvaux, *On Loving God*, in *Bernard of Clairvaux: Selected Works*, trans. G. R. Evans (New York: Paulist Press, 1987), 195.

29. Ibid., 196.

30. Teresa of Avila, *The Interior Castle*, trans. Kieran Kavanaugh, O.C.D., and Otilio Rodriguez, O.C.D. (New York: Paulist Press, 1979), 86.

31. Ibid., 152, emphasis added.

32. This paradoxical equality also serves to illustrate once again the inadequacy of splitting the so-called active life from the contemplative life.

33. Meister Eckhart, *Sermon Six*, in *Meister Eckhart: The Essential Sermons, Commentaries, Treatises, and Defense*, trans. Edmund Colledge, O.S.A., and Bernard McGinn (New York: Paulist Press, 1981), 186–87.

34. Ibid., 187.

35. This and the following citation are from Thérèse of Lisieux, *Story of a Soul: The Autobiography of St. Thérèse of Lisieux*, trans. John Clarke, O.C.D., 2nd ed. (Washington, DC: Institute of Carmelite Studies, 1976), 219–20.

36. Thomas à Kempis, *The Imitation of Christ*, trans. John Rooney (Springfield, IL: Templegate, 1979), 53.

37. Jean-Pierre de Caussade, *The Sacrament of the Present Moment*, trans. Kitty Muggeridge (San Francisco: HarperSanFrancisco, 1966), 53–54.

38. Bernard McGinn, *The Flowering of Mysticism: Men and Women in the New Mysticism, 1200–1350* (New York: Crossroad, 1998), 44.

39. McGinn outlines the philosophical roots of Plotinus's hypostatic system: "the One or Absolute Unity being a development of the Parmenidean-Platonic tradition, the Intellect (One-Many) a combination of the Aristotelian and Middle Platonic elements, and the World Soul (One and Many) partly Platonic and partly Stoic" (46). McGinn comments that this does not render Plotinus simply a compiler of methods, nor does it speak to the continuity of his thought but rather to an "ever-questing mind." In this, he is not unlike many of his most creative followers in the High Middle Ages.

40. Additional citations in the text are from the treatise "Beauty," the earliest of the treatises from the *Enneads*, in Plotinus, *The Essential Plotinus: Representative Treatises from the Enneads*, trans. Elmer O'Brien, S.J. (Indianapolis: Hackett Publishing, 1964), 34–43.

41. Kenneth Leech, *True Prayer: An Invitation to Christian Spirituality* (San Francisco: HarperSanFrancisco, 1980), 13–14.

42. Based on Diogenes Allen, *Philosophy for Understanding Theology* (Atlanta: John Knox, 1973), 138–41.

43. Pseudo-Dionysius, *Divine Names*, in *Pseudo-Dionysius*, 54.

44. Pseudo-Dionysius, *Mystical Theology*, in *Pseudo-Dionysius*, 138–40.

45. Ibid., 140.

46. Ibid., 141.

47. The work can be found as Anonymous, "A Letter on Prayer," in *Pursuit of Wisdom*, 166–73.

48. Anonymous, "A Letter on Prayer," 171.

49. Ibid., 172.

50. Nicholas Lash, *Easter in Ordinary: Reflections on Human Experience and the Knowledge of God* (Charlottesville: University Press of Virginia, 1988), 206.

51. Augustine of Hippo, *Confessions*, trans. R. A. Pine-Coffin (New York: Penguin, 1961), 198.

52. Calvin, *Institutes*, 3.20.2.

53. Ibid., 3.20.51.

Chapter 7

1. Cf. Karl Barth, *Prayer*, ed. Don E. Saliers, trans. Sara F. Terrien (Louisville: Westminster John Knox, 2002), 4.

2. Margaret Guenther, *The Practice of Prayer* (Cambridge, MA: Cowley, 1998), 43.

3. Anthony de Mello, S.J., *Contact with God: Retreat Conferences* (Chicago: Loyola University Press, 1991), 47.

4. See Thomas H. Green, *When the Well Runs Dry: Prayer beyond the Beginnings* (Notre Dame: Ave Maria Press, 1998), 127.

5. See Anonymous/Hugh of St. Victor, *On the Six Wings of the Cherubim,* in *Angelic Spirituality: Medieval Perspectives on the Ways of Angels,* trans. Steven Chase (New York: Paulist Press, 2002), 125–46.

6. Charles de Foucauld, *Meditations of a Hermit,* trans. Charlotte Balfour (Maryknoll, NY: Orbis, 1981), 122.

7. See Evelyn Underhill, *Mysticism: The Nature and Development of Spiritual Consciousness,* 12th ed. (Chatham, NY: Oneworld Publishers, 1993).

8. Friedrich von Hügel, *The Mystical Element of Religion: As Studied in Saint Catherine of Genoa and Her Friends,* 2nd ed. (New York: Crossroad, 1999).

9. Bernard McGinn, *The Presence of God: The Foundations of Mysticism,* vol. 1 (New York: Crossroad, 1991), 293.

10. See John Donne, *The Way of All Earth: Experiments in Truth and Religion* (Notre Dame: University of Notre Dame Press, 1972).

11. Eric McLamb, "The Quiet Evolution of Trees," http://www.ecology.com/feature-stories/quiet-evolution-of-trees (accessed March 23, 2005).

12. Ibid.

Bibliography

Achard of St. Victor. *Achard of St. Victor: Works.* Edited and translated by Hugh Feiss, O.S.B. Kalamazoo, MI: Cistercian Publications, 2001.

Aelred of Rievaulx. *Spiritual Friendship.* Translated by Mary Euginia Laker, S.S.N.D. Kalamazoo, MI: Cistercian Publications, 1974.

Allen, Diogenes. *Philosophy for Understanding Theology.* Atlanta: John Knox, 1973.

———. *Spiritual Theology: The Theology of Yesterday for Spiritual Help Today.* Cambridge, MA: Cowley, 1997.

Anderson, Herbert, and Edward Foley. *Mighty Stories, Dangerous Rituals: Weaving Together the Human and the Divine.* San Francisco: Jossey-Bass, 1998.

Angela of Filigno. *Complete Works.* Translated by Paul LaChance, O.F.M. New York: Paulist Press, 1993.

Anonymous. "A Letter on Prayer." In *The Pursuit of Wisdom and Other Works by the Author of the Cloud of Unknowing,* translated by James A. Walsh, S.J., 157–82. New York: Paulist Press, 1988.

Anthony the Great, St. [by attribution]. "On the Character of Men." In *The Philokalia: The Complete Text,* vol. 1, translated and edited by G. E. H. Palmer, Philip Sherrard, and Kallistos Ware, 329–56. Boston: Faber & Faber, 1979.

Athanasius. *The Life of Anthony and the Letter to Marcellinus.* Translated by Robert C. Gregg. New York: Paulist Press, 1980.

Augustine of Hippo. *The Augustine Catechism: The Enchiridion on Faith, Hope, and Love.* Translated by Bruce Herbert. Hyde Park, NY: New City Press, 1999.

————. *Confessions.* Translated by R. S. Pine-Coffin. New York: Penguin, 1961.

————. *Letter CXXX, to Proba.* In *Nicene and Post-Nicene Fathers of the Christian Church,* vol. 1, edited by Philip Schaff, 459–69. Grand Rapids: Eerdmans, 1956.

————. *The Trinity.* The Works of Saint Augustine, vol. 5, translated by Edmund Hill, O.P. New York: New City Press, 1990.

Bakke, Jeannette A. *Holy Invitations: Exploring Spiritual Direction.* Grand Rapids: Baker, 2002.

Barbour, Ian G. *Myths, Models, and Paradigms.* New York: Harper & Row, 1974.

Barnes, M. Craig. *Searching for Home: Spirituality for Restless Souls.* Grand Rapids: Brazos, 2003.

Barry, William. *Paying Attention to God.* Notre Dame: Ave Maria Press, 1993.

Barth, Karl. *Prayer.* Edited by Don E. Saliers. Translated by Sara F. Terrien. Louisville: Westminster John Knox, 2002.

Bass, Dorothy C., ed. *Practicing Our Faith: A Way of Life for a Searching People.* San Francisco: Jossey-Bass, 1997.

Bernard of Clairvaux. *Bernard of Clairvaux: Selected Works.* Translated by G. R. Evans. New York: Paulist Press, 1987.

Bevans, Stephen B., S.V.D. *Models of Contextual Theology.* Maryknoll, NY: Orbis, 1997.

Black, Max. *Models and Metaphors.* Ithaca, NY: Cornell University Press, 1962.

Boase, Leonard, S.J. *Prayer of Faith.* Chicago: Loyola University Press, 1985.

Bocavcin, Helen, trans. *The Way of the Pilgrim.* Garden City, NY: Image Books, 1978.

Bonaventure. *The Soul's Journey into God, The Tree of Life,* and *The Life of St. Francis.* In *Bonaventure,* translated by Ewert Cousins. New York: Paulist Press, 1978.

Bondi, Roberta C. *Memories of God: Theological Reflections on a Life.* Nashville: Abingdon, 1995.

Bonsaint, Rameo J. "Silence and Transcendent Presence." *Spiritual Life: A Journal of Contemporary Spirituality* 50, no. 2 (Summer 2004): 99–112.

Bradshaw, Paul F. *Two Ways of Praying.* New York: Abingdon, 1995.

Brown, Patricia D. *Paths to Prayer: Finding Your Own Way to the Presence of God.* San Francisco: Jossey-Bass, 2003.

Calvin, John. *Institutes of the Christian Religion*. Library of Christian Classics. Edited by John T. McNeill. Translated by Ford Lewis Battles. 2 vols. Philadelphia: Westminster, 1960.

Catherine of Siena. *The Dialogue*. Translated by Suzanne Noffke, O.P. New York: Paulist Press, 1980.

Chan, Simon. *Spiritual Theology: A Systematic Study of the Christian Life*. Downers Grove, IL: InterVarsity, 1998.

Charry, Ellen T. *By the Renewing of Your Minds: The Pastoral Function of Doctrine*. Oxford: Oxford University Press, 1997.

Chase, Steven. *Angelic Wisdom: The Cherubim and the Grace of Contemplation in Richard of St. Victor*. Notre Dame: University of Notre Dame Press, 1995.

———. *Contemplation and Compassion: The Victorine Spiritual Tradition*. Maryknoll, NY: Orbis, 2003.

———. "What Happens Next? Biblical Exegesis and the Path of the Soul's Journey in Origen and Gregory of Nyssa." *Patristic and Byzantine Review* 10, nos. 1–2 (1991): 33–45.

———, trans. *Angelic Spirituality: Medieval Perspectives on the Ways of Angels*. New York: Paulist Press, 2002.

Collins, Pat. *Prayer in Practice: A Biblical Approach*. Maryknoll, NY: Orbis, 2001.

Conn, Joann Wolski. *Women's Spirituality: Resources for Christian Development*. 2nd ed. New York: Paulist Press, 1996.

Constable, Giles. "The Interpretation of Mary and Martha." In *Three Studies in Medieval Religious and Social Thought: The Interpretation of Mary and Martha, The Ideal of the Imitation of Christ, The Orders of Society*. Cambridge: Cambridge University Press, 1995.

Cousins, Ewert. *Bonaventure and the Coincidence of Opposites: The Theology of Bonaventure*. Chicago: Franciscan Herald Press, 1977.

Cunningham, David S. *These Three Are One: The Practice of Trinitarian Theology*. Oxford: Blackwell, 1998.

Davies, Oliver, and Denys Turner, eds. *Silence and the Word: Negative Theology and Incarnation*. Cambridge: Cambridge University Press, 2002.

de Caussade, Jean-Pierre. *The Sacrament of the Present Moment*. Translated by Kitty Muggeridge. San Francisco: HarperSanFrancisco, 1989.

de Mello, Anthony. *Contact with God: Retreat Conferences*. Chicago: Loyola University Press, 1997.

———. *Sadhana: A Way to God*. Anand, India: Gujarat Sahitya Prakash, 1983.

de Sales, Francis. *Treatise on the Love of God*. In *Light from Light: An Anthology of Christian Mysticism*. 2nd ed. Edited by Louis Dupré and James A. Wiseman, 367–73. New York: Paulist Press, 2001.

de Waal, Esther. *A Commentary on the Rule of St. Benedict*. Collegeville, MN: Liturgical Press, 1995.

Dittes, James K. *Pastoral Care: The Basics*. Louisville: Westminster John Knox, 1999.

Downey, Michael, ed. *The New Dictionary of Catholic Spirituality*. Collegeville, MN: Liturgical Press, 1993.

Dulles, Avery, S.J. *Models of Revelation*. Maryknoll, NY: Orbis, 1999.

———. *Models of the Church*. Expanded ed. New York: Image Books, 2002.

Dupré, Louis, and James A. Wiseman, eds. *Light from Light: An Anthology of Christian Mysticism*. New York: Paulist Press, 2001.

Eckhart, Meister. *Meister Eckhart: The Essential Sermons, Commentaries, Treatises, and Defense*. Translated by Edmund Colledge, O.S.A., and Bernard McGinn. New York: Paulist Press, 1981.

Edwards, Jonathan. "Personal Narrative." In *Light from Light: An Anthology of Christian Mysticism*. 2nd ed. Edited by Louis Dupré and James A. Wiseman, 390–400. New York: Paulist Press, 2001.

Elie, Paul. *The Life You Save May Be Your Own: An American Pilgrimage*. New York: Farrar, Straus & Giroux, 2003.

Emery, Elisha, Obl. O.S.B. "The Postmodern Desert: Solitude and Community in Cyberspace." American Benedictine Academy Preconvention Papers, http://www.osb.org/aba/aba2000/every.html (accessed March 20, 2005).

Erasmus, Disiderius, of Rotterdam. *Novum testamentum omne*. Basel: I. Froben, 1519.

Erikson, Erik. "Reflections on Dr. Borg's Life Cycle." *Daedalus* 105 (Spring 1976): 1–28.

Evagrios the Solitary [Ponticos]. *On Prayer*. In *The Philokalia: The Complete Text*, vol. 3, translated and edited by G. E. H. Palmer, Philip Sherrard, and Kallistos Ware, 55–71. Boston: Faber & Faber, 1984.

Forsyth, P. T. *The Soul of Prayer*. London: Independent Press, 1949.

Foster, Richard J. *Prayer: Finding the Heart's True Home*. San Francisco: HarperSanFrancisco, 1992.

———, and James Bryan Smith, eds. *Devotional Classics*. San Francisco: HarperSanFrancisco, 1993.

Fowler, James W. *Stages of Faith: The Psychology of Human Development and the Quest for Meaning.* San Francisco: Harper & Row, 1981.

Fox, George. *The Journals of George Fox.* Edited by John L. Nickalls. Cambridge: Cambridge University Press, 1952.

Friedman, Richard Elliott. *The Disappearance of God: A Divine Mystery.* Boston: Little, Brown, 1995.

Gallen, John, S.J. *Christians at Prayer.* Notre Dame: University of Notre Dame Press, 1997.

Gilligan, Carol. *In a Different Voice: Psychological Theory and Women's Development.* Rev. ed. Cambridge: Harvard University Press, 1993.

Goldsmith, Malcolm. *Knowing Me, Knowing God: Exploring Your Spirituality with Myers-Briggs.* Nashville: Abingdon, 1997.

Green, Thomas, S.J. *When the Well Runs Dry: Prayer beyond the Beginnings.* Notre Dame: Ave Maria Press, 1998.

Gregory of Nyssa. *The Life of Moses.* Translated by Abraham J. Malherbe and Everett Ferguson. New York: Paulist Press, 1978.

Gregory the Great. *Homily 34.* In *Angelic Spirituality: Medieval Perspectives on the Ways of Angels,* translated by Steven Chase, 91–106. New York: Paulist Press, 2002.

Guenther, Margaret. *Holy Listening: The Art of Spiritual Direction.* Cambridge, MA: Cowley, 1992.

———. *The Practice of Prayer.* Cambridge, MA: Cowley, 1998.

Guthrie, Suzanne. *Praying the Hours.* Cambridge, MA: Cowley, 2000.

Hadot, Pierre. *Philosophy as a Way of Life: Spiritual Exercises from Socrates to Foucault.* Translated by Michael Chase. Oxford: Blackwell, 1995.

Hall, Thelma, R.C. *Too Deep for Words: Rediscovering Lectio Divina.* New York: Paulist Press, 1988.

Hart, Patrick. *Thomas Merton, Monk: A Monastic Tribute.* New York: Sheed & Ward, 1974.

Heiler, Friedrich. *Prayer: A Study in the History and Psychology of Religion.* Oxford: Oxford University Press, 1932.

Henry Suso. *The Exemplar.* Translated by Frank Tobin. New York: Paulist Press, 1989.

Hodgson, Peter C. *The Mystery beneath the Real: Theology in the Fiction of George Eliot.* Minneapolis: Fortress, 2001.

Hollywood, Amy. *The Soul as Virgin Wife: Mechthild of Magdeburg, Marguerite Porete, and Meister Eckhart.* Notre Dame: University of Notre Dame Press, 1995.

Hugh of St. Victor. *The "Didascalicon" of Hugh of St. Victor.* Translated by Jerome Taylor. New York: Columbia University Press, 1991.

James, William. *The Varieties of Religious Experience: A Study in Human Nature.* New York: New American Library, 1958.

John Climacus. *The Ladder of Divine Ascent.* Translated by Colm Luibheid and Norman Russell. New York: Paulist Press, 1982.

John of the Cross. *The Collected Works of St. John of the Cross.* Translated by Kieran Kavanaugh, O.C.D., and Otilio Rodriguez, O.C.D. Washington, DC: ICS Publications, 1973.

Johnston, William. *Mystical Theology.* London: HarperCollins, 1995.

Jones, Cheslyn, Geoffrey Wainwright, and Edward Yarnold, S.J., eds. *The Study of Spirituality.* Oxford: Oxford University Press, 1986.

Jones, Gregory L. "Beliefs, Desires, Practices, and the Ends of Theological Education." In *Practicing Theology,* edited by M. Volf and D. C. Bass, 185–205. Grand Rapids: Eerdmans, 2002.

Julian of Norwich. *Julian of Norwich: Showings.* Translated by Edmund Colledge, O.S.A., and James Walsh, S.J. New York: Paulist Press, 1978.

———. *Showing of Love.* Translated by Julia Bolton Holloway. Collegeville, MN: Liturgical Press, 2003.

Jung, C. G. *Symbols of Transformation.* In *The Collected Works of C. G. Jung.* Vol. 5. Translated by R. F. C. Hull. Princeton, NJ: Princeton University Press, 1976.

Jung, Shannon. *We Are Home: A Spirituality of the Environment.* New York: Paulist Press, 1993.

Karris, Robert J. *Prayer and the New Testament: Jesus and His Communities at Worship.* New York: Crossroad, 2000.

Keating, Charles J. *Who We Are Is How We Pray: Matching Personality and Spirituality.* Mystic, CN: Twenty-Third Publications, 1987.

Keating, Thomas. *Intimacy with God.* New York: Crossroad, 1999.

———. *Open Mind, Open Heart: The Contemplative Dimension of the Gospel.* New York: Continuum, 1986.

Keifer, Ralph A. *Blessed and Broken: An Exploration of the Contemporary Experience of God in Eucharistic Celebration.* Wilmington, DE: Michael Glazier, 1990.

Kelsey, Morton T. *Healing and Christianity: A Classic Study.* Minneapolis: Augsburg, 1995.

———. *The Other Side of Silence: A Guide to Christian Meditation.* New York: Paulist Press, 1978.

Kempe, Margery. *The Book of Margery Kempe*. Translated by B. A. Windeatt. New York: Penguin, 1985.

Lane, Belden C. "Merton's Hermitage: Bachelard, Domestic Space, and Spiritual Transformation." *Spiritus* 4, no. 2 (Fall 2004): 123–50.

———. *The Solace of Fierce Landscapes: Exploring Desert and Mountain Spirituality*. Oxford: Oxford University Press, 1998.

Larkin, Ernest, O.Carm. *Silent Presence: Discernment as Process and Problem*. New York: Dimension Books, 1981.

Lash, Nicholas. *Easter in Ordinary: Reflections on Human Experience and the Knowledge of God*. Charlottesville: University Press of Virginia, 1988.

Law, William. *A Serious Call to a Devout and Holy Life; The Spirit of Love*. Edited by Paul G. Stanwood. New York: Paulist Press, 1978.

Lawrence of the Resurrection, Brother. *Writings and Conversations on the Practice of the Presence of God*. Translated by Salvatore Sciurba, O.C.D. Washington, DC: ICS Publications, 1994.

Leech, Kenneth. *True Prayer: An Invitation to Christian Spirituality*. San Francisco: HarperSanFrancisco, 1980.

Levinson, Daniel J. *The Seasons of a Man's Life*. New York: Knopf, 1978.

———. *The Seasons of a Woman's Life*. New York: Knopf, 1996.

Lévinas, Emmanuel. *Ethics and Infinity: Conversation with Philippe Nemo*. Translated by Richard A. Chohen. Pittsburgh: Duquesne University Press, 1985.

Liebert, Elizabeth, S.N.J.M. *Changing Life Patterns: Adult Development in Spiritual Direction*. 2nd ed. New York: Paulist Press, 2000.

———. "Seasons and Stages: Models and Metaphors of Human Development." In *In Her Own Time: Women and Developmental Issues in Pastoral Care*, edited by Jeanne Stevenson Moessner, 19–44. Minneapolis: Fortress, 2002.

Lienhard, Marc. "Luther and the Beginnings of the Reformation." In *Christian Spirituality: The High Middle Ages and Reformation*, edited by Jill Raitt, Bernard McGinn, and John Meyendorff, 268–99. New York: Crossroad, 1987.

Loder, James. *The Transforming Moment*. 2nd ed. Colorado Springs: Helmers & Howard, 1989.

Lonsdale, David. *Listening to the Music of the Spirit: The Art of Discernment*. Notre Dame: Ave Maria Press, 1992.

Lossky, Vladimir. *The Mystical Theology of the Eastern Church*. Crestwood, NY: St. Vladimir's Seminary Press, 1976.

Louth, Andrew. *The Origins of the Christian Mystical Tradition: From Plato to Denys.* Oxford: Clarendon, 1981.

Luther, Martin. "Treatise on Good Works." In *Devotional Classics,* edited by Richard J. Foster and James Bryan Smith, 132–37. San Francisco: HarperSanFrancisco, 1993.

Macquarrie, John. "Prayer: I. Adoration." In *The Westminster Dictionary of Christian Spirituality,* edited by Gordon S. Wakefield, 307–8. Philadelphia: Westminster, 1983.

Marion, Jean-Luc. *God without Being: Hors-Texte.* Translated by Thomas A. Carlson. Chicago: University of Chicago Press, 1991.

May, Gerald G. *The Awakened Heart: Opening Yourself to the Love You Need.* San Francisco: HarperSanFrancisco, 1991.

———. *The Dark Night of the Soul: A Psychiatrist Explores the Connection between Darkness and Spiritual Growth.* San Francisco: HarperSanFrancisco, 2004.

Maximus the Confessor. *Maximus Confessor: Selected Writings.* Translated by George C. Berthold. New York: Paulist Press, 1985.

McFague, Sallie. *Metaphorical Theology: Models of God in Religious Language.* Philadelphia: Fortress, 1982.

McGinn, Bernard. *The Flowering of Mysticism: Men and Women in the New Mysticism.* Vol. 2, *1200–1350.* New York: Crossroad, 1998.

———. *The Presence of God: The Foundations of Mysticism.* Vol. 1. New York: Crossroad, 1991.

———, and Moshe Idel. *Mystical Union and Monotheistic Faith: An Ecumenical Dialogue.* New York: Macmillan, 1989.

McGrath, Alister E. *Christian Theology.* Oxford: Blackwell, 1994.

Meninger, William, O.C.S.O. *1012 Monastery Road: A Spiritual Journey.* Petersham, MA: St. Bede's Publications, 1989.

———. *The Process of Forgiveness.* New York: Continuum, 1996.

Merton, Thomas. *Bread in the Wilderness.* New York: New Directions, 1997.

———. *The Inner Experience: Notes on Contemplation.* San Francisco: HarperSanFrancisco, 2003.

———. *New Seeds of Contemplation.* Norfolk, CT: New Directions, 1962.

Michael, Chester P., and Marie C. Norrisey. *Prayer and Temperament: Different Prayer Forms for Different Personality Types.* Charlottesville, VA: Open Door, 1991.

Milbank, John. *Being Reconciled: Ontology and Pardon.* New York: Routledge, 2003.

Miller, Patrick D. *They Cried to the Lord: Forms and Theology of Biblical Prayer.* Minneapolis: Fortress, 1994.

Moltmann, Jürgen. *God in Creation: A New Theology of Creation and the Spirit of God.* Translated by Margaret Kohl. Minneapolis: Fortress, 1993.

Naranjo, Claudio. *On the Psychology of Meditation.* New York: Viking Press, 1971.

Niebuhr, H. Richard. *Christ and Culture.* New York: Harper Touchstone, 1951.

Nine Ways of Prayer of St. Dominic, The. http://www.op.org/domcentral/ trad./domdocs/0005.htm (accessed March 20, 2005).

Nouwen, Henri, J.M. *Reaching Out: The Three Movements of the Spirit.* New York: Image Books, 1986.

Origen. *An Exhortation to Martyrdom, Prayer, [and Selected Works].* Translated by Rowan A. Greer. New York: Paulist Press, 1979.

Pauw, Amy Plantinga. "Attending the Gaps between Beliefs and Practices." In *Practicing Theology,* edited by M. Volf and D. C. Bass, 33–50. Grand Rapids: Eerdmans, 2002.

Payne, Leanne. *The Healing Presence.* Wheaton: Crossway, 1989.

———. *Restoring the Christian Soul: Overcoming Barriers to Completion in Christ through Healing Prayer.* Grand Rapids: Baker, 1991.

Pennington, M. Basil. *Centering Prayer: Renewing an Ancient Christian Prayer Form.* Garden City, NY: Image Books, 1982.

———. *Lectio Divina: Renewing the Ancient Practice of Praying Scriptures.* New York: Crossroad, 1998.

———. *A Place Apart: Monastic Prayer and Practice for Everyone.* Liguori, MO: Liguori/Triumph, 1998.

Peter of Damaskos, St. *A Treasury of Divine Knowledge.* In *The Philokalia: The Complete Text,* vol. 3, translated and edited by G. E. H. Palmer, Philip Sherrard, and Kallistos Ware, 74–206. Boston: Faber & Faber, 1984.

Picard, Max. *The World of Silence.* Washington, DC: Regnery Gateway, 1988.

Plotinus. *The Essential Plotinus: Representative Treatises from the Enneads.* Translated by Elmer O'Brien, S.J. Indianapolis: Hackett, 1964.

Pseudo-Dionysius. *Pseudo-Dionysius: The Complete Works.* Translated by Colm Luibheid. New York: Paulist Press, 1987.

Rahner, K., and J. Ratzinger. *Revelation and Tradition.* New York: Herder & Herder, 1966.

Ramsey, Ian T. *Models for Divine Activity.* London: SCM, 1973.

Ramsey, Michael. *Be Still and Know: A Study in the Life of Prayer.* Cambridge, MA: Cowley, 1993.

Reiser, William. *Seeking God in All Things: Theology and Spiritual Direction.* Collegeville, MN: Liturgical Press, 2004.

Reninger, Gustave, ed. *The Diversity of Centering Prayer.* New York: Continuum, 1999.

Richard of St. Victor. *The Twelve Patriarchs; The Mystical Ark; Book Three of The Trinity.* Translated by Grover A. Zinn. New York: Paulist Press, 1979.

Rilke, Rainer Maria. "Sonnet One to Orpheus." *In Selected Poems of Rainer Maria Rilke,* translated by Robert Bly. New York: Harper & Row, 1981.

Rolheiser, Ronald. *The Holy Longing: The Search for a Christian Spirituality.* New York: Doubleday, 1999.

———. *The Shattered Lantern: Rediscovering the Felt Presence of God.* New York: Crossroad, 2001.

Ross, Maggie. *The Fountain and the Furnace: The Way of Tears and Fire.* New York: Paulist Press, 1987.

Rupp, Joyce. *Dear Heart, Come Home: The Path of Midlife Spirituality.* New York: Crossroad, 1996.

Schneiders, Sandra M. *Written That You May Believe: Encountering Jesus in the Fourth Gospel.* New York: Crossroad, 1999.

Scholem, Gershom. *Major Trends in Jewish Mysticism.* New York: Schocken Books, 1946.

Seamands, David. *Healing of Memories.* Wheaton: Victor, 1985.

Sells, Michael A. *Mystical Languages of Unsaying.* Chicago: University of Chicago Press, 1994.

Sheldrake, Philip. *Spirituality and Theology: Christian Living and the Doctrine of God.* Maryknoll, NY: Orbis, 1998.

Short, William, O.F.M. *Poverty and Joy: The Franciscan Tradition.* Maryknoll, NY: Orbis, 1999.

Simoni-Wastila, Henry. "*Unio Mystica* and Particularity: Can Individuals Merge with the One?" *Journal of the American Academy of Religion* 68, no. 4 (December 2000): 857–78.

Spener, Philipp Jakob. "God Pleasing Prayer." In *Pietists: Selected Writings,* edited by Peter C. Erb, 88–93. New York: Paulist Press, 1983.

Steiner, George. *Real Presences.* Chicago: University of Chicago Press, 1991.

Stewart, Columba, O.S.B. *Prayer and Community: The Benedictine Tradition.* Maryknoll, NY: Orbis, 1998.

Tamburello, Dennis E. *Union with Christ: John Calvin and the Mysticism of St. Bernard.* Louisville: Westminster John Knox, 1994.

Taylor, Barbara Brown. *When God Is Silent.* Cambridge, MA: Cowley, 1998.

Taylor, Brian C. *Becoming Christ: Transformation through Contemplation.* Cambridge, MA: Cowley, 2002.

Teresa of Avila. *The Life of Teresa of Jesus: The Autobiography of Teresa of Avila.* Translated by E. Allison Peers. New York: Image Books, 1991.

———. *The Interior Castle.* Translated by Kieran Kavanaugh, O.C.D., and Otilio Rodriguez, O.C.D. New York: Paulist Press, 1979.

Thérèse of Lisieux. *Story of a Soul: The Autobiography of St. Thérèse of Lisieux.* Translated by John Clarke, O.C.D. 2nd ed. Washington, DC: Institute of Carmelite Studies, 1976.

———. *St. Thérèse of Lisieux: Essential Writings.* Selected with introduction by Mary Frolich. Maryknoll, NY: Orbis, 2003.

Thomas à Kempis. *The Imitation of Christ.* Translated by John Rooney. Springfield, IL: Templegate, 1979.

Thomas Gallus. *Commentaires du Cantiques des Cantiques.* Edited by Jeanne Barbet. Paris: J. Vrin, 1967.

Thompson, J. G. S. S. "Prayer." In *New Bible Dictionary,* edited by J. D. Douglas, N. Hillyer, and F. F. Bruce, 958–61. 2nd ed. Wheaton: Tyndale, 1982.

Tillich, Paul. *Systematic Theology.* Vol. 1. Chicago: University of Chicago Press, 1951.

Tracy, David. *Blessed Rage for Order: The New Pluralism in Theology.* New York: Crossroad, 1978.

Trexler, Richard C., ed. *The Christian at Prayer: An Illustrated Prayer Manual Attributed to Peter the Chanter (d. 1197).* Binghamton, NY: Medieval & Renaissance Texts & Studies, 1987.

Troeltsch, Ernst. *Social Teaching of the Christian Churches.* Translated by Olive Wyon. 2 vols. New York: Macmillan, 1931.

Ulanov, Barry, and Ann Ulanov. *Primary Speech: A Psychology of Prayer.* Atlanta: John Knox, 1982.

Vennard, Jane E. *Praying with Body and Soul: A Way to Intimacy with God.* Minneapolis: Augsburg, 1998.

Vest, Norvene, ed. *Tending the Holy: Spiritual Direction across Traditions.* New York: Morehouse, 2003.

Volf, Miroslav, and Dorothy C. Bass, eds. *Practicing Theology: Beliefs and Practices in Christian Life.* Grand Rapids: Eerdmans, 2002.

von Balthasar, Hans Urs. *Christian Meditation.* Translated by Sr. Mary Theresilde Skerry. San Francisco: Ignatius, 1989.

———. *Prayer.* Translated by Graham Harrison. San Francisco: Ignatius, 1986.

Ward, Benedicta, S.L.G., trans. *The Sayings of the Desert Fathers.* Kalamazoo, MI: Cistercian Publications, 1984.

Weems, Renita J. *Listening for God: A Minister's Journey through Silence and Doubt.* New York: Simon & Schuster, 1999.

Weil, Simone. "Forms of the Implicit Love of God." In *The Simone Weil Reader,* edited by George A. Panichas, 469–91. New York: David McKay, 1977.

———. "Reflections on the Right Use of School Studies with a View to Love of God." In *The Simone Weil Reader,* edited by George A. Panichas, 44–52. New York: David McKay, 1977.

Wright, John H., S.J. "Prayer." In *The New Dictionary of Catholic Spirituality,* edited by Michael Downey, 764–75. Collegeville, MN: Liturgical Press, 1993.

Wright, Wendy M. *Seasons of a Family's Life: Cultivating the Contemplative Spirit at Home.* San Francisco: Jossey-Bass, 2003.

Wuthnow, Robert. *Creative Spirituality: The Way of the Artist.* Berkeley: University of California Press, 2001.

Index